Arbroath On This Day

High Seas at the appropriately named Danger Point

Arbroath On This Day

David W. Potter

Kennedy & Boyd
an imprint of
Zeticula Ltd,
Unit 13,
196 Rose Street,
Edinburgh,
EH2 4AT,
Scotland.

http://www.kennedyandboyd.co.uk
admin@kennedyandboyd.co.uk

First published 2022

Text Copyright © David W. Potter 2022
Photographs Copyright © original owner 2022
Illustrations from *Arbroath Harbour, A Book of Drawings*
    © Ian S. Murphy 2020, 2022
Cover based on a drawing by Ian S. Murphy © Ian S. Murphy 2022

Hardback ISBN 978-1-84921-231-1
Paperback ISBN 978-1-84921-232-8

All rights reserved. No part of this publication may be reproduced, stored in a retrieval system, or transmitted in any form or by any means, electronic, mechanical, photocopying, recording or otherwise, without the prior permission of the publishers.

Acknowledgements

Arbroath is lucky in having two excellent newspapers in *The Arbroath Herald* and *The Arbroath Guide*. Research has been an absolute pleasure!

The author would like to gratefully acknowledge
Friends at Arbroath Cricket Club for their help,
The Angus Archives at Restenneth,
The Abbey Theatre Club, Arbroath,
Ian S. Murphy
The other photographers, regrettably not all of whom are known.
The Dundee and Arbroath Joint Railway Report
    by J.W. Pringle, H.M.S.O. 1907.

The town plans and advertisements are reproduced with the kind permission of the National Library of Scotland.

Arbroath High Street, 1937

Contents

January	1
February	37

Traders in Arbroath in 1890 71

March	185
April	225
May	265
June	299

Traders in Arbroath in 1915 333

July	427
August	463
September	497
October	531

Traders in Arbroath in 1925 569

November	655
December	691
Index to Traders	729
Index	739

Arbroath Abbey Church

Illustrations

High Seas at the appropriately named Danger Point	ii
Arbroath High Street, 1937	vi
Arbroath Abbey Church	viii
Aerial view, in the 1950s, with Gayfield prominent	xii
Bradshaw's railway timetable for January 1842	2
Locomotives Victoria and Albert	5
Dick Campbell	11
Arbroath Public Library	16
Arbroath Abbey	27
David Storrier	30
Funeral of James Cobb	32
Auchmithie wedding	36
Bradshaw's railway timetable for February 1906	38
Abbey Theatre Club poster	43
I'll be back before midnight cast	44
I'll be back before midnight programme	45
Proclamation of Queen Elizabeth II, February 1952	47
Catastrophic collapse of the Tay Bridge.	48
Arbroath police force, 1932	53
Sir Francis Webster	54
Staff at Arbroath Infirmary, 1905.	57
Arbroath 1822	186
Keptie Pond	190
The Abbey Theatre backstage crew.	196
Gaslight - the Abbey Theatre programme	197
The importance of Being Earnest - the Abbey Theatre Programme	200
The cast of the production of The Importance of Being Earnest.	201
Arbroath Abbey Pageant	212
Arbroath Burns Club	213
A horse-brake trip to celebrate the Jubilee	215
At the slipway of Mackays yard on Monday 26 March 1990.	217
Ruxton Memorial	221
Corn Exchange	222
Part of Arbroath, from Pont, 1600	226
Lord Inchcape receives the Freedom of the Burgh in 1922	228
Sir Harry Lauder with his old friend John Stewart	230
Colin Grant, Provost 1895 to 1904	241
Arbroath Civil Defence, 1939	262
View of Arbroath in 1693	266
The dredger, Fairport	270
Arbroath Railway Station Staff, 1910	271

Aerial view of Lochlands	272
R. W. Sievwright	276
George Salmond	283
Darren Burnett	294
Sir Robert Hutchison	295
Bradshaw's railway timetable for June 1846	300
War Memorial Unveiling ceremony.	303
Kerr's Miniature Railway	318
Lieutenant Walter Garnet Rait	323
Presentation of Strathmore Cricket Union Trophy by Earl of Strathmore	324
Bradshaw's railway sleeping car timetable for July 1951	428
Bradshaw's railway timetable for July 1951	430, 431
Don Bradman and Bob Sievwright.	438
The Sunday Post, July 13, 1947. Death of R. W. Sievwright	443
Arbroath v Forfar Tennis Club. 1889	455
Kelly Clark	460
Arbroath 1832	464
James Cuthbert	477
Mary S. Young	479
Mrs Lindsay-Carnegie	480
Captured German Heinkel aircraft, 1943	485
Sir Harry Lauder's Jubilee Lunch	489
ARP Wardens	495
Open air pool	504
Queen Mary in Arbroath in 1921	506
Ramsay MacDonald in Arbroath in 1924	507
Arbroath United Cricket Club were league champions in 1932.	509
Arbroath-Bon Accord Centenary	511
Across the Outer Harbour towards the town from the Breakwater	526
Bradshaw's railway timetable for October 1888	532
Andy Stewart	543
Ramsay MacDonald. MP, at the Memorial to J W Herald	549
On Saturday 19 October 1991, Marigold A52 and Sapphire AH79	553
Charles Webster Corsar	555
Brian Bruce and Irene Stott	557
Abbey Theatre programme for "Who saw Him Die?"	558
Charles Corsar and Marion R. Hutchison	561
Arbroath 1839	656
At Auchmithie, woman leaning against boat, 1881	662
Auchmithie Harbour	663
On the beach, Auchmithie	663
John "Ned" Doig	665
Arbroath Instrumental Band in new uniform	669

Portrait of Mrs Janet Webster	687
Reverend D Melville Stewart	690
Arbroath Harbour, 1883	692
Bungalow for the Arbroath Town Improvement Association	710
Sketch plan of Dundee and Arbroath Joint Railway, showing Elliot Junction	722
Scene of the Elliot Junction railway disaster	724
From the Breakwater on Monday 30 December 1991, with a tide so low that some boats were resting on the bottom.	726
Cardinal Beaton - Abbot of Arbroath Abbey in 1524, later Archbishop of St Andrews	728
Dickman's Den	738
Mason's Cove	738

Aerial view, in the 1950s, with Gayfield prominent

Introduction

Arbroath is a remarkable Scottish town. It can be one of the coldest places in Christendom when the wind is coming from the wrong direction, as anyone who has ever been to a cricket match at Lochlands at the start of the season can testify, and it has often been a source of wonder to many visiting supporters that Gayfield has not been swept away by the angry North Sea.

The town punches away above its weight in terms of history. The Declaration, much quoted and indeed misquoted from by enthusiastic rather than meticulous historians, is a study in itself and one leaves it to medieval historians to mull over its significance, and of course the Stone of Destiny made an appearance at Arbroath Abbey as well – and many people feel that it should have been allowed to stay there.

There was also the rascally and much famed Ralph the Rover (is he the principal character in the alliterative "round and round the rugged rock the ragged rascal ran"?) who realised all too clearly one day that crime simply does not pay. Literature has had a field day with Ralph.

Sport has always played a great part in the life of the town. Both the football team and the cricket team have had their ups and downs, but both remain strong. Far too many cricket teams (and not a few football ones) have gone to the wall, but neither of the Arbroath two is likely to do so, for they are well run by strong minded individuals, own good and famous grounds at Gayfield and Lochlands and are well versed in their traditions, whether it be the 13 goals of Jockie Petrie in 1885 or the day that Bob Sievwright skittled the Aussies in 1912.

But there is a great deal more to the town than that, and this book will reflect that in mundane things like whist drives, talks about China, extensions to the Infirmary and people being done for parking offences. There will also be some of the real horrors – the Elliot Rail Disaster of the early 20th century for example and several maritime disasters – but happy days as well of Diamond Weddings and celebrations of Coronations, and the end of wars.

Famous people have connections with the town. Neither Harry Lauder nor Andy Stewart are technically Arbroathians in that they were not born there, but they have strong connections with the town, and the people of Arbroath are quite right to rate each of them as being "one of our own".

It is no easy task to choose one event for every day of the year. Some days are "crowded", others are "sparse" but I have endeavoured to find something of some interest.

This book is emphatically not, and would never claim to be, a history of Arbroath. Such a task would need many encyclopaedias, for the history is huge. Nevertheless, there is enough history in this book for the author to quote the Ancient Greek historian Thucydides, who is very keen that people should read history, so that if similar things occur again in the future, people might be better able to understand and deal with them.

Wars of course figure prominently, particularly the two terrible ones of the 20th century, for they undeniably had a huge effect on the town and its inhabitants, and the author would like to think that some day the human race might see the folly of war. But there are other things as well – the railways, hospitals, motor cars, aeroplanes, for example, which also feature in the development of the town and have an effect on it.

The sad side of life is also there – crimes, drunkenness, frauds, even murders – because one is living in a fool's paradise if he believes that such things do not exist. In particular, the author will confess a particular hatred of the idea that crime is in some way a new thing, and he experiences a frisson of horror when someone talks about the ways of the world *now* when everything is awful, as distinct from what it was like *then* when everyone apparently behaved themselves, stayed sober, kept their hands off other people's wives and husbands.... This is utter rot, and I hope that this book will prove that.

But as in all ages, and in all towns, good usually prevails. Folk do dive into the harbour and rescue people, pupils do succeed in Schools, and mothers do bring up their children, sometimes in the most appalling of circumstances.

This book will succeed if people find it interesting, at least in parts. I hope they also find it informative, stimulating and rewarding. And I hope they know a little more about Arbroath than they did before.

January

TAFF VALE

Cardiff to Merthyr, 8 a.m., and 1 & 4 p.m.—Merthyr to Cardiff, 8 35 a.m., and 1 35 & 4 20 p.m.—FARES—From Cardiff to Merthyr, 1st Class, 6s.—2nd class, 4s—3rd class, 2s.—On *Sundays*, from Cardiff, 9 a.m., and 4 p.m., and from Merthyr, 9 20 a.m., and 4 20 p.m.

GLASGOW AND AYR.

Glasgow to Ayr, $7\frac{1}{2}$, $10\frac{1}{2}$, a.m., $1\frac{1}{2}$, & $4\frac{1}{2}$ p.m.
Ayr to Glasgow, 8 and 11 a.m, and 2, & 5 p.m.

Glasgow to Johnstone, $9\frac{1}{2}$ a.m. and $6\frac{1}{2}$ p.m.
Johnstone to Glasgow, $10\frac{1}{2}$ a.m. and $7\frac{1}{2}$ p.m.

Fares from Glasgow to Johnstone, 1s. 6d., 1s., and 6d., Lochwinnoch, 2s. 6d., 1s. 8d., and 1s. 2d.; Beith, 2s. 9d., 2s.; and 1s. 3d.; Kilbirnie, 3s., 2s. 2d., and 1s. 6d.; Dalry, 3s. 6d., 2s. 3d., and 1s. 8d.; Kilwinning, 4s., 2s. 6d., and 2s.; Irvine, 4s. 6d., 3s., and 2s. 2d.; Troon, 5s., 3s. 6d.. and 2s. 6d.; Monkton and Prestwick, 5s. 6d., 3s. 9d., and 2s 9d.; Ayr, 6s. 4s., and 3s.

ARBROATH AND FORFAR.

Forfar, 7, $10\frac{1}{4}$ a.m. and $1\frac{1}{2}$ & $4\frac{1}{4}$ p.m. Arbroath, $8\frac{1}{2}$ and $11\frac{3}{4}$ a.m. 3 and $5\frac{1}{2}$ p.m.
FARES, 2s. 3d., 1s. 9. and 1s. 3d.

DUNDEE AND ARBROATH.

From Dundee $7\frac{1}{4}$, $10\frac{1}{4}$ & $11\frac{1}{4}$ mail, a.m., $1\frac{1}{2}$, $4\frac{1}{4}$, (and $7\frac{1}{4}$ p.m. to Broughty Ferry only.)
From Arbroath $8\frac{1}{2}$ and $11\frac{3}{4}$ a.m., 1 mail, $3\frac{1}{2}$, $5\frac{1}{2}$, (and $7\frac{3}{4}$ p.m. from Broughty Ferry)
Fares. Dundee to Arbroath, 2s. 6d .2s 1s. 6d. Mail 3s, 2s 6d.
Passengers wishing to proceed. will find a coach waiting to convey them, free of charge, between the Arbroath station of the Forfar Railway and the Arbroath station of this Railway.

Bradshaw's railway timetable for January 1842

January 1 1919

It was a very special New Year this year in Arbroath.

The weather was dry and reasonable as crowds gathered in Kirk Square to welcome in 1919, the first year of peace. It was the most crowded New Year since 1914.

Many Arbroathians, although not yet demobbed, were spending New Year at home on leave to the delight of their families. Lights were on this year (they had not been allowed in previous years for fear of shelling from the sea) but there were still some severe restrictions on alcohol with the result that the "stuffie" or the "cratur" (as it was euphemistically called) was "not absent, but not in great supply", and *The Arbroath Herald* was pleased to mark an improvement in behaviour with a dearth of cases in Court.

Yet amidst all the celebrations, it was far from a time of happiness for Arbroath. Final figures were not yet available but it appeared that some 500 Arbroathians had failed to return, and many others were badly injured or wounded (some of them still fighting for their lives in hospitals in France, England or a few lucky ones in Scotland, which made it possible for mothers and wives to visit them).

But there was also the flu which attacked Arbroath as much as anywhere else. The future was uncertain, but at least the war had stopped, bringing some sort of normality with concerts, films and football.

A makeshift Arbroath team went to Station Park, Forfar and drew 2-2. The Olympia Cinema, now decorated with the flags of all nations (except Germany!) and a huge cartoon character of Charlie Chaplin, was showing next week "Ye Banks And Braes" with stunning photography of the Burns Country, and at one point in the performance the song would be sung by a local artiste.

January 2 1917

The war has brought many evils in its wake, let alone the killing of so many young men and the serious wounding of others.

Today Bailie David T Wilson, presiding in the Police Court, delivers a severe tirade against drunkenness among women.

It has often been said that the Great War liberated women from domestic drudgery. This has an element of truth in it, but it also has a side effect as well in that they now have more money because they have jobs and can spend it on undesirable things like drink, for example.

Today Bailie Wilson had the unpleasant task of fining a woman 15 shillings or 10 days in jail for being drunk and incapable in Keptie Street, where she had tried unsuccessfully to gain admission to a public house on Saturday December 30.

She was not a young woman. She was the mother of three serving soldiers, and presumably the strain of worrying about them had been too much for her.

Bailie Wilson makes the general point, that, although the Government had made a few faltering steps towards restricting alcohol, a lot more needed to be done to "sweep away this great blot on our social and material life" which was impairing our war effort.

He might have approved of recent changes in Downing Street where Asquith (commonly known as "squiffy" because of his fondness for a gin and tonic) had been replaced by Lloyd George who, for all his faults, was a teetotaller.

January 3 1839

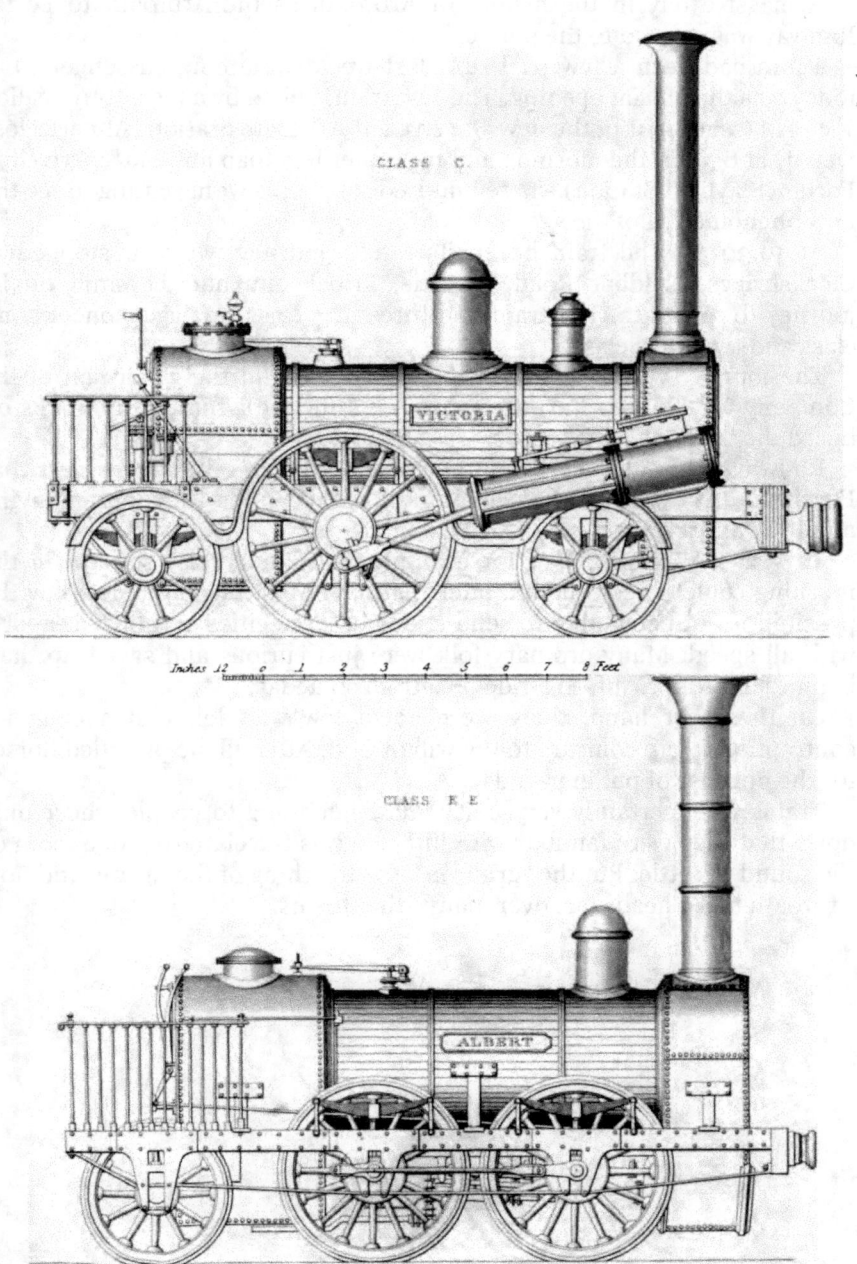

Locomotives Victoria and Albert

January 3 1839

A massive day in the history of Arbroath as the Arbroath to Forfar Railway was opened to the public.

There had been a few trial runs last week containing passengers, but today was the official opening. The first train, pulled by a locomotive called *Victoria* (in honour of the new Queen), left Arbroath Station (Almerlecloss Depot) at 8.30 in the morning and in "rather less than an hour", arrived in Forfar (Playfield Station) where hundreds of people were waiting to see the new phenomenon of the age.

At 10.30 am the train began its return journey where it stopped at Clocksbriggs, Auldbar Road, Guthrie, Friockheim and Leysmill on its journey to Arbroath. The train had three first class carriages, one second class and two third class.

The journey was repeated in the afternoon, and the Chairman of the Company Mr Lindsay Carnegie provided a meal for some of the VIPs on board the train.

Railways had only been around for about ten years, and it was clear that Forfar and Arbroath were ahead of most of the United Kingdom in having a railway and a station.

It was now hoped that, for example, fish landed in Arbroath in the morning could be sold inland later that day! Most business men saw the possibilities of being able to send goods to large cities and busy seaports with all speed. Many ordinary folk were just curious and saved up their pennies in order to afford a ride on a train someday.

On the other hand, there were not a few who felt that such noisy contraptions were contrary to the will of God. After all, he provided horses for the purpose of pulling goods.

Trains were certainly very noisy and frightening to people whose only noise that they were familiar with hitherto was the clattering of a loom or the sound of cattle. But the "gridiron" was the thing of the future, and now Arbroath had a head start over many other towns.

January 4 1904

Fortunately no-one was injured, but a considerable amount of damage was caused in an alarming incident in Arbroath harbour today.

The large steamer "Cumbrian" of Bo'ness, bringing a cargo of 200 tons of flax from Pernau in Estonia had been lying outside the harbour since Hogmanay because of adverse weather, but today at high tide decided to attempt entrance.

There was still a considerable swell on the sea, and the ship rolled from side to side. Her starboard bow collided rather violently with the west quay of the harbour. Just as she got past the pierheads she came with tremendous force against the wall of the quay. A large number of stones were dislodged and the wall was broken in parts.

A large hole was knocked into the bow of the vessel, some of the iron plates were damaged, and the blades of the propeller were badly damaged as well. The ship was examined the following day and it was decided that the ship would have to return to dry dock in Grangemouth for repair.

The Harbour Trustees were also examining the damage to the wall, but it was understood that the pilot was totally exonerated from blame. The incident created a huge interest, and the following day saw a huge influx of local people to the harbour to see the damage. The crew were now safely ashore, but it was not yet clear who was going to pay the substantial costs involved.

January 5 1932

Can and should Arbroath smokies be canned?

This question is exercising the minds of quite a few people at the moment. On the one hand, there are those who react with horror at the very suggestion, for surely the attraction of the Arbroath smokie (and indeed any kind of fish) is that it is fresh?

Indeed one of the many reasons for visiting Arbroath is to enjoy a smokie in the very town which has made them famous. On the other hand, "canning" smokies would allow them to be on sale in places like the USA, Europe and even Australia.

Provost Chapel has been in communication with Mr Edgar Hodges and Sir Edgar Jones of the Empire Marketing Board, samples of the product have been sent and the reply has been that "there is no reason why these could not be canned, but one great reason that would operate against this is the fact that the cost would apparently be too much for a profit to be made after the canning process had been completed".

This all seems to be boil down to the fact that there would not be enough money in this idea. The idea was therefore dropped, at least temporarily, and the purists breathed a large sigh of relief that smokies would not be "canned" for export and gain, and that the smokie industry would remain in the town and would indeed be a tourist attraction.

Yet it was an avenue that had to be explored. This was 1932 and the world was in economic recession.

January 6 1844

The New Year seems to have passed peacefully in Arbroath according to the first edition of the year of *The Arbroath Guide*.

The day was observed as a holiday. The streets were quiet and quite a few people had decided to visit relatives outside the town, something that the railway now made more possible.

There was a report of boys in Montrose wandering around the streets using "improper language", but nothing like that happened in Arbroath! The Churches of the town were still in a state of confusion and flux with so many local churches having seceded from the established Church in what became known as the great Disruption of last year.

There is a movement to set up a Museum in Arbroath, something that would enhance the town, but there is a basic problem in that no-one seems able to find suitable premises to house the large collection of objects that have already been donated. These range from the exotic, e. g. a bust of Cleopatra, to the gruesome whale's teeth and a huge quantity of coins from various sources.

More pertinently the weather has now taken a turn for the colder following a very mild and congenial December, but *The Arbroath Guide* is confident that the town will win the battle against the cold, for coals and blankets have been donated by many kind people for the benefit of the poor.

The Soup Kitchen Committee is working hard to ensure that Field Marshall Winter, who is aided by officers like Lieutenant-General Fever, Major-General Low Wages, Captain Drink and Colonel Despair will be defeated on the battle field of Arbroath!

January 7 1955

Arbroath Amateur Dramatic Society this week put on three One Act Plays in the Webster Memorial Hall.

It was described by *The Arbroath Herald* as "enjoyable if restrained entertainment". The critic could be said to be "damning with faint praise" although his criticisms are less of the actors than of the choice of plays.

The first play, for example, "The Six Wives of Calais" is described as having "little to recommend it other beyond the chance for nice costumes and the opportunity for providing parts for an all-women cast"

The acting was generally good although the eagle-eyed critic noticed a "distinct lack of wedding rings" which of course the "Six Wives of Calais" should have been wearing.

The second play was more meaty. It was called "Baps", and it was a Scots comedy set in a baker's shop. It went well, although one of the characters, an Englishman, clearly had problems with the Doric dialect.

The third play "Fair Rosamund" was about a love affair involving Henry II and his paramour with a tragic ending. It was well done, and the setting was particularly impressive.

The attendance was not what it could have been, and causes one to wonder whether the first week in the New Year is the best time for putting on drama, but full marks to a talented cast of about 25 people over the whole three plays with George Shepherd, Margaret Swankie and a young girl called Helen Turnbull in particular singled out for praise.

January 8 2022

All good things have to come to an end sometime and today saw the end of Arbroath's unbeaten run in the Championship, as they went down to a 0-1 defeat to Ayr United at Somerset Park.

Dick Campbell's men had been unbeaten since October 2021, and this defeat was unexpected although it perhaps owed something to "new Manager bounce" as it is called, for Ayr United had just appointed a new Manager called Lee Bullen.

It was a disappointment for the Red Lichties however, because they had come close in the first half through Scott Stewart and James Craigen before Ayr scored through taking advantage of what was basically a defensive error. Arbroath then pressed hard all the second half but simply lacked the penetration to get through a "parked bus" defence.

It was odd to see the home team employing tactics like that. This result was a big disappointment to the sizeable Arbroath support who had made their way to the other side of the country, but nevertheless, they were still top of the table with 38 points from 21 games, and they were still in the Scottish Cup.

The Championship was a strange League this season with a sub-division of five teams at the top, then a big gap before five struggling to avoid relegation. The other team in the "top" section were Kilmarnock, Partick Thistle, Raith Rovers and Inverness.

Dick Campbell

January 9 1918

"Resigned acceptance" seems to be the general mood prevailing in Arbroath these days with the question of "When will it ever end?" not far from the lips of many people.

New Year is now well and truly over and the Station has seen the departure of those lucky Arbroath soldiers who were given some few days leave over the holiday period. There were tearful departures and the real thought that the loved ones might not be seen again, as the local press continues to print melancholy details of casualties of local soldiers and sailors, where a wound is looked upon as "good" news!

Meanwhile the Palace Cinema tries its best to cheer everyone up with its silent films (everyone is looking forward to the next Charlie Chaplin!) and good wholesome local music.

The weather has been grim as well, but everyone knows that once the weather breaks and the spring appears, there will be another of those "pushes" which have promised so much, but have left so many soldiers dead or unaccounted for.

Food is less of a problem in Arbroath with the abundance of fish and a blind eye turned to the undeniable black marketing that goes on. The character of the war has changed. Russia is now out of the war and Germany has won in the East, but the Americans are now with us.

Ah yes, the Americans! But where are they? For Arbroathians, it is hard to disagree with the sentiments of the popular song made so popular by soldiers, usually sung in a maudlin, plaintive melancholic way, when they were home on leave at New Year

> When this lousy war is over
> No more soldiering for me
> When I put my civvy clothes on
> Oh, how happy I will be!

January 10 1914

The monthly meeting of Arbroath School Board was held tonight under the Chairmanship of Mr George Reid.

Attendance figures at the various schools were read out for the month of December 1913, with the average attendance about 87.5. There was also a report on the amount of clothes distributed to poor children. Up to the New Year, 60 pairs of boots, 26 pairs of stockings and 95 articles of undergarments had been distributed.

It was decided after some debate that the Supplementary Classes should continue to be taught at Keptie School even though it meant more accommodation would have to be sought, and plans were discussed for a new block at Arbroath High School to contain a gymnasium and a music room.

There was a proposal to buy a small steam engine and boiler for the instruction of the fourth year engineering class at the Evening Continuation Classes held at the High School, and that one might be available for £25.

There had been an objection from the Angus Education Department about an 80-hour session for dressmaking, stating that they would only pay for 40 hours.

The Clerk was instructed to write to the Department to state that this year's arrangements had been agreed, and should not be interfered with. It appears that the Department were wishing millinery, dressmaking and cooking to be amalgamated into a course called household management.

January 11 1896

The Arbroath Total Abstinence Society held its usual Saturday night meeting in the Victoria Hall.

It was of course the habit to meet on a Saturday night quite deliberately as a counter attraction to the alcohol consumption that was going on elsewhere, and next Saturday night, there was going to be a special treat with the Montrose Premier Troupe of Minstrels coming to entertain.

Tonight, in spite of the somewhat inclement weather, there was a reasonable attendance to hear some solos from Miss Jessie Hogg, Miss Lownie and Mr Mathers, accompanied on the piano by Miss Spink.

Two young men Master Clark and Master Robbie combined to give a splendid display of solo dancing to pipe music. Then Mr D G Dorward, a school teacher, gave an address, advocating temperance, and remarked that in his job he had seen so many of the bad effects of alcohol on members of a drunkard's family, and how important it was to ensure that young children should learn the true facts of the deleterious effects of strong drink.

A by-election was coming in Arbroath, and he hoped that everyone, no matter what their political beliefs were, should vote for a party and a candidate that was in favour of legislation to limit the consumption of alcohol.

There was certainly enough cause for concern about alcohol, but a few people questioned whether limiting the sale of alcohol would in itself solve the problem. Did not the problem lie in poverty and deprivation, and the need of so many people to forget the horrors that surrounded them?

January 12 1937

Today Arbroath Town Councillors were entertained by Messrs Carnegie Soutar and Sons Ltd at their new Café Moderne which had just opened.

The Councillors were also taken on a tour round the premises which were the last word in 1930s standards of hygiene and cleanliness. Provost Sir William Chapel congratulated the firm on their enterprise and said that the town would always do its best to encourage firms of this kind in their attempt to make Arbroath a very attractive venue for visitors.

Things were now beginning to boom in the area with the holiday industry, and he was sure that the new Café would be a great asset to the town in the summer. There was also in his speech a little by-play between himself and Provost Hugh H Soutar of Montrose who was a Director of the firm Carnegie Soutar.

There had always been a little rivalry between the two towns on the Angus coast, but on this occasion the firm had decided to go for Arbroath rather than Montrose because Arbroath, of course, had its new swimming pool, which was likely to attract many visitors to the town.

It was a competition that Arbroath was always more likely to win because Arbroath was bigger and because of the direct rail link to Forfar, more likely to attract local tourists. There was however a market for tourism in Montrose as well, and it was hoped that both towns could co-exist harmoniously.

January 13 1945

The weather is still dark and grim, and the war continues with relentless ferocity, although the feeling is growing that there must be an end to it soon.

The Arbroath Herald still contains a few notices about soldiers killed in action or dying as a result of wounds sustained earlier, but also a few happier notices about men being awarded honours for bravery or gallantry.

There is a lighter side to life as well as today Lady Chapel opens an exhibition of paintings in the Public Library Art Galleries. There were about 70 such paintings and they are from the Scottish Modern Arts Association, and it was rare to see such a large collection in a provincial museum.

Lady Chapel and Mrs Kemp, the organiser, both said that they hoped that the people of Arbroath, including school children and members of the Armed Forces would come and enjoy the pictures, because it was important to be able in such times of stress to enjoy paintings.

The arts – music, drama, cinema, painting, opera and ballet – boomed in war years with the idea that there was no point in winning a war if one of the rewards was not going to be the beautiful things in life, which really must now be brought to all levels of society and enjoyed by everyone.

It was hoped that the good people of Arbroath would avail themselves of the opportunity to enjoy these paintings, and a few tours would be arranged.

Arbroath Public Library

January 14 1897

Today in San Francisco, California, an Arbroath ship reached its destination after having been at sea for a total of 183 days!

This was the iron barque "Elliot", 1050 tons, registered in Arbroath and belonging to Mr W Bowen junior. It had previously belonged to Provost James Muir.

It had enjoyed many adventures, the worst being a snowstorm, blizzard and hurricane as she rounded Cape Horn in August 1896. The decks were buried under heavy snowfalls and the rigging was clogged with frozen snow in sub-zero temperatures as the sea ran "mountains high".

The ship sustained major damage and its cargo "shifted" (ie slid all over place) causing damage to the deckhouse, doors and bulwarks. The ship might have gone under, but it was rescued and towed to the haven of Port Stanley in the Falkland Islands by a British cruiser. There they were able to repair the damage and discharge some of the cargo, and the injured members of the crew were able to be treated, before resuming the voyage to California.

Thanks to the miracles of modern communication by telegraphy, Arbroath was able to keep in touch with its progress (or the lack of it) but it was still a relief to hear that the barque had reached port. For a long time, nothing had been heard and relatives of those on board feared the worst.

But now there was the return journey to be faced. Work had stalled on the Panama Canal, and it would be 1914 before it was opened.

January 15 1922

Quite the worst fall of snow for about 40 years since the 1880s fell on Arbroath and other parts of Scotland this Sunday.

The intensity and suddenness of it all was quite frightening and it rather dispelled the commonly held belief that because of what would 100 years later be called "climate change", snowstorms were a thing of the past!

It had been very frosty overnight, but then just as Arbroath was going to Church, it came "oan-ding", as the saying goes, and by the afternoon, the town was virtually paralysed with travel in and out of the town impossible, but local Ministers were all delighted at the number of people who managed to trudge through the snow (many of them enjoying the novelty of it all!) for the evening services.

When night fell, the snow abated a little but continued intermittently throughout the night. Telephone and telegram communication was badly disrupted, but the trains were able to run as far as Montrose and Dundee at least, thanks to the services of a snowplough.

In the ongoing 1920s debate as to whether rail transport was better than road transport, on this occasion at least, rail won! But Arbroath being Arbroath, the salt in the sea air came to its rescue. The snow melted a little quicker than it did elsewhere, although this caused fresh problems with slush and flooding, and it was in any case a day or two before anyone could venture by road inland to either Forfar or Brechin.

January 16 1923

The "wireless" is the coming thing in the 1920s.

Tonight in Arbroath, the few possessors of wireless installations were "delighted and astonished beyond measure" at the wonderfully clear reception by their instruments of the beautiful strains of orchestra and vocalists from the Opera House at Covent Garden in London.

This is a particularly good night because it is calm and Arbroath is believed to be particularly well placed because of being on the coast and because the sound waves travel better over the sea than they do over mountains and hills.

Some nights the reception has not been so good and fog seems to have an adverse effect on the radio waves. It is clear that there are many possibilities here – we might, for example, hear the King speaking from London or even someone commentating on a football match.

The Arbroath Herald is very keen to let everyone know about the role played by local man James Bowman Lindsay in the invention of telegraphy without wires.

Lindsay was born in Carmyllie and lived from 1799 to 1862. Among other things in an eventful life he managed to send messages across the Tay at Glencarse without using wires but by a primitive form of electricity.

Although Marconi is correctly regarded as the inventor of radio communication, local boy James Bowman Lindsay played his part in the amazing new invention which allows people at their fireside in Arbroath to listen to concerts and operas in London!

January 17 1960

This weekend at the Seaforth Hotel a "school" was held by the South Angus Liberal Unionist Association.

The name itself was confusing because the "Liberal Unionist" were in fact Conservatives whose MP Sir James A L Duncan "took the whip" and voted for the Conservatives in the House of Commons. The name was possibly a piece of camouflage in an attempt to pick up the Liberal vote, which of course was very strong in Arbroath and in Angus in general. The Liberal Unionists had in the 1920s been the "Coalition" Liberals of Lloyd George.

In any case, 55 students attended and they had talks from various MPs, a Brains Trust on Saturday night, and this Sunday, Mr T W Strachan gave a talk on "Problems In The Colonies" while Mr I W Mowat gave a more mundane talk on "Problems In Organisation".

The talk on the colonies was very relevant to 1960. Indeed there were some who even found the word "colonies" patronising and offensive, for it was round about this very time that Prime Minister Harold MacMillan was talking about "The Winds Of Change" which were blowing through Africa, and that the day was fast approaching when Britain's imperial posturing would have to stop.

It was a challenging time for those who believed in the British Empire, but its day had passed. What the future was going to bring, no-one knew. The weekend however was generally believed to have been a success.

January 18 1904

Today John Morley, Liberal MP for Montrose Burghs, was granted the Freedom of the Burgh of Arbroath and thus became its most recent Burgess.

Such a ceremony was now looked upon as more than a little archaic and lacking in any real meaning, but it was a token of how highly he was regarded as an MP in the constituency which he had now served since the 1896 by-election.

He had just recently finished writing a biography of the late William Ewart Gladstone. It was highly acclaimed, but it also subjected him to a few harsh barbs about how he had possibly spent too much time working on the book to the detriment of his constituency work.

He had not been seen all that often in Arbroath of late, but he graciously accepted the award at a ceremony in the Town House that afternoon, and then he addressed a meeting in the Public Hall that evening. He spoke well, and not without humour but he never allowed himself to be distracted by "hecklers or dissidents".

Naturally he was very critical of the Conservative Government of Arthur Balfour and felt that there had to be a General Election fairly soon so that the good people of Arbroath would be able to make their protest against the Chinese Slave Labour scandal that had recently been unearthed, as well as the general corruption and nepotism of the Conservatives.

Arthur Balfour had recently taken over from Robert Salisbury as Prime Minister. And how was that? Well, "Bob's your uncle"! Morley was given a polite, and in some cases, enthusiastic hearing from his audience.

January 19 1957

It is very seldom that football in Arbroath has such a bad day as it had today.

It would have been a great deal better, one feels, if the frost had been just that wee bit harder and the games had all been off.

As it was, nine Arbroath teams took the field today and all nine retired beaten. Arbroath FC themselves were at that most desolate of grounds, Albion Rovers, where they lost 0-2 to the Coatbridge side with the small band of dedicated fans now reconciled to the certainty that, yet again, there was to be no promotion this year.

Ashdale, Vics, Youth Clubs, both Lads Clubs and the three High School FPs teams all went down as well. There were a few hard luck stories. Ashdale had to start with only nine men at Gayfield because two of their players who lived in Brechin were held up by a late bus.

One of the High School FP teams suffered really hard luck by going down to Morgan Academy FPs 2-6 – but two of the goals were clearly offside and another came about when a friendly dog ran on to the field and impeded the Arbroath goalkeeper from getting to the ball!

So, there were no open top buses and showings off of trophies in Arbroath tonight! Even smiles were scarce among the footballing fraternity, and it was scant consolation that night to read *The Sporting Post* singing the praises of two Arbroathian goalkeepers playing with distinction for other teams – Bill Brown for Dundee and Jimmy Mowat for Forfar!

January 20 1912

As the dark days of January are slowly beginning to show a little more daylight in the morning and the afternoon, it is good to think that cricket will, in a few months, be returning to Lochlands.

Cricket fans have been following with interest the England tour of Australia by reading about it in the evening newspapers, and the deeds of Wilfred Rhodes and Jack Hobbs have provided a great deal of happiness.

But *The Arbroath Herald* also has news of two one-time Arbroath United players doing well for themselves in South Africa, in particular the ex-professional Charlie Boyes, who had hit a score of 73 for his team.

As his partner he had D L Ferrier, who was also an old Lochlands favourite. The two of them had not partnered each other for the past 20 years since their happy days at Lochlands when they used to treat the spectators to some terrific hitting.

Also in the same South African team was another man with Arbroath connections and this was Dave Nourse who, in 1907, when the South Africans were in England with their famous spin bowlers, played as a guest for Arbroath at Lochlands and ran up a century against Brechin.

It is always good to hear about cricket in winter, for it encourages people to think that summer is not far away, and this year the omens are good for Arbroath cricket, particularly with that devastating spinner Bob Sievwright around!

January 21 1894

Sunday in Arbroath and indeed in Victorian society generally was still a quiet day, considered to be a day of rest.

Not everyone agreed, of course, and there were some activities that went on — to the tut-tutting of the religious. Occasionally, one saw boys playing football and women hanging out their washing!

There were now signs however that the Churches were striking back by organising their own Sabbath activities. Today for example the Mission Hall had over 220 children at their free Sunday breakfast, which was then followed by a talk from the Missionary and several hymns were sung "the whole meeting being particularly bright and cheerful". This clearly says a lot for the Mission Hall, and it also says a lot about the poverty in the town if 220 children were there for a free breakfast.

There were however a lot fewer than 220 people at the Sunday night concert in the New Public Hall in the evening. The programme embraced some solos from oratorios and some popular songs as well as sacred, religious music but failed to attract a large audience, even on a night which, for January, was not all that bad.

One assumes that this was because the programme fell between two stools – had it been entirely religious music with stirring redemption songs, it might have attracted a larger audience, mainly of Churchgoers. But Arbroath was clearly not yet ready for Music Hall type entertainment on a Sunday.

January 22 1901

Round about 7.30 pm tonight the Town Bell began to toll for no obvious reason, but everyone suspected that they knew what it meant.

The Queen was dead. A telegram reached the Post Office, the offices of *The Arbroath Herald* and the Town Hall with the news that affected everyone so much.

It was no real surprise for she was well into her eighties and had been ill for some time. She had died in Osborne House on the Isle of Wight surrounded by her family, including ironically (in view of later events) her grandson, the Kaiser of Germany.

A couple of days later, *The Arbroath Herald* appeared with black edges round its news stories and paid eloquent tribute to her, with best wishes to her son King Edward VII who had now acceded to the throne after a very long wait!

It would be true to say that she wasn't universally loved in Arbroath. Her excessive wealth, her self-indulgent sulk after the death of Prince Albert, and the fact that she was seldom (more or less never!) seen in these parts made her not as totally popular as the local press would have us believe.

Nevertheless, she had been Queen since 1837, and those who remembered her predecessor King William IV were few and far between in Arbroath, and due respect was paid to her in the days leading up to her funeral on February 2.

In the meantime the war in South Africa was continuing and causing a fair amount of anxiety to those Arbroath mothers and wives who had sons serving there.

January 23 1937

This was the last night of Arbroath Amateur Operatic Society's production of "A Country Girl" which finished tonight in the Webster Memorial Hall.

It was with a sigh of relief that the final curtain fell this Saturday night, one feels, for the Society had been stricken with a difficult problem on the week of the show.

George Morris, who played the part of the Rajah of Bhong, fell ill with influenza and could not play his part on Wednesday and Thursday. For these two nights, young Ian Hunter ably deputised at short notice and his doing so was much appreciated by the audience who forgave him the occasional understandable blemish.

George Morris was able to perform on Friday and Saturday, something that also earned him a special round of applause from the audience. At the end, appreciation and thanks were paid by President Neil Robertson to Producer Addison Will, who had himself been ill as well, Conductor William Hunter and Pianist Miss Ramage.

It had been a cheerful sort of a show with fine costumes and a vindication perhaps of their decision a few years ago not to focus exclusively on Gilbert and Sullivan operas. "A Country Girl" is a simple tale, and none too demanding for the audience, and the cheerful setting provided a pleasant contrast to a bleak Scottish town like Arbroath in January.

The illness among the cast was perhaps inevitable for a production at this time of year, and raised the question of the wisdom of putting on a show in January.

January 24 1445

Today took place the Battle of Arbroath for control of the Abbey, which effectively meant control of the whole area.

On the one side were the Crawfords and the Lindsays, and on the other were the Ogilvys. What seems to have happened is that the monks of Arbroath Abbey appointed Alexander Lindsay, Master of Crawford as their "Bailie of the Regality", mean effectively their landlord and leader.

Unfortunately, Lindsay did not exercise his powers wisely and among other things, billeted his soldiers in the Abbey without paying for them, and the soldiers with their drinking and whoring brought the Abbey into disrepute. Thus the monks sacked Lindsay and appointed Alexander Ogilvy, Baron of Inverquharity in his stead.

The Lindsays and the Crawfords did not take kindly to all this and recruited various other clans to join their side before they attacked the Abbey on this day. Apparently the Earl of Crawford tried to mediate to prevent unnecessary bloodshed, but one of the Ogilvys saw him, threw a spear at him and killed him, thus precipitating the battle in which the Ogilvys were routed and driven out of the Abbey.

A few days later after they had tried to rally at Leysmill, the Ogilvys were defeated again, and were not seen back in Arbroath for a long time after that, tending to settle in what is now the Kirriemuir area of Angus.

As was the wont in medieval times, the idea of compassion to the vanquished was a non-starter, and the Crawford and Lindsays embarked on a prolonged campaign of pillage and slaughter.

Arbroath Abbey

January 25 1902

Arbroath had seldom seen anything like this.

It was a cold day (well, it isn't very often warm at Gayfield in January!) with an icy blast coming from the north, as Glasgow Celtic took on the locals in the Scottish Cup in what was Arbroath's biggest ever game to this point.

Celtic had tried to buy ground rights for this game in return for a very substantial bribe, but the Arbroath Directors laudably turned it down and they were awarded with a crowd which yielded over £111 9/2d and another £20 for the stand.

A heavy fall of snow just before kick-off might have deterred a few from attending, but the grandstand was full and about 10,000 gathered round the ropes with both the local maroons and the green and white vertical stripes well supported.

The snow had been quite fierce, "falling like pancakes" according to one unlikely account, but had stopped by the time that the teams took the field.

Arbroath's team was McKenzie, Carrie and Clark; McGlashan, Cargill and Ferguson; Black, Middleton, Axford, Willocks and Dilly.

To the horror of those who were supporting the green and white brigade, Arbroath scored first through Dilly. Indeed Arbroath went into the lead again after Campbell had equalised for Celtic, this time through Black after he had got the better of Battles.

This time Orr brought Celtic level to make it 2-2 at half time, but then Celtic scored the winner in the second half as part-time Arbroath tired, centre half Henry "Beef" Marshall being the "shootist" as *The Arbroath Herald* describes him.

January 26 1955

It is no great secret that the railway service from Arbroath to Forfar is going to close soon.

It is a shame for the railway link has been running since 1839 and has done a great job. But it is no longer "viable" and will be closed down. No point in complaining really, but what does one do now if one wants to go to Forfar?

Well, Alexander and Sons Ltd run a daily service, but it is far from satisfactory with very few buses, all at the wrong time etc. In particular there is no service at night, so the various Dance Halls of Arbroath are deprived of their customers from Forfar and the inland areas.

Today the small Forfar firm Davidson and Smith was applying to the Licensing Authority for Public Service Vehicles for a licence to run one bus from Forfar to Arbroath on a Saturday night and back leaving Arbroath no later than 11.45 pm.

Naturally the Dance Halls supported this idea but amazingly, this petition was opposed by Alexander and Sons Ltd who felt some sort of threat to their monopoly. Yet, the question was reasonably asked what business was it of theirs, if they had no intention of providing a service at the same time?

Their objections were overruled and there would now be a Dancers Bus from Forfar to Arbroath on a Saturday night. A more valid objection might have been raised on the ground of the likelihood of trouble on these buses. "Incidents" were not unheard of!

January 27 1910

Today the great Arbroath sportsman Davie Storrier died of tuberculosis at the age of 37. He was a licensed grocer in Panmure Street, and left a wife but had no children.

David Storrier

His career in both football and cricket had been remarkable. He had started off playing for Ardenlea, a junior football team, then Arbroath, Everton, Celtic, Dundee and Millwall.

When with Celtic, he won two Scottish Cup medals at left back in 1899 (McArthur, Welford and Storrier) against Rangers, and at right back (McArthur, Storrier and Battles) in 1900 against Queen's Park, and also in 1899 he played for Scotland in the 1-2 defeat to England at Villa Park.

He was one of two Arbroathians playing for Scotland that day, the other being goalkeeper Ned Doig, now playing for Sunderland. He also played against Ireland and Wales that year. As a cricketer, he played for Arbroath United and Forfarshire, suffering a serious blow to the head from a cricket ball in June 1902 and playing for Forfarshire the day of the North Inch disaster at Perth in 1903.

He remained a keen player and supporter of Arbroath United until his death but had suffered from "indifferent health" for some time. He was an amiable, modest and well-liked man, but had cause to feel bitter about his departure from Celtic in 1901 when he was suspected of "malingering", when in fact he may have been genuinely ill.

January 28 1978

Not for the first time in history were Arbroath people thankful that they lived on the coast, as the worst blizzard in living memory hit the Highlands, Aberdeenshire and, closer to home, the inland area of Angus. The roads to Forfar and Brechin were blocked at various points during the day and the snow ploughs fighting a losing battle.

In Arbroath the wind and the precipitation were just as severe, but it was more like sleet rather than snow and it did not lie to the same extent as it did inland.

Arbroath even managed to play their Scottish Cup tie at Gayfield against Motherwell, but they must have wished that they hadn't, for they were on the wrong side of a rather severe 4-0 defeat.

The weather is seldom great at Gayfield in January, and this was a collector's item of horror. It was one of those days where the comedians said "Four nil, and they were lucky to get nil!", but there was real concern at the end about how the sizable Motherwell support were to get home, for reports were coming in all afternoon about roadblocks etc.

That night as the news programmes became more and more pessimistic with the news about the rest of Scotland, there was however a certain smugness about how good it is to live in Arbroath in the wind and the rain!

On a serious note, quite a few people lost their lives in the snow in the Highlands. One man, famously, a commercial traveller in undergarments, marooned in his car, saved himself by putting on about 20 pairs of ladies tights!

January 29 1912

The funeral took place of Sergeant James Cobb, a veteran of the 93rd Foot in the Crimean Peninsular battles.

He was born in Menmuir, Caterthun, Angus on 12th June 1826, the son of David Cobb. Encouraged by a veteran, a Mr Davidson, he enrolled at the of 15. He spent five years in Canada, then sailed for Malta, then Varna, and finally to the Crimea.

At Balaclava, he witnessed the "The Charge of the Light Brigade". At Sebastopol, he lay with the 93rd for months in trenches, where he was wounded in the thigh, and retired from active service.

The well-attended funeral saw the cortege, accompanied by "The Flowers of the Forest", move from the house to the grave in the north-west of the cemetery.

The pall-bearers were his sons, James Cobb, 33 Jamieson Street, John Cobb, 4 Lochland Street, and Alfred Cobb, 30 Kyd Street, together with his brother John Cobb, of Brechin, and his grandsons James Cobb, and Cobb of Jamieson Street, James Cobb and Murray Cobb of Lochlands Street.

Funeral of James Cobb

January 29 1936

Friendly local rivalry between the towns of Arbroath, Forfar and Brechin is very common, particularly in the sports of football (at senior, junior and school levels) and cricket with the occasional other sport as well.

Today a less common sport saw its introduction in a competition sponsored by the Arbroath Physical Culture Club at the Red Triangle Hut. This was Weight Lifting, a sport which, it would be fair to say, was not widely practised in either Arbroath, Forfar or Brechin.

But tonight before an audience of family, friends and a sprinkling of interested and curious spectators of both sexes, B Butchart, P White and W McRae appeared for the Red Lichties against the Loons of Forfar and a team from the Cathedral City of Brechin.

The contest was refereed by the famous Dundee weight lifter Willie Simpson who was at pains to explain the complicated rules of the competition to the audience.

In an exhibition, Simpson himself gave a demonstration by raising 245 lb on the "Two Hands and the Clean Jerk", a feat which involved lifting the weight above his head. The three categories were the "Military Press", the "Two Hand Snatch", and the "Snatch and Clean Jerk".

Forfar won, Arbroath were second and Brechin third with the best individual performance being that of J Downie of Forfar who lifted a weight of 210 pounds on the "Clean Jerk".

It was an interesting competition, and the opinion was impressed that none of the local toughs was likely to give the Forfar and Brechin boys any bother as they made their way to their train!

January 30 1906

The reporter of *The Arbroath Herald* was given a sneak preview of The Yeomen Of The Guard, an opera of Gilbert and Sullivan to be put on by the Arbroath Amateur Operatic Society soon.

This was clearly an attempt to boost sales of tickets, and the reporter does so, saying that is just as well that the General Election is over, and that the Scottish Cup tie has passed (Arbroath sustained a heavy 1-4 defeat to Bo'ness United), for both would have had to take second place to what the reporter is convinced will be a very good show indeed.

He has been to the previous three productions of the Society and every time has been very impressed. He gives a synopsis of the plot – a necessary thing, one feels, for Gilbert and Sullivan plots are often hard to follow. Although he says that the Yeomen Of The Guard does not compete with The Mikado for "sheer fun", there is no lack of enjoyment in the show, and he predicts that this, the fourth production of the Society, will be the best so far with the song "I Have A Song To Sing, Oh" well worth the entrance money on its own.

Emma Geddes is very good as Phoebe, David Scott likewise as Wilfred Shadbolt and Mary Strachan does a good Elsie. He is confident that when he comes back to see the performance, he will rate this one the best of all.

January 31 1953

Although Arbroath escaped the worst of the storm today and thankfully there was no loss of life, there was still a great deal of damage done to the town and the surrounding district.

No part of the British Isles was totally exempt, but the East Coast seems to have got off comparatively lightly. The major disaster was on the Irish Sea where 133 people were drowned on the Princess Victoria but loss of life was reported all over England and Scotland.

The main damage done to Arbroath and the surrounding district was the blowing down of trees with the consequent disruption to electric supplies. Almost every street in town had at least one chimney pot blown down either on to the street or on to the roof of the house. For example, at 8 Keptie Street a chimney head built of large blocks of masonry was blown into the attic bedroom of the house, but fortunately no-one was in there asleep.

Sections of the glass roof at the swimming pool were shattered but fortunately the swimmers had been cleared and part of the side of the old stand at Gayfield (it was indeed very old) was blown away, and damage done to the perimeter fence.

The following day the town looked like "it had been in a war film" in the graphic account of one bystander, and driving a car through the town was more or less impossible without having to take many detours. It was just as well that a wind of such ferocity had not been coming from the East, for Arbroath would then have been totally exposed.

Auchmithie wedding

February

Bradshaw's railway timetable for February 1906

February 1 1930

As strong a gale as anyone could remember whipped the East Coast today, rendering social life and sporting fixtures virtually impossible in Arbroath.

Golf tournaments had to be abandoned, and it was as well that Arbroath were playing at Celtic Park that day.

In Glasgow conditions were described as "gusty", but they were certainly better than in Arbroath where the major spectator sport of the afternoon seemed to be standing to watch the waves which were quite spectacular as long as you were on the shore!

One or two local fixtures at Junior level took place but in farcical conditions and at least one was abandoned at half time. Fishing was clearly out of the question for today (it had been the same yesterday) but the reinforcement of the sea wall with timber and sandbags seemed to have had its effect.

A curious phenomenon however was the gravel beach. A couple of weeks ago, when the weather was similar but the wind was blowing from a different direction, the gravel had disappeared. Today it came back!

The storm lasted for several hours, but in spite of it causing a great deal of anxiety, no loss of life was reported and only very minimal damage to property. February was clearly off to a stormy start, but it had followed a January which was, by most standards, not too bad with an absence of real winter conditions like snow and ice, but a plethora of rain and damp, unpleasant conditions.

February 2 1892

The Arbroath Presbytery met in the Town Hall tonight to discuss, among other things, the vexed question of Sabbath observance and whether there were any people carrying out work on a Sunday.

For some time, the Church had felt that it had been losing this battle, as one or two horses and carts had been seen around Arbroath apparently transporting goods.

Sunday newspapers had not yet made an appearance – at least not in Scotland – but it was obvious that Monday newspapers could not appear on Monday morning without quite a lot of work on the Sunday.

There were quite a lot of other people who simply had to work on a Sunday, for example farm labourers who had to feed the animals. Should doctors attend the sick on a Sunday? Should the Arbroath lifeboat go out to rescue a boat in distress on the sea on a Sunday?

Generally speaking the working classes in factories agreed with and supported the Church, for a day off on Sunday was the only break from their dull monotony that they were likely to get. Local ministers reported a varied picture, but there was such a thing as "essential workers" who had to work on a Sunday – including, of course, ministers!

Curiously for a society that was so obsessed with the Bible, no-one felt like raising the basic question of when the Sabbath actually was. Could a strong case not be put forward for saying that, in Biblical terms, the Sabbath was actually Saturday?

February 3 1817

The Caledonian Mercury reports a meeting on the Town Common in Arbroath of a considerable number of persons "mainly of the working classes".

The protesters had been summoned by bills posted on Church doors about their grievances and in particular the need to reform the lower House of Parliament.

They included a fair amount of war wounded – men with one leg, or bits of an arm missing — and they were generally welcomed and cheered as they arrived. These were not easy times in Arbroath. The defeat of Napoleon a couple of years ago had not been accompanied by any great prosperity.

Indeed as often happens, there had been a slump in trade, and with Parliament being as corrupt as it was, there seemed to be very few legitimate ways of complaining. The authorities, obsessed with what had happened in France in 1789, naturally feared violence and disorder and would have been prepared to deploy troops, but in Arbroath, the Provost and the Town Council agreed to support the protesters.

In fact, there was a huge amount of legitimate grievances — the high price of corn, the inability to resettle veteran soldiers and the reckless behaviour of the Prince Regent. Even a small Scottish coastal town like Arbroath was not immune to such tensions, and indeed this would be a constant motif for the next few years.

There was however a general agreement that Parliament itself needed to be reformed, and this would be the dominant theme of the Arbroath protest to Edinburgh and London.

February 4 1946

Tonight the Police Committee of Angus County Council rejected an ambitious plan for the building of a Greyhound Racing Track on a site to the north of the Eastern Cemetery.

The plan had been controversial, with many people all for it, on the grounds that it would bring jobs to the town and possibly make Arbroath a mecca for greyhound enthusiasts from all over the country.

The counter argument tended to come from the religious wing of the town and people who felt that it was undesirable to have such an institution so close to the Dale School. Moreover it would encroach on Arbroath's Green Belt.

The application was made on behalf of William Harvey Small of Inverleith Road, and opposed by the Town Council, the Kirk Session of St Vigeans and the Commander of the Royal Naval Air Service, Arbroath School Management Committee and Hopemount Church Sunday School.

The opposition was a "mighty strong" one and the application was rejected unanimously. The decision was not necessarily agreed with by traders in the town, for it would have been a good development with the ground to hold 10,000 people, and a grandstand of about 1,000.

It would have made "the dogs at Arbroath" a great Saturday night attraction for people from Dundee, Forfar and even as far away as Aberdeen and would have been a boost to the tourist and the hospitality industry in the town.

But the moral argument won the day and Arbroath did not "go to the dogs".

February 4 2013

February 4 2013

Jan (Hilary Tasker) and her husband (Aaron Bain) rent a remote cabin from an odd farmer (Gordon Holder). Then her

February 4 2013

I'LL BE BACK BEFORE MIDNIGHT

a thriller by Peter Colley

2013

CAST

Jan	-	Hilary Tasker
Greg	-	Aaron Bain
Laura	-	Nadia Grace Steel
George	-	Gordon Holder

Producer/Director **Alan Johnston**

EVENTS

ACT I
Scene 1 – An evening in early spring
Scene 2 – The next morning
Scene 3 – That night

INTERVAL

ACT II
Scene 1 – A few moments later
Scene 2 – Evening, a week later
Scene 3 – That night, just before midnight

WARNING

There will be several
GUN SHOTS & unexpected LOUD NOISES in this production

PRODUCTION CREW

STAGE MANAGERS
William McKenzie, Heather Osborne

SET DESIGN
Alan Johnston

SET BUILDERS
Dave Ferguson, Ian Anderson, Ginny Graham, Tony Bogulack, Bob Johnston, Jim Ratcliffe

SET PAINTERS
Caroline Pennant Jones, Dorothy Parfitt, Pat Stewart, Bill McKenzie

LIGHTING & SOUND
Stephen Gilbert, Debbi Proctor, Selina King, Cath Eddie, Doug

COSTUMES
Lex Sawley, Maria Masson, Fiona Burnett

PROMPT	PUBLICITY
Pat McInroy	**Anne Smith**
FRONT OF HOUSE	CATERING
Bob Sawley & Theatre Members	**Kirsty Gibb & Theatre Members**

EXHIBITION IN THE UPPER LOUNGE

by **TONY BOGULACK**

February 5 1919

The influenza epidemic has been raging in Arbroath since before the end of the war, and today it claimed a notable casualty in the death of John Douglas Kilpatrick, Geographical (sic) Teacher at Arbroath High School when his influenza developed into pneumonia.

He was only 27. He had been enlisted in July into the King's Own Scottish Borderers in the "comb out" of 1918 and was demobilised in early January.

He returned to Arbroath High School only last week on Monday, fell ill with flu last Wednesday and died of pneumonia this Wednesday. He was to be buried in his home town of Stranraer and the school was given a half day so that teachers and pupils could follow his cortège from his lodgings in Hill Street to the Station.

It was one of Arbroath's many sad days at this time, and it highlighted the major problem that Arbroath High School and its associated primaries were facing about staffing because of the Spanish flu pandemic.

Strenuous efforts had been made to get teachers in the services demobbed early, and appeals were made for retired teachers to come back and help out. There was even the suggestion that the Leaving Certificates could be postponed until later in the year because of the amount of teachers and pupils who were ill.

The hope was expressed that the virus might lose its effect with the warmer weather, and thankfully not every bout was as severe as that which laid low poor Mr Kilpatrick.

February 6 1952

Early this morning, King George VI passed away.

It was hardly unexpected for he had been an ill man for several years and had recently undergone an operation for lung cancer. He had been a heavy smoker all his life. Yet the death itself was sudden, and when rumours began to spread round Arbroath, they were dismissed as just that – rumours.

But then flags were flown at half-mast from public buildings, and the steeple bell began to toll at noon, and the wireless (the radio) gave the sad news interspersing the news with solemn Bach music.

Provost John F. Webster sent a telegram to the new Queen, currently in Kenya. There was a certain affinity for the King in Arbroath because his wife was from Angus, from Glamis Castle, and a certain sympathy for the man who was never meant to be King but who had nevertheless steered the country through the most difficult times imaginable.

All Arbroath cinemas closed for a night as a matter or respect, and the Operatic Society's performance of "No! No! Nanette" was postponed until next Monday with tickets already bought valid for that night.

A couple of days later, the new Queen was proclaimed at the Market Cross opposite the Town House. King George VI had been King since December 1936 when his brother abdicated, and he was well respected in the town even by those who had a few republican or socialist sympathies.

Proclamation of Queen Elizabeth II, February 1952

February 7 1872

At least 20 Arbroath men are currently engaged on the construction of the new Tay Railway Bridge near Dundee. Work began in 1871, and the bridge designed by Dr Thomas Bouch is being built by the Hopkin Gilkes firm of Middlesbrough, who are heavily dependent of local labour, including these men from Arbroath.

It is even considered to be an honour to be allowed to work on this project which will make a huge revolutionary change the railways in general and the area on the Tay in particular.

Bridges of this size are not common at this time, but it is hoped that this will eventually allow travel from Arbroath all the way to Edinburgh through Fife.

No-one would anticipate the difference that it would make to Dundee which now overtook Perth as the more important port on the Tay. The work was difficult and dangerous for the 20 local men employed there as it working at a height, but the advantage was that a worker could get to his work (by train) and back every night, and of course it was very well paid.

The idea was that, once the Bridge was built, jute and other goods can be transported a lot more quickly. Jute production might well spread to Arbroath as well. The bridge now has seven "piers" in position and a start had been made to span the gap with girders. Some Arbroath people have even travelled on the train to Dundee just to see this marvel which is being built and which is dominating conversation.

Unfortunately, on 28th December, 1879, the bridge was destroyed in a storm.

Catastrophic collapse of the Tay Bridge.

February 8 1958

For climatic reasons, it is not often that Arbroath suffers from a lot of snow.

Normally if all of Angus is blanketed in snow, Arbroath and Montrose escape the worst, but today was different because the bad weather came from the east.

In fact, it was part of the same weather system which had played a part in causing the crash of the aeroplane bringing the Manchester United team home at Munich on Thursday.

There had been a fall of snow on Thursday and Friday but it really reached a blizzard on Saturday at lunch time, so much so that the town was paralysed, with only a very few people venturing out to go to the cinemas which laudably remained open.

Cars and even buses had to be abandoned. Trains continued but made slow progress and some passengers decided that enough was enough when they reached a station, and were thus forced to make emergency arrangements for an overnight stay.

A party of Arbroath workers doing construction work in Brechin got as far as Friockheim on the way home, but had to stay there. Saturday night more or less saw Arbroath cut off from the outside world.

Daylight however on Sunday saw the snow stop and this allowed the snow ploughs to do their job and travel to other towns like Montrose and Dundee was possible. But by Monday, the slow thaw became a rapid one, and rain took over.

February 9 1961

More teachers are needed in Arbroath schools with Arbroath High School and most primaries reporting a shortage in key areas. And the situation is hardly likely to get any easier with the proposed opening of a new secondary school in the town next year.

It is of course a national problem and in some ways it is a problem brought about by prosperity. The immediate post war years saw a rise in the birth rate with soldiers coming home from the war and starting a family.

This coincided with the arrival of the National Health Service, which meant that the survival rate of these children improved beyond all recognition, and the result was that there was now a huge number of teenagers – "the baby boomers" — in the world.

Not only that, but there was an intention to raise the school leaving age to 16 rather than 15, a decision that was not popular in the teaching profession! The answer to the problem, according to some members of the education authority, was to bring back more married women whose families had now grown up, and they could now take up a job, even on a temporary basis.

The problem was that so many women teachers in the 1950s "left school to get married", being expected to stay at home to make their husband's tea and wait for the inexorable processes of biology to take place.

But now life had changed. We needed more teachers and women themselves were needing to take a job. Apart from anything else, the money would be quite handy for even, perhaps, the new luxury of the age of affluence — a holiday abroad!

February 10 1922

It was almost a family affair at the Police Court.

Ex-Bailie David Wilson quoted from the Book of Proverbs, to the effect that "Wine is a mocker, strong drink is a brawler and whoever is led astray by it is not wise" to a married couple who had clearly overstepped the mark.

Sadly drunkenness was not a totally uncommon cause of misery in Arbroath in the difficult days of the early 1920s.

Colin and Helen Farquharson of 40 Green Street were charged with having behaved in a disorderly manner in Park Street while drunk, contrary to the Licensing (Scotland) Act. It appears that it was the lady in question who was more inebriated and the instigator of the disorderly conduct.

They both pleaded guilty with Helen saying that it all started when her husband was insulted by another young man who "put his dog on him". Nothing more was heard of the man and his dog.

Ex-Bailie Wilson turned his attention on Colin, saying that he was the son of a respectable father (Arbroath being Arbroath, everyone knew each other!) and that he ought to be ashamed of himself. It was up to him to make sure that his wife didn't drink more than what was good for her.

In the hope that this would be a lesson to them, he was going to let them off lightly with a fine of 10 shillings each or the alternative of seven days in prison. Interesting this idea in 1922 that the man was expected to control his wife!

February 11 1918

There was little doubt that alcohol and its misuse were a major impediment to Great Britain winning the war.

King George V had banned alcohol from all Royal premises, and Prime Minister Lloyd George, himself a teetotaller, imposed tough conditions on the sale of alcohol.

One of them was a "No Treating" rule which meant that you were not allowed to buy drink for anyone else, and you couldn't therefore have "rounds", the Government reckoning correctly that more alcohol was consumed that way.

Today at Dundee Sheriff Court, Sheriff Neish dealt with the case of James Hunter Paterson, spirit dealer of Millgate, Arbroath who was accused of having, in his licensed premises, served to William Lyall, farm servant at Monfieth a pint of beer, which had been purchased by Thomas Matthewson, labourer, Arbroath. This transaction had presumably been spotted by a plain clothes policeman or Government spy.

Rather ungallantly, Mr Paterson, the publican, tried to blame it all on his wife. At the time in question he was upstairs having his tea, and his wife was in charge. It was possible, he conceded, that his wife, in the heat of the moment and under pressure from other customers, may have made this mistake, and therefore he decided to plead guilty but to ask for leniency.

Sheriff Neish was not impressed and imposed a fine of £5, a not inconsiderable amount in 1918 and, to be fair, a somewhat draconian punishment for a fairly trivial offence, which may indeed have been a genuine mistake. But things are different in war time.

February 12 1934

Chief Constable James MacDonald, in his Annual Report, announces that there has been a decrease in crime in Arbroath. 30 fewer crimes have been reported than the previous year, leaving a total of 222 offences in which criminal proceedings have been instituted.

Fines have totalled £106 in 1933 as distinct from £254 in 1932. Property and articles stolen amounted to £53, £19 of which had been recovered.

Chief Constable MacDonald paid a great deal of tribute to Arbroath's unemployed, some of whom had been out of work through no fault of their own but they had resisted the temptation to augment their meagre income through dishonest means.

He also paid tribute to the officials of the Working Men's Club who had done so much to provide social and recreational activities for those out of work. Chief Constable MacDonald also commented on the number of premises, both business and domestic, which did not seem to have been adequately locked or secured during the night, leaving an open invitation to crime.

There were 74 road accidents in 1933, 56 of them involving motor vehicles but, mercifully, only one fatal accident. The present strength of the police force in Arbroath at the moment is one Chief Constable, one Inspector, three Sergeants and fourteen Constables.

Generally speaking, law and order was seldom a major problem in Arbroath. Saturday night was always the problem night with drunks, and now and again holiday makers in the summer could get out of hand, but Arbroath had in 1933 been generally a peaceful place.

Arbroath police force, 1932

February 13 1922

There was a disappointing turnout of people at the fifth of a series of lecture recitals held by the YMCA and Social Institute at the Webster Memorial Hall.

This was a shame, for it was a lecture by Lady Parrott on "Some Women Characters From Dickens". Sir Francis Webster presided and remarked scathingly to the meagre audience that it seemed to be a rule in Arbroath that "the better the lecturer, the smaller the audience". (This was put slightly more earthily by a member of the audience who muttered under his breath that "Arbroath's taste is a' in its erse!").

Sir Francis remembered hearing from those who had been alive at the time of the queues that awaited the arrival of the serialisation of The Pickwick Papers, and said that you could only get such queues at football matches now.

Lady Parrott spoke well, saying that Dickens was a "knight errant", seeing the appalling problems in society concerning poverty and other things and attacking them through his writings. He had been unhappily married however and this possibly reflected his portrayal of women.

Nevertheless there were some great characters like the brusque but large hearted Betsy Trotwood in David Copperfield, and Dickens was capable of idealising women as well.

The Vote of Thanks was given by George Stewart, and in reply Lady Parrott said that she was not too disappointed in the turnout tonight because it was compensated for by the quality of the audience, and that she would be delighted to come back to Arbroath some time.

Sir Francis Webster

February 14 1953

Tonight the Arbroath Amateur Operatic Society finished its performance of "The Mikado" in the Webster Memorial Hall.

The Hall building was gifted by Sir Francis Webster and his brothers William and James to Arbroath Town Council, in memory of Sir Francis' son Lieutenant Joseph F Webster, killed 30th October 1914 at Zaandvoorde Ridge.

A painted portrait of Lieutenant Webster hangs inside the Assembly Hall of the Theatre. The building was originally used for entertainment, with meeting rooms for various societies and as a home for the collections of the Arbroath Museum Society.

It was the first time that the Operatic Society had done a Gilbert and Sullivan opera since 1933, and the last time that they had done "The Mikado" was 1929. There were still some veterans of that show in the Chorus and a few more in the audience.

The Arbroath Guide reports that the spontaneous movements were a pleasant change from the more regimental form of choral dancing which had been common since the end of the war. There was a Chorus of about 50, and they were all well costumed and choreographed.

"The Mikado" is the best of the Gilbert and Sullivan operas, according to the critic, but the principals rose to the challenge and much praise was bestowed on Margaret Robb, Robert Brown, John Corbett, Wilfred Forrester and others, and it was a very pleasant occasion for lovers of music.

The whole thing was well orchestrated and co-ordinated, according to the theatre critic of *The Arbroath Guide*. This was their Jubilee performance, for they first appeared on an Arbroath stage in February 1903, but for obvious reasons of wars and other things, this was not their 50th annual performance.

The Press pays tribute to the group for their hard work and determination not to fall by the wayside as so many other dramatic/operatic groups had done.

February 15 1942

This Sunday brought the worst news of the war, although it was a few days later before it was confirmed. Singapore had fallen to the Japanese.

This disaster was brought about by British incompetence on a colossal scale. Fingers were rightly pointed at Lieutenant-General Arthur Percival, but also at Prime Minister Winston Churchill himself who, apparently, did not realise that all the defences were concentrated on the sea side of Singapore, and the peninsula was virtually undefended.

He had also demanded that Percival should fight to the last man, but Percival disobeyed him and agreed to unconditional surrender in the face of all the air raids. It was the biggest surrender in British military history.

All this of course happened on the other side of the world and did not immediately threaten Great Britain, but there were many Arbroath men serving, for example, in the Gordon Highlanders who were now in captivity and now subject to the vilest of ill treatment.

Mothers and wives had already heard stories of Japanese brutality – and what subsequently happened was every bit as bad as the worst rumours.

In the meantime, history was made in Arbroath with the first ever appointment of a female Minister to any Church. This was May Findlay who had received a "unanimous call" to the Queen Street Congregational Church.

One of her first duties would have been to pray for the many Arbroath soldiers now facing several years of the hell of a Japanese Prisoner of War camp, and to comfort anxious relatives of these men.

February 16 1905

The medieval crime of sheep stealing has returned to Arbroath.

Not for a very long time has this crime been recorded, but today at the Police Court, Bailie John Duncan had to deal with such a case.

Before him appeared George Robb, baker, George Street and James Duff, shepherd, West Common, charged with having stolen from a flock of which Duff was in charge, two sheep with Robb on the additional charge of reset for trying to sell them on.

Mr McNeil, prosecuting, stated that the sheep belonged to Mr Archibald Clark, Saucher Farm, Collace, Fife, and they had been wintering near Arbroath in the charge of James Duff.

There were 441 in the flock but four were now missing. Mr Clark had now come to take charge of the flock. How the men were caught is not clear, but it seems that there was a plan to misappropriate a few sheep hoping that they would not be missed.

Both men were remitted to the Sheriff Court because of the severity of the charge. It was also clear that Robb was having some serious personal problems for he had apparently tried to take his own life in the police cells using the buckle of a belt.

He had been taken to the Infirmary, and had been brought from there to the Court in a cab, having had to be helped upstairs. All in all, it was one of the more unusual of cases to appear at Arbroath Police Court.

Staff at Arbroath Infirmary, 1905. Dr Dewar, left; Miss Gordon and Dr Laing at the back.

February 17 1925

Motor accidents are not common in Arbroath, but today there occurred one which highlighted the problems of the increasingly common motor bicycles on icy roads in winter.

It happened on Keptie Road early this morning before the sun had been able to melt the ice. It concerned a man called Arthur Rennie of 34 Damacre Road, Brechin who was returning home after working his night shift as a linesman at the Arbroath General Post Office.

While in the vicinity of the Gallowden Laundry, he was seen to be thrown over the handle bars of his motor cycle. No other vehicle, motorised or horse drawn was near him when it happened. Several people rushed to his aid and discovered him in an unconscious condition with wounds and bruises on his head and face.

A van was immediately procured from the nearby Laundry and he was conveyed to Arbroath Royal Infirmary, where he was immediately examined by the resident physician amidst great fear for his life.

At about mid-day however, he regained consciousness and there doesn't seem to be any brain damage. His injuries, though extensive and painful, are not considered to be a threat to his life but he will be kept in the Infirmary for several days.

This incident provoked a discussion in several circles in the town about the safety or otherwise of motor cycles. The problem was that they travelled so fast. It was felt that speed limits should be rigorously enforced, and that crash helmets should be introduced and made compulsory.

As for ice on the road, there was little that could be done, although someone did suggest sprinkling the surfaces with sand or grit.

February 18 1919

The Spanish flu epidemic which had lain comparatively dormant since Armistice Day in Arbroath has returned with a vengeance.

It hit the town with 16 people having died in the past few days. Rarely, if ever, says *The Arbroath Herald* has it been its sad duty to report quite so many deaths. The bulk of the deaths has been among the old as the flu has turned very quickly into pneumonia or bronchitis, and very many of "our residenters" have passed away.

It does affect the young people as well, although not so badly, and there seems to be no 100% safeguard against the illness. Medical advice is to make sure that all rooms are reasonably well heated and ventilated (two things that were very difficult to do simultaneously in the houses of Arbroath in 1919) and to stay away from crowded places, again something that was not easy to do.

The long term causes are, of course, the malnutrition and poor diet of the war years, plus the psychological effect of the war on so many people.

The medical profession in 1919 was slow to spot a link between mental and physical health, but it was a potent factor, for one of the things that everyone kept saying was to keep cheerful and to ignore the depressing propaganda of the "four horsemen of the apocalypse" brigade who kept pointing out that war, pestilence, hunger and death were all happening in 1919!

February 19 1887

Today saw the International debut of John Edward Doig (commonly known as "Ned") in the goal for Scotland at Hampden Park against Ireland.

Doig had been very impressive for Arbroath all this season, and it was a great honour for him to be "capped" for Scotland in this way, becoming the first Arbroath player, as far as can be established, to play for his country.

Although most supporters preferred to stay at home to watch Arbroath playing Montrose, a few went to Glasgow to see him play in the 4-1 win.

Football was not yet common in Ireland being only played in the area around Belfast, while the rest of the country, in so far as they played sports at all, preferred other, more traditional Irish games.

Scotland usually beat Ireland (and Wales) with a degree of ease, and the opportunity was often taken to give players a trial, as it were, for the "big" International against England.

Ned played well today "keeping a quiet goal" as the idiom went, and the only goal that Scotland conceded was from a "scrimmage".

The crowd was a big one of about 3,000 and it was a great experience for Ned to play in front of a crowd much larger than he was used to. Playing alongside players of Queen's Park, Hearts, Vale of Leven and St Bernards was a learning experience for him as well.

He would eventually play five times for Scotland, not a bad achievement for the boy from Letham.

February 20 1903

Never let it be said that *The Arbroath Herald* does not care for its women readers!

This week's edition has a whole Ladies Column in which it gives some wholesome advice to ladies. After all, a great deal of its readership is female, and quite a few of them, frankly have little to do with their lives.

We are, of course, here talking about the middle classes. Women of the textile industries and the fishing community have enough to do to keep body and soul together!

But here, for example, we have *The Arbroath Herald* telling women how to polish new boots (with a little lime juice, apparently), advises on a use for old table cloths, and how to renovate a brown Gladstone bag by using a bizarre combination of the inside of a banana skin, skimmed milk and methylated spirit.

But the main advice this week concerns knitting. It is a very beneficial and therapeutic exercise for women who have rheumatic or arthritic problems in their hands and fingers, but also for those women (and you can almost hear the voice being lowered here) who suffer from insomnia and depression.

In some sanatoriums, women are encouraged to use brightly coloured needles and the work is very pleasant and much enjoyed by them! And there are times in the year and even in the day when it is best to try on new shoes, and a lot depends on the kind of stockings that the lady is wearing!

One almost hoped that the good ladies of Arbroath paid attention to all this, and did not allow themselves to be diverted by subversive influences like Suffragettes!

February 21 1950

Arbroath tonight had a visit from one of Scotland's most famous writers of the day in Helen W Pryde.

She was the creator of the famous "McFlannels" series on the radio in the 1940s and early 1950s, a soap opera about working class Glasgow folk with all their famous sayings like "We've never died o' winter yet" and "a terrible tribulation".

Helen, who had a cottage near Forfar, was in town tonight at the Webster Memorial Hall to support John Jenkins, the Liberal candidate in the coming General Election.

Jenkins appeared on the platform with his mother and Mrs Pryde in a clear attempt to win the vote of the women. Jenkins himself spoke well and then so did his mother, but it was generally agreed that Mrs Pryde stole the show.

She start by making a joke that the country was suffering from a bad disease called "electionitis" which could occasionally result in one losing one's friends. She said that the Tories wanted to make a land fit for the wealthy to live in, and that Labour wanted to make a land fit for bureaucrats to live in, but the Liberal idea of profit sharing was a good one.

One of the reasons that she supported the Liberals however was that they were interested in self-government for Scotland. She proved to be charming and was quite happy to talk to people afterwards about the McFlannels. But alas for her efforts! The Election was held a few days later and the Conservatives won in Arbroath.

February 22 1898

Conservative and traditional Arbroath opinion would have been shocked, one feels, by the meeting that took place tonight in the Bank Street Hall.

There were several aspects of this meeting which would not have happened even 10 years previously.

In the first place it was organised by the new political party called the Independent Labour Party, a party that was formed only five years before out of frustration with the slow gradualism of the Liberal Party; in the second place the meeting was addressed by a woman, Mrs Olive M Aldridge.

The third novel, or at least unusual feature was the use of a lantern which showed some "beautiful" lime light views. The subject was hardly "beautiful" though because it was about slum life in a talk entitled "The land and its relation to the health and comfort of the people".

Before a large attendance, presided over by Mr W Hood, the baker, Mrs Aldridge spoke eloquently about the present land system and the iniquities which prevailed in the overcrowding of large sections of city life.

Most Arbroath people would have been unaware of most of this. A small town did not have the extremes of overcrowding, although there were very many houses unfit for human habitation. Quite a few of the audience would have seen the sort of thing she was talking about in Dundee, for example.

Mrs Aldridge was given a loud round of applause and a vote of thanks for what she had told them. It was an aspect of Victorian Society that so many people tried to prefer not to know about!

February 23 1947

There is little doubt about what the main topic of conversation is in Arbroath these days.

It is the terrible weather. Arbroath and Montrose because of their proximity to the sea have avoided the absolute worst of the weather in a way that Brechin and Forfar haven't, but the town has not been without its blizzards and its severe frost.

A football has not been kicked in anger for many weeks, for example and Arbroath High School has had to tell its pupils to go home because of its inability to heat them adequately.

Churches have a similar problem. Today one had to be sorry for the shivering figure of the Rev Albert Connon of Knox's Church who was taking his departure to a new charge in Victoria Park Church, Partick West.

His freezing Boys Brigade were there to see him off and his Session Clerk, in presenting him with a wallet of notes, expressed the hope that his new Church would be a little warmer!

The Arbroath Herald, Conservative as always and occasionally blinkered, cannot quite place the cold weather at the feet of any politicians, but nevertheless blames all the current misery on the Labour Government which has "not had a single success to date"!

Sadly for all concerned, although the days are visibly getting longer, the cold spell still has a while to run yet and it will be well into March before anyone can say that this awful winter is over!

February 24 1932

Times are hard in Arbroath these days, as Arbroath in common with other towns and communities throughout the world feels the chill blast of recession.

The Arbroath Herald is a little too pessimistic, one feels, with its heading "Is There Hope For Arbroath?" but concludes that there is! It is however difficult to see any easy way out of what is a global problem.

The National Government in Great Britain seems to think that cuts in Government expenditure is the answer, and Arbroath is suffering. There is also the scourge of the 1930s, the disease called tuberculosis or phthisis. It is slightly easier in Arbroath because of the sea air than in horrendous places like Dundee's slums, but is still a problem.

Tonight at the Phthisis Hut in the Public Health Hospital, some local artistes provide a concert for patients, something that takes a great deal of courage, given that tuberculosis, phthisis or consumption can be infectious, but full marks to the Inverkeilor Players, under Mr Joss, and singers like the Riddle sisters, John Blair and John Bell who provided some entertainment for the poor sufferers from this killer disease.

Mr Hunter was the accompanist and Mrs Setten organised it all. It was a ray of light in the midst of so much gloom. There may one day be a cure of sorts for the economic depression, and scientists are working on a cure for tuberculosis.

February 25 1908

The annual *soirée* of the Ladyloan United Free Church Mission Sunday School was held tonight in the Mission Hall with the Rev J Moffat Scott presiding.

It was a very pleasant occasion. After tea, the Rev Scott spoke and contrasted the welfare of children in the locality 25 years ago with now.

He said that 25 years ago children would come to Mission ill-clad, some without stockings and boots and with their faces unwashed, all of them grateful to get a bun or a piece of bread from the Mission.

Rev Scott claimed that things were much better now with most children cleaner and better clad. He attributed this to the improved education of the people (education had been compulsory in Scotland since 1872) and their improved social conditions.

Most people agreed with Rev Scott but also said that there was a long way to go yet. There had also, he said, been an improvement in the "moral tone" of the youngsters. That was a questionable statement according to some of his listeners, but he was applauded.

Then after addresses from Mr Nicoll of the Band of Hope and from Mr Duncan, the superintendent of the Sunday School, the entertainment began with various songs and recitals mainly from young folk, and indeed from anyone who cared to contribute.

The entertainment was all the better, it was felt, for the fact that it was from the Mission's own folk and in some cases spontaneous. It was an excellent *soirée* and much enjoyed by all.

February 26 1913

Something remarkable was seen in the skies above Arbroath today, namely aeroplanes!

It was the first time that any such thing had flown over the town, and they were observed by the locals with a mixture of wonder, curiosity and some fear. Some religious people still denied that it was possible to fly in the air!

Five planes were seen coming from Edinburgh to their new base in Upper Dysart beyond Lunan Bay. The first one was spotted at about 10 o'clock and the town fell silent so that the whirring noise of the engine and the propellers was heard.

It was estimated that the plane was only 600 feet above the ground. An hour and a half later, another one appeared and although he was higher up, a better view was obtained because the sky was a lot clearer.

Only four were expected, but a fifth one came along as well, travelling so low that some people claimed they actually saw him manipulating the steering wheel.

It was quite a remarkable experience and people expressed amazement at how they were able to move through the air so easily. More wondered how the aeroplanes were able to keep up in the air without collapsing, and someone even ventured to make a joke to the effect that if there were two men on board and they quarrelled, they had better make sure that they did not "fall out"!

February 27 1899

Today before Bailie Alexander, John Fettes, flax dresser, 45 Gravesend, was charged at the instance of the School Board with failure to provide elementary education for his daughter Jessie or to secure her regular attendance at school.

His defence was that he had no opportunity to send his children to school because he was working, his wife had left him and if he went to her, she would get the police to him.

He was asked if he had ever given his wife anything for her upkeep, and he said that she never needed anything from him.

It also appeared that Mr Fettes had a string of conviction for offences like breach of the peace and had paid about £6 in fines. It also transpired that Mrs Fettes had attended a School Board meeting on the subject of the failure to send the children to school.

She had given a good account of herself. She was a respectable woman who had been brought to poverty by her husband's behaviour and now earned a living by teasing ropes because she had not received a penny from her husband for years.

Bailie Alexander felt that Mr Fettes's bad treatment of his wife aggravated his failure to educate his children and such a situation was intolerable. He imposed the full penalty, namely £1 fine or 14 days in prison.

Such cases were sadly very common in Victorian Arbroath, and all the more deplorable because education was now free.

February 28 1974

This was General Election day. Arbroath was part of the South Angus Constituency along with Forfar, Carnoustie and Monifieth. It was traditionally Tory held since the 1940s when the Tories had won it from the Liberals (this was when the constituency was called Montrose Burghs).

The sitting MP was Jock Bruce-Gardyne; this time he was under pressure, not from Labour, but from the Scottish Nationalists who this time fielded a strong candidate called Malcolm Slesser.

The country was in a crisis of inflation and a miners' strike had precipitated this General Election with the country on a Three Day week. Slesser fought hard, particularly in Arbroath itself which he identified as the place where he could pick up most votes from fishermen in particular, and he was not slow to talk about the historical significance of the Declaration of Arbroath.

Bruce-Gardyne, normally seldom seen in town, held a few meetings as well and there were clear signs that he was rattled. If the jute workers of Forfar and Arbroath had realised the potential and opportunities presented by tactical voting, then Slesser might have won. As it was, Bruce Gardyne won, but his vote did not beat the combined total of Labour and SNP.

The SNP managed to get seven MPs in Scotland, as a minority Labour Government took over in Westminster. By the next Election in October, the penny had dropped and the crucial Labour vote transferred to the SNP and enabled them to win.

Jock, Baron Bruce-Gardyne, died in 1990 from a brain tumour.

February 29 1956

The Arbroath and District Music Festival was held tonight in the Webster Memorial Hall tonight.

It was the 24th Annual Festival and it was declared open by the Provost of Montrose, Mr Joseph Calder Cameron, who recalled having been in one of the winning choirs in the first Festival!

Provost Cameron recalled a Spanish adage which said that "he who loves music can do no ill" and that he wished that more nations spent their money on music.

If this happened, the world would be a better place, but he specified that he did not mean "modern spineless music that is a headache". Choirs, Scottish Country Dancing, Singing and Instrumental Playing delighted the audience but the hero was Morris Pert, eight year old son of local music shop proprietor Mr and Mrs J Pert.

Both father and son were suffering from influenza, and Morris was only allowed by his doctor to play in the Piano playing section as long as he returned home immediately after his piece. He played "What Shall We Do This Lovely Day" which won for him the Miss Mary A Dowall Challenge Cup! He went home and told his father, which was a lovely tonic for him!

Also taking part in the Tenor Section of the Singing was Jim Stormont, centre forward of Arbroath FC. He made a bad start to one of his songs but kept going. "He must be quite a sportsman" said the adjudicator.

In this year
Traders in Arbroath in 1890

ii. *Arbroath Year Book Advertisements.*

☞ ALL COMMUNICATIONS TO BE ADDRESSED
"D. & A. COMPANY, LD.,"
ARBROATH.

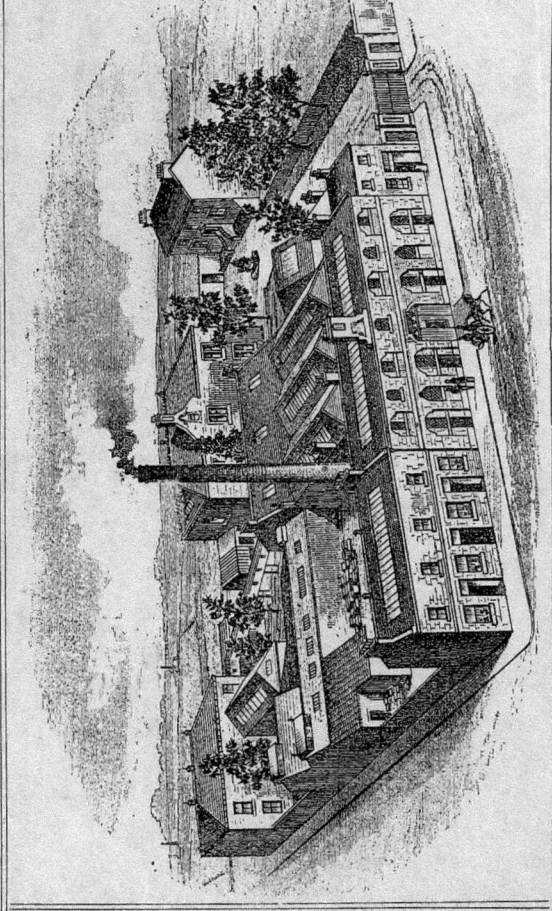

Telephone—DUNDEE, No. 863 : ARBROATH, No. 6
Telegraphic Address—"PRESERVES," ARBROATH.
R. M. TAYLOR, *Managing Director.*

The Dundee & Arbroath Confections AND Preserve Manufacturing Co. Ld.

Manufacturers of Confections, Marmalade, Jams, Jellies, Orange and Lemon Peel, &c.
DUNDEE and ARBROATH.

Established over Fifty Years.

CRAIG'S
GLASS & CHINA WAREHOUSE,
37 MILLGATE, ARBROATH.

THIS Establishment has had the Confidence of the Public for over Half-a-Century, and we still intend to keep to the front by having

The Largest and Best-Selected Stock in Town.

J. B. CRAIG

OFFERS THE BEST VALUE MONEY CAN BUY IN ALL DEPARTMENTS.

NOTE THE ONLY ADDRESS—

CRAIG'S,
37 Millgate, Arbroath.

Commercial Union Assurance Company, Limited.

FIRE—LIFE—MARINE.

CAPITAL FULLY SUBSCRIBED,	£2,500,000
LIFE FUND in Special Trust for Life Policy-Holders,	£1,183,000

Total Invested Funds Exceed Two and a Half Millions.

TOTAL Net Annual Income,	£1,250,000

HEAD OFFICE, - 19 and 20 Cornhill, London, E.C.
EDINBURGH OFFICE, 37 Hanover Street

FIRE DEPARTMENT.

Manager, E. ROGER OWEN. | Assistant Manager, GEO. C. MORANT.

Undoubted Security. Moderate Rates. Prompt and Liberal Settlements.

LIFE DEPARTMENT.

Actuary, T. E. YOUNG, B.A.

The LIFE FUNDS invested in the names of Special Trustees. The ASSURED wholly free from liability.

FOUR-FIFTHS of the Entire LIFE PROFITS belong to Policy Holders.

INTERIM BONUSES are paid.

The EXPENSES OF MANAGEMENT limited by Deed of Settlement.

Liberal SURRENDER VALUES guaranteed; and CLAIMS paid immediately on proof of death and title.

MARRIED WOMEN'S PROPERTY ACT (1882).—Policies are issued to husbands for the benefit of their wives and children, thus creating, without trouble, expense, stamp duty, or legal assistance, a FAMILY SETTLEMENT, which Creditors cannot touch.

Agents in Arbroath—
BENNET & SMITH, Solicitors, 81 High Street.

DAVID ✠ BYARS

Has always in Stock the Latest Novelties
— IN —

MANTLES

MILLINERY   **DRESSMAKING**

Marriage and Mourning Orders Punctually attended to.

Ladies waited upon at their own Residences if desired.

The Central Millinery & Mantle Warehouse,
151 HIGH STREET, ARBROATH.

A. C. Dargie,

House Painter,

4 Dishland Street, Arbroath.

Stained Glass from 1s 6d per Square Ft.   Paper-Hangings from 3d per Piece.

Designs and Estimates on Application.

MISS WHITTON,
The House of Novelties,
147 HIGH STREET, ARBROATH.

Bazaar Goods, Fancy Wools, Silks, Art Goods, Work Baskets, Fancy China, Writing Cases, Purses and Bags, Dolls, Perambulators, Mail Carts, Rocking Horses, &c.

Always in Stock Latest Novelties of Fancy Goods.   High-Class Needlework.

Alexander Petrie,
FAMILY GROCER,
6 WEST PORT, ARBROATH.

FINEST TEAS that can be procured.
Finest **COFFEES** always Fresh Roasted and Ground on the Premises.
Best Quality of Groceries and Provisions at Lowest Prices.
All Orders punctually attended to.   Goods delivered to any part of the Town.

STEVENSON BROTHERS,

The Dundee Dye Works

DYERS, CLEANERS,

→❋ CARPET BEATERS. ❋←

ARBROATH OFFICE:

BROTHOCK BRIDGE.

By leaving Notice or sending Post Card our Vans call for and Deliver Goods.

Feathers Dyed and Curled.

Agents in Arbroath:

MISS LAING, MILLGATE LOAN.
MRS ARCHER, KEPTIE STREET.
JAMES BROWN & Co., 261 HIGH STREET.

The Carse of Gowrie Dairy Company,

(LIMITED),

WHOLESALE & RETAIL DAIRYMEN,

AND

Bakers of all Kinds of Milk Bread.

PURE CREAM.   DEVONSHIRE CREAM.
REFRIGERATED CREAM.

MILK—Creamed and Uncreamed. Butter Milk. Churned Milk and Whey.

FRESH BUTTER. SALT BUTTER. CHEESE—*Various Kinds.*

❧ FRESH EGGS. ❧

Milk Loaves, Milk Biscuits, Pastry, Oat Cakes, and Scones Daily.

OPEN ON SUNDAYS FROM 8 TO 10 A.M.

❧ Luncheon ❋ Rooms : ❧

AT THE
CREAMERY, WARD ROAD,
14 Crichton Street, & 67 Perth Road,
DUNDEE; and at

283 HIGH STREET & BROTHOCK BRIDGE,
ARBROATH.

Where Hot Coffee and Cream, Tea, and other Refreshments, are to be had Daily.

TELEPHONE NUMBERS—DUNDEE, 371; ARBROATH. 15.

Special Orders from Arbroath are Telephoned to THE CREAMERY *and Despatched with all Speed.*

The Public are invited to inspect the Goods and see the process of Manufacture at THE CREAMERY, WARD ROAD, DUNDEE.

WM. SMITH, Manager and Secretary.

Arbroath Year Book Advertisements.

Bibles, Books, Stationery, &c.

W. & J. Boath (Successors to J. BRODIE) have always on hand a Large and Carefully-Selected Stock in all Departments, to which they respectfully invite attention. Agents for RAPHAEL TUCK & SONS' ARTISTS' MATERIAL. Fine Variety of COPIES for Hire. All sizes of OPALS and PLACQUES for Painting &c.

AUTHORISED and REVISED PEW and POCKET BIBLES and TESTAMENTS. Church Services, Prayer Books, Hymn and Tune Books. WORKS OF STANDARD AUTHORS, and BOOKS of GENERAL LITERATURE in Plain and Handsome Bindings.

CALENDAR for 1891.

1891	Sunday	Monday	Tuesday	Wednesday	Thursday	Friday	Saturday
Jan.	...	...	...	...	1	2	3
	4	5	6	7	8	9	10
	11	12	13	14	15	16	17
	18	19	20	21	22	23	24
	25	26	27	28	29	30	31
Feb.	1	2	3	4	5	6	7
	8	9	10	11	12	13	14
	15	16	17	18	19	20	21
	22	23	24	25	26	27	28
Mar.	1	2	3	4	5	6	7
	8	9	10	11	12	13	14
	15	16	17	18	19	20	21
	22	23	24	25	26	27	28
	29	30	31	...	...	...	...
April	...	...	...	1	2	3	4
	5	6	7	8	9	10	11
	12	13	14	15	16	17	18
	19	20	21	22	23	24	25
	26	27	28	29	30	...	...
May	...	...	...	...	...	1	2
	3	4	5	6	7	8	9
	10	11	12	13	14	15	16
	17	18	19	20	21	22	23
	24	25	26	27	28	29	30
	31	...	...	...	...	...	...
June	...	1	2	3	4	5	6
	7	8	9	10	11	12	13
	14	15	16	17	18	19	20
	21	22	23	24	25	26	27
	28	29	30	...	...	...	...

1891	Sunday	Monday	Tuesday	Wednesday	Thursday	Friday	Saturday
July	...	...	...	1	2	3	4
	5	6	7	8	9	10	11
	12	13	14	15	16	17	18
	19	20	21	22	23	24	25
	26	27	28	29	30	31	...
Aug.	...	...	...	...	...	...	1
	2	3	4	5	6	7	8
	9	10	11	12	13	14	15
	16	17	18	19	20	21	22
	23	24	25	26	27	28	29
	30	31	...	...	...	...	...
Sep.	...	...	1	2	3	4	5
	6	7	8	9	10	11	12
	13	14	15	16	17	18	19
	20	21	22	23	24	25	26
	27	28	29	30	...	...	...
Oct.	...	...	...	...	1	2	3
	4	5	6	7	8	9	10
	11	12	13	14	15	16	17
	18	19	20	21	22	23	24
	25	26	27	28	29	30	31
Nov.	1	2	3	4	5	6	7
	8	9	10	11	12	13	14
	15	16	17	18	19	20	21
	22	23	24	25	26	27	28
	29	30	...	...	...	...	...
Dec.	...	...	1	2	3	4	5
	6	7	8	9	10	11	12
	13	14	15	16	17	18	19
	20	21	22	23	24	25	26
	27	28	29	30	31	...	...

PURSES, POCKET BOOKS, WALLETS, CARD CASES, CIGAR CASES, &c. Immense Variety of Fancy Goods, suitable for Souvenirs, &c. WRITING DESKS, WRITING CASES, WORKBOXES, and INKSTANDS in a Variety of Designs.

ADDRESS—BROTHOCK BRIDGE.

North British and Mercantile
INSURANCE COMPANY.
ESTABLISHED 1809.

Incorporated by Royal Charter and Special Acts of Parliament.

FIRE.   LIFE.   ANNUITIES.

Total Assets   -   -   -   £10,075,213

The Funds of the Life Department are not liable for Obligations under the Fire Department, nor are the Funds of the Fire Department liable for Obligations under the Life Department. In this Company, therefore, the Investments for the Life Department are kept entirely separate from those for the Fire Department, as set forth in the Balance-Sheet.

President—HIS GRACE THE DUKE OF ROXBURGH.
Vice-President—HIS GRACE THE DUKE OF SUTHERLAND, K.G.

LIFE DEPARTMENT
IMPORTANT FEATURES.

All Bonuses now vest on Declaration, while, in the event of a claim arising under a participating policy even before a Declaration of bonus, the usual intermediate bonus will be paid.

The period during which a lapsed policy may be revived is extended to one year, and the fine payable on revival is much reduced.

The Surrender Value of a lapsed policy is now held to the credit of the assured during the extended period of ten years ; and during that period the option is allowed of taking a paid-up policy calculated on very favourable terms.

The Suicide clause is abolished.

The form of policy has been shortened and simplified so that the true meaning of the contract may be readily ascertained.

Claims paid immediately *on proof of death and title.*

Premiums adjusted to each *half-year* of age.

Minimum Surrender values fixed.

Policy not forfeited by error in Proposal Papers, unless accompanied by fraud.

General freedom of policies from restriction in Residence, Occupation, and Travel.

Nine-Tenths of the Whole Profits of the Life Assurance Branch are allocated to Participating Policies.

ANNUITY BRANCH—**Annuities**, Immediate, Contingent, or Deferred, are granted on favourable terms.

FIRE DEPARTMENT—Property of nearly every description insured at Home and Abroad at the lowest rate of Premium corresponding to the risk.

LOSSES PROMPTLY AND LIBERALLY SETTLED.

Prospectuses may be had at the Chief Offices, Branches, or Agencies.

CHIEF OFFICES—

EDINBURGH—64 PRINCES ST. | LONDON—61 THREADNEEDLE ST. E.C.
DUNDEE BRANCH OFFICE—13 PANMURE STREET.

Agents in ARBROATH—

J. A. DICKSON & J. M. M'BAIN, British Linen Co. Bank.
R. C. KINLOCH, Bank of Scotland.
MILN & DALGARNO, Solicitors.

NORMAN M'BAIN, Solicitor.
DAVID SMITH, Solicitor.
J. FERGUSON, Accountant.

Arbroath Year Book Advertisements.

J. P. GREWAR & SON,

FUNERAL UNDERTAKING

(Established 1862).

We devote Special Personal Attention to this Department of our Business.

The entire Funeral Arrangements conducted, to suit all Classes, both in Town and Country.
Night and Day Attendance at 62 GRAVESEND.
EVERY REQUISITE SUPPLIED.

GRAVESEND and PANMURE ST., Arbroath.

J. ALEXANDER,

General Linen and Woollen Draper,

HATTER, HOSIER, & GLOVER,

NEW BUILDINGS, HIGH STREET,

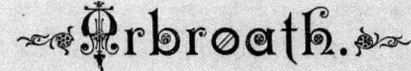

Arbroath.

FLANNELS	SHEETINGS	HATS, CAPS	BRACES, UMBRELLAS
BLANKETS	TICKS	SHIRTS, FRONTS	HANDKERCHIEFS
PLAIDINGS	SHIRTINGS	COLLARS, CUFFS	GLOVES, HOSIERY
BED COVERS	STAYS	SCARFS, TIES	UNDERCLOTHING

A. ✛ JENKINS,

Confectioner,

26 ❋ KEPTIE ❋ STREET,

Nearly Opposite the Railway Station,

ARBROATH.

Fancy Biscuits and Finest Teas, Fruits and Confections of the Finest Quality.

MRS ❋ MACPHERSON,

BROTHOCK BANK,
ARBROATH,

HAS always on hand a Fine Selection of Gold, Silver, and Jet Jewellery, Watches and Clocks, Electro and Silver Plate, Table Spoons, and Best Sheffield Cutlery.

Also, a Large Variety of Fancy and Other Goods.

SPECTACLES  FOLDERS
Adapted to all Sights.   At all Prices.

PRICES IN ALL DEPARTMENTS VERY MODERATE.
INSPECTION RESPECTFULLY INVITED.

JEWELLERY & FANCY WAREHOUSE,
BROTHOCK BRIDGE, ARBROATH.

HEALTHY HOUSES.

"Nothing is so Costly as Disease, nothing is so Remunerative as the Outlay which Augments Health."

Ashphalte. — Is impervious to Damp, Sewage Gases, Vermin, and Dry Rot. Will not crack with setting of building. Properties protected by Asphalte are much increased in Value.

REGISTERED.

Syenitic.—*An Improved Granolithic* Paving Material. Specimens can be seen at Lochshade, Keptie Hill, St Vigeans, and New Inverbrothock Schools, Walker Place, Sydney Street, &c., and in many other towns.

WILLIAM BRIGGS,
ARBROATH and DUNDEE.

Estimates Furnished Gratis.

SMITH'S FURNITURE STORES,
5 & 7 HAMILTON GREEN, ARBROATH.

The only House in Town where you can get Really Substantial Second-Hand Articles of Furniture at Moderate Prices.

FURNITURE, CARPETS, ETC., BOUGHT, SOLD, OR EXCHANGED.

For the Convenience of Parties not able to attend Sales in Town or Country, R. SMITH is ready to Purchase Furniture, &c., at 5 per cent. commission.

FINEST SCOTCH WHISKY.

Matured in Sherry Wood, and Blended in Bond under Excise Supervision.
17s per Gallon ; **2s 10d** per Bottle.

CHARLES A. LOW,
Family Grocer & Wine Merchant,
44 KEPTIE STREET, ARBROATH.

"THE CORNER"
HAT AND CAP SHOP.

HATS.   HATS.   HATS.

Favourite Prices, 2s 6d, 3s 6d, 4s 6d, and 5s.   Better Qualities also kept.

SHIRTS—A Large Assortment in every Material and Size.

CAPS—Hundreds to choose from—6d to 2s 6d—Every Style.

Fronts, Collars, Cuffs, Handkerchiefs, Gloves, Braces, Scarfs, Ties, Umbrellas, Hand-Bags, & Portmanteaus.

Always on Hand a Grand Selection in every Department.

Sole Agent for D. M. MELDRUM & Co., Dundee.   Umbrellas Repaired and Re-Covered on Shortest Notice.

The Corner Hat & Cap Shop,
2 WEST PORT, ARBROATH.

JAMES BRAND, Manager.

ANDREW M'KAY,
FISH DEALER,
WEST PORT, ARBROATH,

HAVING acquired the Business carried on by MRS CHRISTIE, desires to say that it will be his endeavour to give every attention to the wants of his Customers, and by keeping the Best Qualities of Fish, and charging a Moderate Price, he hopes to retain MRS CHRISTIE's Customers, and secure a share of Public Support.

Fresh Fish on Arrival of Boats.

THE IVANHOE,
VERY OLD SCOTCH WHISKY.

☞   A More Honest Whisky cannot   got

To be had from all Grocers and Spirit Merchants, in our Labelled and Capsuled Bottles.

Sole Proprietors — D. A. RHIND & Co., Leith.

SMALL PROFITS AND QUICK RETURNS

JAMES ✛ SEATON,

Family Grocer & Provision Merchant,

IMPORTER OF, AND DEALER IN

TEAS, WINES, AND SPIRITS,

BROTHOCK BRIDGE, ARBROATH.

Excellence of Quality is the True Test of Cheapness.

DAVID COOK & SONS,
Registered Plumbers, Tinsmiths, and Gasfitters,
219 HIGH STREET, ARBROATH.

DAVID COOK, Sen., in thanking his numerous Customers for the very liberal support he has received during the Thirty-three years he has been in business, begs to announce that he has assumed his two sons as partners. His eldest son, JAMES COOK, holds a full Master's Certificate, after a practical examination in Plumbing and Sanitary Engineering Work, at the City and Guilds' London Institute; while DAVID COOK, Jun., has had large experience as a practical Tinsmith and Gasfitter.

The new firm trust that by devoting the greatest care and attention to all work entrusted to them, and by supplying the best possible material at the lowest remunerative prices, to have a continuance of the wide public patronage so long accorded to DAVID COOK.

ADDRESS—
219 HIGH STREET, ARBROATH.

Arbroath Year Book Advertisements.

GEORGE FINLAY,
Purveyor of the Best Butcher Meat,

282 HIGH STREET, ARBROATH
(Opposite the Abbey Tower.)

R. STRACHAN & SONS,
Tailors & Clothiers,
58 HIGH STREET, ARBROATH.

Choice Selection of Cloths always on Hand.   Perfect Fit Guaranteed.

PRUDENTIAL ASSURANCE Co. Ld.

ESTABLISHED 1848.

Annual Premium Income exceeds £4,500,000.
Invested Funds exceed   -   -   £12,000,000.
Bonus Additions average 50 per cent.

All Profit Policies effected before close of 1891 will share in the Division of Profits to be made at close of Financial Year.

Annual Reports and Balance Sheets on application to the Agents, or from

J. SMAIL, *Superintendent*,
11 BANK STREET, Arbroath.

Assistant Superintendent—D. WALLACE, 23 Ladyloan.

Established 25 Years.

Mrs R. G. RUXTON,

Clothier and Outfitter,

21 COMMERCE STREET, Arbroath.

Ladies' Jackets and Mantles in all the Latest Fashions.

EVERY DEPARTMENT UNDER THE MOST EFFICIENT MANAGEMENT.

CLOTHING MADE AFTER DR JAEGER'S SANITARY SYSTEM.

PEOPLE'S BOOT & SHOE ESTABLISHMENT.

Large Stock of BOOTS and SHOES always on hand at Very Low Prices.

Goods made of the Best Material, and Neat Fitting Guaranteed.

HAND-SEWED BOOTS AND SHOES made on the Premises.

☞ CHARGES STRICTLY MODERATE.

James Smith & Son,

38 GUTHRIE PORT, Arbroath.

A. Strachan & Son,
Tailors and Clothiers.

THIS Old-Established Business, which has been successfully conducted for over Half-a-Century, is still being energetically carried on by Mrs STRACHAN. She is being assisted in the Management of the Business by

MR DAVID GUILD,

who has had a lengthened experience in several of the Best Houses in the Trade, and Customers may therefore have every confidence that all Orders entrusted to A. S. & SON will be executed with every regard to Style, Fit, and Finish.

**MOURNING ORDERS
EXECUTED WITH CARE AND PROMPTITUDE.**

LADIES' DEPARTMENT.

Fine Selection of Cloths suitable for LADIES' JACKETS, DOLMANS, and ULSTERS. These can be Made to Measure on very Short Notice. Ladies can have their own Cloth made-up if desired.

128 HIGH STREET, ARBROATH.

JAMES MILNE,
Portrait and Landscape Photographer,

ST RUTH'S, ARBROATH,

AND

ST NINIAN'S SQUARE, BRECHIN.

Studio Work always carefully attended to.

Orders for Photographing RESIDENCES in Town and Country, WEDDING, LAWN TENNIS, CROQUET PARTIES, &c., have careful and prompt attention.

THE ARBROATH AND DISTRICT
ECONOMIC BUILDING SOCIETY

(Registered under the "Building Societies Act, 1874.")

Will make Advances

To its Members by Ballot, for the Purchase or Erection of Houses, or on the Security of Heritable Property in the Sums of £100, £150, up to £500, to be repaid WITHOUT INTEREST in from 1 to 16¾ Years.

Shares £100 each.

Subscriptions, at the rate of 6d per Share, payable Weekly, Monthly, or Quarterly, as may be arranged. These Subscriptions are held as part payment of the advances made.

The Directors

Are appointed annually by the Members, and the whole Management is directly under the control of the Shareholders.

Members

Are Enrolled at the Society's Office, BROTHOCK BANK HOUSE, every FRIDAY EVENING, between Eight and Nine o'clock, by the Secretary, JAMES R. AITKEN, 5 St Vigeans Road, and as the Shares are rapidly being taken up, early application is necessary.

The Last Year's Bonus

Of the Society was equal to a Dividend of fully FIVE PER CENT.

N.B.—The Public are particularly requested to keep in view the fact that in this Society the Advances by Ballot are Repayable WITHOUT INTEREST.

ALEXANDER MATTHEW,
51 GUTHRIE PORT, ARBROATH.

MANUFACTURER OF TOBACCO PIPES AND TOPS, BLUE, WHITE, AND TAILORS' CLAY, POLISHING PASTE, HEARTH STONES, &c.

JAMES SMITH,
ROPE SPINNER,
EAST LINKS & WEST LINKS ROPEWORKS, ARBROATH.

All Orders Carefully and Promptly executed.

Arbroath Year Book Advertisements.

CHARLES S. COPLAND,
(From Stanley's, London),
Watchmaker and Jeweller,
183 HIGH STREET, ARBROATH,

(Sign of the Clock.)

Highest Class of London-Made LEVER WATCHES always in Stock, or Made to Order, and Cased in Gold or Silver.
MARBLE CLOCKS FOR PRESENTATION.
WEDDING AND KEEPER RINGS.

Special attention paid to Watch and Clock Repairing.

LADIES' AND GENTS' HAIRCUTTING SALOON.

Real HAIR SWITCHES from 2s 6d upwards. Ladies' OWN COMBINGS, or CUT HAIR made up in any Style at 1s 6d per Oz.

❦ J. ✻ P. ✻ GIBB, ❧
(From J. Allen & Son, Dundee).
284¼ HIGH STREET, ARBROATH.

ALEXANDER ✢ FYFE,
Joiner, Van Builder, &c.,
9 PONDERLAW STREET,
ARBROATH.

All Kinds of Joiner and Cabinetmaker Work Punctually and Carefully Attended to.

SELECTED STOCK of INDIAN, CHINA and CEYLON TEAS,
Always on Hand—Pure as Imported—at

A. & D. BATCHELOR'S,
Wholesale Tea, Wine, and Spirit Merchants,
BROTHOCK BRIDGE, ARBROATH.

Life, Fire, Accident, & Plate Glass Insurance.

North British and Mercantile Insurance Company—Fire and Life Insurance.

United Kingdom Temperance & Provident General Institution—Life Insurance.

The Accident Insurance Company, Limited.

- Accident Insurance.
- Plate Glass Insurance.
- Fidelity Guarantees.

Agent—NORMAN M'BAIN, Solicitor.

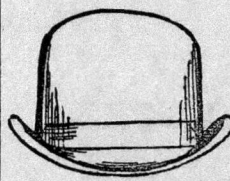

CAMPBELL'S
CELEBRATED
Hat and Cap Depot,
280 HIGH STREET,
ARBROATH
(Sign of the Red Hat).

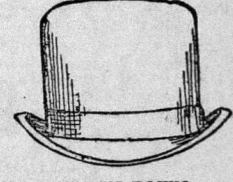

IS DECIDEDLY THE CHEAPEST HAT AND CAP ESTABLISHMENT IN TOWN.

NOTHING BUT FIRST-CLASS GOODS KEPT IN STOCK. EVERY ARTICLE SOLD AT THE LOWEST REMUNERATIVE PRICE.

HATS, CAPS, SCARFS, TIES, COLLARS, CUFFS, FRONTS, DRESS, REGATTA, OXFORD, AND TWEED SHIRTS, GENT.'S HOSIERY, AND GLOVES.

280 HIGH STREET, ARBROATH.

E. & J. MACLURE,
ARBROATH DYE WORKS,
68 HELEN STREET, ARBROATH.

George A. Campbell,

PLASTERER,

15 MILLGATE LOAN, ARBROATH.

Every Description of PLAIN and ORNAMENTAL PLASTER and CEMENT WORK Carefully and Expeditiously Executed.

All Orders promptly attended to in Town and Country.

Estimates given for all Styles of Work.

Victoria Public Buildings Company,
LIMITED,
Victoria Halls, James Street.

Halls for Balls, Concerts, Soirees, Theatre, Public Meetings, Society and Committee Meetings, Marriage and other Festive Parties.

LARGE HALL HOLDS 600 TO 650.   SMALL HALL HOLDS ABOUT 300.
SMALLER ROOMS FOR COMMITTEES, &C.

Particulars of Charges &c., may be had on Application to the Curator,
Sergt. WOOD, 31 Guthrie Hill, Arbroath.

Arbroath Year Book Advertisements.

ALEX ✻ BOATH,
Tailor & Clothier,
66 MARKETGATE, ARBROATH.

SUITS MADE TO MEASURE
FROM 30/-

TROUSERS MADE TO MEASURE
FROM 10/6.

**GENTS' OWN MATERIAL MADE UP
at Moderate Prices.**

SPECIAL.

Gentlemen getting their Clothes made in other Towns, but wishing Repairs or Alterations, can't do better than send to above Address.

Repairs & Alterations, Cleaning, &c., at Moderate Charges.

WILLIAM BRAND,
Slater and Slate Merchant,
30 DISHLAND STREET,
ARBROATH.

☞ All Kinds of Jobbing punctually attended to.

46   *Arbroath Year Book Advertisements.*

Established over 30 Years.

R. A. CUTHILL

(*Successor to Mrs M'Kay, Confectioner*),

KEPTIE STREET POST OFFICE,

Finest CONFECTIONERY at Keenest Prices.

SEED, PLANT, & BULB WAREHOUSE.

Garden and Flower Seeds of every description may always be had Fresh and Reliable.

Plants—Always on Hand a Large Selection. Any Plant not in our Greenhouses may be procured in a Few Days.

Bulbs—a Specialty—**Bouquets, Wreaths, Crosses, &c.**, made to Order on the Shortest Possible Notice.

Bird Seed—Loose and in Packets, Gravel, &c. Tallies, Standens, Manure, &c.

LETTER ORDERS PROMPTLY ATTENDED TO.

R. A. CUTHILL,
KEPTIE STREET POST OFFICE.

CHARLES MITCHELL,
SLATER,
34 HILL STREET, ARBROATH.

All Orders in Town or Country Promptly Attended to.

ESTIMATES GIVEN.

CENTRAL
HAIRDRESSING ESTABLISHMENT.
201 HIGH STREET, ARBROATH.

MESSRS CROWE & Co.,

Have Opened those Nice Central Premises where the Public can with Confidence rely on having their Best Wishes Attended to regarding SHAVING, HAIR-CUTTING, SINGEING, and SHAMPOOING. COMFORT and CLEANLINESS. Nice Assortment of BRUSHES, COMBS, RAZORS, POMADES, &c. Parties can be Attended at their own Residences if Required.

NOTE THE ADDRESS—
201 HIGH STREET, ARBROATH.

DAVID ✣ KERR,

BUTCHER,

250 HIGH ST.,  ARBROATH.

A LARGE STOCK OF
PRIME BEEF, MUTTON, & PORK
Always on Hand.

ALL ORDERS HAVE PROMPT AND CAREFUL ATTENTION.

❊ MISS LEWER, ❊

Milliner and Dressmaker,

130 HIGH STREET, ARBROATH.

LATEST STYLES ALWAYS ON HAND.

DAVID S. TAYLOR,

Photographer,

Studio: 7 GOWAN STREET, ARBROATH.

Enlargements in Bromide and Carbon.

GEORGE CROWE,
HAIRDRESSER,
18 COMMERCE STREET, ARBROATH.

SHAMPOOING AND HAIRBRUSHING.
CLEAN HOT WATER TO EVERY CUSTOMER.
RAZORS, SCISSORS AND GENERAL CUTLERY GROUND AND SET.

H. WESTWATER,
Pastry Baker,
3 ELGIN PLACE, ARBROATH.

All Kinds of FANCY BREAD.
SOIREES, BALLS, and PICNICS Supplied on the Best Terms.
BRIDES' CAKES made from the Finest Material at Lowest Prices.
TRADE SUPPLIED.

GEORGE HUTTON, Shoemaker,
4 ALLAN STREET.

Boots and Shoes made to order on Shortest Notice. Repairing in all its Branches. Best Material and Workmanship. Charges Strictly Moderate. Always in Stock a Large Supply of Ladies', Gent.'s, and Girls' Boots and Shoes from the Best Scotch Manufacturers.

NEW DOCK TAVERN,
53 AND 55 LADYBRIDGE STREET,

DRAUGHT AND BOTTLED BEER IN PRIME CONDITION.

PROPRIETOR—
WILLIAM F. M'HARDY,
(Late of the Black Horse Inn, Montrose).

GEORGE H. STRACHAN,
Sheriff Officer, J. P. Constable, & Burgh Officer.
1 HILL STREET, ARBROATH.

CALDER ❋ BROTHERS,
LOCHLAND STREET,

Builders, Pavement Merchants, & Monumental Masons.

JOBBING OF EVERY DESCRIPTION.
TOMBSTONES IN GRANITE, MARBLE, OR FREESTONE.
INSCRIPTIONS CUT IN TOWN OR COUNTRY.

ESTIMATES GIVEN FOR ALL SORTS OF WORK.

All Orders Promptly Attended to.

D. R. CALDER, LICENSED VALUATOR, undertakes Valuations in Town or Country.

MURRAY & Co.,
Silk Mercers, Montrose.

❋ DRESSMAKING, . . .
❋ MILLINERY, ...
   MANTLEMAKING, . . .
❋ LADIES UNDERCLOTHING,
   BED & TABLE LINEN, &c.

Importer of Foreign Fancy Goods.

Arbroath Year Book Advertisements.

Established 1860.
J. FAIRWEATHER,
Tobacconist, &c.,

Has always on hand a GRAND SELECTION of Goods comprising the following :—
Silver-Mounted Briars, Meerschaums, Asbestos, Clays, Cigars, Pouches, Cut and Bar Tobaccos.
SPECIALTY.—BRUSHES, BASKETS, COMBS, TOYS, BOXES, WALKING STICKS, NICK-NACKS for Presents in Great Variety. INSPECTION INVITED.

207 HIGH STREET, ARBROATH.

ALEXANDER SMITH,
THE LORNE
17 COMMERCE STREET,

Where to get the LION-BRANDED STOUT of which the qualifications go a long way to please the Taster.

Smith's LION-BRANDED STOUT, 2s 6d per doz. Pints.
FAC-SIMILE OF LABEL (LION'S HEAD) ON EACH BOTTLE.

ALEX. SMITH, LORNE BAR, Arbroath.

Goulding's Celebrated Manures.

AGENT—
ROBERT FORBES,
189 HIGH STREET, ARBROATH.

ROBERT DYER,
Registered Plumber, Gasfitter & General Zinc Worker,
BROTHOCK BRIDGE, ARBROATH,

Has always on hand a Large Stock of all kinds of GARDEN and SUCTION Hose.
HOT WATER AND SANITARY APPLIANCES
Supplied or Repaired on the Shortest Notice, and Most Reasonable Terms.

Drains and Sewage Escapes Tested with Patent Apparatus.

Best Home Investment—4, 4½d, & 5 per Cent. Interest Clear of Income-Tax.

THE LIBERATOR PERMANENT
BUILDING AND INVESTMENT SOCIETY,
20 Budge Row, Cannon Street, London, E.C.

Paid-up Capital,—£1,500,000.

President—THE RIGHT HON. THE VISCOUNT OXENBRIDGE.
Vice-President and Honorary Director—J. SPENCER BALFOUR, Esq., M.P.

Directors—
S. R. PATTISON, F.G.S., 11 Queen Victoria Street, E.C., **Chairman.**
GEORGE DIBLEY, 19 Bury Street, E.C., **Vice-Chairman.**
J. BINFIELD BIRD, F.S.I., 14 Queen Victoria Street, E.C.
G. E. BROCK, 20 Budge Row, E.C.   L. B. BURNS, 2 Bond Court, Walbrook, E.C.
J. TEESDALE DAVIS, St Margaret's, Twickenham.
MAJOR WRIGHT, R.E., A.I.C.E., 16 Carlisle Mansions, S.W.

Secretary—J. C. TEMPLE.

Bankers—THE NATIONAL PROVINCIAL BANK OF ENGLAND (LIMITED),

Shares.
SHARES, £30 each, receive Interest at Five per Cent., and Bonus as stated in Prospectus.

Deposits.
DEPOSITS (£5 and upwards) are a First Charge on all the Assets of the Society, and rank prior to over £1,500,000 of fully Paid-up Shares. Interest Four per Cent., repayable on One Month's Notice.
Deposits of £100 to £500 for 1 Year, 4½ per Cent; £500 upward, 5 per Cent.

TABLE SHOWING PROGRESS OF SOCIETY.

For the Year ending	Amount to Credit of Investors.	Amount due by Mortgagors.	Reserve Fund.
	£ s. D.	£ s. D.	£ s. D.
30th June, 1869	7,398 3 10	7,724 2 3	150 0 0
30th June, 1872	159,636 17 1	168,360 14 3	6,000 0 0
30th June, 1878	1,081,867 18 8	1,091,949 13 5	30,000 0 0
30th June, 1880	1,264,510 14 0	1,285,860 13 7	44,000 0 0
30th June, 1883	1,565,773 3 1	1,618,964 9 8	55,000 0 0
30th June, 1886	2,083,231 7 4	2,164,210 15 9	70,000 0 0
31st Decr., 1887	2,275,746 14 6	2,359,860 10 3	75,000 0 0
31st Decr., 1888	2,487,525 14 9	2,568,110 12 5	80,000 0 0
31st Decr., 1889	2,712,777 1 2	2,814,045 18 4	85,000 0 0

Town and Country Members enjoy Equal Facilities, and all Business Communications are Treated as Strictly Confidential.

Interest Paid Half-Yearly Free of Income Tax. Shares and Ordinary Deposits Withdrawable at One Month's Notice.

ADVANCE DEPARTMENT.
Liberal Advances made on Heritable Securities in any part of the United Kingdom. The amount advanced last year was **£589,525 7s 10d** per annum.

The Whole Investments are on Approved Mortgages over Heritable Property within the United Kingdom.

THERE IS NOTHING OF THE BALLOT OR GAMBLING ELEMENT IN THE WORKING OF THIS SOCIETY.

Reports, Prospectuses, and all Particulars Free on Application to

E. J. LESLIE, Solicitor, 1 Hill Street, Arbroath,
DISTRICT AGENT.
Deposits Received at any time.

Ample Security and Good Interest.

The Annual Income exceeds £1,024,000.
The Reserve Fund now amounts to £85,000.

DAVID ❋ ANDERSON,

India, China, and Ceylon Tea Merchant.

BLENDED TEAS
Rich, Pure, and Fragrant.

AFTERNOON TEAS
Delicious Taste and Delicate Flavour.

FAMILY TEAS
Full Flavoured, Rich, and Syrupy.

5, 10, 15, and 20 Lb. Tins, and 20, 40, and 60 Lb. Boxes, at Reduced Rates.

Delivered Daily to all parts of the Town and Country, and Despatched to any Railway Station in the County Free of all Charges.

Sample Free by Post or on Application at the Warehouse.

PRICE LIST OF OVER 1000 ARTICLES ON APPLICATION.

KEPTIE STREET, Arbroath.

TOSH'S STORES,

Cheapest Establishment for Hardware, Tinware, Trunks, Bonnet Boxes, Lamps, Best Oils, Chimneys, Wicks, Cutlery, Combs, Baskets, Dress Stands, Brushes, Door Mats, Mattresses, Feathers, Glass, China, Fancy Wares, Toys, &c. Spectacles to suit all sights from 6d per pair. Lamps, Tinware and Woodware Repaired. Locks and Keys Fitted.

INSPECTION CORDIALLY INVITED.

TOSH'S WHOLESALE STORES, 31 WEST PORT,} ARBROATH.
TOSH'S BRANCH STORES, 67 GUTHRIE PORT,

D. & J. NAPIER,

Practical Sanitary Plumbers, Gasfitters, Bell-Hangers, &c.

34 MAULE STREET, ARBROATH.

SANITARY APPLIANCES ALWAYS IN STOCK.

All Orders in Town and Country Promptly Attended to.

ESTIMATES GIVEN.

MISSES E. & J. ROBERTSON,

Hairdressers and Tobacconists,

19 GUTHRIE PORT, ARBROATH,

Have on Hand a Large Stock of PIPES, TOBACCOS, WALKING STICKS, COMBS, BRUSHES, &c., all of Best Quality at Moderate Prices.

LADIES AND GENT.'S HAIRCUTTING.

Life, Fire, Employers' Liability, and Accident Assurances

 ARRANGED WITH UNDERNOTED COMPANIES.

SCOTTISH WIDOWS' FUND AND LIFE ASSURANCE SOCIETY

COMMERCIAL UNION FIRE AND LIFE ASSURANCE SOCIETY

SCOTTISH EMPLOYERS' LIABILITY AND ACCIDENT ASSURANCE COMPANY, LIMITED

SCOTTISH ACCIDENT ASSURANCE COMPANY, and NORTHERN ACCIDENT ASSURANCE COMPANY

And other Long-Established Companies.

IMPORTANT TO FISHERMEN.

INSURANCE OF BOATS & APPURTENANCES

ARRANGED WITH

NORTH BRITISH FISHING BOAT INSURANCE COMPANY, Limited,

ON MOST LIBERAL TERMS.

ALL PARTICULARS FROM

BENNET ❋ & ❋ SMITH,
SOLICITORS, AGENTS.

SNOW ✢ FLOUR.

SNOW FLOUR is one of the Finest and most Convenient of Self-Raising Flours. It is of very Fine Quality, and the Ease with which it can be used at all times makes it very valuable. For Home-Made Sultana, Madeira or Light Cakes, Plum Puddings, Blanc-Mange, Sandwich Cakes, and all other Dainties.

SNOW FLOUR, 4d PER POUND

Is the Best and most easily-used Material. To be had only from

Mrs BOATH,

Grocer and Fancy Dealer,

78 MARKETGATE, ARBROATH.

GAME AND POULTRY.

Established for a Quarter of a Century.

MRS ✢ CHRISTIE

Has always the Largest and Best Supply of **POULTRY** and **GAME** in its Season.

178 HIGH STREET, Arbroath.

ERNEST SCOTT,

Painter and Decorator,

6 MILLGATE LOAN, ARBROATH.

Painting, Paperhanging, &c. ✢ ✢ Estimates Given.

David Hutchison,
GENERAL DRAPER & SILK MERCER,
1 WEST PORT, ARBROATH.

Every Description of First-Class Drapery kept of the Best Makes at the Lowest Possible Price.

Daily Arrivals of the Latest Novelties in
MANTLES & MILLINERY.

Funerals Conducted in Town or Country.
W. FARQUHAR & Co.,
FUNERAL UNDERTAKERS,
46 AND 48 GUTHRIE PORT, ARBROATH.
ALL ORDERS PROMPTLY EXECUTED.
Charges Strictly Moderate.

The National Bar.
WILLIAM ✢ LYALL,
WINE AND SPIRIT MERCHANT,
286 HIGH STREET, ARBROATH.

Dispensing

OF

PHYSICIANS' AND SURGEONS' PRESCRIPTIONS.

SPECIAL FEATURES.

I.—All Prescriptions compounded with the Purest Drugs and Chemicals, Manufactured strictly according to the various Official Formulæ of the British Pharmacopæia. All inferior Preparations rigorously excluded.

II.—Dispensing charges fixed as low as possible, consistent with the employment of the Best and Purest Drugs obtainable.

III.—All New Remedies Procured and Stocked as soon as introduced.

IV.—Urgent Medicines have immediate attention, and are despatched by Special Messengers.

V.—Medicines forwarded promptly to all parts of the Town, or by Parcel Post to all Parts of the Country.

VI.—No other Business interfered with outside that of a legitimate Chemist and Druggist.

A. ✣ NAYSMITH,

DISPENSING CHEMIST

(From Savory & Moore, Chemists to the Queen, London),

211 HIGH STREET, ARBROATH.

THE BEST HOUSE IN TOWN
FOR EXTRA VALUE IN
Groceries, Provisions, Teas, Wines, Spirits & Malt Liquors

GEORGE ✴ CUTHILL,
Family Grocer, Tea, Wine & Spirit Merchant,
47 KEPTIE STREET (Corner of Helen Street), Arbroath.

JAMES SMITH,
37 WEST PORT,
ARBROATH,

Has always on Hand a Large Selection of the Choicest Fruits. Also, Decorative Plants, Choicest Cut Flowers, Bouquets, Dress Sprays, &c.

Wreaths and Crosses made to Order on a Few Hours' Notice.

37 WEST PORT, ARBROATH.

R. Farquharson,
GLAZIER,
BROTHOCK BRIDGE, ARBROATH,
AND MURRAYGATE, DUNDEE.

CARVER & SYMON,
Architects & Surveyors,
BROTHOCK BANK,
ARBROATH.

WILLIAM TARBAT,

Family Grocer, Tea, Wine, & Spirit Merchant,

36 LOCHLAND STREET,
ARBROATH.

FINEST TEAS, WINES, SPIRITS, &c.

MALT LIQUORS Bottled on Premises and always in Splendid Condition.

☞ PRICE LIST ON APPLICATION. ☜

GEORGE ✢ ESPLIN,
FRUITERER AND GAME DEALER,
27 MILLGATE, ARBROATH.

Largest Dealer in GAME and POULTRY in Town. FRUITS, VEGETABLES, &c., Fresh Daily.

NOTE CHANGE OF ADDRESS—
27 MILLGATE, Arbroath.

J. F. BURNESS,
Family Butcher,

PURVEYOR OF GOOD BEEF AT CHEAP PRICES.

WEST PORT,
ARBROATH.

Arbroath Year Book Advertisements.

GLASS AND CHINA.

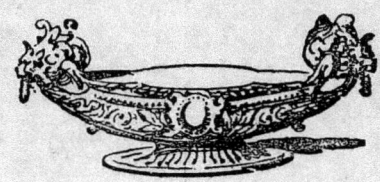

Tea Sets.
Dinner Sets.

Bedroom Sets.
Fancy Goods.

Extensive and Carefully-Selected Stock at Lowest Prices.

ANDREW W. GRAY,
244 HIGH STREET,
ARBROATH.

M. & M. Clark,
BOOT & SHOE WAREHOUSE,
87 HIGH STREET.

Every Variety of Boots, Shoes, and Slippers, kept in Stock.
HYGIENICS, ANATOMICAL & STRAIGHTS,
MADE ON THE NEWEST AND MOST FASHIONABLE LASTS.

DRESS SHOES and SLIPPERS in Great Variety from Best Makers.
Ladies', Misses', and Gent.'s BAGS. Large Stock kept.

Hand-Sewed Work Specially attended to. Repairs Promptly Executed,
AT
87 HIGH STREET, ARBROATH.

Sole Agent for Scafe's Patent Leather and Rubber Combination Boots; also, the Waterproof "K" Boot.

MRS ✢ LITTLEJOHN,
Tobacconist.

Splendid Assortment of TOBACCOS, CIGARS, *and* CIGARETTES.

LARGE VARIETY OF

- Meerschaum and Briar Pipes
- Fancy Goods
- Walking Sticks, Canes, &c.

13 WEST PORT, ARBROATH.

George Duthie,

Tailor and Clothier,

93—HIGH STREET—93

ARBROATH.

Material and Workmanship of the Best Description.

STYLE AND FIT GUARANTEED.

(ARBROATH HERALD OFFICE LITHOGRAPHIC PRINTING MACHINE.)

Plans, Schedules, Circulars, and all other Work in fac-simile promptly executed.

For Specimens and Prices of Plain and Artistic Lithographic Printing apply at the Herald Office.

The HERALD OFFICE is the only Office in Forfarshire (out of Dundee) where Lithographic Printing is done Artistically by Modern Machinery.

BRODIE & SALMOND, Proprietors.

JAMES CUTHBERT,

Wholesale and Retail Ironmonger and Seedsman,

8, 10, AND 12 COMMERCE STREET, ARBROATH.

HOUSE FURNISHING IRONMONGERY

IN great variety, including Kitchen Grates and Ranges; Parlour, Dining, and Drawing Room Registers, finished in Berlin Black; Bronze and Brass Work, fitted complete with Tile Hearths, Kerbs, and Brasses; Coal, Oil, and Gas Heating and Cooking Stoves; Fenders, Fire-Irons, Coal Vases, Kitchen Utensils of every Description; Washing and Wringing Machines, Mangles; Brass and Iron Bedsteads, Mattresses; Hall and Umbrella Stands, Baths, Travelling Trunks, Deed Boxes; Fire and Thief-Proof Safes, Lamps, &c.

Cutlery, Britannia-Metal, Nickle Silver & Plated Goods of the Best Sheffield Manufacture only.

AGRICULTURAL DEPARTMENT.

Clovers, Ryegrasses, Natural Grasses, Turnips, and General Garden Seeds; Sacks, Spades, Scythes, Forks, Rakes, Fencing Wire and Netting; Sheep Nets and Dips; Sheep Shears, Hay Knives, Horse Clippers; Sack Weighing Machines; Plough, Halter, and Cart Ropes; Plough and Cart Chains; Hames, Harness Composition, Lanterns, Burning and Lubricating Oils, Greases, &c.

Large and Varied Stock of Joiners' and Blacksmiths' Furnishings always on Hand.

All Purchases delivered Free in Town and Country per own Vans, or Carriage Paid to nearest Railway Station.

84   *Arbroath Year Book Advertisements.*

JAMES CUTHBERT, Furnishing Ironmonger, &c.,

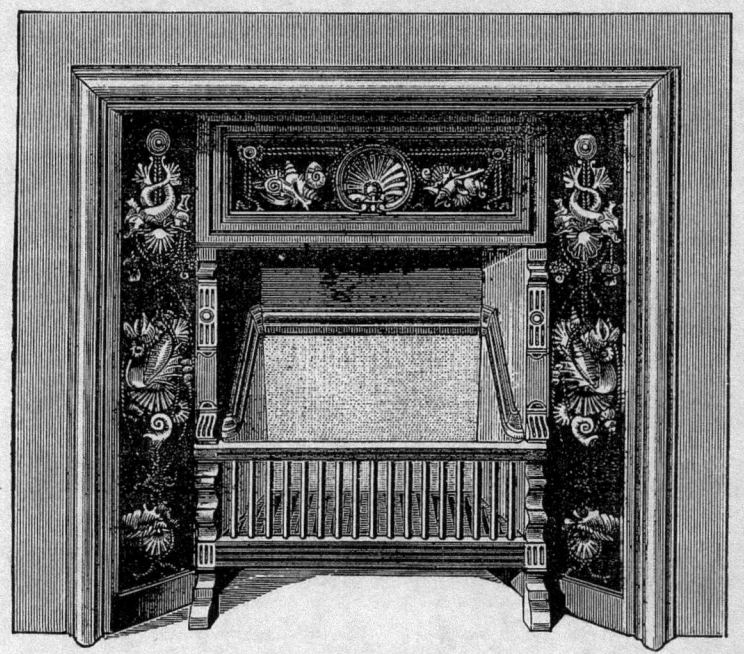

BERLIN-BLACKED REGISTERS and KINNAIRD GRATES.

With TILES and BRONZES in Cheek and Canopy, Bronze and Brass Mouldings, &c.

Patent Smoke-Preventing Registers.

TILE HEARTHS Laid. REGISTERS and RANGES Built in by Experienced Workmen.

8 to 12 Commerce Street, Arbroath.

JAMES CUTHBERT, Furnishing Ironmonger, &c.,

CONVERTIBLE, CLOSE, & OPEN FIRE RANGES
Of Various Designs, with Newest Improvements,
INCLUDING
THE SIMPLEX, EXPRESS, DOW'S PATENT, CARRONA,
THE ROSEBERY, PORTDOWNIE, &c., &c.

Estimates Furnished Gratis.

8 to 12 Commerce Street, Arbroath.

JAMES CUTHBERT, Furnishing Ironmonger, &c.,

Large Stock of Patent Safety and other Lamps.

Five to One Hundred Candle Power to suit all Purposes.

RIPPINGILLE'S OIL STOVES
In Great Variety.   Prices and full Particulars on Application.

8 to 12 Commerce Street, Arbroath.

GEORGE ✻ SALMOND,

Bread and Biscuit Manufacturer and Confectioner.

G. S. HAS to thank his numerous Customers throughout Forfarshire for the liberal patronage bestowed upon him during the last Quarter of a Century.

The Principle of our Trade is to produce a REALLY FINE ARTICLE at a MODERATE PRICE, and our success is proved by an ever-increasing demand for all our Manufactures.

All Materials used are of the Finest Quality, and are specially Selected and Prepared under Personal Supervision. Our premises are fitted up with the most modern Machinery and other appliances, and this enables us to produce all kinds of Cakes, Biscuits, &c., in the most expeditious and economical way, and of a quality equal to the Finest produced in Edinburgh or Glasgow.

Cakes.	SALMOND'S BISCUITS AND CAKES	Biscuits
PLAIN TEA	Are constantly used throughout Forfarshire.	TEA
FRUIT TEA		WINE
CITRON		ABERNETHY
LEMON	SALMOND'S	MIXED
SEED	SHORTBREAD	WATER
MADEIRA	Cakes from a Penny to a Pound. Ornamented and Plain. Our SCOTCH SHORTBREAD will be found delightfully Fine and Crisp.	MACAROON
SULTANA		RICE
SPONGE		SPONGE
COCOA-NUT, &c.		WALNUT, &c.

199 HIGH STREET, Arbroath.

ESTABLISHED 1867.

Tell me where is Fancy Bread?

AT SALMOND'S

Our Fairport Gingerbread

Is one of the Finest Scotch Fancy Cakes. In Cakes, 5d, 10d, 15d, and Larger if Ordered.

VANS VISIT

CARNOUSTIE, FRIOCKHEIM,
COLLISTON, CARMYLLIE,
FORFAR, BRECHIN,
MONTROSE, INVERKEILOR.
AND SURROUNDING COUNTRY DISTRICTS

EVERY WEEK

SCOTCH, ENGLISH, FRENCH & AMERICAN FANCY CONFECTIONERY

NOVELTIES.

Fresh Supplies every Week of the Best Selling Sorts of HALF-PENNY and FARTHING FANCIES at Lowest Cash Prices.

Shipping Orders Supplied on Best Terms.

EVERY REQUISITE FOR
SOIREES, MARRIAGE & SUPPER PARTIES,
PICNICS,
AND ALL OTHER FESTIVE AND SOCIAL GATHERINGS.

199 HIGH STREET, Arbroath.

THE Arbroath Coffee House Coy., LIMITED,

⇾✸ 30 MILLGATE. ✸⇽

BREAKFASTS, DINNERS, TEAS,
SOIREE, PICNIC, AND
OTHER FESTIVE PARTIES

Carefully Attended to at Lowest Charges.

BILLIARD ROOM AND ROOMS FOR MEETINGS.

WILLIAM FRASER, Manager.

MIDDLETON & DONALD,

Plasterers,

41 LINDSAY STREET, ARBROATH.

Every Description of Plaster and Cement Work; also, Lathing Work.

Ornaments of every Description Supplied to the Trade.

ORDERS IN TOWN AND COUNTRY PROMPTLY ATTENDED TO.

ESTIMATES GIVEN.

House Address—

⇾✸ ALEXANDER DONALD, ✸⇽

ALEXANDRA COTTAGE, CARNEGIE STREET.

COALS.

For the Best Qualities of all Kinds of Coal for all Purposes, try

T. Muir, Son, & Patton,

Colliery Agents, Coal Merchants, and Steamship Owners,

Whose Reputation for Supplying a Good Article at a Fair Price they will always endeavour to sustain.

Orders Booked and Prices arranged at all their Branches and Depots.

District Depots—

39 HELEN STREET AND 69 WEST GRIMSBY,
ARBROATH;

AND AT

RAILWAY STATIONS—

CARNOUSTIE and INVERKEILOR.

LARGEST GLASS & CHINA ROOMS
IN THE NORTH OF SCOTLAND.

DEPOT FOR
WORCESTER, CROWN DERBY, WEDGWOOD, MINTON, DRESDEN, &c., &c.

Wholesale and Retail.   Established 1811.

WM. FRAIN & SON,

BEG to solicit Inspection of their Choice and Varied Stock including every Requisite for Household Use and Adornment from the Cheapest to the Most Expensive.

From their connection for upwards of half-a-century they are enabled to give Exceptional Advantages as to Quality, Stock and Price.

    DINNER SETS from 18s 6d (61 pieces) to £35.
    TEA SETS from 11s (39 pieces, China) to £23.
    TOILET SETS from £4 10s (5 pieces) to £10.
    DESSERT SETS from 18s (18 pieces) to £30.

From W. F. & SON'S position these are necessarily much more Choice and Trustworthy than can be obtained in any other class of Establishment.

TABLE GLASS AND DECORATIONS
In Great Variety, and including the Best of the Newest Styles and Patterns.

GOODS FOR PRESENTATION,
Useful and Ornamental.

Afternoon Tea, Trinket, and Toy Dinner and Tea Sets, Vases, Flower Pots and Bowls, Table Decorations, Rose Leaf Jars in various Choice Styles; White China Fancy Trays, &c., in Endless Variety; Fairy and Other Lamps, &c.

FRAIN'S * BUILDINGS,
CASTLE STREET (OFF HIGH STREET) DUNDEE.
SHUT ON SATURDAYS AT FOUR O'CLOCK.

THE ROSEBERY FILE
SCRAP BOOK.
REGISTERED.

A novel combination of Scrap Book and File for the ready classification of Private Papers, Notes of Speeches, Newspaper Cuttings, and Memoranda of all kinds.

Prices 3s 6d and 5s 6d.

A MOST USEFUL PRESENT TO GENTLEMEN.

Ask your Stationer for it.

New * Note * Papers.

Economical and Satisfactory for Business and Private Correspondence.

Imperial Parchment Note Paper and Envelopes.

Thick Vellum Wove. Mill Surface, and Highly Glazed. A most Useful and Highly Satisfactory Paper.

The Posthorn Vellum Laid Note Paper and Envelopes.

With Medium Surface, having much of the appearance and qualities of Hand-Made Papers, and at a Moderate Price.

Ask your Stationer for Samples.

George Waterson & Sons,
EDINBURGH AND LONDON.

THE
Scottish Widows' Fund

(MUTUAL) LIFE ASSURANCE SOCIETY.

MAGNITUDE OF THE OPERATIONS.

Policies Issued, . . . £48,000,000	Claims Paid, . . . £17,500,000
Bonus Additions, . . 10,800,000	Accumulated Funds, . . 10,750,000
Policies in Force, . . 30,000,000	Annual Revenue, . . 1,250,000

PROFITABLE CHARACTER OF THE BUSINESS.

Cash Profit for Seven Years to 31st December, 1887, £1,727,659
Bonus Additions for the Seven Years, . . 2,785,611

THIS was the LARGEST DISTRIBUTION OF PROFIT made by any Life Office in the Kingdom during the period. It yielded Bonuses ranging from £1 14s to £4 6s 7d per cent. per annum on the Original Sums Assured, according to the duration of the Policies—facts which clearly prove

The Intrinsic Value of the Society's Mutual System, and
The Highly Profitable Character of its Business.

LIBERAL CONDITIONS OF ASSURANCE.

Surrender Values allowed after payment of one year's premium.	**Loans** granted within a small margin of the Surrender Value.
Paid-up Policies allowed in lieu of Surrender Values.	**Extensive Foreign Residence** free of charge in all cases.

Claims Payable on Production of Proof of Death and Title.

Persons desiring to effect LIFE ASSURANCES for the benefit of their Families, or in connection with Business Transactions, are invited to **Read the Society's Prospectus**, which contains general information of use in selecting an office, and particulars of the principles and liberal practice to which the Society owes its success.

Agents in Arbroath—
ANDREW BENNET, Solicitor, High Street.
JAMES A. DICKSON, British Linen Co. Bank.

WHITE HART HOTEL,

HIGH STREET, ARBROATH.

(The Only First-Class Family and Commercial Hotel in Town).

THE Proprietor has recently acquired an adjoining property which has enabled him to add to his Hotel a Large Bar Room, which has been fitted with all Modern Conveniences.

THE COMMERCIAL AND COFFEE ROOMS
Are most Comfortably and Attractively Furnished.

THE RESTAURANT AND DINING ROOMS
Are Fitted and Furnished in the Best Style.

The Finest Brands of Champagne, Sherry, Port, Whisky, Claret, and all other Liquors always in Stock.

Finest ALES and STOUT kept on Draught and in Bottle.

"Boots" and 'Bus attend all Trains. Charges Strictly Moderate.

J. G. EHRLICH, Proprietor.

WHITE HART LIVERY STABLES

Hiring Establishment

Is now Complete in all its Branches.

Brakes, Waggonettes, Gigs, Dog Carts, Open and Close Carriages,

For Private, Picnic, and Marriage Parties.

Horses kept at Livery under Careful Management.

Hearses and Mourning Carriages.

As all Orders are carefully attended to, Customers can rely on getting every care and attention.

GEORGE FLEMING, Jun., Manager.

Telegrams, "*HOTEL.*"

Beware of misleading titles, as New Dyeing Companies trade on the words, **Campbell** and **Perth**. All Authorised Persons display our Initials.

P. & P.

For Superior Dyeing and Cleaning of Ladies' and Gentlemen's Apparel, Curtains, and other Furnishings.

"The Oldest and Best Dyers."—*Myra's and Sylvia's Journals.*

P. & P. CAMPBELL,
SOLE PROPRIETORS OF
THE PERTH DYE WORKS.
Established 1814.
PRICE-LISTS FREE.

DUNDEE OFFICE—33 NETHERGATE.

DISTRICT AGENTS.

ARBROATH, - - Miss BURRELL, Fancy Wool Repository, 19 Millgate.
BARRY, - - - Mr JOHN SCOTT, Post Office.
CARNOUSTIE, - Mr A. REID, Stationer, Dundee Street.
Do., - - Mrs MARTIN, Milliner, Lochend House.

Goods may be sent through Receiving Offices, or Agencies, carriage free, or direct by Post or Rail to

P. & P. CAMPBELL, PERTH.

SECOND TO NONE
FOR A QUARTER OF A CENTURY.

✢ JAMES ✢ DOIG, ✢

71 AND 73   71 AND 73

GUTHRIE PORT, ARBROATH.

DOIG'S OLD MALT WHISKY.

DOIG'S FAMILY BLEND.—The Finest of Old Scotch Whisky. Blended and Bottled on the Premises. A Sample Bottle of this Excellent Whisky has been submitted to the Public Analyst, who reports as under :—

Laboratory of the Public Analyst, Dundee, 14th May, 1885.

"This is to certify that I have examined a Sample of Whisky marked 'DOIG'S FAMILY BLEND,' sent to me by Mr JAMES DOIG, Family Grocer and Wine Merchant, Arbroath.

"I have to report that the Spirit is strong and pure. It has every quality of an old and thoroughly sound Whisky, being practically free from fusel oil, and containing no poisonous ingredient.

"(Signed) G. D. MACDOUGALL,

"*Public Analyst for the County of Perth, and the Burghs of Dundee, Forfar, Montrose, and Arbroath.*

IF YOU WISH TO USE ONLY THE BEST OLD SCOTCH WHISKY,
ASK FOR

DOIG'S FAMILY BLEND.

DOIG'S Stock of INDIAN, ASSAM, and CEYLON TEAS are always of the very Finest Qualities, being Selected and Blended with the greatest Care. They combine the greatest Strength, with Delicacy of Flavour, and are all Absolutely Pure.

FOR THE BEST VALUE IN ALL KINDS OF PROVISIONS, SPIRITS, BEER PORTER, &C.
CALL AT

DOIG'S, GUTHRIE PORT.

For Press Opinions see Page 110.

JAMES DOIG,

Family Grocer, Tea, Wine, and Spirit Merchant.

Opinions of the Press—

DOIG'S TEA.—*The Mercantile Age* of April 16th says:—Mr JAMES DOIG is a great believer in Indian, Assam, and Ceylon Teas; and rightly so, for not only has he, but all the most competent judges, proved their superiority over those Teas grown in China. There is a uniformity of body in DOIG'S TEAS as well as a richness of Quality, and analytic tests prove that there is little mineral matter, the tannin, nitrogen, and other properties being excellently balanced, so as to avoid undesirable astringency. I am glad to know that an appreciative public very highly value Mr JAMES DOIG'S Teas. His annual returns show a very marked increase in the sales, and I am quite convinced that, if he continues to keep up the standard of quality—which he seems determined to do—he will some day ere long occupy a foremost position as a tea-dealer in Scotland. His policy is a generous one; he has entered upon and is pursuing a safe enterprise, one calculated to benefit himself as well as the public, and I am glad to know of his success— a success highly merited.

Doig's Whisky, Beer, &c.—The *Mercantile Age* of April 16th, says:—DOIG'S Malt, Wine, and Spirit Cellars are, on the whole, the best I have seen north of Glasgow—and I have visited hundreds of Establishments—very lofty, have an abundance of light, and the temperature is very carefully regulated for maturing and conditioning the valuable stock of Malt Liquors. The Bottling cellar is fitted with hot and cold water, and other appurtenances for effectually cleansing the bottles, and filling in a cleanly manner from the casks, Barclay Perkin's Stouts and Bass & Co.'s Ales. Proceeding to the Spirit Department, I found a Whisky, a surprisingly good blend of pure old Scotch Whisky, known as "Doig's Family Blend." This blend of Whisky deserves to be extremely popular. It is a very old, pure Whisky, free from fusel oil, smoke, or wild flavour, and to connoiseurs of Whisky, as well as those whose health requires this article, I can confidently recommend it as a pleasant, honest stimulant of good age and purity. (See Public Analyst's Opinion on Page 108.)

Doig's Provisions, Feeding Stuffs, &c.—The *Mercantile Age* says:—DOIG'S stock and management of his establishment displayed many evidences of good and experienced generalship. Everywhere energy and order seem to have been happily combined. The Goods seemed fresh throughout, and chosen from the markets and manufacturing centres that I have visited a hundred and one times, and know, therefore, their pure, dietary properties. The third storey of DOIG'S Warehouses is used as a general reserve-stock warehouse for fruit, jellies, jams, biscuits, &c. Mr Doig also conducts a very large trade for feeding stuffs, such as Oats, Barley, Oilcake, &c.

ESTABLISHED FOR OVER A QUARTER OF A CENTURY.

JAMES DOIG,
71 & 73 GUTHRIE PORT, ARBROATH.

DUNDEE AND NEWCASTLE, MIDDLESBRO', HARTLEPOOL, AND SUNDERLAND.

The Fine Iron-Screw Steamer

"PLADDA,"

A1 AT LLOYD'S

Captain ROBERT LATTO.   Carrying Steward and Stewardess.

Leaves Dundee for Newcastle Every Tuesday.   From Newcastle for Dundee Every Friday

When it is found necessary to alter Day of Sailing notice thereof is given by Advertisement.

Goods and Live Stock on deck carried at Shipper's risk. Not responsible for returned empties unless booked and freight prepaid.

Sailing to Middlesbro', Hartlepool, Sunderland, and Montrose as Cargo Offers.

Fares—Per "Pladda."—Dundee and Newcastle—First Cabin, 9s; Second Cabin, 6s.   RETURN TICKETS—Available for One Month—First Cabin, 13s 6d; Second Cabin, 9s.
Children under twelve years of age (when in charge of their friends only) half-fare.   Infants in arms, free.   Not responsible for Passengers' Luggage.

Freight of Goods, Carriages, Horses, Cattle, &c., on the Lowest Scale.

This Conveyance affords a cheap and rapid means of communication with NEWCASTLE, SHIELDS, SUNDERLAND, HARTLEPOOL, SEAHAM, STOCKTON, MIDDLESBRO', DURHAM, DARLINGTON, CARLISLE, MORPETH, BERWICK-ON-TWEED, and all the NORTH OF SCOTLAND.

There are also frequent Steamers loading in the Tyne for NEW YORK, BOSTON, PHILADELPHIA, MONTREAL, ROTTERDAM, ANTWERP, COPENHAGEN, STETTIN, DUNKIRK, GENOA, NAPLES, LEGHORN, VENICE, TRIESTE, FIUME, ODESSA, ·&C.

1 Commercial Street, Dundee.   HENRY PLENDERLEATH, Manager.

WILLIAM S. OGG,
Hairdresser and Manufacturing Perfumer,
2 and 4 HAMILTON GREEN,
ARBROATH.

Finest Fitted Premises in the district.   Dealer in WALKING STICKS; also, COMBS, BRUSHES. and other Toilet Articles.
Newest Designs in HAIR ORNAMENTS.

ESTABLISHED 1862.

FURNITURE. ⇢✴⇠ **BEDSTEADS.**
CARPETS. **BEDDING.**

Extensive   Latest

Stock   Designs

J. P. Grewar & Son,
Cabinetmakers and Upholsterers.

EXCELLENCE of QUALITY has always been our aim, and we at present see no need to diverge from this line of conducting our Business. The Quality of our Goods is correct, the Prices are Extremely Low, and we would invite those Furnishing to favour us with their Orders. The Stock we hold is extensive, and embraces

    DINING-ROOM, PARLOUR, BEDROOM,
        LOBBY, OFFICE, & KITCHEN FURNITURE.
  BEDDING, FLOORCLOTHS, CARPETS, CURTAINS, &c.

JOBBING Carefully attended to, and receives Special Attention.

☞ *FURNITURE EXCHANGED.* ☜

FUNERAL UNDERTAKING—See page 18

J. P. GREWAR & SON,
Picture Furniture & Bedding Warehouse,
Frame Corner GRAVESEND & PANMURE St., Arbroath.

JOHN TULLIS & SON,
St Ann's Leather Works,
GLASGOW,

Tanners, Curriers, & Manufacturers

OF

Oak-Tanned Leather Belting
Orange-Tanned Leather Belting
Leather Link Chain Belting
Llama Hair & Cotton Canvas Belting
Buffalo Skips and Temperbands
Roller and Pump Butts
Laces and Loom Pickers
Leather Fire-Hose Pipes

AND ALL KINDS OF

MECHANICAL LEATHER.

ANDREW SCOTT,

Grocer, Wine, and Spirit Merchant,

195 HIGH STREET,
ARBROATH.

PERFECTION * IN * TEA,
AT 2s 4d PER LB.
Better Value cannot be given.

SCOTCH ✢ WHISKY.

We desire to call attention to our OLD SCOTCH WHISKY, which, for Purity, Mildness, and Delicious Flavour is unsurpassed.

This Whisky is distilled from the Finest Malt (all deleterious matter being extracted in the process of distillation) and fully matured by age.

MALT LIQUORS.

Special attention is devoted to this Department, and Customers may rely upon the Ales, &c., being sent out in the best possible conditition

ALLOA ALE, Bitter and Sweet. Pilsener **LAGER BEER**.
LONDON PORTER.
Bass & Co's and Allsopp's **PALE INDIA ALE**.

195 HIGH STREET, ARBROATH.

Arbroath Year Book Advertisements.

The People's Friend.

The Favourite Scottish Miscellany,

WEEKLY, ONE PENNY.   *MONTHLY, SIXPENCE.*

CONTAINS

Serial Tales.	Essays on Popular Subjects.
Helps and Hints to Civil Service Candidates.	Scientific Notes and Jottings
	Original Poetry.
Standard Popular Readings.	Original Music.
Competitions for all Classes of Readers.	Wit and Humour—the Brightest and Best.
Choice Household Letters.	Notices to Correspondents—Entertaining and Useful.
Helps in Home Management.	
Brilliant Biographical Papers	Complete Tales.

"An admirably conducted Serial."

SOLD EVERYWHERE.

The People's Journal.

The People's Favourite Newspaper.

The Best Scottish National Weekly Paper; Radical Politics; Foremost in every Reform for the Benefit, Enlightenment, and Elevation, of the People; Complete News of the World. One Million Readers every Week.

NOW IS THE TIME TO READ THE PEOPLE'S JOURNAL.

SPECIAL FEATURES.

Aunt Kate's Gossips wi' Guidwives.	Opinions of the People.
Weekly Competitions—A Prize Silver Watch Every Week	New Scotch Stories—By Favourite Authors.
Legal Jottings by a Lawyer.	Fullest Local & Widest General News.
Children's Column.	Draughts Column.

THE PEOPLE'S JOURNAL

Is Read in all Parts of the World.

SATURDAY, ONE PENNY.   SOLD EVERYWHERE.

CASH ✢ PRICES
FOR
Drugs, Pharmaceutical Preparations,

- Patent Medicines . . . .
- Proprietary Articles . . .
- Toilet Preparations . . .
- Household Requisites . . .

Infants' and Invalids' Food,
SPONGES & BATH REQUIREMENTS,

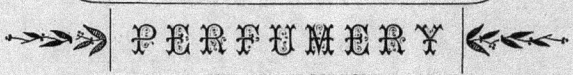
PERFUMERY

&c., &c., &c.

For Prices and Full Information see Price List, which may be had on Application,

FROM

Shield, Will, & Jack,
Chemists, Arbroath.

Arbroath Year Book Advertisements.

PRICE ONE PENNY.

he Arbroath Herald

EVERY THURSDAY MORNING,

IS THE

Best and Cheapest Advertising Medium for Arbroath, Carnoustie, Friockheim, and Surrounding Districts.

As others see us.

One of the Best Provincial Newspapers for a town like Arbroath I have ever seen—*Member London School Board.*

The Fullest and Freshest Family Newspaper that crosses the Atlantic.—*Vide Andover Townsman.*

One of the Healthiest and most Successful Journals in this County.—*Piper of Dundee.*

THE PUBLISHERS of the *Arbroath Herald* have pleasure in directing attention to the special characteristics of the *Arbroath Herald* as a Newspaper. In addition to full and impartial reports of all District Meetings of importance, the *Herald* contains an Epitome of all matters of general interest transpiring during the Week.

No Effort spared to make it

T he Fullest, Freshest,
And Most Readable
Family Newspaper
 In the District.

**Proprietors and Publishers—BRODIE & SALMOND,
BROTHOCK BRIDGE, ARBROATH.**

Musical ∗ Instruments.

GRAND AND COTTAGE PIANOS
BY

ALLISON	BREWER	HOPKINSON	KELLY
BROADWOOD	COLLARD	HILTON	RODGER
BROWNE	CHAPPELL	HUMMELL	SAMUELS
	&c.,	&c.	

From £9 to £120.

AMERICAN ORGANS,

To hand a Large Consignment of the above Popular Instruments by the following Makers, viz.,

BELL	DOHERTY	KELLY	PELOUBET
CLOUGH & WARREN	KARN	MASON & HAMLIN	STIRLING

&c., &c., from £5 to £50.

HARMONIUMS.

By all the Best Makers, from £4 to £60.

A few Second-Hand Instruments always in Stock.

All Instruments purchased will be delivered Free and kept in Tune for One Year, and changed within that time if desired.

Tuning in all its Branches expeditiously attended to.

Instruments on Three Years' System—Monthly or Quarterly Instalments taken.

An Inspection is Earnestly Solicited.

| 5 and 7 Hill St. ARBROATH. | **T. ∗ BOOTH** | 2 & 4 Pleasant Pl. BRECHIN. |

The Only Place in Town where your can Furnish Complete.

G. Rutherford Thomson & Son,

Cabinetmakers, Upholsterers, Linoleum and Carpet Warehousemen,

43 MARKETGATE, ARBROATH.

Largest and Finest Stock of

Household Furnishings
In the County.

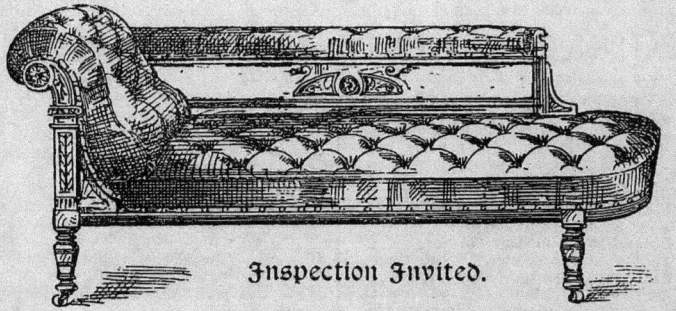

Inspection Invited.

G. RUTHERFORD THOMSON & SON,
43 MARKETGATE, ARBROATH.

Arbroath Year Book Advertisements.

The only Place in Town where you can Furnish Complete.
G. Rutherford Thomson & Son,
Cabinetmakers, Upholsterers,
Carpet and Linoleum Warehousemen, and Removal Contractors,
43 MARKETGATE, ARBROATH.

BEDSTEADS & BEDDING DEPARTMENT.

Over 200 BEDSTEADS in Stock.

50 Different Designs.

From 11s 6d to £9 10s.

This Special Department has our most careful attention, and has assumed such large proportions that we have been compelled to make out Special Rooms for the making of Hair and Wool Mattresses, Feather Beds, Bolsters and Pillows, &c. Only absolutely pure materials used in the making up.

Hair and Wool Mattresses Cleaned and Recovered by Practical Upholsterers on the Premises.

PATENT DOUBLE WOVEN WIRE SPRING MATTRESS.

Price 16s 6d.   Price 16s 6d.

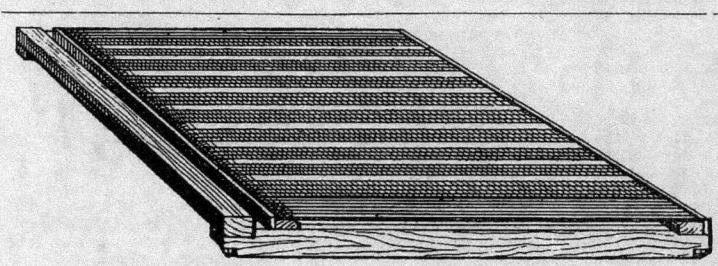

After having tested every kind of Spring Mattresses made, we can with confidence recommend the above as the Cleanest, Healthiest, and Best Mattress yet produced.

W. & A. GILBEY,
Wine Growers and Distillers.

Consumption of Wines and Spirits in 1888.

The Quantities on which duty was paid in the United Kingdom, for year 1888, were, according to the Government Returns:—

Wines,..13,500,109 Gallons.
Spirits,...34,989,843 ,,

| Wines—Sold by W. & A Gilbey. | Spirits—Sold by W. & A. Gilbey. |
| 912,684 Gallons. | 877,622 Gallons. |

QUALITY AND VALUE.—No better Guarantee can be given than the fact that about every FOURTEENTH BOTTLE of WINE and FORTIETH BOTTLE of SPIRITS consumed in the United Kingdom is supplied through W. & A. Gilbey's Agents.

W. & A. GILBEY'S SYSTEM OF BUSINESS.

The Purity of every Article bearing the Seal and Label is guaranteed.
The Quality and Place of Production of each Article is as specified.
Every Six Bottles are guaranteed to contain One Gallon.
The Strength of Spirits is stated upon the Label.
300 Varieties of Wines and Spirits can be obtained from all Agents at fixed London Prices.
Single Bottles, or Larger Quantities, can be procured from Agents in every Town.
All Bottles (except where otherwise stated in their List), are charged 1d each, which is allowed when returned.
Cash Payments are absolutely necessary, as all prices are based on that principle.

Price Lists with Full Particulars, and all Varieties of Wines and Spirits, may be obtained from

Shield, Mill, & Jack,
Chemists, Arbroath.

JOB PRINTING DEPARTMENT
OF THE
⊰ Arbroath Herald Office ⊱

Programmes for
Assemblies,
Concerts,
Soirees, &c.

Marriage
and other
Invitations

Visiting and
Business
Cards

Account,
Memo. and
Letter
Headings

Funeral Letters
and
Memoriam Cards

The TOBACCOS bought at this Establishment can be relied on for Excellence of Quality, combined with Moderate Charges.

Large Variety of Meerschaum and Briar Pipes, Fancy Goods, Walking Sticks, Canes, etc.

All the Leading Brands of CIGARS kept in Stock.

ANDREW BEATT,
Tobacconist,
142 HIGH STREET (Opposite Kirk Square), ARBROATH.

GEO. DORWARD,

Wholesale Grocer,

Wine and Spirit Merchant,

WEST PORT AND BANK STREET,

Arbroath.

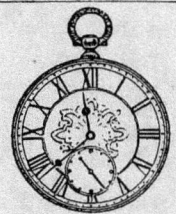 

GOLD AND SILVER WATCHES AND CHAINS.
DIAMOND GOODS.
Marble, Brass, Wood, and Mosaic Clocks,
SOLID SILVER AND ELECTRO-PLATE.

JAMES WILLOCKS,

Practical Watchmaker, Goldsmith, and Jeweller,

(Opposite Town-House)

105 HIGH STREET, ARBROATH.

PRESENTATION COMMITTEES LIBERALLY DEALT WITH.   GOODS SPECIALLY SELECTED AND OFFERED AT LOWEST PRICES.

INSPECTION INVITED.

SCOTTISH BOILER INSURANCE CO., LTD.

HEAD OFFICES:
13 DUNDAS STREET, GLASGOW. CAPITAL, £75,000.
38 LLOYD STREET, MANCHESTER. CAPITAL, £75,000.

Managing Director, - JOHN D. YOUNG.
Local Agent—J. M. M'BAIN, British Linen Co. Bank, Arbroath.

Moderate Rates.   Prompt Settlements.   Sound Advice.
Reliable Reporting.   Thorough Inspection.

ARTISTIC Photographer

FERRIER

1 Tally Street
(NETHERGATE CORNER),
DUNDEE.

THE ANGLO-AUSTRALIAN BANK,
LIMITED
(Registered under the Victorian Companies Statute, 1864.)

Authorised Capital,................................£2,000,000.
Subscribed Capital...................................250,000.
Paid-up Capital,......................................100,000.
Reserve Fund, Reserved Liability, and Undivided Profits, £170,660.

HEAD OFFICE—QUEEN STREET, MELBOURNE.
NEW SOUTH WALES BRANCH—PITT STREET, SYDNEY.
SOUTH AUSTRALIAN BRANCH—ROYAL EXCHANGE, KING WILLIAM STREET, ADELAIDE.
TASMANIAN BRANCH—LIVERPOOL STREET, HOBART.
LONDON BRANCH—J. A. CRAVEN, Manager, 120 CANNON STREET, E.C.

Local Directors for Great Britain—
LORD CAMOY'S, HON. ASHLEY G. J. PONSONBY, J. BLACKWOOD, Esq.

FIXED DEPOSITS of £50 and upwards received at the London Office at the following rates of interest—

One year,.......................................5 per cent.
2 or 3 years,..................................5½ ,,
4 or 5 years,..................................6 ,,

Interest Payable Half-Yearly.

DEBENTURES.

Debentures are issued for a period of Five Years, bearing interest at the rate of 6 per cent. per annum, payable half-yearly by attached coupons.

NOTE.—By a special Clause in the Bank's Articles of Association Depositors and Debenture Holders are secured by having a First Claim upon all the Assets, Securities, and Monies of the Bank.

Balance Sheets and all further information obtainable at the Bank's London Office.

Local Agents—
BENNET & SMITH, Solicitors, Arbroath.

Life, ✣ Fire, ✣ Accident,

OTHER ASSURANCES.

THE LIFE ASSOCIATION OF SCOTLAND
Established 1838.

NORTHERN ASSURANCE COMPANY
Established 1836.

LIVERPOOL, LONDON, AND GLOBE
ASSURANCE COMPANY.

SCOTTISH EMPLOYERS' LIABILITY & ACCIDENT
ASSURANCE COMPANY, Limited.

THE LONDON & PROVINCIAL HORSE & CARRIAGE
ASSURANCE COMPANY, Limited.

Important to Farmers.

Protection against all Liability under Employers' Liability Act and Insurance against Personal Accident arranged for Small Premiums.

All Particulars on Application to

GEORGE ✠ REID,

Agent,

ROYAL BANK, ARBROATH.

It will Pay you Well

✠ ✠ ✠

To Order Your Groceries

Teas, and Provisions

From Us

For Quality, Freshness

And Genuine Value

We are Not Surpassed

In Dundee, let alone Arbroath.

Goods Carefully Packed

And all Cases Free

Terms—Cash with Order.

Full Price Lists

Can be had on Application.

Carriage Paid on all Orders of £2 to any Station within 30 Miles of Dundee.

Peebles ✠ Brothers,
TEAMEN AND GROCERS,
WHITEHALL STREET, DUNDEE.

J. P. SMITH & SON,
Merchant Tailors,
DUNDEE, ARBROATH, AND MONTROSE.

ORDER DEPARTMENT
(One of the Largest in the North of Scotland).

Every Description of Clothing Made to Measure on the Shortest Notice.

SUITS,	from 40s 0d to 80s.
TROUSERS,	,, 13s 6d ,, 25s.
OVERCOATS,	,, 30s 0d ,, 70s.

All Cut and Made-Up by Experienced Cutters and Workmen on our own Premises.

READY-MADE & OUTFITTING DEPARTMENT.

Always on Hand, a Large and Superior Stock of Bespoke Goods in Men's, Youths', and Boys' Clothing.

MEN'S SUITS,	from 30s 0d to 60s.
YOUTHS' SUITS,	,, 16s 6d ,, 40s.
BOYS' SUITS,	,, 5s 6d ,, 20s.

MOURNINGS.

Always on Hand a Superior Stock of BLACK SUITS, all Sizes, in Men's, Youths', and Boys' Suits.

HATS, CAPS, TIES, BRACES, UNDERCLOTHING, GLOVES, SHIRTS, &c., &c., in all Classes.

Arbroath Branch—
165—HIGH STREET—165
(Corner of Kirk Square).

New Drapery Goods.

GRAND DISPLAY
OF

New Dress Materials—Every Description, in all the Fashionable Shades.

New Jackets and Dolmans—Magnificent Stock—Newest Shapes and Colourings.

Waterproof Mantles and Dust Cloaks—Great Variety—all Sizes.

Jersey Jackets—All the Leading Styles.

Mantle Plush—Black and Brown.

DRESS AND MANTLE TRIMMINGS.
Corsets, Gloves, Handkerchiefs, Umbrellas, and Sunshades.

JAMES MACDONALD, 108 HIGH STREET.

James M'Wattie & Sons,

ABBOT BRAND

Tobacco and Snuff Manufacturers and Cigar Importers,

20 & 22 COMMERCE STREET,

ARBROATH

REGISTERED TRADE MARK.

JOHN OGILVIE,

Bookseller and Stationer,

8 WEST PORT, ARBROATH.

Fine Selection of NEW and SECOND-HAND BOOKS always in Stock.

CIRCULATING LIBRARY, 1d per Volume.

☞ BOOKBINDING DONE CHEAP. ☜

Agent for SCOTTISH KEY REGISTRY ASSOCIATION.

WHITE'S
SEMOLINA

(Made from Finest Spring Wheat),

FOR

PUDDINGS, PORRIDGE, &c.

THE BEST AND CHEAPEST IN THE MARKET.

GUARANTEED THOROUGHLY GENUINE.

DUNDEE FLOUR MILLS.

ROBERT FORBES,
BUTCHER,

148 HIGH STREET, ARBROATH
(Opposite Kirk Square).

PRIME BEEF, MUTTON, PORK, &c., ALWAYS ON HAND.

All Orders promptly delivered per Own Van in Town or Country.

Extra Value in TEAS, 1/4, 1/6, 1/10, and 2/4 per Lb.
2d per Lb. Less for 5 Lbs and Upwards.

James Fox,
Family Grocer,
Tea, Wine, & Spirit Merchant,
94 HIGH STREET,
ARBROATH.

Superior Blended COFFEE, 1/-, 1/2, 1/4, and 1/6 per Lb.
Fresh Roasted and Ground.

Old Blended SCOTCH WHISKY, 2/6, 2/8, 2/10 per Bottle; 15/-, 16/-, 17/- per Gallon.

Old Matured WINES, 1/-, 1/6, 2/-, and 3/- per Bottle. Dunville's Old IRISH WHISKY, 3/- and 3/3 per Bottle.

Fire, Life, & Accident Assurance.

Webster & Littlejohn,
SOLICITORS, ARBROATH,

AGENTS FOR

Standard Life Assurance Company.

Northern Fire and Life Assurance Company.

London & Lancashire Fire Assurance Company.

Also for Accident and Employers' Liability Insurance Companies.

NORTH BRITISH
Ærated Water Coy.,
MONTROSE.

Families in Arbroath and District should use only

THE N. B. A. W. COY.'S ÆRATED WATERS.

For Sparkling Brilliancy,
High Æration, &
Absolute Purity,
THEY TAKE THE FIRST PLACE.

☞ Vans Visit Arbroath and District Twice a-Week.

Orders by Post Promptly and Carefully Attended to.

Arbroath Year Book Advertisements.

H. ✱ GOUCK,
Hosier, Hatter, & Woollen Draper,

Has always on hand a Large Stock of

Flannels, Blankets, Plaidings, Skirtings, Shirtings, Sheetings, Bed Covers, &c.,

HOSIERY AND UNDERCLOTHING,
In Every Size and Quality, to Suit any Season or Climate.

HAT & CAP DEPARTMENT
Packed with all the Latest Styles at Prices quite unheard of.

SHIRT DEPARTMENT
One of the Largest Stocks in the County to choose from.

Cricket, Lawn Tennis, and Football Clothing, a Specialty.

Fronts, Collars, Cuffs, Handkerchiefs, Gloves, Braces, Umbrellas, Scarfs, Ties, Hand-Bags, and Portmanteaus, an Endless Variety.

96 HIGH STREET, ARBROATH.

Try ✱ FINLAYSON'S

Famous 5-Year Old WHISKIES and RUMS, 6d and 7d per gill; 2s 6d and 2s 10d per bottle.
THOMSON'S IRISH WHISKY, 7½d per gill; 3s 3d per bottle.
PORT WINES from 1s, 2s, 2s 6d, and 3s per bottle.
SHERRIES, Choicest, 1s, 2s, 2s 6d, and 3s per bottle.
BASS & ALLSOPP'S PALE ALES, 2s 3d per dozen.
YOUNGER'S TABLE BEER and PORTER, 2s per doz. quarts.
COMBE'S IMPERIAL PORTER, only 2s 6d per dozen.
LONDON XX PORTER, Very Fine, 2s 3d per dozen.
LEMONADE, GINGER BEER, and POTASH WATER, 11d per dozen.

NOTE THE ADDRESS—
193 HIGH STREET, ARBROATH.

IMPERIAL HOTEL,
RAILWAY STATION, ARBROATH.

Built expressly as a FIRST-CLASS MODERN HOTEL, and is the only such in Arbroath. It contains—

Commercial, Coffee, Billiard, and Stock Rooms, Private Parlours, Dining-Rooms, &c.

The House is Lofty and Ventilated on the most Improved Sanitary Principles.

HOT, COLD, and SHOWER BATHS. Lavatories on each Floor.

Families and Commercial Gentlemen will find this Establishment replete with every Comfort.

BOOTS IN ATTENDANCE AT ALL TRAINS.

TERMS STRICTLY MODERATE.

FIRST-CLASS
RESTAURANT AND DINING-ROOMS
IN CONNECTION WITH THE HOTEL.

Soups and Hot Joints from 12.30 to 3 p.m.

BASS'S and ALLSOPP'S ALES on Draught and in Bottle.
BARCLAY and PERKIN'S STOUT.
Finest Blend of OLD MALT WHISKY, Guaranteed Five Years Old, 17s per Gallon.
G. & G. SMITH'S GLENLIVET, 8 Years Old.
Pale Dry Gonzalez' SHERRY, 24s per Dozen.

FAMILIES SUPPLIED.

S. AITKEN, *Proprietor.*
Late of White Hart Hotel.

JOHNSTON'S EMPORIUM,

33 & 35 COMMERCE STREET,
ARBROATH.

Special Attention devoted to

HOUSEHOLD HARDWARE,
GLASS AND CHINA WARE.

Always on hand a Good Selection of

MANGLES—28s 6d, 32s 6d, 35s, 40s, 45s each—every Machine Warranted.

Patent WRINGERS—16s, 18s, 20s, 22s, 24s each—Warranted Best Rubber Rollers.

TUBS, TUBSTOOLS, SCREENS, BOARDS, CLOTHES' ROPES, and PINS.

Tinned and Enamelled GOBLETS, POTS, PANS, &c., Superior Make—Sold Cheap.

Close and open FIRE RANGES, all Sizes. Parlour and Bedroom Grates.

FENDERS are a Specialty here—Newest Designs in Great Variety.

ASH-PANS and FRONTS in Great Variety—very Cheap.

TINWARE of every description—Well-made, Strong and Cheap.

BRUSHES of every kind—Large Stock always on hand.

BIRDS' CAGES—Large Stock of various shapes, very cheap.

MELODEONS—the Best Value ever offered-

Cutlery, Spoons, and Britannia Metal Goods in Great Variety.

INSPECTION INVITED
AT

JOHNSTON'S EMPORIUM,
33 & 35 COMMERCE STREET,
ARBROATH.

Dodds & Bathie,

AGRICULTURAL AUCTIONEERS,

Live Stock Salesmen,

VALUATORS AND SURVEYORS,

Manure, Seed and Potato Merchants,

86 * HIGH * STREET,

ARBROATH.

Established 1845.

Arbroath Carriage Factory.

MELVIN & SONS

All our Carriages are Warranted of Newest Style and Best Workmanship.

LANDAUS, BROUGHAMS

PHÆTONS, WAGGONETTES

DOG-CARTS, CHAPEL-CARTS,

GIGS, PONY CARRIAGES

TO ORDER OR IN STOCK.

AT THE LOWEST PRICES.

Vans, Lorries, and Message Carts Built to Order.

All Repairs Promptly Executed.

☞ SECOND-HAND MACHINES BOUGHT & SOLD.

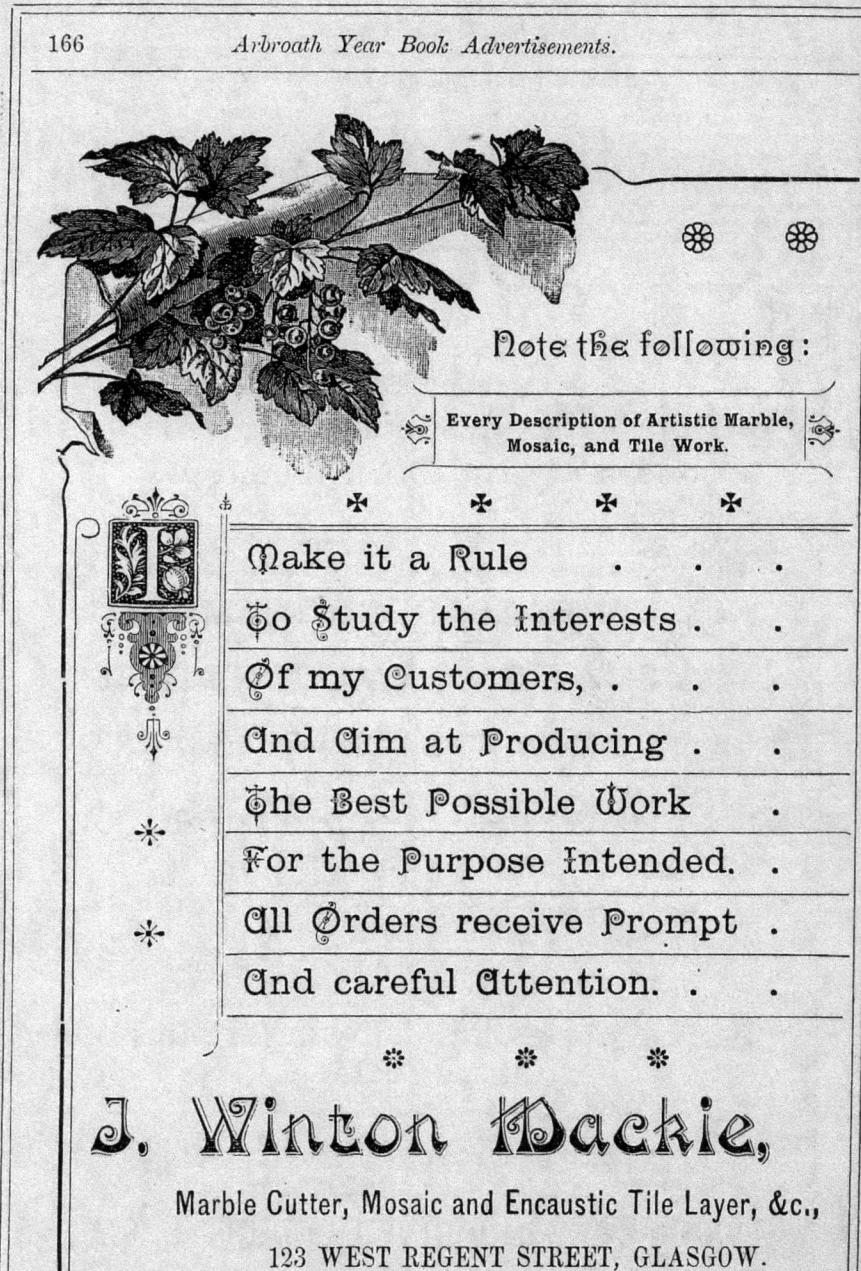

Note the following:

Every Description of Artistic Marble, Mosaic, and Tile Work.

Make it a Rule
To Study the Interests
Of my Customers,
And Aim at Producing
The Best Possible Work
For the Purpose Intended.
All Orders receive Prompt
And careful Attention.

J. Winton Mackie,

Marble Cutter, Mosaic and Encaustic Tile Layer, &c.,

123 WEST REGENT STREET, GLASGOW.

ESTABLISHED 1882.

Northern Accident Insurance Co., Ltd.

CAPITAL, - - - - £100,000

Chairman:
ANDREW J. KIRKPATRICK, Esq. (Messrs MIDDLETON & KIRKPATRICK), Merchant, Glasgow.

PERSONAL ACCIDENT   EMPLOYERS' LIABILITY

Third Party, Plate Glass, and Fidelity Guarantee Assurances effected.

Over £80,000 paid in Claims.

INSURE AGAINST ALL ACCIDENTS.

PERFECT SECURITY   MODERATE RATES

Agents in Arbroath :—
BENNET & SMITH, SOLICITORS.
R. C. KINLOCH, BANK OF SCOTLAND.
WILLIAM ROLLO, COMMERCIAL BANK.
WILLIAM CLUNIE, 54 MILLGATE LOAN.

For full information as to Rates, &c., apply to these Agents, or to
R. W. THOMPSON, General Manager.

Head Office—19 West Nile Street, Glasgow.

Arbroath Year Book Advertisements.

ALEXANDER HIRD,

Drapery and Outfitting Establishment,

28 KEPTIE STREET,

(Opposite the Railway Station),

Has always on hand a Full and Fresh Stock of all Kinds

OF

DRAPERY GOODS.

All Parties Purchasing should see Stock and Prices

AT

HIRD'S, ✻ KEPTIE ✻ STREET.

Elgin Wine & Spirit Vaults.

JOHN MACKENZIE'S NEW ADDRESS

IS

MACKENZIE'S BUILDINGS & (Next Old Church)

(Opposite White Hart Stables) **ELGIN WINE VAULTS.**

TRY

THE ARBROATH WINE & SPIRIT VAULTS,

Where Everything is of the Best.

MUSICAL INSTRUMENTS.

PIANOS—Second-Hand Square Pianos from 30s. Second-Hand Cottage from £8 10s. New Cottage, from £15 10s. Iron Frame, Check Action, Full Trichord, 4 ft. 1 in. high, £19 10s—Cash.
AMERICAN ORGANS—Gothic Case, £6; 5 Stops, Walnut Case, £7 15s; Ten Stops, £10 up to £50.
VIOLINS—$\frac{1}{4}$, $\frac{1}{2}$, $\frac{3}{4}$, and Full Size, from 5s; Strauduarius, 20s.
BOWS—From 1s; Snakewood, Inlaid Ivory Nut, 3s 9d.
VIOLIN CASES—Half Lined, 3s 9d; Full Lined, 5s 6d.
STRINGS—Best Roman, 6d; Second Quality, 4d; Silk do., 4d.
MELODEONS—From 2s 11d; 2 Sets Reeds, 3s 11d; Steel Reeds, from 7s 6d; 3 Rows Reeds, 10s 6d.

J. JOHNSTON,
Music Warehouse, 196 & 198 High St., Arbroath.

HARRIS & KYD,
(*Successors to* D. HARRIS),
Wholesale and Retail Butchers,
29 MILLGATE,
AND
19 BARNGREEN, ARBROATH.

A Large and Fresh Stock of PRIME BEEF Always on Hand.

Orders Delivered per own Van in Town or Country.

The Best & Most Fashionable Drapery Goods.

WM. SALMOND & CO.,
145 HIGH STREET, ARBROATH.

WE avail ourselves of this medium of thanking our numerous Customers for their patronage during a prolonged business connection, and beg to assure all that we shall spare no effort to deserve a continuance of their valued support by keeping

The Best and Latest Novelties

in the various Classes of Drapery Goods, at the Lowest Market Rates.

145 HIGH STREET, ARBROATH.

ROBERT ✢ SHEPHERD,

Wine and Spirit Merchant,

2 ✱ HOWARD ✱ STREET,

ARBROATH.

Families Supplied with Liquors of the Best Quality, in Prime Condition, at Moderate Prices.

USE MASTERTON'S CRYSTALLIZED CONCENTRATED AMMONIA SOAP!

The Only Perfect Cleanser.

It Washes Everything and Injures Nothing.

*A Specialty
For all Kinds of Lace.*

MASTERTON'S PARAFFIN SOAP EXTRACT

THE ONLY GENUINE

LEAVES NO SMELL — SAVES TIME — SAVES LABOUR

SOAP WORKS, HARRIS ST, BRADFORD YORKS.

Ask your Grocer for it, and give it a trial.

*A Specialty
For all Delicate Fabrics.*

Makers also of Extract of Soap, Dry Soap, Musk Paraffin Soap Extract, Lavender Paraffin Soap Extract, &c.

D. S. MASTERTON & Co., Bradford.

Agent for Scotland—JAMES R. AULD, 149 Govan Road, Glasgow.

178   *Arbroath Year Book Advertisements.*

Port Wine from 1s 6d to 3s per Bot.   Sherry from 1s 6d to 3s per Bot. Whisky from 2s 6d to 2s 10d per Bot.

Bran, Sharps, Maise, Whole and Ground; Barley, Whole and Cut; and Corn.

Potatoes for Table Use. Potatoes for Feeding Purposes.

BUTTER AND CHEESE.

I make it a point to personally select my Butter and Cheese.

The Prices for Keiller's Gold Medal Marmalade this Season, is Reduced to 5d per 2 lb. Pot.

⇢ DAVID ✶ ROBBIE, ⇠

Family Grocer, Tea, Wine, & Spirit Merchant,

Corner of Lochland & Keptie Streets, Arbroath.

Arbroath Year Book Advertisements.

SEAMEN'S LIVES AND EFFECTS INSURED AT SPECIALLY FAVOURABLE RATES.

Fire, Life, Marine, ...

Employers' Liability, ...

Guarantee, Accident, and . .

Boiler Assurances, ...

EFFECTED WITH FIRST-CLASS OFFICES,

ON FAVOURABLE TERMS,

BY

J. M. M'BAIN, BANKER, ARBROATH.

The Best Newspaper for Friockheim and District.

The Arbroath Herald

May be had in FRIOCKHEIM

EVERY THURSDAY MORNING.

Agricultural Notes and News. Interesting Record of all Local and District Events. Entertaining Sketches and Stories.

Every Inhabitant of Friockheim should read

The Arbroath Herald

EVERY THURSDAY MORNING. ONE PENNY.

THE STAR HOTEL, FRIOCKHEIM.

D. D. PETRIE

HAS pleasure in thanking his numerous Patrons in Friockheim, Arbroath, and surrounding Districts. The Stock of Liquors at "THE STAR" can always be relied upon as of the Finest Quality, thoroughly Matured, and in the Best Condition.

Whisky, Rum, Port and Sherry Wines, all of the Best Brands.

BASS' and ALSOPP'S ALES, LONDON STOUT, TABLE BEER, &c., always in Prime Condition.

STABLING and POSTING. Orders by Post have Careful Attention.

Customers can rely upon the Best Service and Attention at

✻ **THE STAR.** ✻

EDWARD ✢ & ✢ CO.,

Coal Merchants,

FRIOCKHEIM.

Best Qualities of English, Wishaw, and Fife Coals.

Country Customers can be supplied with Cart-Loads at Friockheim Station on application to **Mr THOMAS STEPHEN**, N. B. Railway Company's Agent there.

☞ *Waggon Loads at Special Rates.*

Arbroath Year Book Advertisements.

William Greenhill,

Livery Stable Keeper and Coach Proprietor.

KINLOCH ARMS HOTEL, CARNOUSTIE.

Dinners, Suppers, Pic-Nic Parties, &c., are Carefully Attended to at Moderate Charges.

ALL LIQUORS OF THE VERY FINEST QUALITY.

Posting in all its Branches.　　Telegrams Promptly Attended to.

During the SUMMER MONTHS a Three-Horse 'Bus runs to AUCHMITHIE and LUNAN BAY every WEDNESDAY.

WILLIAM D. MURDOCH,

Family Grocer, Tea, Wine, and Spirit Merchant,

IRELAND STREET, CARNOUSTIE.

BEST VALUE IN ALL KINDS OF PROVISIONS.

SALMOND'S Arbroath Biscuits, Cakes, Gingerbread, &c., Fresh every Week.

HENRY'S
Favourite Gem Photographs.

VISITORS to CARNOUSTIE should not fail to secure a Sitting for a Dozen of those lovely PHOTOGRAPHS, taken Instantaneously, finished in a few days, and sent by Post to any Address, for 2s 6d per Dozen.

Largest Size Promenade Midget, 3s 6d per Dozen.

Portraits and Groups taken daily, any Style or Size, and Finished in a most Artistic Manner.

SPECIALITY.—Permanent Enlargements on Canvas, Opal, Ivory, or Paper, highly finished in Oil, Water Colour, or Black and White.

Studio—Lochty Bridge, Carnoustie.

Arbroath Year Book Advertisements.

JAMES SOUTER,
NEWSAGENT, TEA MERCHANT, &c.,
BARRY ROAD, CARNOUSTIE.

SOUTER'S CELEBRATED TEAS—

The saying's as old
As the Hills o' Gleniffer,
And as true as it's old
That doctors do differ ;
But there's one vital matter
On which they agree,

'Tis the baneful effects
Of Adulterated Tea.
At SOUTER's Barry Road,
You can have it as pure
As the sparkling dew-drop.
Then it won't kill but cure.

SOUTER'S TEAS
Are admitted by all Users to be the Acme of Perfection.

⇢ BARRY ROAD, CARNOUSTIE. ⇠

⇢ JAMES B. DICK, ⇠
Family Grocer,
WINE MERCHANT & ITALIAN WAREHOUSEMAN,
CARNOUSTIE.

Orders in Town and Country carefully and promptly despatched per our own Van.

DYE ✢ & ✢ FALCONER,
Tailors and Clothiers,
DUNDEE STREET, CARNOUSTIE.

Shirts and Hosiery always on Hand.

CARNOUSTIE
Co-Operative Association,
LIMITED,
Bakers, Grocers, Ironmongers, Drapers, and Tailors,
DUNDEE STREET & KINLOCH STREET.

BRANCHES:
BROWN STREET, CARNOUSTIE. | HIGH STREET, MONIFIETH.

Orders Punctually Delivered in Town or Country per Own Van.

JAMES ANDERSON, Manager.

JOHN KERR,

Grocer and Italian Warehouseman, and Patent Medicine Vendor,

THE CROSS.
CARNOUSTIE.

JOHN M‘ANDREW,
Registered Plumber and Gasfitter,
DUNDEE STREET, CARNOUSTIE.

Estimates given for all Sanitary Work.

☞ ORDERS PUNCTUALLY ATTENDED TO.

ALEXANDER REID,
Bookseller, Stationer, and News-Agent,
DUNDEE STREET, CARNOUSTIE.

Agent for the ARBROATH HERALD—Every Thursday Morning—1d.

CARNOUSTIE
EQUITABLE CO-OPERATIVE SOCIETY
(Limited).
WEST END, CARNOUSTIE,
Supplies the Finest Provisions at the Lowest Prices.

Van Deliveries as follows:

CARNOUSTIE and WEST HAVEN—Mondays, Wednesdays, and Saturdays
BARRY—Mondays, Tuesdays, and Fridays.
ARBIRLOT, EAST HAVEN, SCRYNE, FALLAWS, &c.—Mondays and Thursdays.
NEWBIGGING, KINGENNIE, DRUMSTURDIE, FOUR MILE HOUSE, LUCKY SLAP, MONIKIE—Tuesdays and Saturdays.
CARMYLLIE AND DISTRICT—Wednesdays and Fridays.
GUILDY AND KIRKBUDDO—Thursdays.
MUIRDRUM, PANBRIDE, PANLATHY, SALMOND'S MUIR, CROOKHILL—Tuesdays and Fridays.

W. H. STIVENS, Manager.

ALEX. S. WALLACE,
Veterinary Surgeon,
10 MILLGATE LOAN,
ARBROATH.

WILLIAM FERRIER,

Tailor, Clothier, and Shirt Maker,
DUNDEE STREET, CARNOUSTIE.

HATS and CAPS.—In all the Latest Styles.

HOSIERY and UNDERCLOTHING—Every Size and Quality, to Suit any Season or Climate.

SHIRT DEPARTMENT.—Shirts made to order in all the Best Styles.

BRACES, COLLARS, CUFFS, HANDKERCHIEFS, GLOVES, UMBRELLAS, in Great Variety.

CRICKET & LAWN TENNIS SUITS made on Shortest Notice.

JAMES ROBERTSON,
Grocer, Tea, Wine, and Spirit Merchant,
DUNDEE STREET,
CARNOUSTIE.

Agent for W. & A. Gilbey's Wines.

Established 1849.

JOHN THOMSON,
WHOLESALE AND RETAIL
Ironmonger and Seedsman,
90 HIGH STREET, ARBROATH.

All Orders Promptly
Attended to.

Designs and Estimates
Furnished.

T. SAVEGE,

Painter and Decorator,

HIGH STREET, ARBROATH.

Strachan, Wallace and Whyte,

Wholesale Grocers,
WINE AND SPIRIT MERCHANT,
TOWER NOOK,
Arbroath

Arbroath Year Book Advertisements.

ESTABLISHED 1850.

Numerous Medals and Other Awards.

W. H. GEDDES & SON.

Photographic Department.

PORTRAITS taken in any Style. ENLARGEMENTS in CARBON,
BROMIDE, and OPAL, &c. Portraits Painted in Oil.

Framing Department.

Pictures Framed in all the Newest Mouldings. Real Gold Frames, Oak, Rosewood, Black, &c. Estimates given for Quantities.

Magic Lantern Department

First-Class Exhibitions by Lime Light conducted. Slides supplied on any Subject. Lantern, with Lime or Oil, lent out on Hire. Terms and all Information at

✶ 14, 16, & 18 APPLEGATE ✶

JOHN SUTTIE,

Blacksmith,

41 and 43 WEST ABBEY STREET.

All Styles & Sizes REGISTER GRATES Tile Cheeks & Canopy

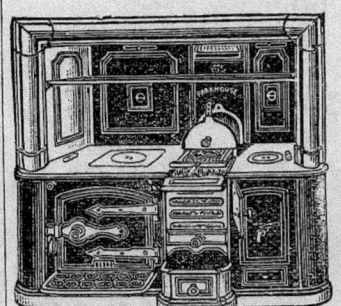

| Grates Carefully Fitted in, and . |
| Tile Hearths Laid by . . . |
| Experienced Workmen . . . |
| Under Personal supervision . . |
| Close and Open Ranges . . |
| Fitted to any size. . . . |

Arbroath Year Book Advertisements.

JAMES STEPHEN
(Late H. GREENHILL),
Horse-Hiring Establishment,
WEST NEWGATE STREET, ARBROATH.

Job and Post Horses, Best Hearses and Funeral Carriages,

Brakes, Waggonettes, and Dog Carts on Hire.

Picnic and Marriage Parties have Special Attention.
Orders Punctually Attended to.

Alex. Swirles & Son,
Tanners, Curriers,

| Wholesale and Retail . . . . . . |
| Leather Merchants, ... |
| Manufacturers of Mechanical Leather |
| Of all Descriptions . . . . |
| For Home and Exportation. . . . . |

Ponderlaw Leather Works,
ARBROATH.

N.B.—Highest Prices given for Cattle and Horse Raw Hides.

ALEX. ✣ WALLACE,

Wholesale & Retail Glass & China Merchant.

Always on Hand a Large and Well-Selected Stock.
Splendid Selection for Marriage Presents.
INSPECTION INVITED.

GOODS ON HIRE WITH CUTLERY.

10½—MILLGATE LOAN—10½
(Near Corner of West Port),
ARBROATH.

WHOLESALE WAREHOUSE—
10 PANMURE STREET, ARBROATH.

Best Prices given for Waste, Rags, Paper, Skins, &c., &c., in any Quantity.

JOHN NAPIER, Jun.,
Family Grocer, Tea, Wine, and Spirit Merchant,
43 EAST ABBEY STREET, ARBROATH.

BANK STREET HALL.

This Handsome and Popular Hall is to Let at very Moderate Terms—for Concerts, Marriage Parties Balls, Soirees, &c.

The Hall accommodates upwards of 300, and is fitted up with all the Newest Improvements to make it the Most Complete and Comfortable Hall in the Town. For Concerts, &c., there is a nicely fitted up Stage, with Scenery, Ladies' and Gentlemen's Dressing Rooms, entering off Stage, Pay Box, &c, For Marriage Parties and Balls, there is Anti-Room, Lavatory, Cloak Room, Tables, &c.

For Terms apply to **A. LORIMER, 14 Keptie Street.**

GEO. D. FLETCHER,

Family Grocer

ITALIAN WAREHOUSEMAN,

Wine, Spirit, & Liqueur Merchant,

18 KEPTIE STREET,
ARBROATH.

Only the Highest and Most Genuine Class of Goods procurable are Sold at the above Warehouse.

ANDREW FIFE,
BUILDER,
29 LINDSAY STREET, ARBROATH.

Estimates Given. Jobbing Work Carefully done. Orders from Town and Country Promptly Attended to.

THE BEST VARIETY AND BEST VALUE IN

HATS & CAPS      HATS & CAPS

OF EVERY DESCRIPTION MAY ALWAYS BE FOUND AT

FULTON'S OLD-ESTABLISHED HAT & CAP MART
152 HIGH STREET, ARBROATH.

Also, all Kinds of Gentlemen's Requisites in the Shape of SHIRTS, FRONTS, SCARFS, COLLARS, GLOVES, HANDKERCHIEFS, BRACES, UMBRELLAS, &c., &c.

ALEX. LOW,

Watchmaker and Jeweller,

WEST PORT, ARBROATH.

Always on Hand a First-Class Selection of CLOCKS, GOLD and SILVER WATCHES, JEWELLERY, ELECTRO-PLATE, DIAMOND, MARRIAGE and KEEPER RINGS.

A Guarantee is given by A. L. with each Watch Sold.

Jobbing of Every Description done on the Premises by Experienced Workmen.
JEWELLERY MADE TO ANY DESIGN.
RE-GILDING EXECUTED IN ALL ITS BRANCHES.
Second-Hand Watches taken in Exchange.

Presentations.—Special Arrangements made with Presentation Committees.

WILLIAM ALEXANDER,

Family Grocer, Tea, Wine & Spirit Merchant,

1 KEPTIE STREET, ARBROATH.

WHISKY

Our Whiskies, Blended from the Productions of the Most Famous Distilleries, are Old and Thoroughly Matured, therefore can be used with safety.

Price per Bottle, 2s 6d, 2s 8d, and 2s 10d.
,, Gallon, 15s, 16s, and 17s.

In RUM, GIN and BRANDY we give Excellent Value
PORT and SHERRY WINES from 1s to 3s 6d per Bottle.

Having given particular attention to TEAS, we are offering Very Special Value at Prices which will compare favourably with any House.

Cheese from Best Dairies.

☞ BEST SMOKED AND MILD-CURED HAMS. ☜
Only Provisions of First Quality kept.

WAVERLEY TEMPERANCE HOTEL.

THIS Hotel is conveniently situated within one minute's walk of Railway Station, and has been specially built to meet the requirements of a COMFORTABLE COMMERCIAL & FAMILY HOTEL.

Breakfasts, Lunches, Dinners, Teas (Plain, or with Fish or Meat), prepared on Receipt of Post Card or Telegram.

KEPTIE ST., ARBROATH
J. SHERET, Proprietor.

Mr & Mrs W. J. Anckorn,
Art Photographers & Publishers,
WEST PORT, ARBROATH.

One of the Largest and Best-Appointed Art Studios.
Specially Constructed for High-Class Photographic Work.

Awarded First-Class Prize Medals and Diplomas wherever we Exhibit, embracing—

Edinburgh	Vienna	Liverpool
London	Philadelphia, U.S.	Oldham
Berlin	Chicago, U.S	Keighley, 3 Awards
Keighley Champion Award	Coventry, 3 Awards	&c. &c.

PORTRAITS—:—LANDSCAPES—:—ENLARGEMENTS.
LANTERN SLIDES and OIL PAINTINGS Copied into Photogravure at Moderate Charges.

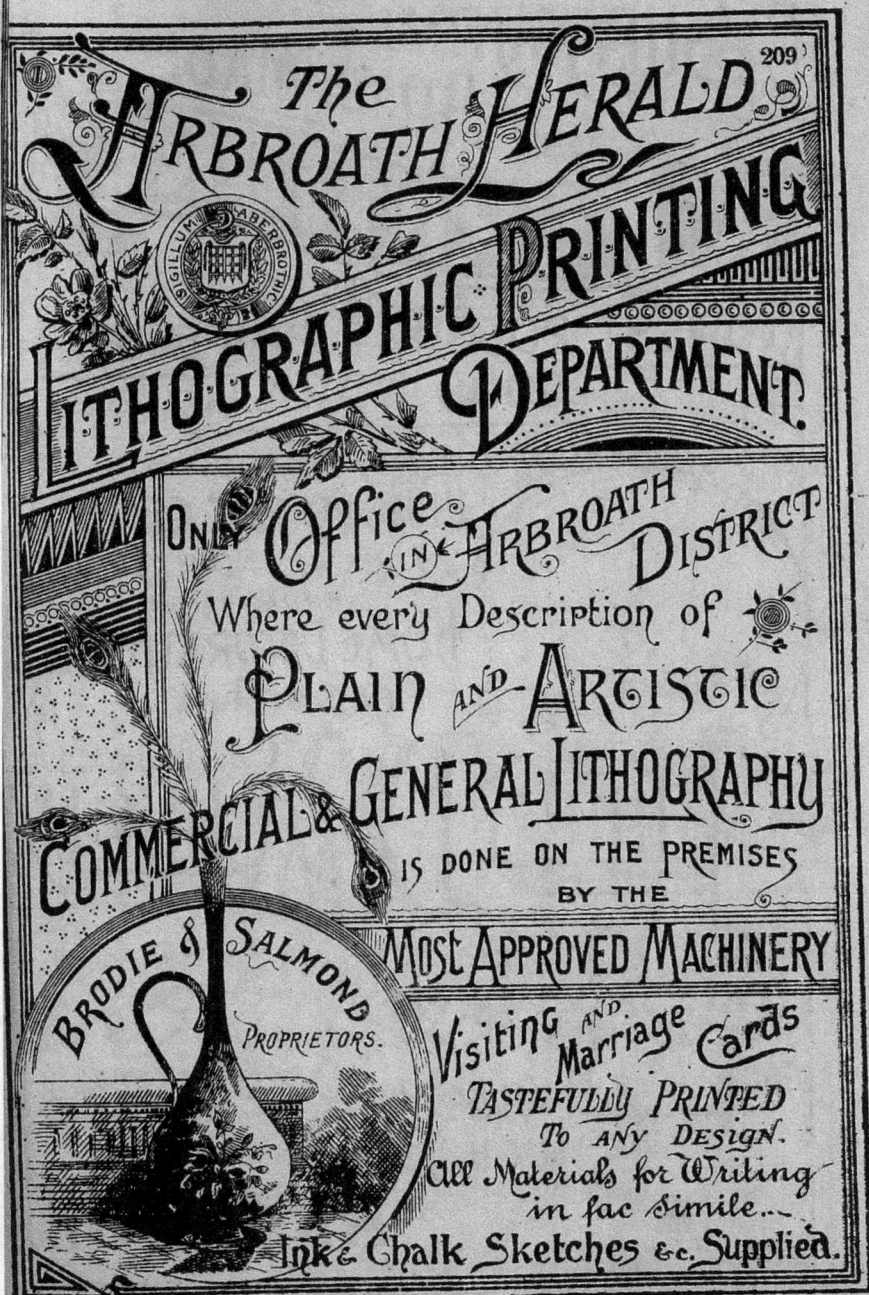

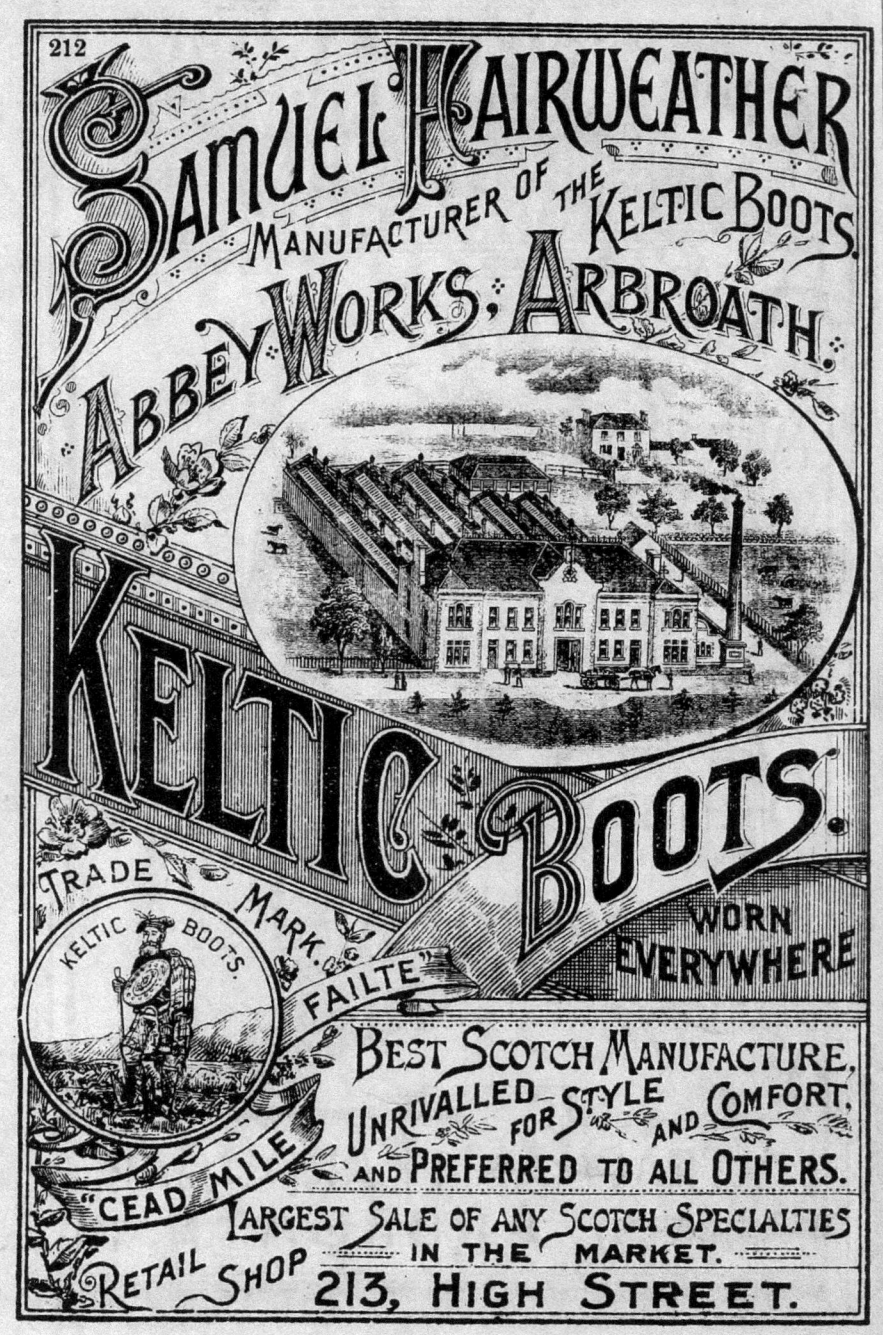

→ IMPORTANT NOTICE TO GENTLEMEN. ←

HAND SEWN BOOTS NO LONGER A NECESSITY.

KELTIC BOOTS & SHOES,

Recognised Standard of Fine Foot Wear.

KELTIC WELTS relieve the public of the expense and necessity of Hand Sewn Boots, which they are rapidly displacing all over the Kingdom. Since their introduction in the Summer of 1890, the most gratifying and flattering testimony to their excellence has reached us from all parts of the World; and practical Bootmakers frankly admit that Keltic Welts have sealed the fate of Hand Sewn Boots. We ask for them only ONE TRIAL, and Keltic Welts will claim you as their own. For Ease, Flexibility, and Comfort they are equal to the Finest Hand Sewn Boots ever made. The principle on which they are made is IDENTICALLY THE SAME AS HAND SEWN—only, instead of the inseam being put in and the Welt stitched by hand, it is done by the most marvellously perfect Machines the Shoe Trade has ever seen. Machinery has long ago superseded hand labour on the UPPERS of Boots; it has now done so on the BOTTOMS.

Read the Annexed Description of the Advantages of Keltic Welts.

- KELTIC WELTS have no Tacks or Wax to destroy or soil the Stockings.
- KELTIC WELTS have a perfectly smooth inner sole.
- KELTIC WELTS are Light and Flexible, and cannot be distinguished from Hand Sewn.
- KELTIC WELTS are Damp-Proof and Perfectly Noiseless.
- KELTIC WELTS are better than the majority of Hand Sewn Boots.
- KELTIC WELTS cost little more than ordinary Machine Sewn, and are as easy and comfortable to wear as Hand Sewn.

SPECIAL NOTICE.

Gentlemen bringing their own Lasts can have their Boots made on them on the Welted principle, and in thanking for their patronage those numerous Gentlemen who have already availed themselves of this privilege, we desire to call public attention to the manifest Advantages of the New System, and to recommend those who have not done so to give it an early trial.

Sole Manufacturer—

SAMUEL FAIRWEATHER,
213 HIGH STREET, ARBROATH.

MYLES' TAILORING ESTABLISHMENT.

CHARLES MYLES

From £3 15s up.

Is enabled by Personal Supervision, and a Large Staff of thoroughly Competent Workmen to Guarantee to every Customer

PERFECTION OF FIT AND STYLE.

Prices and Materials to suit all Classes.

✳ MOURNING ✢ ORDERS ✳

Can be Executed on a Few Hours Notice.

Testimonials from Customers both at Home and Abroad, testify to the Perfection of the Workmanship turned out.

Captains, Engineers, and other Seafaring Friends can have their Wants attended to on the Shortest Notice.

From £2 2s up.

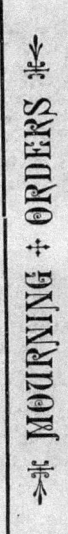

THE ARTISTIC FITTING ESTABLISHMENT, JAMES STREET. Arbroath.

Tailoring Establishment, MYLES, James Street, Arbroath.

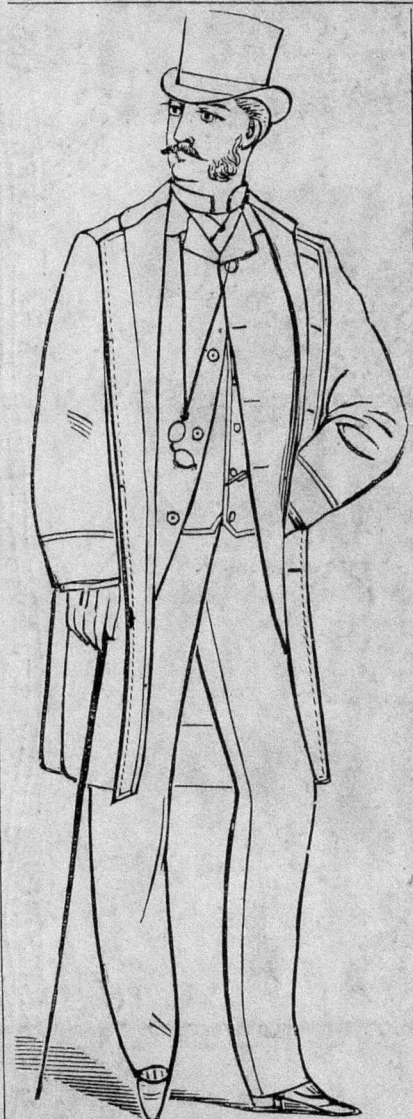

✠ ✠ ✠ ✠

C. ✠ Y. ✠ M. ✠←

Sends Greeting
To Red Lichties
In all Parts
Of the World,
And wishes them
A Happy and
Prosperous 1891.
All Orders
Have Prompt
And Careful
Attention at
His Establishment,
James Street,
Arbroath.

March

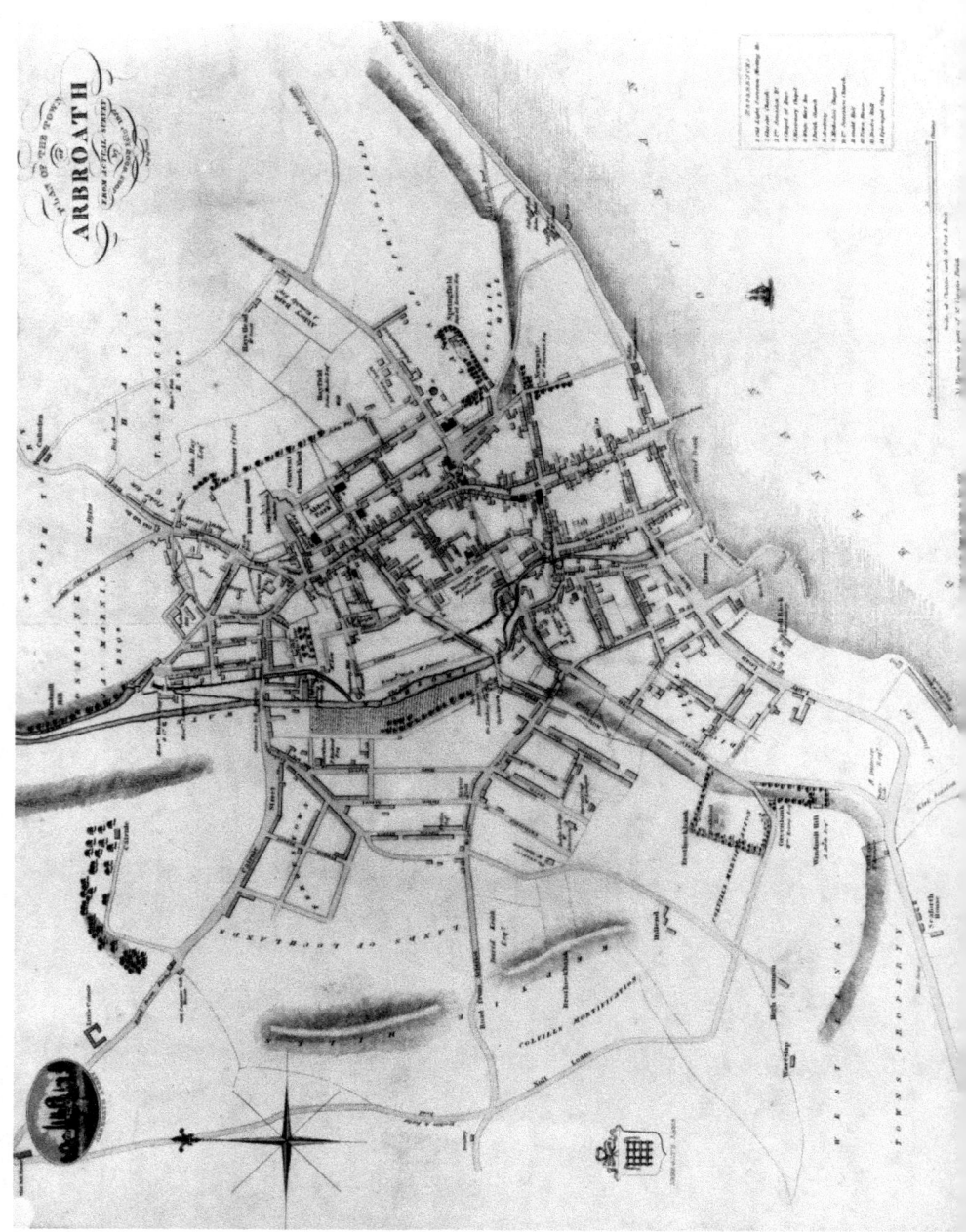

Arbroath 1822

March 1 1890

A major disappointment today for those who suggested that Public Baths should be erected in Arbroath.

Throughout the late Victorian age, more and more towns were building Baths with obvious benefits for cleanliness and health.

There was the additional advantage in Arbroath of public safety because swimming was widely practised in the North Sea, where accidents of drowning and being swept out to sea were not uncommon.

The counter argument was that there was enough water in Arbroath anyway and we did not need anymore. There were other arguments involving expense, and the moral argument (supported by the Churches) that swimming did necessarily involve exposing bits of naked flesh which polite society felt should be covered up!

Today in a public referendum (rare for the times), by a decisive majority of 332, Arbroath voted against the idea with the fishing community and women in particular opposed to the idea, although the main objection was the cost.

This seems to have been a blow to progress, and the word "backward" was used by a few people. *The Arbroath Herald* is disappointed, but makes the telling point that the result might have been a great deal different if the poll had been held in June or July instead of a damp late winter day when the attractions of bathing were not so obvious!

It would however be an issue that would return to the town.

March 2 1921

Today a new and much needed Billiard Hall was opened in Arbroath.

The location was significant. It was in the Young Men's Christian Association building in the High Street and it was opened in the company of many local dignitaries by Thomas Scott, manufacturer and president of the YMCA.

The Chairman, James Nichol, welcomed everyone, praised the YMCA for their enterprise and hoped that the young men of Arbroath would enjoy playing billiards in the YMCA building which he hoped they would use for "friendly intercourse (sic) and gain things which would make for their betterment and welfare".

It was probably true to say that in the dark days after the Great War, the sport of billiards was struggling to gain a respectable name for itself. It was one of these sports, like horse racing, which tended to miss the middle classes, for it was played by "officers and gentlemen" on the one hand and ne'er do wells and criminals on the other.

Usually it was associated with drink and gambling, and here was a chance to make the game respectable and to encourage young men to come to the YMCA instead of "ice cream parlours" and "licensed premises".

It was a fact that other than drink, there was a paucity of things that young men could do in Arbroath, and billiards was an excellent addition to the town.

Mr Scott was then handed a cue and asked to make the first shot on the new tables. After that, tea was served and two famous local billiards players Mr Cadman and Mr McInnes played an exhibition match.

March 3 1944

As spring returns to Arbroath (the weather is as usual up and down at this time of year) it is possible to detect a little optimism in the streets that the worst of the war may well be behind us and that things may be coming to an end soon.

Every day bring news of some progress in Italy and there seems little doubt that this will be the year of the invasion of northern Europe.

It is still an anxious time for many families however and tonight in the Town Hall, Provost John Lamb began making preliminary arrangements for Arbroath's contribution to the "Salute The Soldier" campaign.

It was agreed that the campaign would be targeted on the week between June 3 and 10 (no-one could in March predict that this would be the actual week of the invasion!) and the aimed for investment in War Savings would be £175,000.

Various convenors were appointed for Posters, Propaganda and other things, and it was agreed that the money would be loaned to the Government on an interest free basis, rather than as a free gift as before – a subtle change in emphasis, perhaps!

Such things were of course good for morale because it gave people something to look forward to and to focus on in the dark days of war when sometimes life could become a little drab, and the restrictions could be a little irksome from time to time.

But hope was in the air!

March 4 1936

The Arbroath Curling Club is celebrating its Golden Jubilee this year, and tonight at its Annual Dinner in the Imperial Hotel, among other things, a talk on the history of the club was given by Neil Robertson, Secretary and Treasurer.

About 50 people, including the Provost Sir William Chapel were in attendance and after the meal and the various toasts to the club, the King and The Royal Caledonian Club, Mr Robertson gave his talk.

To a large extent, he used as his source the diaries of an original member called David Greig who wrote in a very pawky and entertaining style about games in the early days and told everyone quite a lot about the first 27 years of the club.

There is of course a basic problem about curling in Arbroath for there is no piece of water that can be guaranteed to freeze on any one particular day, and of course, Arbroath, being on the coast gets a lot less frost than most towns.

There was no great likelihood of a bonspiel in Arbroath very often! Nevertheless on February 6 1886, the Arbroath Curling Club was formed and a plot of ground at Lochlands between Lochside Gardens and Keptie Loch was feued.

It was sub-let to Arbroath Tennis Club during the summer, and in the winter, the "roaring game" was played on tarmacadam in the first instance and then reinforced concrete from 1933 onwards.

The prizes were duly presented and then there was some musical entertainment as well.

Keptie Pond

March 5 1920

Today saw the retirement of John Brodie, editor and proprietor of *The Arbroath Herald*.

He had lived in the town for the past 40 years. He was a native of Selkirk where he learned his trade as a printer and journalist, and arrived in Arbroath in 1880 via Aberdeen, having bought a bookseller's business, which sadly burned to the ground shortly after his arrival.

He then had the happy idea of resurrecting *The Arbroath Herald* which had gone bankrupt in 1839. The first edition of the resurrected journal was in 1885, and in 1887 he went into partnership with J B Salmond.

From then on the newspapers never looked back, surviving blows like the death of Salmond in 1901, a year after the death of Brodie's son. But along with his daughter, Brodie kept the newspaper going, providing detailed and couthy news about what was happening in the town.

Brodie himself more or less did it all, sometimes using pseudonyms like "Jonathan Oldbuck junior" (Jonathan Oldbuck being The Antiquary of Sir Walter Scott), and it was a labour of love for, as he said, he enjoyed every minute of it.

He would admit to being a traditional Victorian who distrusted the rising Labour movement, but that did not stop him from showing compassion to the poor, and he was often prepared to go out on a limb against the Council if he felt that some injustice had been done.

He freely admitted that his saddest job had been writing about all the young men who had recently been lost in France and elsewhere. He left with best wishes and hopes for a happy retirement.

March 6 1922

In some parts of Scotland, Freemasons are looked upon with a certain degree of suspicion.

All their business is secret, they don't like women, they don't like Roman Catholics, they shake hands in a funny sort of way, and they keep all the good jobs on the Town Council and in business organisations to themselves.

They talk about their mystic craft in a secret, subversive sort of way. In Arbroath? Well, no actually! Tonight in the Good Templar Hall, they held a concert and it was open to all, including women!

Indeed, women actually sang and entertained the audience! It was under the auspices of the Inchcape Lodge Number 619, but various Lodges of the town were represented, and this "secret" organisation leaked its activities to *The Arbroath Herald* with everyone's name!

There was singing, dancing, recitations, violin performances and other things. Admittedly, they did called themselves "Brothers" and "Sisters", but what is the harm in that?

Arbroath, a town which was mercifully lacking in any sort of sectarian intolerance even in difficult economic times which often breeds such nonsense, generally looked upon freemasonry with benign acceptance, and even a little amusement at grown men apparently rolling up their trouser legs and poking each other with swords etc.

It was what men did when they were too old for the Boy Scouts and the Boys Brigade! And when the Arbroath Lodges played their Montrose equivalents at football on the Common one day, no-one knew what the score was. It was a secret!

March 7 1947

There are at last signs that the dreadful winter of 1947 may at last be coming to an end.

It is generally agreed that 1947 was the worst winter of them all with frequent blizzards in February after a reasonable January, and now that we are into March with its longer daylight, it is to be hoped that spring may be just around the corner.

Arbroath, being on the coast, tended to be a little better than some of the inland areas but the town itself was not without its problems, and the major problem was getting food to some of the villages in Angus.

Noranside Sanatorium, for example, had to be supplied by an aeroplane dropping food and supplies after being cut off for about a fortnight. The plane could not even take off from HMS Condor as the runway was snowbound, and the emergency supplies had to come from Donibristle in Fife.

The road to Auchmithie was blocked for several days, and even on one day the coast road between Arbroath and Montrose was impassable. Generally speaking the trains were able to run, although the timetable was chaotic.

What has made matters worse has been a shortage of coal with miners unable to get to their pits in Fife and elsewhere, and more problems getting what coal had been mined to its destination.

The Arbroath Herald and *The Dundee Courier*, cheerful and encouraging as always and resisting the temptation to blame it all on the Labour Government, tell of how everyone is looking out for each other, just as they did in the dark days of the war.

March 8 2016

Today Arbroath appointed a new Manager in Dick Campbell.

It was an appointment which raised a few eyebrows for Dick had been around many clubs, most recently Arbroath's traditional rivals Forfar Athletic.

His twin brother Ian also joined the club at the same time as his Assistant. The Campbell twins had been born in Hill of Beath (that well known Fife nursery of men like Jim Baxter and Scott Brown) in 1953.

Dick's playing career had failed to sparkle, although he had played several seasons for Brechin City, but as a Manager he had made an impact wherever he went, apart from a brief and unhappy spell at Ross County.

Most recently he had been Manager for seven years (a long time in football management) at Forfar Athletic, where he had become a cult figure and had in 2015 come close to winning them a place in the Championship.

It was a major surprise (even though Forfar were going through a bad spell) when Forfar sacked him in December 2015.

But he made it clear that he was interested in an immediate return to football management, and when the struggling Arbroath club approached him, he did not take much persuasion, for he detected in Arbroath's fans and Directors a certain ambition that perhaps had been lacking elsewhere.

The next few years promised to be very interesting ones for Arbroath and their supporters.

March 9 1897

It has been a constant refrain for the past fifty years or so in the columns of *The Arbroath Herald* that the Railway Station is simply not up to scratch.

The main problem seems to be that it is just not big enough. It was clearly built at a time when the Railway Company simply had not appreciated just how much the railways were to expand.

By the 1890s, railways were a very large concern indeed with trains leaving for Glasgow, London, Edinburgh and any place in the British Isles through complicated "Change at Perth" or "Change at Crewe" connections, with the joke about the Arbroath man who, as he paid his fare, was told "Change at Dundee" to which he replied "Na! Na! I want my change here!"

It was totally different from the days when a railway trip meant nothing more than a gentle chug along to Forfar!

Trying to deflect some of the criticism from the basic point that it is simply too small, the Railway Company have now repainted and repapered the whole place, waiting room, porter's room, booking office etc. so that it now looks "clean and cheerful" with all the work having been done by the railway employees, other than the glazing which was done by Mr Robert Farquharson, a local tradesman.

The problem of course is that a railway station, by its very nature in the 1890s, cannot really stay clean for very long.

Trains were powered by steam, and travel by train was sometimes a very dirty business! And there remained the basic problem that on busy days, there was simply not enough room.

March 10 1997

The Abbey Theatre backstage crew. From left standing is Dave Smith (Sound and Light Engineer), Evelyn Chaplain (Producer/Director), Pieter Cargill (Assistant Sound and Light), Lex Sawley (Wardrobe Mistress), Margaret Kerr (Theatre Member), Jean Moir (Front of House) and then her husband Frank Moir (Front of House). Sitting from left are Caroline Pennant-Jones and Carol Bruce.

March 10 1997

THE ABBEY THEATRE
Presents
" GASLIGHT "
a *Victorian Thriller*
by Patrick Hamilton

Cast :-
MRS MANNINGHAM .... Fiona Arnot
MR MANNINGHAM .... Brian Bruce
ELIZABETH .... Maureen Hayes
NANCY .... Lorraine Proctor
ROUGH .... Bob Chaplain

PRODUCED BY EVELYN CHAPLAIN

Set designed by .... Evelyn Chaplain
Set constructed by .... Frank Moir, Bill Gilmour & Jim Christie
Set painted by .... Evelyn Chaplain & Theatre members
Stage Managers .... Margaret Kerr and Brenda Martin
Lighting & Sound .... David Smith, Pieter Cargill
Prompters .... Carol Bruce & Caroline Pennant Jones
Wardrobe .... Lex Sawley & Jean Moir
Front of House .... Frank Moir & Theatre members
Coffees .... Theatre members

Playing at The Abbey Theatre, Arbroath, from 10th - 22nd March 1997.

The scene is the living room on the first floor of a four storied house in London, in the latter part of the Last Century.

Synopsis of Scenes

ACT 1 - Early evening.

** INTERVAL **

ACT 2 - No time has passed.

** INTERVAL **

ACT 3 - 11p.m. the same night

THE EXHIBITION in the Coffee Lounge is by -
THEATRE MEMBERS & FRIENDS.

NEXT PRODUCTION from June 16th to 28th 1997
" THE EXORCISM "
by DON TAYLOR
Produced by Alan Christison.

197

March 10 1906

This was possibly the biggest football occasion seen in the county of Angus for some time, certainly since the visit of Glasgow Celtic to Gayfield in 1902.

The venue was Links Park, Montrose and the occasion was the final of the Forfarshire Cup between Arbroath and Forfar Athletic.

Two special trains, as well as the normal service, were used to convey passengers from Arbroath Station, a few sailed up the coast and some even apparently went by horse and cart to the home of the Gable Endies.

It was clear, though, that Arbroath supporters were in the minority, for there was a very large contingent from Forfar as well, and the local Montrose crowd seemed to side with Forfar, possibly still feeling sore about their 0-5 hammering from the Red Lichties earlier in the season.

And it was Forfar's day, their winning goal coming soon after half-time. Arbroath pressed hard and felt that they were deprived of a penalty kick by referee Mr Walker of Falkirk, but it was not to be.

The cup was presented at the Commercial Hotel, Montrose in a room which was far too small for the occasion, and it took an unconscionable time for tea to be served.

There was some consolation for the Arbroath men, however, for "three cheers for the gallant losers" were called for and some of them sang to entertain the company.

The "gallant losers" were Johnstone, Clerk and Ferguson; Jimmy Petrie, Bob Petrie and Gordon; Easson, Proctor, Gray, Dorward and Crockatt.

March 11 1924

It is not often that high class musical entertainment appears in Arbroath but that was definitely what those who attended the Palace Theatre experienced this Tuesday night.

The bonus was that it was all home produced by a new organisation calling itself the Arbroath Symphony Orchestra. The Orchestra was formed only last year and is yet another example of the town fighting back from the horrendous years of the Great War and its immediate aftermath.

The leader is a woman (another comment on the rise of women in the 1920s) called Miss Walker, and the Conductor is the well-known local musician called Mr W Bell, and both deserve praise for the way they have assembled such a huge and talented Orchestra.

They were rewarded by a large attendance of family and friends and also a few others who simply like good music. Singled out for special praise were the singing of Miss Dorothy Pugh, and the violin playing of Mr Horace Fellowes. Miss Pugh sang items like the Jewel Song from Faust and the Skye Fisher's Song and the Enchanted Forest. Mr Fellowes, not a local man but not unknown in Arbroath also delighted the audience with numbers like Coronach and the Slavonic Dance.

The local critic in *The Arbroath Herald* goes out of his way to describe the Beethoven Romance in G "as near perfection as even the most critical audience could desire".

THE IMPORTANCE OF BEING EARNEST
By Oscar Wilde

March 12 2001

Cast in order of appearance :-

LANE - a manservant	Stewart Cassidy
ALGERNON MONCRIEFF	Alan Johnston
JOHN WORTHING	Alan Christison
LADY BRACKNELL	Maureen Hayes
HON GWENDALEN FAIRFAX	Moira Paterson (at short notice)
MISS PRISM	Rosemary Fussey
CECILY CARDEW	Sharon Milne
REV CANON CHASUBLE D.D.	Frank Gilbert
MERRIMAN the BUTLER	Jack Laing (at short notice)

PRODUCER - BOB CHAPLAIN

Set design	Bob Chaplain, Neil Ritchie
Set Constructed by	Neil Ritchie, Bob Sawley, Dave Ferguson,& Ian Anderson.
Set painted by	Roz Armstrong Bob Chaplain, Caroline Pennant-Jones , Dorothy Parfitt, Brian Bruce.
Stage management	Brenda Martin & Douglas Middleton.
Prompters	Evelyn Chaplain & Michelle Gordon.
Lighting & Sound	Stephen Gilbert, Dave Smith.
Wardrobe	Lex Sawley , Evelyn Chaplain.
Front of House	Theatre members
Catering	Theatre members

Synopsis of Scenes :-

TIME - SUMMER 1894.

ACT ONE   Algernon Moncrieff's Rooms, London.

INTERVAL

ACT TWO   The Gardens of the Manor House, Woolton.

INTERVAL

ACT THREE   The Drawing Room of the Manor House, Woolton.

EXHIBITION in the Coffee Lounge - By FRANK McDIARMID'S WEDNESDAY CLASS

NEXT PRODUCTION from April 30th to May 12th
THE BUSINESS OF MURDER
BY Richard Harris
Produced by Anne Smith.

Two young gents have taken to bending the truth in order to put some excitement into their lives. Worthing (Alan Christison) has invented a brother, Earnest, whom he uses as an excuse to leave his dull life behind to visit Guendolyn (Moira Paterson).

March 12 2001

The cast of the Abbey Theatre's production of The Importance of Being Earnest. From the left are: Stewart Cassidy, Frank Gilbert, Rosemary Fussey, Moira Paterson, Alan Christison, Alan Johnston, Sharon Milne, Maureen Hayes, Jack Laing, Michelle Gordon

March 12 1951

The dumping of rubbish had always been a serious problem in Arbroath.

There did not seem to be a public "coup" or a "tip" available, and it would be many years in the future before anyone thought of using a term like "recycling centre". People were simply dumping what they did not want on the strip of foreshore between the harbour and Gayfield – household waste, industrial waste, old beds, mattresses "wi mair o horrible and awful that even to name wad be unlawful" as Burns might have said.

The effect was distinctly unhygienic, unhealthy, smelly and a deterrent, according to Provost John Ford Webster, for people wanting to come to Arbroath.

It could be seen from the railway, and some of it could get washed out to sea on high tide. Something had to be done about it, said the Provost at tonight's Town Council meeting, otherwise the town would lose the fine reputation that it had built up over the years as a clean and health giving holiday resort.

There was a problem with the land however, for no-one seemed to know to whom if anyone this strip of land belonged, but steps were being taken to negotiate with the District Valuer to either buy the ground or simply take it over.

The real solution to the problem would of course to be to develop the land and put something on it; the other thing that really needed to be done soon was for a public dumping ground to be found, preferably outside the town and well away from the tourists.

Arbroath needed to "turn the bonny side tae the Minister", as the saying went!

March 13 1962

Having been accused of being too lax and lenient in this respect in the past, the Arbroath Licensing Court turned strict and repressive today in the matter of issuing licenses to sell alcohol.

An outright refusal of a licence was dispensed in the case of Mr James Bremner of the National Bar, 298 High Street, after an objection by the Chief Constable J J Dingwall, who claimed that Mr Bremner was not a fit and proper person to hold a licence after he had been found guilty of being drunk in his own premises.

Mr Bremner argued unconvincingly that he had bought the alcohol elsewhere and that he was only in charge of the premises for a short time, awaiting his wife to come and take over.

They were slightly more tolerant of two women in licensed premises in Keptie Street, Mabel Hand of the Station Hotel and Maureen Peters of the Imperial Hotel.

They had been found guilty of serving alcohol on a Sunday, through their employees, to people who were neither guests nor *bona fide* travellers. They were allowed to keep their licenses but were censured and warned about their future conduct.

The last clause about *bona fide* travellers was something that caused a little amusement. In order to be travellers Arbroath people would travel to Montrose for a drink on a Sunday, and Montrose people would naturally return the compliment.

It was of course good for bus companies who made money out of "the boozers's bus" and British Railways, but it did seem rather silly. The law would soon be changed.

March 14 1921

Possibly Arbroath is slightly better off than many places in the country at the moment, but at the moment 868 people are completely unemployed and 1610 on short time.

The main cause is of course the textile industry, which has seen a slump in trade largely because of the war and in particular the collapse of the German market (Germany is of course bankrupt) and the Russian market (where civil war is still going on). The tragedy is that so many ex-soldiers, who served their country well, are now out of work.

There are of course no easy solutions to all this but tonight a deputation from the Arbroath Trades Council approached the Town Council to see if there was anything that could be done, even on a short time basis, to alleviate matters.

It was generally agreed that there were loads of jobs needing done – the streets were acknowledged to be an "a deplorable" condition – but the problem lay in getting grants from central Government.

A few small jobs like the widening of roads would be considered but that would hardly cater for the 868 local unemployed people.

There was, for example, a tract of land on the Brechin Road which could be taken over by the Council and used for growing vegetables, either for sale or to be distributed among the poor.

It was agreed that a Relief Committee should be formed to look into this difficult problem.

March 15 1907

The success of the Arbroath Evening Continuation Classes was marked by the prize giving and concert held in Arbroath High School tonight.

All the teachers were present, as indeed were a large group of young people. These Classes had been in existence for several years now and the idea had been to give young lads and lasses a "second chance" if they had not done too well at school.

The idea was that one could work, say in a factory during the day, but then learn something like Engineering at night.

"It is never too late to learn" was the gist of what Chairman Mr Arthur King (inevitably called King Arthur and asked about his Round Table!) said in his address.

The subjects taught included English, Art, Engineering, Maths, Carpentry, Wood-Carving, Singing and Ambulance.

The Ambulance and the Singing classes were this year to be examined by external examiners because the Committee were of the opinion that certificates awarded by an external body had far more validity than internal ones, simply because internal certification could lead to allegations of collusion on the one hand or victimisation on the other!

The two duxes of the school Jemima Forsyth and John Mathieson were each presented with a copy of "Inverbrothock Illustrated", and the proceedings were concluded with a concert involving pupils of the Music class and supplemented by other local talent while Mr Adamson, the Music teacher accompanied on the piano.

March 16 1962

Today, *The Arbroath Herald* notes with sadness the decision of Bailie Mrs J C Ross to stand down at the end of the Municipal year, by which she means that she is not seeking re-election in May.

In an age where women still did not take as large a part in public life as they perhaps ought to have done, Mrs Ross had proved the "value of a woman's approach" (whatever that delightfully vague piece of phrasing in *The Arbroath Herald* might have meant!) in matters of education and health, and as a Magistrate, she was always a "fair and impartial" judge.

Sadly in recent times, she has been stricken by a "painful illness" which has imposed a severe limitation on what she has been able to do.

Provost David Gardner also expressed his regret on hearing about her decision, but hoped that her illness would not preclude her from taking part in the many voluntary activities with which she was associated in the town, and hoped she would enjoy better health.

She was by no means the only woman on the Council in 1962, but she had been one of the most forthright and the most vocal. Women politicians in the 1960s were often considered to be pushy, unpleasant creatures, sexual predators and generally not really as bright as their male counterparts.

The cause of female equality clearly had a long way to go yet! But Mrs Ross was generally considered to be one of the better and more trustworthy local politicians. She had been awarded the MBE in 1951.

March 17 1919

The cosy little hall at St Thomas RC Church was packed to its utmost capacity tonight to celebrate St Patrick's Night.

The situation with Ireland in these first few months after the Great War was fraught and tense.

The Sinn Fein party, who had won almost every Irish seat in the General Election of December 1918, had now effectively seceded and formed their own Dail in Dublin. However, the British Government would not recognise their right to self-determination, something that seemed to contradict all the cant the Irish had heard about "gallant little Belgium".

Violence was not unknown, and would get a great deal worse in the nest few years. Every effort was made to keep politics out of this nice concert in Arbroath.

The small Irish enclave in Arbroath was vibrant, but also well integrated into Scottish society, unlike in other parts of the country where they were made to feel a great deal less welcome.

The Rev W McCurragh welcomed everyone and they all sang "Hail Glorious St Patrick" (otherwise known as "Erin's Green Valleys"). Other Irish songs were sung, including "The Dear Little Shamrock" and the ever popular "Tipperary".

The young people also took part with action songs of an International flavour like "Little Japs at Play", "Dutch Chorus" and "Deep in Canadian Woods".

Mr P Brannan called for a Vote of Thanks to everyone, spoke of how well the Irish in Arbroath had enjoyed St Patrick's Day before everyone joined in an impassioned rendering of "God Save Ireland".

March 18 1931

Tonight at the Red Triangle Hut in Hill Street under the auspices of the YMCA and the local group of Toc H, a talk was given by the Rev D C Wiseman of Hopemount Church on his visit to Oberammergau.

The famous Passion Play, which had been held there in its modern form every ten years from 1860, was one of the few plays which was allowed to break the general convention that no actor ever played the part of Jesus Christ.

Oberammergau in the Bavarian Alps was a small village of about 2,300 inhabitants, all of whom were very keen to take a part in the play. Rev Wiseman lived with a family in the village, and was well informed about the play which was produced on alternate days and lasted all day.

It began at 8.00 am, continued until about 12.00 then had a lunch interval of about 2 hours before beginning again until 6.00 pm.

Laudably, the villagers had resisted any attempts at commercialisation, having turned down the advances of an American film company last year.

Rev Wiseman said that he would love to take a party from Arbroath to Oberammergau one day, but it would be an expensive undertaking, and there was not another scheduled performance until 1940.

No-one could say this at the time, but there would be a major obstacle called the Second World War in 1940! The talk by Rev Wiseman was well received by the Arbroath audience.

March 19 1953

The Second World War had been over for several years now, and there was every sign that things were beginning to improve in every respect.

The day of universal foreign holidays had not yet arrived but there were already indications that some people were beginning to say "Why not?"

A resolution to form an association between Arbroath and the Normandy town of Pont L'Eveque was passed at the Town Council tonight.

Proposed by Honorary Treasurer D A Gardner the resolution was also unanimously supported by members of local organisations.

The idea had come from Mr R L Mackie, West Newport, the honorary general secretary of the Franco-Scottish society. Pont L'Eveque is a small town of about 3,000 inhabitants situated in the middle of an agricultural area of Normandy.

The idea would be that information would be exchanged about between the two towns with a view to visiting each other on summer trips. In particular they would exchange information about holidays and leisure activities.

Those Arbroathians who had taken part in the D Day landings of less than ten years ago would be very interested in going back. Pont L'Eveque had been in the middle of the action but had recovered and had been virtually rebuilt.

Office bearers were elected for this new Association with Provost James Kydd Moir being the President, and the Rector of Arbroath High School Mr D D Wilson being Vice President, as well as Mr T Matheson representing ex-Servicemen's organisations.

March 20 2022

This was Census night in Scotland. In England and Wales the Census was held on March 21st, 2021.

There had been a Census in the United Kingdom held every 10 years since 1841 with the exception of the war year of 1941.

This year the Census had been delayed (perhaps unnecessarily) by a year because of the Coronavirus outbreak, which had inflicted a great deal of disruption throughout the country in 2020 and 2021.

There could be no doubt that it was a necessary evil (if evil it was) and the historian is always rewarded by a look at the Arbroath Census records of bygone ages, even if they are not released until 100 years have passed.

This year it is different. Unlike on previous occasions, when house-to-house with the Census being done on-line – something which causes a great deal of additional stress for those who are not completely computer literate or whose laptops cause them trouble!

As a result, it appears that more than 500,000 households had failed to file a census return a fortnight after the original deadline.

By May 1st, the completion rate had reached 77 per cent, with 604,000 forms outstanding. By Sunday 15 May, the National Records Office were awaiting returns from 460,000 households, with 82.6 per cent complete.

In addition, one wonders whether all the questions about one's income and even one's ethnicity are necessary or desirable, although there are of course all the guarantees that the information will not fall into the wrong hands!

One is often shocked to read some of the past Census records. Some ancestors are perhaps not as rich nor as moral as they were sometimes portrayed, and there is often a genuine horror at the sheer number of people who had to live so close together in some awful housing on the High Street or near the Harbour, for example.

It was little wonder that TB and other horrors were so prevalent!

March 21 1900

This being the spring equinox, the quarterly "exercise" of the Lifeboat took place today. This was a statutory requirement.

The sea was very heavy, as often happens at his time of the year, but that made the exercise all the more valid, because it is usually in heavy seas that Lifeboats are required.

The boat was launched at ebb tide, and as there was no water at the Boat House, the vessel had to be wheeled down and it was some time before it was actually floated under the command of Coxswain William Smith and under the supervision on Lieutenant Tracey, RN Inspector of Lifeboats.

Most of the Arbroath fishermen were there to watch the 12 oarsmen of the crew row her out. Somewhat alarmingly, on several occasions an ugly breaker swept the boat from stern to stern and drenched the crew, but the crew were able to cruise and then to row back into the harbour.

In the afternoon a meeting of the Committee was held and Lieutenant Tracey reported that he was satisfied with the Lifeboat and that the Boat House was in good order.

He also stated that he was still in communication with the Dundee and Arbroath Joint Railway Company with a view to widening the gateway at Elliot Junction in order to provide a passageway for a boat at that point in case of emergency.

Funds recently raised for the Lifeboat Institution were handed over with thanks.

March 22 1961

The Arbroath Abbey Pageant will go ahead again, as from next year 1962!

This was the good news that came from the Society's Executive Committee which met tonight in the Town House, and was generally greeted with joy and enthusiasm in the town.

The Pageant had sadly been allowed to lapse after 1956, thanks to a succession of unfortunate experiences with the weather and a few weak pusillanimous Committee decisions, but it was felt that the Pageant should be resurrected.

Church Ministers, Drama Societies, the Burns Club and other bodies including people from the Abbey itself expressed interest with the telling fact being the amount of visitors to the town and the Abbey who came along and expressed disappointment that there was no Pageant anymore.

The Arbroath Herald also expressed its qualified approval at the change of heart. There was no doubt that the character of the town, particularly in the summer months, had changed radically with the constant influx of tourists which seemed to be growing year by year, but it was always a good idea for a town to remember its past.

"A town which does not remember its past cannot expect to have much of a future" and the Declaration of Arbroath, although now a distant event with little apparent relevance to the modern world, was nevertheless significant enough to deserve commemoration.

Apart from anything else, it was all good fun to see well-known local characters dressed up as Bishops and Royalty!

Arbroath Abbey Pageant

March 23 1949

Arbroath is shocked today with the news that Provost John Lamb has resigned.

He told the Town Council of his decision last night. There was nothing sinister about his decision, simply that he had been invited to become President of the Scottish Football Association.

He would resign as from May 2nd, when in any case a new Town Council would be appointed. It would be impossible to give the job of Provost the amount of time that it needed, if he were also doing the very demanding SFA job.

He announced his intention to step down with a great deal of regret, for he had been on the Town Council for 20 years and had made many friends there, while working hard to attract new industries to the town.

He probably deserved a great deal of credit for the work he and the rest of the Council did in the 1930s to make Arbroath a great holiday resort particularly for the large Glasgow market, but also for the rest of Scotland as well.

Provost Lamb paid tribute to First Bailie McGlashan for the help and support he had given him. For his part Bailie McGlashan said that the Provost was a man of very keen business ability who had administered the affairs of the Town with sound judgement and common sense.

He would be much missed, but the decision had been made, and all that remained to do was to wish the Provost every success.

Arbroath Burns Club

March 24 1870

It seems now that the strike of seamen in Arbroath Harbour is over with everything settled reasonably amicably.

Strikes in the manufacturing industry are by no means uncommon in Arbroath or anywhere else, but is unusual to hear of seamen striking work.

By the very nature of the work, strikes can only really take place when the sailors are on shore. If everyone "struck" when on board ship, not only would the ship simply drift away, but it would be what was called a "mutiny" and that would have very serious consequences indeed!

Seamen are paid monthly, and normally received £3 10 shillings per month. The Arbroath sailors asked for £4 quoting examples of sailors from other ports who earned this amount, but the owners refused, citing the depression in trade and the increased competition from steamers operating from large ports and threatening the livelihood of smaller ports.

For a day or two there was a stand-off with no ships sailing and an attempt was made to bring in sailors from Dundee who were apparently being offered £3 12 6.

This attempt proved fruitless, and after a few other attempts at negotiation with the Arbroath sailors on strike, an agreement was reached whereby the sailors would receive £3 15 shillings per month, payable in advance before the ship sailed.

Confusingly, a rumour had also reached the ears of *The Arbroath Guide* to the effect that some sailors had actually sailed earlier, having negotiated their £4 per month. Anyway, the matter was settled.

March 25 1897

1897 is Diamond Jubilee year and preparations are well in hand in Arbroath and elsewhere to commemorate the sixty years that Queen Victoria has been on the throne.

The good lady, now not far away from her 80th birthday, will obviously not be present in Arbroath, but arrangements are well advanced.

There can be little doubt that she has been a great deal better than quite a few of her horrendous predecessors, and that her 60 years have been an era of progress in terms of railways, industry and the steadily expanding Empire, even though it is said that she herself is more and more prone to irrational bouts of sulking and sheer awkwardness.

Today *The Arbroath Herald* reports with sadness the death at an advanced age of John Hean, the tanner, a man who was quite outspoken in his opposition to royalty.

The paper recalls the time in the old Trades Hall when he delivered a talk on "The Cost Of The Crown" when "between the Bible and a blue book, Mr Hean gave the Royal Household a rousing night of it" and when heckled by some of the audience he replied "with characteristic pith".

This is good evidence to suggest that Victorian Society was by no means monolithic, and that affection for the Queen was far from universal. *The Arbroath Herald* regrets the passing of the old agitator and remarks that society is so much the poorer for the comparative dearth of such men today.

Whatever else Hean said or did, he "kept people interested". But so too does the Queen, and the summer is much looked forward to.

A horse-brake trip to celebrate the Jubilee

March 26 1937

Arbroath people, and particularly those of who lived around Arbirlot would have been saddened to hear of the death of the Reverend Edward Vernon at the advanced age of 84.

He had been Minister of Arbirlot Church from 1879 to 1914, a total of 35 years, a considerable number of years in a time of rapid social change. He was born in 1853 in Edinburgh and graduated from Edinburgh University with the rare combination of Mathematics and Hebrew.

He had done some of his early ministry at Crathie and then Doune, before he was called to Arbirlot in 1879. Soon after that, he married his wife in Edinburgh in 1880 and she was a great support to him as Sunday School teacher.

Both Rev and Mrs Vernon were involved in a movement called Onward and Upward, an organisation interested in the moral welfare of the nation and locality. They had four sons and a daughter.

He was deeply involved in Presbytery work, as well as his parish work, but sadly a protracted period of ill health round about the start of the Great War obliged him to demit office in Arbirlot.

After a brief time in Edinburgh, he returned to Angus, to Edzell, where his health improved and allowed him to preach in various pulpits in the area.

Although more than 20 years had passed since he had been Minister at Arbirlot, he was buried there with a large attendance of mourners who remembered him with a great deal of affection.

March 26 1990

At the slipway of Mackays yard on Monday 26 March 1990. The boat is Fidelity AH113 completed in 1946. The hull was black, lined out in yellow. Notice the fine old wooden foremast. Notice also the simple shelter deck at the

March 27 1953

Tonight at the Webster Memorial Hall was held a wonderful concert in aid of funds for the Arbroath Instrumental Band.

It would be fair to say that although the Band played its part well, the two stars of the show were the soloists Elizabeth Dall and Conway Stuart.

Elizabeth Dall is a well known Arbroath singer and she entertained the company with such favourites as "Little Polly Flinders", "The Last Rose of Summer" and "John Anderson My Jo, John", displaying a wide repertoire and recalling the days when the child prodigy little Betty Dall used to entertain in concerts. She has now grown to maturity.

Conway Stuart, an Arbroathian only by adoption, in spite of suffering from the after effects of flu, entertained the audience with some lovely numbers including Handel's "Where'er you walk" especially when he did a duet with Elizabeth Dall.

The band themselves, resplendent in their new uniforms of navy blue, scarlet and gold, drew many appreciative comments of approval from the audience.

One of the members of the band was John McEwan of 25 Panmure Street, a founder member of the band in 1893 and still playing, sixty years later! There are another four founder members of the band still alive, but Mr McEwan is the only one still active of the Arbroath Instrumental Band.

The Arbroath Instrumental Band were formed when they broke away from the Arbroath Artillery Band because they resented having to do military drills, like marching and saluting, as well as playing their instruments!

March 28 1923

A rather distressing case came to Arbroath Sheriff Court today.

Sheriff Gordon and a jury had to enquire into the circumstances of the death of a cattleman called James Kirkland, aged 58, of Hillhead, in the employ of Mr Hume.

Both the next of kin and Mr Hume were legally represented and Mr T Hart the Procurator Fiscal represented the Crown.

Mr Kirkland had died in Arbroath Infirmary on March 7. On December 23 the deceased had been jammed against a stall by a bullock and from then on complained intermittently of pains in his left side.

In January Dr Yule was called to Hillside to see Mr Kirkland and after several visits decided that he should be taken to hospital where he underwent an operation on January 29.

In this operation a tumour was discovered, and Dr Yule was of the opinion that the tumour had been there before the accident with the bullock. The accident on its own would not have killed Mr Kirkland but the tumour might well have in any case, even without the accident.

It was possible that the encounter with the bullock accelerated his death, and the incident helped to draw attention to the problem that was already there, but there were no grounds for believing that Mr Kirkland died solely through the incident with the bullock.

The callous may even have said that the unfortunate incident did him a favour. Mr Hume was exonerated of all blame.

March 29 1933

An old lady had a remarkable escape today when part of her roof in Philip Street, collapsed.

The rafters of the roof had given way (through sheer old age, presumably, for it was not a stormy day) and had crashed through the ceiling bringing down a great deal of slates onto the bed and damaging some of furniture.

Miss Elizabeth Taylor, aged about 70, presumably deaf, who had lived in this house for over fifty years (and her parents had lived there before her!) had been sitting, apparently unaware, in another part of the house.

It was only through the prompt action of a neighbour, Mr Buick, a retired confectioner, that she was removed from the house before more of the roof collapsed.

The adjoining house was occupied by a Mr and Mrs Mill who only lived there during the summer months. Mr Hogg, the slater, was immediately engaged to repair the roof, and he was there most of the evening.

Questions were immediately raised about the long term viability of the house. It was like many houses in the district at this time which had served honourably for many years (in this case, for possibly more than a century) but which either needed major attention or to be demolished.

There was a fair amount of house building going on, but clearly a lot more needed to be done, even in these times of economic stringency.

March 30 1851

The 1851 Census for Scotland was taken on the night of 30/31 March 1851. The following information was requested:

Place (name of street, place, or road, and name or number of house)
Name of each person that had spent the night in that household
Relation to head of family; Marital Status; Age; Sex (indicated by which column the age is recorded in); Profession or occupation; Birthplace; Whether blind, or deaf and dumb.

The population of Arbroath was 16,986.

Alexander was born to James Ruxton and Mary Low on 31st August 1839. in St Vigeans. In 1851 they lived at 67 Keptie Street, St Vigeans, Inverbrothock, with his siblings Elizabeth, Helen, John, Martha, Fredrick and Jean.

In 1861 he was described as an Engine Smith. By 1870 he was living with John Ruxton, a Locomotive Machinist, in Schenectady. In 1880 he is married, to Ann, from Scotland. By 1900 he has moved to Yonkers, and is married to Hannah, from New Jersey. By 1910 he has been widowed.

He became a naturalised US citizen on 20 October 1879, in Schenectady.

He visited the UK frequently, including a trip in 1907.

Alexander Ruxton sailed on the Lusitania from Liverpool on 17th September 1910 to his home in 77 Lindon Street, Yonkers, New York, with Mary Ruxton, now aged 66, and listed on the ship's manifest as a house keeper.

He was back in Britain, returning to the US on August 17 1911, and again, from 8th July to 13 September 1912. He died later that year and is buried in Vale Cemetery, Schenectady.

Ruxton Memorial

March 30 1964

Tonight Noel Coward's "Private Lives" opened at the Abbey Theatre.

It was a professional performance put on by five young people, all second year students at the College of Dramatic Art, and they had full houses at six performances and two matinees.

Admittedly, it was a small theatre – indeed it was sometimes referred to as "the little theatre" – but they were surprised and delighted by the amount of Arbroath people who wanted to see Noel Coward.

The attraction, however, was that the actors were all local people. There are two outsiders, if Aberdeen and Fife can be referred to in those terms, in Caroline Hedderwick from Fife and Pat Ramsay, the daughter of Bill Ramsay, who was well known in Aberdeen dramatic circles.

From closer to home came Stuart Mungall who had performed with Forfar Amateur Dramatic Society and had already appeared professionally in Arbroath. His parents had a garage in Forfar.

There were also two former pupils of Arbroath High School in David Kane who was brought up in Carnoustie and also Isobel Gardner who could not be more centred on Arbroath, for her father was the Provost!

It was good to see these local young people do well, particularly Isobel Gardner who was the Stage Manager and Producer as well as taking a small part in the play.

There was certainly talent there, but making progress in the world of professional acting was very much a hit or a miss business. "Many are called, but few are chosen" and a lot depended on sheer luck.

Corn Exchange

March 31 1901

The 1901 Census for Scotland was taken on the night of 31 March/1 April 1901. The population had reached 22,997.

The following information was requested: place, name, relationship to head of family, marital status, age, gender, profession, birthplace, and whether blind, deaf, and dumb.
This information helps to identify people with similar names.

David Cargill, 78, lived at 14 West Newgate with his wife Nellie, 61, a sewing machinist, and his daughter Nellie, 20, a tow preparer.
David Cargill, 52, a flax dresser, lived at 16 Smithy Croft with his wife Jane, 52, and children Peter, 24, a flxdresser, Christina, 21, a flax mill worker, and robert, 18, a flax mill worker.
David Cargill, 52, a fisherman, widowed, lived with his daughters Maggie, 20, a housekeeper, and Jane, 15, a servant.
David Cargill, 42, a fisherman, lived at 26 Seagate with his wife Margaret Shepherd, 50.
David Cargill, aged 39, a coal carter, lived at 11 Hannah Street, St Vigeans, with his wife Mary, aged 30.
David Cargill, aged 15, lived with his mother, Elizabeth Watton, 45, his brothers James, 4, and Isaac, 26, in 3 Marketgate.
David Cargill, 11, lived at 8 Ladybridge street. The son of James Cargill, fisherman, 40, and Catherine, 38, his siblings were Betsy, 17, Catherine, 15, James, 12, Jane, 12, Robina, 7, Helen, 5, Thomas, 2, and Cecilia, 1.
Some more:
David Cargill,39, a fisherman, of 28 Union Street East; David Cargill, 33, a fisherman of 21 Old Shore Head; . David Cargill, 31, a fisherman of Old Shore head; David Cargill, 25, a fisherman, of 7 South Street; David Cargill, 23, a plasterer of 6 Union street East; David Cargill, 23, a flax weaver of 23 Ladybridge Street; ; David Cargill, 22, fisherman, of 32 High Street; David Cargill, 19, mill machinist of 30 High Street; David Cargill, a bleacher flax, of 30 High street; David Cargill, 15, not working, of 3 Marketgate; David Cargill, 13, fisherman, of 12 South Street; David Cargill, 9, a scholar, of 31 Seagate; David Cargill, 6, a scholar, of 25 Seagate; David Cargill, 5, a scholar, 9 Old Shore head; newly born David Cargill of 29 Union Street East; David Cargill, aged 13, a scholar of 7 Seagate.
Nine more David Cargills in St Vigeans, two in Panbride and one in Arbirlot.

March 31 1928

It was the start of a trend which would grow and grow over the next fifty years and more.

For the first time a small group of Arbroath fans decided to go and watch Scotland playing at the famous Wembley Stadium.

A trip to London and back for a weekend was, of course, way beyond the pocket of most 1920s Arbroathians, so it involved a great deal of financial sacrifice.

About 20 tartan clad people, including some women, left the station last night to arrive in London early this Saturday morning.

Some of them would be seen to be carrying a paper bag which made a clinking sound like bottles bashing against each other.

This was what was called the "Kerry-oot" and was a *sine qua non* for the trip. They would spend two nights on the train, and thus they didn't need to spend money on accommodation in London.

When they arrived in London, the weather was absolutely dreadful, but they did spend the morning looking at Trafalgar Square and Buckingham Palace before heading out to the great, impressive stadium that was Wembley.

Some were lucky enough to see the Duke of York (who was "merriet oan yon lassie fae Glamis") and the King of Afghanistan, both of whom attended the game and saw the famous Scotland "Wembley Wizards" beat England 5-1!

The football edition of the *London Evening Standard* gave the no less vital news that the Red Lichties, who could be tactfully described as "experiencing a season of mediocrity", had drawn 2-2 with East Stirlingshire at Gayfield.

April

Part of Arbroath, from Pont, 1600

April 1 1939

War was fairly obviously approaching – a matter of months or even just weeks away – but more pertinent for Arbroath was whether they could retain their First Division status.

Today's result, a 0-2 defeat at Celtic Park did not help, but this was the day that would haunt Attilio Becci for the rest of his life.

Born in 1914 of Italian origin, he had played for Arbroath since 1932, was commonly known as "Teel" and both he and his family, who had a fish and chip shop in Dishlandtown Street, publicly disowned Mussolini and his blackshirts.

Today he was involved in an incident with the great Jimmy Delaney when he fell on top of Delaney and accidentally stood on Delaney's arm, not so much breaking it as shattering it.

Although Delaney would absolve Becci from blame, Becci was booed by the Celtic supporters who even threatened to stone the Arbroath bus. Arbroath did save themselves from relegation.

When war ensued, "Teel" was allowed to serve in the British Army, played as a guest for Notts County in 1942 and was chosen to play in a British Army XI in Naples in 1945 — where he was cheered on by quite a few Arbroathian soldiers who remembered him. He could never forget the Delaney incident.

Delaney was out of the game for two years, but having recovered, he then scored the famous winning goal in the Victory International of 1946 to the delight of Becci who remained on friendly terms with Delaney.

Becci returned to the family chip shop and died in 1980.

April 2 1871

The 1871 Census for Scotland was taken on the night of 2/3 April 1871. The following information was requested:

> Place (name of street, place, or road, and name or number of house)
> Name of each person that had spent the night in that household
> Relation to head of family
> Marital Status
> Age
> Sex (indicated by which column the age is recorded in)
> Profession or occupation
> Birthplace
> Whether blind, or deaf and dumb.

The population had risen to 22,682

Jane Paterson Shanks, born on 25 April 1861, lived in Woodley Cottage, Service Road, Arbroath. Her parents, James, 40, an engineer who employed 136 men and 52 boys, and Margaret Jane Cargill, 34, had six children, of whom Jane was second eldest. they had three servants.

On 10 July 1883 she married James Lyle Mackay, born on 11 September in 1852, son of James Mackay, shipmaster, and Deborah Lyle.

They had five children.

James Lyle Mackay became the first Baron Inchcape in 1911.

He received the Freedom of the Burgh on 3rd June, 1922.

He died on 23 May, 1932

Lord Inchcape receives the Freedom of the Burgh in 1922

April 2 1911

The 1911 Census for Scotland was taken on the night of 2 April 1911

There were new questions relating to fertility of marriage: on duration of marriage; the number of living children born to each marriage; and the number alive at the time of the census.

The population had dropped, by 267, from the last census to 22,730

There were changes to several others:

categories for people with disabilities were revised and the introductory section to the third report on the 1911 census refers to the intended use of the terms as:

lunatic - in cases where the infirmity had been acquired during life

imbecile - in extreme cases where the infirmity had existed from birth or an early age

feeble-minded - in milder cases where the infirmity had existed from birth or an early age.

the question on occupation was extended to find out which industries or services a worker was connected to in addition to their personal profession or occupation

the question on place of birth was extended to include nationality for those born in a foreign country, that is, outwith British territory, colonies and dependencies.

The police were asked to assist with the enumeration of persons in barns, sheds, caravans, tents and in the open air.

April 2 1919

Arbroath is, on the surface, vibrant these days, but *The Arbroath Herald* is right to see problems here.

The streets are crowded and it is a positive delight to see so many boys who have now become men after their years in the khaki.

Quite rightly do they walk the streets, proud of what they have done, but there does remain a major problem of what they are going to do now.

Military life has not really equipped them for civilian life, which is possibly less dangerous but a great deal more complex, and there can be little doubt that the end of the war has been accompanied by a major slump in trade in the textile industries on which Arbroath relies.

How could it be otherwise? The war demand has now gone, and there is undeniably the long-term collapse of the German market, which is not really good news for this country, for an impoverished Germany is in no position to buy goods.

So what is there for a young man? Even a fit and healthy one?

Not all young men have returned unscathed; in fact, casualties are a lot heavier even than they have been portrayed, for so many ex-soldiers are carrying with them the horrible mental scars of some of the things that they have seen.

And there is also the flu' still wreaking havoc and death.

So behind all the "Welcome Home, Boys" parties and Arbroath's own Harry Lauder singing about "The Laddies That Fought And Won", there remains a great deal of anxiety about the future.

Arbroath is far from "the land fit for heroes to live in".

Sir Harry Lauder with his old friend John Stewart

April 3 1881

The 1881 Census for Scotland was taken on the night of 3/4 April 1881. The following information was requested:

Place (name of street, place, or road, and name or number of house)
Name of each person that had spent the night in that household
Relation to head of family
Marital Status
Age
Sex (indicated by which column the age is recorded in)
Profession or occupation
Birthplace
Whether deaf and dumb, blind, imbecile or idiot, or lunatic

The population, 24,475, showed a healthy increase over the last ten years.

Charles Webster Corsar, 46, a Sailcloth manufacturer employing 200 men and 260 women, lived with his wife Agnes, 45 at Seaforth, Dundee Road, Arbroath, with children David, 20, William, 15, Marjory, 13, Jane, 11, Charles, 9, Henry, 8, and Agnes, 7.

The servants were cook Catherine Callum, 23, from Banff, housemaid Georgina Petrie, 23, from Perth, and laundress Mary Coull, 24, from Forfar.

April 3 1925

A strange, unnerving and still unexplained event occurred in Arbroath tonight.

The Arbroath Herald tells the story gleefully of how a couple, either recently married or about to be, entered "the dark and forbidding tunnel" which connects Spink Street and Hume Street.

They were coming home from "a place of entertainment" (the cinema, one presumes) and had just entered the tunnel when they saw a couple of steers or bullocks entering from the other end and charging towards them.

The couple turned tail and fled, just reaching the stairs at the end of the tunnel as the creatures charged past them and disappeared into the gloom of Hume Street.

Where the beasts came from, no-one knows, although it may have been from a loading bank adjacent to Robert Street, and more to the point, no-one seems to know where they went to, for they were never seen again!

Naturally an occurrence like this caused no little alarm in the town, but there was also a certain amount of doubt cast on the reliability or veracity of the witnesses.

Had they perhaps been not to the cinema, but a public house instead? And had they perhaps "exaggerated" the story?

Perhaps it was a couple of dogs they had seen? Or maybe like Tam O' Shanter they had seen witches, when we all know that such things do not exist.

It was a strange story, and no-one ever came up with a credible explanation.

April 4 1832

The country is in a ferment at the moment about the passing of the Reform Act.

Arbroath will be in a constituency to be called Montrose Burghs and there will be 1,494 electors in Arbroath, Forfar, Brechin, Inverbervie and Montrose.

The years since the end of the Napoleonic Wars have not been easy with unemployment, poverty and the occasional riot about things like the price of corn.

It is to be hoped that the Reform Act will at least be a first step to making sure that Parliament is fairly representative of public opinion, because, otherwise .... every one knows what happened in France in 1789.

There have been reports of "incendiaries" at Lathermuir near Montrose with five houses set on fire, whether by supporters of Reform or opponents to Reform, or simply "lawless elements", no-one can be sure.

One rumour, however, current in Arbroath, *The Perthshire Courier* is at pains to deny. The rumour is that a woman has died of cholera.

There have been outbreaks of cholera from time to time in Arbroath as it could be brought in by sailors from abroad, although the usual cause is a polluted water supply. However, in this case the woman is alive and well, and reports of her death have been much exaggerated.

"To allay the fears of the timorous", *The Perthshire Courier* quotes the medieval poet Thomas the Rhymer talking to the jolly monks of Aberbrothock

> From the Sidlaws eastward to the sea
> Pest or plague will never be

April 5 1891

The 1891 Census for Scotland was taken on the night of 5/6 April 1891. The following information was requested:

>Place (parish and name of street, place, or road, and name or number of house)
>Name of each person that had spent the night in that household
>Relation to head of family
>Marital Status
>Age
>Sex (indicated by which column the age is recorded in)
>Profession or occupation
>Whether an employer, employed, or working on own account
>Birthplace
>Whether speaks Gaelic or Gaelic and English
>Whether deaf and dumb, blind, or lunatic, imbecile, or idiot
>Number of rooms in house with one or more windows.

The population had fallen to 22,993.

In Hill Street, there were 30 householders, of whom 18 were born outside the Burgh.

In Lindsay Street, St Vigeans, there were also 30 householders, of whom also 18 were born outside.

April 5 1856

The Arbroath Guide today carries news of the end of the Crimean War.

The war officially ended on March 30, but news did not reach Arbroath until the following day; immediately the town began to rejoice with flags, parades of local instrumental bands and a bonfire on the Common.

There have been several local men killed in Crimea, and many more who have not been heard of for some considerable time. This does not of course necessarily mean that they have been killed, for communications have been poor and very slow, but there are quite a few anxious Arbroath wives and mothers.

The war has lasted more or less exactly two years and other than learning a few geographical terms like Balaclava and Sebastopol, it has been difficult to work out what is going on. It has been odd to have the French on our side and the Russians against us for a change!

In the meantime as it will be some time before the soldiers can come home, life continues as normal in the town with meetings of the Arbroath Presbytery and a meeting of the Arbroath–Forfar Railway Company indicating a slight profit.

But there was also a hoax when a group of young men spread a rumour that an "Equestrian Company" were coming to the Common to celebrate the end of the war with a firework display.

Sadly, the day was April 1.

April 6 1320

Today was signed in Latin what was called *Declaratio Arbroathis* or the Declaration o' Aiberbrothick, in which Scots barons wrote a letter and sent it to the all-powerful Pope John XXII in Rome.

King Robert the Bruce had been excommunicated in 1317 for refusing to agree to a truce in the War of Independence. This was seen as the reply of the people of Scotland, asserting Scotland's right to an independent existence free from the attempts of the English to invade or control Scotland.

The declaration was drafted in Arbroath Abbey by Bernard of Kilwinning, then the Abbot of Arbroath, and was signed by 51 Scottish nobles. It certainly put Arbroath on the map and contains the following famous lines

> *"for, as long as but a hundred of us remain alive, never will we on any conditions be brought under English rule. It is in truth not for glory, nor riches, nor honours that we are fighting, but for freedom – for that alone, which no honest man gives up but with life itself".*

Historians have argued about how much the Declaration actually affected future history.

The fact that it involved the Pope meant that for a few centuries, it was marginalised in Presbyterian Scotland, (which tended in any case to side with those of the Unionist persuasion).

In the 20th and 21st centuries politicians have not been slow to grasp its significance as evidence of the rich and powerful wanting independence for Scotland in medieval times.

April 7 1861

The 1861 Census for Scotland was taken on the night of 7/8 April 1861. The following information was requested:

Place (name of street, place, or road, and name or number of house);
Name of each person that had spent the night in that household;
Relation to head of family; Marital Status; Age; Sex (indicated by which column the age is recorded in);
Profession or occupation; Birthplace; Whether blind, or deaf and dumb;
the number of children aged between five and 15 attending school or being educated at home;
the number of rooms with one or more windows (reflecting concerns about housing and sanitary conditions and not to be confused with the window tax which had been abolished in 1851).

The population, including St Vigeans, was 17,657, living in about 90 streets.

William Simpson from Dundee, aged 59, a blacksmith, and his wife, Mary, 58, were boarding in one of the 84 households in Lord Burn with Elizabeth Robertson, 38, a married woman, and her daughter, Mary Baxter, 9, and her two-year-old twins, Susan and William Langlands.

Another William Simpson, one month old, was boarding with his parents at the house of George Henderson, 66, at 41 St Mary Street. His father, James Simpson, was a Railway Engine Smith from Methven in Perthshire, who had married Mary Crawford from Arbroath in 1859.

William Peter, 50, a carter, was boarding, together with four other people, in the lodging house of Christian Law at 19 Dickfield Street.

William Charles, 47, from St Vigeans, a flax canvas weaver, was boarding with flax weaver Samuel and his wife Mary Hunter at 17 North Grimsby.

William Davidson, 45, from Arbirlot, a general labourer, was boarding with Jessie Carnegie, 48, a flax mill worker, and her two children at 19 North Grimsby.

April 7 1953

Who said that Christianity was all about loving one's neighbour?

Is there not also something in the Bible which says that the Church is the body of Christ, and that all parts should move harmoniously?

If so, someone forgot to tell Arbroath Presbytery, for this afternoon we had a very public hanging out of dirty washing.

It concerned the Reverend Matthew McPhail, Minister of Arbirlot and one time clerk to Arbroath Presbytery Clerk who alleged that a deliberate attempt was being made to persecute him.

Mr McPhail had been sacked by the Presbytery as Presbytery Clerk but had appealed to the Synod of Angus and had been reinstated. Once reinstated, McPhail had immediately resigned!

Such behaviour was inconsistent and indeed curious. It all seemed to concern McPhail's recording of the Presbytery minutes, which were inaccurate and contained a few omissions, in one case of a call to a Minister and his induction.

Reverend W W M Bell of Hopemount Church seemed to be spearheading the movement against McPhail, and it was apparent that some of the minutes had been doctored.

It was clear that this was a long story of bitter personal hatred, and *The Arbroath Guide* reports that "the attendance during the discussion was attenuated". Many members had gone home, as the matter had gone on for three hours!

The matter promised to run and run for a while without any signs of the situation being resolved. To be brutally frank, this business did not do the Church any good at all! Actually, "forgiveness" might not have been a bad idea!

April 8 1921

A very rare phenomenon indeed today in Arbroath with a total eclipse of the sun.

This being a Friday, the schools were in, but the pupils were allowed to come out to watch the event, all armed with smoked glasses or negatives of a film to allow them to look at the sun without damaging their eyes.

There could not have been a better day to watch the eclipse, for it was a superb spring morning, and wonder was expressed that those who had predicted when it would occur had got it exactly right.

Many people watched it from the beach, others found some other vantage points.

At about 8.52 a.m. a small bit of the sun "in the top right hand corner" was seen to be missing. This patch grew and grew over the next hour as the light grew mustier and mustier, producing almost a green colour at the same time as the temperature dropped, until about 9.52 am almost exactly an hour later, the sun had almost disappeared.

There were clear signs of animals being disorientated by what was going on, and it was easy to understand why primitive man associated an eclipse with the end of the world, whereas we all knew that it was the moon getting between the sun and Arbroath.

Slowly the sun came back, the light got better, the heat returned and Arbroath returned to normal life. It would be a very long time before anyone talked about eclipses again.

April 9 1882

Easter Sunday was today celebrated with a great deal of joy and relief in the various Churches of Arbroath.

There was relief that the recent storms which had swept Scotland over the past few days and had caused a certain amount of damage, had not been worse; in fact they were now subsiding, having affected the exposed West coast of the country far more than the slightly more sheltered East coast.

But yesterday had seen a certain amount of drama at the Harbour, and of course everyone was aware that yesterday was Black Saturday, traditionally an unlucky day because it came between Good Friday and Easter Monday and was therefore the one day in the year when Christ was dead.

Be that as it may, the *SS Nautilus* of Lubeck arrived from Riga in Latvia with a full cargo of flax destined for the Burnside Works and ran aground at the western side of the harbour leaving 333 tons of shipping trapped and in a dangerous position until the evening tide.

The crew were safely taken off, and the cargo was loaded into a stream of "lighters" which were able to take the flax into the Harbour and place on the quayside.

An anxious crowd gathered to watch the ship successfully get afloat again without any apparent damage and able to sail away to Leith Docks for a full survey.

Apart from natural concern for the ship and its crew, the cargo of flax was also vital for Arbroath's fragile economy, and therefore the hymns were sung this Sunday morning with all the more gusto.

Colin Grant, Provost 1895 to 1904

April 10 1900

The Liquor Licensing Court met today for the purpose of granting licenses to those who wished to sell alcohol.

The Court was held in the Sheriff Court House under Provost Colin Grant and Bailies Robert Melvin and John Duncan, and was well attended. Most applications went through on the nod.

There are now five hotel licences, 32 public house licenses, 55 licensed houses and three porter and ale licenses, making a total of 95 in all. (*The Arbroath Herald* miscounts and says 105!)

95 seems an awful lot of licensed premises for a town the size of Arbroath, but that was common for the time, and explains the massive drink problem that existed in the town.

Some were unsuccessful in their application for a licence, e.g. John Thomson of 17 Elliot Street wanted a "porter and ale" licence for 52 Helen Street. It was felt that there were enough of such places in that area in any case, and that "porter and ale" houses were "a mongrel sort of thing".

There was a major problem about the George Hotel which had been the subject of a complaint from the Chief Constable who claimed that it was "not a hotel in any sense of the term".

Mr McLeod, the proprietor, strongly denied that, said he had had 200 "sleepers" since last May, and invited the Court to come and visit his premises. The decision was adjourned for a fortnight to allow this to happen.

April 11 1951

One of the more eventful days of Arbroath's long history.

It began at lunch time. Some men arrived in a car at Arbroath Abbey, took something large out of the car.

They conveyed it on a wheelbarrow, into the Abbey near the tomb of William the Lion, close to the spot where the Scottish Declaration of Independence was signed solemnly every year in the Abbey Pageant, and deposited it.

The large object, draped in the Scottish flag, turned out to be nothing less that the Stone of Destiny, which had been stolen from Westminster Abbey on Christmas Day 1950 and had not been seen since.

It was of course the Stone on which Kings of Scotland had sat while being crowned, but had been stolen by King Edward I in 1296 and taken to Westminster Abbey.

Beside the Stone was a letter which admitted the theft and stated that they simply believed that the Stone should be in Scotland.

What followed next showed a certain amount of indecent haste on the part of the Abbey authorities and the police who clearly feared an awful lot of trouble about this harmless looking lump of masonry.

In the middle of the night it was conveyed to Forfar Police Station where it stayed in a cell (!) until such time as it was removed back to London.

One cannot help wondering whether the authorities missed a trick here. It would have been a great attraction, and would the Government have ever dared to try to remove it?

April 12 1927

Poor radio reception in Arbroath has been a problem for some time.

Wirelesses or radios began to appear in the town round about 1923, but sales have dropped considerably over the past year or two, to an extent because people cannot afford them, but mainly because the reception is simply not good.

It varies in different parts of the town. Generally the hillier part of the town gets a slightly better reception although a few houses very close to the sea also report good reception particularly at night when things are quieter.

But those who hoped to be able to listen to Scotland v England at Hampden a couple of Saturdays ago had a serious disappointment with the voice of the commentator sounding "like a foghorn", and music lovers have had similar blows, even when the concert is coming from Edinburgh!

Last week Tom Johnston, the Labour MP for Dundee, raised the question in the House of Commons and received the customary reassurance that "it would be looked into", but the truth is that no-one really understands a great deal about how to guarantee good radio reception.

Much is the discussion about whether new masts being erected might help matters, but in the meantime the radio lovers of Arbroath, a large potential audience, must put on their radio and hold their breath to see if they are going to be able to enjoy their favourite programme or not.

Others shake their heads and say that they managed fine without these noisy things anyway!

April 13 1935

A glory day for Arbroath at Gayfield today as, before a large crowd of enthusiastic supporters, they completed their season with a 5-0 win over East Fife.

They had gained promotion last week at Recreation Park, Alloa in a curiously anti-climactic fashion in a 0-0 draw, the 0-0 draw meaning that they would almost definitely end up second behind Third Lanark.

This was the farewell day to the Second Division for Bert McGlashan's men and they thanked their fans for supporting them by turning on a superb display of attacking football over the luckless Fifers.

It was the first time that the Red Lichties had gained promotion and even people like Scots singer Harry Lauder sent them his congratulations.

Today the goals were scored by Brand scoring a hat trick and Carver and Duff one each, but the star was Atilio Becci at left back.

The team were applauded off the park at the end, but no-one was under any illusion that next year in the First Division against the likes of Celtic and Rangers would be a different matter altogether.

In fact, many of their supporters questioned whether promotion was a good idea for a part-time team like Arbroath, but for the moment, everyone was celebrating.

The team was Cumming, Fordyce and Becci; McNab, Paterson and Urquhart; Lowe, Duff, Brand, Jamieson and Carver.

In spite of a few pessimistic prognostications about how they would do in the First Division, they did in fact stay there until the declaration of war in 1939, and they were never officially relegated at this time.

April 14 1912

While the world's attention was drawn to the maiden voyage of the Titanic across the Atlantic, no less remarkable a trip was organised by two local motor cyclists

They rode their bicycles across the country from east to west and back again from Arbroath to Oban, a round total of 300 miles, all achieved in three days!

It would be fair to say that motor bikes which had been seen in Arbroath for several years now enjoyed a mixed reception in town.

There was little doubt that they were quick with people reaching Dundee from Arbroath well within the hour of setting out. On the other hand they were noisy, frightening children, animals and old people and they were also highly dangerous with several accidents being reported.

Nevertheless they were the things of the future. Along with these motorised cabs now appearing in town, it was beginning to look as if the days of the horse were numbered!

This Monday evening (the end of the Holiday weekend) the two motor cyclists arrived back in town to a great reception from their friends, some of whom had advised them against such a foolhardy expedition on a motor bike and side car.

They came back and told their story in detail to *The Arbroath Herald,* with stories of punctures, funny looks from locals and surpassing scenery on a nice weekend. The news from the Titanic was not quite so good, though!

April 15 1946

What's in a name?

An awful lot, actually. Reporting back to the Town Council on his recent attendance at the Scottish Convention of Local Burghs in Edinburgh, Provost John Lamb said that he had suggested that the name "Aberbrothock" should be discontinued in official language, and that the town should be known as "Arbroath" as it had been commonly known for the past few centuries.

The problem was that other towns did not know it by that name, and on one famous occasion, a councillor from Forfar (only 16 miles away) had given the impression that he thought that "Aberbrothock" was a "Hieland village up near Inverness". This councillor was admittedly renowned for his stupidity, but it made a point.

For these reasons, Provost Lamb wanted to be known as the Provost of Arbroath. Not everyone agreed. His predecessor, Sir William Chapel, had insisted on Aberbrothock, pointing out the historical significance of "aber" meaning "at the mouth of" the river Brothock.

Also, those who didn't like the English in 1320 and who signed the famous declaration had never heard of any place called Arbroath.

It was Aberbrothock, and that was also the place that the notorious thieving pirate Ralph the Rover kept stealing bells from.

Nevertheless, this was now 1946, and the team that played at Gayfield was one of the three football teams in Scotland that began with the letter R – Rangers, Raith Rovers and AaaaRbroath!

Traditionalist shook their head, but Aberbrothock was no more!

April 16 1917

It was the Spring Holiday, the "fast" as it was called, normally a day of cheerfulness and enjoyment of the approach of spring. Not so today!

The weather was foul with wind and rain, and any sort of outdoor entertainment was simply out of the question with even gardening, a hobby much encouraged these days, impossible.

In addition, there was simply too much misery and anxiety in the town at the moment with the news of yet another "annual" British offensive and no reason to believe that this one would be any more successful than the previous two of 1915 and 1916.

In addition the war had taken an uncertain turn with the news of the overthrow of the Czar in Russia, a clear indication that the Germans were winning in the East.

But there was also the news that the Americans were now in! A huge country with loads of resources, but how would they cope war in European conditions?

Such things were much discussed by Arbroathians as they attended their "aquatic gala" in the Public Baths this Monday. Some holiday makers had gone to the cinema, but an "aquatic gala" was a novel event involving swimming races between local primary schools, for example.

Provost Rutherford Thomson welcomed everyone, saying how nice it was to see so many people in such awful weather, and what a great institution that Baths had turned out to be for the town. He even stated that it should be compulsory that everyone should have to learn how to swim.

April 17 1746

The battle is now over, and an uncertain future faces what is left of the Jacobite Army.

Many are now dead, many are captured facing a life of slavery or execution depending on the whim of the merciless Duke of Cumberland.

The Prince himself has fled to the west, but for the men from Arbroath who fought in the Forfarshire Regiment of Lord Ogilvy, the retreat was to the south east over Highland pathways.

Most of the Regiment managed a reasonably orderly retreat, everyone realising that, although casualties were inevitable, there was more chance if they stuck together.

Some made for the northern coast, where there were still some sympathisers, hoping that a ship might be able to take them to Aberdeen, and thence to Montrose or even Arbroath itself, but Aberdeen itself was now very much in the hands of the Hanoverians.

Most followed their leaders over the inland route. Food was always a problem, and many of the wounded simply had to be left to the mercy of Redcoat patrols.

Perth was to be avoided, but some managed to reach Clova Glen, and thence to Forfar or Brechin, still sympathetic and thence home, where the secret was "haud yer wheesht". But the persecution continued for another decade or more.

Many were able to resume their trade as brewers, tailors, even schoolmasters and priests (in the Episcopalian Church), but had the good sense not to talk about the dark events of 1745 and 1746 until much later – when of course they could exaggerate and romanticise!

April 18 1929

A massive scandal in Arbroath today with the news that a charge of embezzlement has been brought against an official of the Arbroath Mill and Factory Workers' Union.

Such charges are by no means uncommon in the 1920s, but this one seems to be a major one.

It is all the more alarming because the accused has been doing the job since before the Great War and is a well-known figure in town, having been at one point a member of the Town Council, from which he resigned in 1923.

He is Edward Spink of 13 Bank Street, Arbroath, described as a clerk.

Bailie David Wilson at the Police Court heard the charge that between January 1 1926 and April 6 1929, he had, while acting as Treasurer to the Arbroath Mill and Factory Workers' Union, 43 East Abbey Street, Arbroath, embezzled the sum of £877 4 shillings and 11 pence, being the funds of the said union.

What seems to have happened is that Spink on several occasions had taken money out of the funds, never too much at any one time to arouse suspicion, and appropriated it for his own use, possibly even intending to pay it back but never actually doing so.

The other officials of the Union had gradually become more and more suspicious and had investigated the matter.

Chief Constable MacDonald felt the affair had to be investigated further and asked that Spink should be remanded for a few days until inquiry could be made. The Sheriff agreed.

Connected by Telephone for Quick Despatch of all Orders.

Alexander Hird,

DRAPER AND OUTFITTER,

28 Keptie Street (OPPOSITE RAILWAY STATION,)

AND **258 High Street, Arbroath.**

Departments

Flannels, Blankets, and Plaidings, Grey and Bleached Cotton, Plain and Twilled Linens, Bed Ticks, Hessians, Apron Cloths, Galateas, Flannelettes, Prints, Linings, Gloves, Corsets, Umbrellas, Plain and Fancy Hosiery, Wrap Shawls.

Small Wares of Every Description.

A Leading Department with us is

OUR READY-MADES,

Which are Noted for Style, Finish, and Durability, combined with Moderation in Price.

HOUSE-FURNISHING DEPARTMENT COMPLETE WITH EVERY REQUISITE.

Drapery & Outfitting Establishments,

KEPTIE STREET AND HIGH STREET.

April 19 1907

The death took place today of Mr Alexander Hird, owner one of the oldest and most successful Drapery businesses in the whole of Angus.

He died at the age of 67 at his house at Inchcape, Nolt Loan Road. His death was sudden but not entirely unexpected, for he had been in declining health for some time.

Realising the onset of tuberculosis a couple of years ago, Mr and Mrs Hird had set out on a sea voyage to the southern hemisphere and had been able to visit his sons Robert, a banker in Ceylon, Alexander junior, a soldier in Australia and David, a pastor in New Zealand.

The sea voyage was very enjoyable but did not bring any long term benefit for Mr Hird's health and he was seldom seen out of his house in recent months.

Born in Dunnichen, he was a sailor for a spell until an eye injury compelled him to give that up. He returned to work in his father's shop in Letham, but then decided to branch out himself as a Draper.

He leased a shop in Keptie Street, strategically placed near the railway station, then in 1891, took over another shop in the High Street, where he soon built up a reputation for honesty and service.

His two younger sons Walter and Alfred now run the business. He was laid to rest in the Western Cemetery in the presence of a huge crowd of mourners.

April 20 1950

Today saw the retirement of a man who had, apart from war service, worked with the General Post Office for 47 years.

This was William Crowe, who was Inspector of Postmen in Arbroath. He was born in Arbroath but had started to work in Montrose in 1903 as a boy messenger. He then became a Postman in 1908 in Laurencekirk before returning to his native Arbroath in 1912.

He served from 1916 to 1919 as a Sapper in the Royal Engineers (Signals Division). Returning to his job in Arbroath after the war, he became involved in the Co-operative Movement, something that he still is very much part of.

In 1927 he became a committee member of the West Port Co-operative Association and in the fullness of time became its Chairman, and when the West Port amalgamated with the United Co-operative Society to become the Arbroath Co-operative Society, he was appointed Chairman to the new organisation.

He is also a former Secretary of the Workers Educational Association and has held various posts in the Association of Postal Inspectors.

He retired not because he wanted to but because he was of the age that he had to, and was succeeded by John Ramsay. The retiral of this man will be a blow to the Postal Service in Arbroath, it is felt, for he had a wide variety of experience behind him.

April 21 1908

Another case of smallpox was confirmed today and the patient removed to the epidemic hospital.

This makes seven patients in Arbroath. The latest case was a young woman and the sister of one of the existing patients, something that is a little reassuring because it means that the outbreak seems to be able to be contained.

All seven patients seem to have a mild dose of the disease, but they must of course be isolated until such time as the symptoms disappear.

All the proper precautions have been taken by the Medical Officer of Health and the Sanitary Inspector, and there is, as yet, no panic in town.

There have been outbreaks of smallpox in Arbroath before, but the disease does seem to be less of a killer than it used to be. The outbreak however did once again raise the argument in the town of the value or otherwise of vaccination.

It seems to work in either preventing the disease altogether or mitigating the effects of the disease if someone has it. It all started over a hundred years ago when Dr Edward Jenner noticed that those who had been exposed to cowpox did not develop smallpox, so he developed a vaccine (so called from the Latin word "vacca" meaning "cow") which effectively began the slow process of eradicating this foul disease.

For all these reasons it was hoped that the Arbroath outbreak would be a mild one, and would soon disappear, but it was worrying nevertheless.

April 22 1938

The AGM of the Directors of the Dale School was held in the Town Hall tonight with Dr W J Dewar presiding.

The Rev J Spence Cuthill submitted the Annual Report, in which he said that there were at present 19 boys, including one voluntary case, and they were all being educated at Inverbrothock School.

Rev Cuthill paid tribute to a long list of people who had helped the school out by paying for food, outings and clothing, and the many local institutions including the Olympia Theatre and Arbroath FC, who allowed the boys in free on occasion.

The boys had been allowed to attend the Parish Church picnic and had been given a treat on Coronation Day last year.

Dr Dewar remarked on the change that had come over the School in the past fifty years. At one point, the School had been seen as a tough institution for bad boys.

Now it was still a well-disciplined institution certainly, but one in which the emphasis was on the School being looked upon as a home where the boys were to be loved and encouraged to make the most of the opportunities offered them for future life. They integrated well into Inverbrothock School.

The Dale School was often looked upon with suspicion by Arbroathians and occasionally a little jealous resentment about how "they get things that we don't" etc, but once people found out the truth of what the boys had experienced in their early life, attitudes often changed for the better.

Arbroath had reason to be proud of what The Dale School was achieving.

April 23 1931

Tribute was paid tonight to Miss McElney for her 25 years of service to Arbroath Infirmary tonight, when she was presented with a dressing case and 30 volumes of Robert Louis Stevenson for her long service.

1906 was a long time ago, and the Infirmary had come along with leaps and bounds since those days. The most difficult time had of course been the war years when there had been more patients, mainly recovering war casualties and the subsequent pandemic, and fewer nurses, as some had joined the military or had been involved in other war work.

But the Infirmary had expanded since 1906. When Miss McElney arrived, she had a staff of three nurses. Now she had an Assistant Matron, four Sisters and twenty nurses.

The premises had been much improved and enlarged as well, and there were vast improvements in the medicines and treatments available, particularly in the early treatment and diagnosis of the scourge of the 1920s and 1930s, tuberculosis or "consumption" as it was sometimes called.

Francis Bacon was quoted to the effect that "felicity and long service together surely make nursing one of the noblest and most self-sacrificing of all services to a community".

For her part, Miss McElney acknowledged the help that she had been given by many people, some of whom no longer around, and the hope was expressed that she could continue to serve the community for many years yet.

April 24 1948

The weather was just a little unsummery, but no doubt it would get better.

The football season was at last fizzling out, and the cricket season was getting underway – the first, of course, for many years in which the colossal figure of RW Sievwright would not be featuring.

Today was the start of the Bowls season at both the Arbroath club at Dishlandhill and at the Newgate Club. Tradition always demanded that the first game of the season should be between the President's team and the Vice President's team.

At Dishlandhill, President William Stark defeated the Vice President, and at Newgate the President's daughter, Miss LR Donald threw the first jack before her father beat his Vice-President.

Bowls had a long tradition in Arbroath and had been played at several sites over several hundreds of years. Often perceived as an old man's sport, every effort was being made to attract young men and women to the sport as well these days.

The other misconception of the sport— that it was only for the middle classes — had now been well and truly torpedoed, for all social classes were now represented there.

What was true, however, was that it was a sport which required good weather. Today was OK but a little cold. At least it was fair and it was a start to the sport which would bring so much joy to so many people over the summer.

April 25 1958

There was magic in the air in Arbroath this weekend.

The Scottish Association of Magical Societies held its annual convention in the Windmill Hotel where they were very appreciative of Arbroath hospitality and said that they did not feel in any way like strangers in the town.

Within a few hours of some of them arriving last night, they went to Arbroath Infirmary to do a few tricks for the patients

On the lawn of the hotel in front of the hotel staff, and any people who happened to be passing, volunteer waitress Helen McFarlane was suspended in mid-air three feet from the ground, the plank on which she had been lying having been whipped away from her.

This morning a special show was given in the Webster Memorial Hall for old age pensioners and children. In the evening came the *pièce de resistance* when at the Webster Memorial Hall in front of an audience of several hundred, Provost David A Gardner was sawn in half!

Before the crowd could cry "Murder" or lament for their beloved Provost, he was returned in one piece, none the worse apparently for his ordeal!

It was very impressively done by Marjorie Waddell from Berkshire who was wearing an "L" plate throughout!

The President of the Association, Mr Hynd from Kirkcaldy talked warmly of Arbroath at the presentation ceremony and Provost Gardner and his wife were made very welcome at the luncheon on the Sunday.

And then on Monday, no-one really knew what happened because the magicians... simply disappeared! (But they did pay their hotel bill first!)

April 26 1920

The Great War is still very much alive in the consciousness of Arbroath, and indeed all other towns of Scotland, but amidst all the poverty and unhappiness, there is certainly no lack of social activity in the town.

Tonight at the Webster Memorial Hall under the chairmanship of Bailie David Wilson, there was a concert in aid of funds for Arbroath Infirmary.

The Infirmary had of course played a large part (and continued to do so) in rehabilitating wounded soldiers and depended to a very large extent on activities like this for its funding, for there was precious little coming from the central government or indeed anywhere else in 1920.

The concert also served the purpose of encouraging ex-Servicemen, some of them still severely traumatised, to attend and enjoy some local entertainment.

The audience contained a large proportion of women on their own, sometimes with young children, sometimes without. These were the war widows of whom there were an awful lot in Arbroath and elsewhere.

The programme consisted of dancing by the pupils of the Misses Scott and their pupils, a few recitations by local people, some songs, and a short play called "My Turn Next" with two young ladies and four young men.

It was followed by a dance. The previous night, Sunday 25, had seen at the same venue a concert of religious music, also in aid of funds for Arbroath Infirmary and sponsored by employees of the Westburn Foundry.

April 27 1929

Today was meant to be a historic day in local cricket circles.

It was meant to be the start of the Strathmore Union, a new League for local teams.

But it was the usual enemy of cricket, particularly at the start of the season, the weather which had the last (or should that be the first?) word, and the game against Strathmore was rained or rather snowed off on a particularly foul day!

The start of the Strathmore Union was delayed until next week. The Union had been formed on November 21 1928 at a meeting in Forfar, and it would consist of six clubs – Arbroath, Brechin, Strathmore, Meigle, Blairgowrie and Montrose, where the club had been more or less out of commission since the Great War, but had been given a boost with the arrival of League cricket.

In fact, it was not really a radical change because the teams played each other in friendlies anyway, but it was felt that things should be formalised.

It had also followed a few abortive attempts to form a Midland League including teams like Cupar, Kirkcaldy and Alloa, but the problem seemed to be the distance and travelling expenses.

As it was, travel was heavily dependent on the railway system. Bob Sievwright felt that competitive League cricket was necessary to provide a stimulus for young cricketers to develop.

In fact, it was Brechin who would win the Strathmore Union this year and for the next four years before Arbroath eventually won it.

April 28 1945

A free gift sale and an indoor carnival held by the Arbroath Civil Defence Service on behalf of the local Welcome Home Fund raised £410 this Saturday.

The idea was to give every ex-Service man and woman a gift of appreciation for what they had done. The war was not yet over, but all those who attended the Arbroath v Dundee North-Eastern League game knew that it was not far away.

Arbroath won 2-1 that day, but everyone was awaiting the announcement. No-one knew exactly what was going on, but everyone knew that the Russians had driven them back and that the Russians were now about two streets away from the Bunker.

No-one knew it at the time but today was probably the day that Hitler committed suicide.

In any case the surrender announcement was imminent. In fact it would be another week and a bit yet, but the town was already behaving as if the war was over.

Unlike 1918 when everyone was more relieved than anything else, 1945 saw a little exuberance and triumphant behaviour with possibly as much happiness brought about by the fact that the town had not been bombed, nor the beaches used for any German landing.

And of course the boys would soon be home – except of course those who wouldn't. Their parents and relatives found the joy hard to bear, but of course they had reason to be proud.

Arbroath Civil Defence, 1939

April 29 1959

A bumper crowd of 5,229 were at Gayfield to welcome Arbroath's recent promotion to the First Division.

Tonight's game was against St Johnstone and was a 3-1 win but it was irrelevant because on Monday Dumbarton had failed to collect any points against Champions Ayr United, and Arbroath were promoted.

This had followed a weird series of results in which Arbroath had gone down 0-7 to Stenhousemuir at Ochilview, then 0-4 to Hamilton Accies at Douglas Park, before beating the same Hamilton Accies 6-0 at Gayfield!

It was unpredictable form like this that led to cynical remarks about "not wanting promotion" and "throwing games" among the supporters, and to strong hints in the local Press that playing in the First Division next year might see Arbroath a little out of the depth.

However that may be, the Red Lichties were cheered to the echo as Williamson, McLevy and Young; McLean, Fraser and Sinclair; Shirreffs, Brown, Easson, Anderson and Quinn took the field and beat the Perth men 3-1 after trailing for most of the game.

The Arbroath Herald is at pains to point out that Arbroath were NEVER relegated from the First Division in the first place. When war broke out in 1939, Arbroath were a First Division side alongside all the big clubs.

When the Scottish League was reformed in 1946, Arbroath were not voted in. It was not one of Scottish football's happiest moments, but now at least justice had been done, and Arbroath, for good or ill, were back in the First Division.

April 30 1955

Some 90 people from Arbroath attended the Closing Service of Dr Billy Graham's Scottish Crusade tonight.

The Service was held at Hampden Park in the open air, possibly the only place in Scotland capable of holding the amount or people who wanted to listen to him.

A week ago the ground had held the Scottish Cup final between Celtic and Clyde, and now it was being used for a different purpose altogether, although it did generate an equal amount of passion!

At least there was no necessity to clear up beer cans after this occasion! The Arbroath people travelled by special bus to Dundee to get a train which took them straight to King's Park Station which was within walking distance of Hampden Park.

They came back full of enthusiasm for Billy Graham whose tour of Great Britain had been a thundering success. Opinion was divided about Billy Graham, not least in Christian circles. Some felt that he was sent by God to change the world; others thought that he was a dangerous charlatan who played too much on people's emotions.

Some of the established Church Ministers in Arbroath commended him; others saw him as a threat to their fairly cosy existence because Graham, a brilliant orator, had the ability to change lives, and this was not necessarily something that the Church really wanted!

On the other hand, he was looked upon as a great person by the fishing community in particular in Arbroath.

May

View of Arbroath in 1693

May 1 1883

An important day in the history of railways in Scotland when the stretch of line from Arbroath to Montrose was opened for passenger traffic.

It had already existed for freight traffic for a couple of years, but the opening of this stretch of line meant that there was now a direct connection from Aberdeen to Dundee down the coast.

It was single track line, but hopes were expressed that it would be "doubled" soon. There were passing points at Inverkeilor and Lunan Bay.

The first train left Montrose as early as 5.57 that bright May morning. Some got off at Lunan Bay and spent some time there before catching the train back, but others went all the way to Arbroath.

It is probably true to say that this meant more to Montrose than it did to Arbroath, for Arbroath was already well connected to Dundee (and the south) and Forfar (and from there to Perth and Glasgow).

Montrose's joy was reflected in the decorations of Montrose Station, but it was also a major step forward to Arbroath in that Aberdeen was now only about an hour away.

The intention would be to schedule a train at 2.00 pm on Wednesday from Arbroath to Montrose for the benefit of the shopkeepers enjoying their half day and on Saturday for the working classes now that all mills and factories tended to close at 12.00 noon on Saturdays.

Rail travel had taken a dunt with the Tay Bridge Disaster in 1879, but there was still a manic desire for speed!

May 2 1951

Arbroath today attracted a great deal of national attention as nearly 1,000 people flocked to the Webster Memorial Hall and an overflow meeting in the Assembly Hall.

The speakers were two of Scotland's leading protagonists for self-government, Dr John MacCormick, Lord Rector of the University of Glasgow, and Mr Ian Hamilton, a young man described quote succinctly as the "man who stole the stone", a reference to the recent "theft" or "reclaiming" or "liberation" of the Stone of Destiny from Westminster Abbey on Christmas Day 1950.

The main purpose was to form an Arbroath branch of the Scottish Covenant Movement with the idea of Scottish self-government. One of the resolutions was one deploring the "hasty and unseemly manner or removal" of the Stone of Destiny from Arbroath Abbey.

Mr Hamilton raised a laugh by pointing to a policeman at the back of the hall and saying that it was a good thing that "a vulgar vandal" like himself and a "sergeant of the police" can look each other in the eye.

The meeting was enthusiastic, but it was probably true to say that although Arbroath welcomed being in the limelight, opinion was divided on the wisdom of the actual theft of the Stone.

Many people were of the view that it was really rather amusing and silly, although everyone felt that Arbroath Abbey (or Scone or Edinburgh) was a suitable resting place for the Scottish Stone.

The stone had rested in Rochester, Kent, before it was moved to Bonnybridge, then to Cambuskenneth, before being left in Arbroath Abbey until 11th April 1951. Ian Hamilton died, aged 97, in October 2022.

Certainly the feelings engendered in Arbroath on this occasion were not really translated into political action for more than 20 years, for the Scottish Nationalist movement tended in 1951 to be dismissed as somewhat eccentric!

May 3 1901

This Saturday at Letham Grange, Arbroath Fire Brigade had a chance to show off its new "toy".

This was a fire engine which had just arrived.

The Brigade were invited to provide an exhibition at Letham Grange by Mr Fletcher.

The men assembled at the Fire Station in their new and very impressive uniforms. Fire Master Major Corsar then inspected the men, gave them a short drill, and then they moved on to Letham Grange in their horse drawn fire engine.

A fire was lit at Ward Dykes. The engine was then run alongside the lake near the main drive and the suction pipe was dropped into the water. About 2,000 feet of hose was run out from the lake with a view to showing how the engine could run a long way from the scene of the fire.

The engine was then brought round to the front of the big house to where the Brothock passes within 150 yards. Then the Brigade were able to scoot a jet of water from the lawn right over the flagstaff on the centre tower. They were directed in their operations by Fire Instructor Dorward.

All this was watched by Mr and Mrs Fletcher and Mr and Mrs Lindsay-Carnegie, then Mrs Fletcher invited the firemen into the Dining Hall for refreshments.

The fire engine was drawn by the "Antiquary" team of horses from the White Hart Stables. A large crowd was very appreciative of this demonstration.

May 4 1816

Today in Edinburgh was published "The Antiquary" by Sir Walter Scott. It was generally looked upon as a great success and it was always Scott's own favourite.

Situated to a very large extent in a fictitious Scottish port on the East coast called Fairport, it was believed to be based on Arbroath, which Scott had visited several times before the book was written; he never denied the identification with Arbroath.

Set in 1794, the book has a fairly complicated plot (as do several of Scott's novels) but it gives a good account of the tensions in the country at the time of the Revolutionary War and the genuine fear of invasion from France.

The antiquary, a collector of historical items and facts, called Jonathan Oldbuck is an amalgam of a man that Scott met in Arbroath and a self-portrait.

The hero is a man called Neville who uses the pseudonym Lovel. He has fallen in love with a girl who lives in Fairport, but the girl has rejected him because he was born out of wedlock. After a series of unlikely adventures, he is allowed to marry the girl.

In some ways the hero of the book is the beggar Edie Ochiltree who provides humour and kindness as he brings the two people together, and he may be based on a well known Arbroath character.

Possibly a bit ponderous for our modern taste, the book sold well in its day and was much studied in schools as a text for Higher English in the 1950s and 1960s.

The dredger, Fairport

May 5 1911

The Arbroath Herald today announces the knocking down of the last portion of the Keptie Street Bridge at the new Railway Station this week, something that indicates that the job is now nearly over.

Work has been going on for some two years and more, and care has been taken not to disrupt too much the running of the trains.

The work has been organised by a Mr George Campbell of Glasgow, and it will not be totally completed until December, but there is little doubt that a fine new modern railway station is being built.

It is on the same site as the previous one which had been built in 1848 to allow the joining of the lines from Forfar and Dundee, but although the railway lines remain the same, everything else has been changed.

The problem with the old station was, quite simply, that it was too small and dingy, and did little to enhance the impression that one got of the town as they came off the train.

There had been any complaints every year, especially at holiday time, of the station being seriously and dangerously overcrowded with people missing their trains simply because they could not get to the train through all the baggage and suitcases in a limited area.

But now that had changed and Arbroath had a station to be proud of, and one that was appropriate to the number of holiday makers who were now visiting the town.

Arbroath Railway Station Staff, 1910

May 6 1772

Today John Wesley, of what became known as the Methodist Church, came to Arbroath to found the St John's Methodist Church, the second oldest Methodist Church in Scotland.

Situated in Ponderlaw Street, it is often nicknamed the Totum Kirkie because it is shaped like a "totum", an eight sided spinning top, and the interior of it is indeed octagonal in shape. It was extended in 1882 but the interior has not been changed since the day that Wesley was here.

John Wesley of course travelled all over Great Britain in his evangelical zeal to spread the Methodist word. His brother Charles wrote many hymns, many of which e.g "And can it be that I should gain" are still sung in Church today.

Methodists were looked upon as the progressives of the 18th century with their desire to abolish slavery and their opposition to unnecessary foreign wars. Essentially non-Conformist, they made great headway in England and particularly Wales, but Scotland where Calvinism was deeper rooted was a more difficult nut to crack.

Presumably Wesley chose Arbroath because it was on the coast and thus far easier to reach than inland areas, and it is to his credit that the Totum Kirkie lasted for so long.

Its most famous scion, apart from Wesley himself, is George Railton who was the son of Methodist missionaries, was born in the Manse in 1849 and became second in command of The Salvation Army, second only to William Booth.

Aerial view of Lochlands

May 7 1926

The General Strike seems to be passing Arbroath by.

The Arbroath Herald is reduced from eight pages to four this week, possibly indicating that some of its printers or compositors are on strike, but it is able to tell us that some trains have been running.

To a certain extent, life is fairly normal, even though Brechin Cricket Club who are playing at Lochlands tomorrow are taking the precaution of travelling by motor rather than rely on the train.

There is an advertisement on page one for "Male Citizens" who feel they can help in the current emergency to appear at the Town Hall or the Police Station, and there is also an appeal not to overuse coal.

As was the way with most provincial newspapers, *The Arbroath Herald* is very right wing. Clearly with the spectre of Russia in 1917 in the background, it uses phrases like "anarchy" "challenge to constitutional authority" and "a declaration of war on the people" while making no attempt to criticise the obduracy of the coal owners who wish to lengthen the day and cut the wages of the miners!

In the event, the General Strike collapsed after 10 days, but the miners carried on alone until November before being eventually starved into submission.

People in Arbroath had already seen strikes and labour unrest in 1921, and were generally glad to see the General Strike collapse and things return to normal, but the miners did not entirely lack sympathy particularly among the railway workers and transport workers.

May 8 1945

It is finished at last! VE Day!

The unconditional surrender by Admiral Doenitz to General Eisenhower meant that the war which had been going on since 1939 was now over.

Rightly did Churchill say "In all our long history we have never had a day like this", and Arbroath, like everywhere else, celebrated with the King's Speech being broadcast at the Picture House.

The weather was awful, but that did not deter enthusiasm as impromptu dances were held in the streets, Church bells rang out. Rockets were fired. The town was decorated with red, white and blue.

The fishing boats flying patriotic flags. Shops displayed pictures of Winston Churchill, the King and his Scottish Queen, who came from not far away at Glamis Castle.

But a bonfire which was meant to be lit at Springfield Park was cancelled just in case there were a few rogue Nazi U Boats still operating in the North Sea!

Yet in the middle of all this euphoria and joy, there were still a few Arbroath families receiving the bad news of loved ones killed, injured or missing.

And of course although Germany was "Kaput", there was still Japan undefeated in the Far East and holding large numbers of British prisoners captive.

No-one yet had even begun to talk about the post-war world in which the Soviet Union, our "allies" now held half of Europe. And what kind of society was Britain going to have?

There was no desire to go back to the old pre-war days of unemployment, poor health and slum housing. It was time for a change.

May 9 1900

There has been such a great deal of gloom of late concerning the economic situation and the war in South Africa that it is good to relate that the Brothock Mill has now been more or less totally restored.

It is hoped that it can be re-opened on Saturday on a limited basis but with full restoration not far away.

Six months ago, a large part of the flax spinning mill had been destroyed by fire, throwing 300 people out of a job. With great enthusiasm and energy, the mill has been restored and indeed improved, with some people in town talking darkly about "insurance" and the local Press not entirely above hinting in the same direction.

The reconstruction has all been done by local contractors and with commendable speed. Be that as it may, it has been a miserable time for the 300 workers, not all of whom managed to find alternative employment in the meantime, although some did get a job labouring for the contractors at the rebuilding.

One finds it hard to believe that "the increased comfort of the workers has not been forgotten" in the new interior, although one definite improvement has been the installation of electric light throughout.

Generally speaking the building has been expanded and the capacity for production has been enhanced. 200 workers will be able to restart working on Saturday, and it is confidently believed that all 300 will be back in position by the end of next week.

R. W. Sievwright

May 10 1919

Cricket returns to Lochlands!

The weather was good enough without being warm or hot, and to the relief and delight of all Arbroathians, the game has now returned.

The crowd was about 500 – more might have been expected perhaps in more normal circumstances, but there were still an awful lot of men abroad, particularly those who had been in Mesopotamia and the Persian Gulf.

The great R W Sievwright, already a legend throughout Scotland, was the key man. Because of his role in running his joinery business, he had been demobbed in January and had spent a lot of time and effort to get the ground ready and players available.

This was, of course, no easy task because the Spanish flu was still raging, and because several years of youngsters had been lost to the game through military service, and of course, so many had been killed or badly wounded.

However, the groundsman, Mr Pyott, and Sievwright had prepared "the carpet" for the game, and the ground which had been used for all sorts of purposes other than cricket was more or less prepared.

The opposition were the soldiers at the Royal Garrison Artillery at Broughty Ferry, and they were simply swept aside for 23 all out as Sievwright with his slow left armers took 8 for 4!

Chisholm and Mann then hit the runs without much bother, but as was the custom at the time, they batted on to reach 62.

The crowd, sadly several of them now in wheel chairs or walking with difficulty, clapped and cheered.

At the end, Sievwright made a point of talking to another group of men who had been at the cricket but had not seen it. They were the blinded but they had still followed the game as people shouted information like "Boab's got anither een. Catched ee slips this time!"

May 11 1940

Today, Stoker James Falconer of 35 Townhead Road arrived home in Arbroath after a series of incredible adventures in Norway during which he had been bombed and machine gunned almost incessantly over the previous fortnight.

He brought with him a piece of shrapnel from a German bomb. He had been wounded slightly in the ear. Stoker Falconer was one of the lucky ones to escape the ill-fated Norwegian campaign in April and May 1940.

Ironically, the man responsible for this catastrophe, First Lord of the Admiralty Winston Churchill had yesterday been appointed Prime Minister!

Stoker Falconer would have found an Arbroath not entirely dissimilar to pre-war years. Cinemas and dancing were still going strong, and it being summer, cricket was being played but there was evidence of fortifications on the beach.

Shops were all open and doing a good trade with loads of soldiers and sailors in the town, and everyone with more money in their pockets. (War often brings an increase in prosperity!)

The winter of 1939/40 had been known as the "phoney war" because of little going on, but that was soon to change. Yesterday, as well as the appointment of Churchill as Prime Minister, had seen Hitler launch his invasion of Belgium, Holland and Luxembourg.

The war was getting a great deal closer. At the moment Stoker Falconer was one of the very few Arbroath servicemen who had seen any action. He would soon be joined by very many more.

May 12 1908

Arbroath had been in an uproar for the past few days, and today was the day of the by-election in Montrose Burghs.

The Liberals were in power and had begun to introduce a series of much needed reforms to tackle the appalling poverty which existed as much in Arbroath as anywhere else.

The by-election had been occasioned by the elevation to the peerage of John Morley.

For the Liberals Robert Vernon Harcourt was being opposed by Briggs Constable for the Conservatives and Joseph Burgess for the Socialists, the new force that had appeared on the political horizon over the past few years and who were attracting fishermen and jute workers to their creed with their utopian vision of equality.

A complicating factor was that the Prime Minister Herbert Asquith had only been in power for a few weeks after his predecessor the respected Campbell Bannerman had died.

Harcourt had faced his electors several times and preached the values of Free Trade and the reforms, but he was worried about Burgess who was strong in the Abbey and Guthrie Port area of town and also among the Forfar jute workers.

Suffragettes had apparently disrupted things in Montrose but everything was peaceful, if animated and excited in Arbroath. The polls closed at 8.00 pm. and the ballot boxes were taken away on the 8.38 train to Montrose.

The result was telephoned to *The Arbroath Herald* shortly after midnight and hand bills were quickly printed and distributed to the waiting crowd. Harcourt had 3083, Burgess 1937 and Constable 1576.

May 13 1891

One of the quiet successes of Victorian society in general was the number of people who used the library service.

"The best things in life are free" everyone said and the library was an excellent example of this, Arbroath being particularly lucky. In the past week 317 books and 70 magazines had been issued.

The librarian announced that a large number of new books had been purchased for the library, notably Stanley's *Darkest Africa*, Sir Walter Scott's *Journal*, Paton's *New Hebrides*, Dilke's *Problems of Greater Britain*, Booth's *Darkest England* and the Queen's Prime Minister Series.

In addition another sixty volumes of fiction had been added – the works of G A Henty, Edna Lyall, Anne Swan, Mrs Henry Wood and James Grant.

The librarian was confident that all these things would be enjoyed by the Arbroath public. Indeed, it was something to be encouraged, and it was one of the benefits of the Education Act of twenty years ago that so many more people were now able to read.

It was no uncommon sight to see men in working clothes walking home from the library with a pile of books under their arm. Some disapproved of all this, but there seemed to be little doubt that we were living in an "improving" society.

There was still a long way to go, however, in some respects, when one looked at the shocking housing and lack of health facilities, but there was now at least the opportunity for someone to "improve himself" through reading.

May 14 1857

News from India has been disturbing recently with reports of some sort of rebellion or mutiny in that distant land.

The stories of shootings, burnings of buildings and massacre have been particularly disturbing to people in Arbroath who have relatives living or working there, particularly those young men serving in the Army who look so handsome in their uniform.

Not many people know an awful lot about the country, however, other than that it is shaped like a triangle, is huge and is a long way away, at least a fortnight on a ship.

But the recent news has triggered an interest and the Treasurer of the Arbroath Museum has recently received from an anonymous donor a number of interesting articles from India.

They are articles worn by the ladies of Cawnpore – two pairs of metal bracelets, one pair or anklets, two pairs of Cashmere stockings, two caps in the shape of Glengarries manufactured by Cawnpore shawl weavers, a rich gold-mounted velvet jacket worn by the rajahs, and an ivory model of the Golden Mosque at Lahore.

These articles were looked at by quite a few local people who commented on their unique nature. Hope was repeatedly expressed that the trouble in India would soon be settled.

Apparently the Indians are suspicious of the British building railways. This struck a chord with some Arbroath people who remembered that some people objected to the railway to Forfar being opened in 1839 because trains were frightening, noisy, dirty things!

May 15 1931

An absolutely heinous offence had been committed by Alfred Webster, a chimney sweep of 28 Cairnie Place.

He was charged with having deposited a quantity of soot in Bank Street contrary to the Burgh bye-laws. The sweep admitted that charge but said that it was absolutely impossible for any sweep to do his job conscientiously without in the process getting some soot on the street.

All he had done was shake his cloths. He normally kept his soot in bags and later disposed of them. Having been warned once before not to leave his soot bags on the street, Webster said that he now left them in alleyways but people still complained.

The Cleansing Superintendent had said that although the streets were always cleaned every morning, nevertheless some bags of soot found their way to the streets after the cart had passed. The bye laws apparently stated that anyone with soot which they desired to have removed should inform the scavengers where the soot was placed, and they would then put it on the bottom of the dust cart.

Bailie David Wilson who had been listening to this less than totally riveting local wrangling about a fairly insoluble problem, which was a lot worse on a windy day, admonished Webster.

Soot would continue to be a problem on the streets of Arbroath until such time as coal fires would give way to other, more modern ways of heating a house!

May 16 1999

One of the many historic dates of Arbroath cricket this Sunday at Worcester when George Salmond led Scotland out to her first One Day International in the World Cup against Australia.

George, born in Dundee, but having learned the trade and played almost all his cricket in Arbroath was a right-handed batsman, unlike his brother John who played left-handed. He had risen to become captain of Scotland, and it was a great honour for him and his family and friends at Lochlands.

Almost inevitably, Scotland lost to the team who would eventually win the World Cup that year, but Scotland under Salmond's leadership put up a fine performance reaching 181 for 7 before Australia hit the runs with 5 overs to spare.

Salmond himself hit 31 in an innings that *Wisden* describes as "perky" and twice "skipped down the pitch" to Glenn McGrath before being caught by wicket keeper Adam Gilchrist off Steve Waugh.

The atmosphere in the game seen by *Wisden* as "boozy but cheery" was typified by the image of a fan with split loyalties, but who turned up wearing an Australia top and a kilt.

George had been captain of Scotland since 1995 and had captained the side in the historic defeat of Worcestershire in the 60-over tournament at The Grange the year before. He later went on to become a football referee, and Headmaster of George Watson's Junior School.

George Salmond

May 17 1921

An agreement has been reached in the Arbroath building trades dispute, but it is hardly an agreement that will be widely welcomed by the workers!

The problem is that this is 1921, and the world is still in the grip of global economic recession caused by the Great War.

In Great Britain the miners, for example, have been on strike for a long time, and although the effects are not so noticeable in Arbroath in May, they are still visible in a shortage of coal and the curtailment of railway services.

The problem is, basically, during the war, workers were paid at a rate that employers now claim they cannot afford.

Not everyone believes that, of course, but today we have the return to work of masons, slaters, builders, joiners and plasterers who have to agree to accept a reduction in wages.

These trades will work for a penny an hour *less* than the national rates as, for example, what is paid in Dundee for doing the same job! To modern eyes, this may seem nothing short of astonishing.

It appears that there was little alternative or choice in that many local firms would have gone bankrupt if they had continued to pay the rates of wages that had obtained during the Great War when so much was subsidised by the Government.

Unemployment remains high, even in a coastal town like Arbroath, and the attitude seems to be that you should consider yourself lucky if you have any sort of job!

May 18 1957

The Scottish Liberal Party are holding their Annual Conference in Arbroath this week-end.

Their Parliamentary Leader, Joe Grimond, led the attack on the Conservative Government and the Labour opposition.

They had been welcomed at the Webster Memorial Hall by Provost J K Moir and local Liberal members, and it was clearly a great honour for the town to host this event.

All the local hotels did well, particularly the Hotel Seaforth where a number of meetings would be held. Provost Moir expressed the hope that the delegates would find time to visit Arbroath Abbey as long as they were here, and stressed how important the town was in Scotland's independence.

In 1957, there was as yet no strong Scottish National Party, and the Liberals "flirted" with Scottish Nationalism, although they possibly stopped short of outright independence, preferring instead to concentrate on a strong federal structure with Scotland having a large degree of what would now be called devolution.

Mr John Bannerman, leader of the Scottish Liberal party, said that liberalism was gaining ground in the country as people tired of the Conservative obsession with accumulating private wealth and the Labour predilection for nationalisation.

The Liberals tended to be "nice people" and were very welcome in Arbroath, but they were at a low point of their existence in 1957 with only six MPs.

Nevertheless, some of what they said was quite encouraging and worth listening to, although the days in which the Liberals were significant in British politics were a long time ago now, and it would be many years in the future before they became significant again.

May 19 1900

You couldn't exactly say that Arbroath was short of news today.

Late yesterday came the news that Mafeking in South Africa had been relieved.

Life was not boring in Arbroath, but the main thing, of course, was the relief of Mafeking. Quite a few Arbroath men were serving in the Army in South Africa, and news had been scarce of late, and everyone had worried about the fate of the garrison at Mafeking.

This was well received and it could not have come at a more appropriate time for Arbroath, for today was the official opening of the lovely new Arbroath Post Office.

Provost Colin Grant, whose wife had performed the ceremony, declared that the first Telegram to be sent from the new Telegraph Office in the Post Office would read "To Colonel Baden-Powell, Mafeking – Town of Arbroath sends heartiest congratulations".

There was thus double celebration in the town. But there was also something else. The town was all agog about a murder.

Earlier this morning in the Infirmary, Mr John Smail of Dalhousie Place, Arbroath passed away after being shot yesterday in his office in the Prudential Insurance Company at Brothock Bridge by an ex-employee called Arthur Hingston Elliot of Leonard Street, Arbroath.

Today Elliot appeared in Arbroath Police Court and was duly remitted to Dundee Sheriff Court. There was no robbery or anything other than what appeared to be a revenge killing for Elliot being sacked some time ago.

May 20 1893

The Soup Kitchen had been kept open over the past five months since just before Christmas by the committee in charge of the aid to the Unemployed Fund.

Today it was formally closed down, at least for the time being. There does not seem to have been any obvious reason for this, because unemployment and poverty had certainly not gone away.

In this very week there was news that both the Netherward and the Alma jute and linen works would be going down to a 33 hour week.

Douglas Fraser and Sons, who made canvas shoes, have shortened their week to four days.

Those who had run the kitchen were thanked for their efforts in supplying over the winter 16,460 meals at the cost of less than 2d per head.

Possibly the reason for the closing of the Soup Kitchen lay in the fact that the winter was now over, and that there might be less need for hot food in the summer with more people able to get some sort of seasonal work in the fruit or vegetable harvest on nearby farms.

The Treasurer Mr W J Rollo reported that a total of £122 18 8 had been contributed to the fund and it had been totally expended.

David Dobson and William Stewart were thanked for buying all the equipment and raw materials, and Mrs Chalmers for her work in the general running of the kitchen.

May 21 1924

The roaring twenties are now in full spate with the country now slowly recovering from the war.

There are still parts of the country living in appalling poverty, Arbroath not entirely excepted from that general statement.

But in 1924 the word "Wembley" was the last word in exoticism. The stadium had been built in 1923 in the affluent North West part of London as an emphatic statement that "we won the war" (not unlike the Parthenon in Athens in that respect in the 5th Century BC).

The opening ceremony, in 1923 by King George V, was broadcast live on radio, although reception was not all that clear.

This year Scotland's football team had drawn 1-1 with England. Two English Cup finals had been played there, won by Bolton Wanderers and Newcastle United.

But it was more than a football ground. There was an Exhibition Centre there as well, and the Dundee, Perth and London Shipping Company was offering to take folk from Arbroath to Wembley for £6 6 shillings including "victualling" on board ship, sleeping accommodation and two tickets to the Exhibition Centre.

The whole tour would take six days, with two clear days in London and a chance to see the other attractions of London as well like Buckingham Palace and the Cenotaph in Whitehall.

It would be the opportunity of a lifetime but the only problem was that £6 6 shillings was about four times the average weekly wage for a worker in Arbroath in 1924, and not a lot of people would be able to afford it!

May 22 1915

As if the news from France was not bad enough, news reached Arbroath today of a rail disaster early this Saturday morning at a place called Quintinshill near Gretna.

The death toll would eventually reach 227, most of whom were in the Royal Scots regiment in a troop train which had left Larbert that morning.

At least three Arbroath men were known to be in the 5th Royal Scots. When they had returned from leave, they had said they would "entrain" at Larbert to travel south that day.

Anxiety reigned all day but fortunately late in the afternoon, the relatives of Privates Hume and Henderson of Arbroath itself and of Lance Corporal Gibb of Inverkeilor were informed by telegram that they were safe, having travelled south on a previous train.

In addition, Rev J A Tweedie, who was attached to the Royal Scots as a Chaplain was due to travel on the next train.

It would be some time before the full details of this horrific accident were known, but it is generally reckoned to have been one of the world's worst rail disasters.

The fact that no Arbroath people were in that accident was of little comfort to others in the town, because the war, which had been quiescent during the winter, was now beginning to become more active again.

As well as in France, the war was now in the Dardanelles in Turkey. This brainchild (it now appeared to be more of a *brainstorm*) of Dundee's rather eccentric MP Winston Churchill, First Lord of the Admiralty, led to the disastrous events at Gallipoli, for which he was removed from his post.

May 23 1938

It was hardly the biggest secret in Arbroath or even the rest of the world that a lot a gambling and betting went on.

Betting on horses and football matches was technically illegal, although there were many ways round it.

One of them was the employment of a man called a "bookie's runner", a man who would approach people in the street and organise bets between them and what were called "commission agents" or bookmakers.

Such activities were illegal but widely practised and often blatant, but every now and again, the police would make an example of someone.

Thus today David Coull of 76 Helen Street, Arbroath could consider himself to be very unlucky when he was fined £3 by Provost Sir William Chapel on a charge of street betting.

He pleaded guilty to the charge of having loitered in Panmure Street, near a billiards saloon, for the purpose of "bookmaking, betting or wagering", something that he had been doing for some time.

It was often felt that being arrested was an "occupational hazard" for a "bookie's runner" in the murky world of gambling.

It was also a rather dangerous job, for sometimes the loss of a bet was not taken in the most sporting fashion by the aggrieved parties.

Nor were the "runners" themselves always honest and it was not entirely unknown for them to "disappear" with someone's winnings – and of course as the whole practice was illegal, there was no redress.

May 24 1889

Say what you want about the old dear, she did have her uses sometimes!

Queen Victoria, not always as well loved as she was sometimes portrayed, was 70 today, and the occasion was marked by a public holiday.

The weather was reasonable and several trips were organised on the train to the usual places of Forfar, Perth, Dundee and Aberdeen.

One or two horse-drawn carriages were hired by employers to give their employees a treat of a trip to places like Edzell and Kirriemuir.

It was a day on which drink, of course, played a large part as everyone toasted the health of the Queen.

Even one or two douce Church-going matrons and spinsters were seen to imbibe a glass of port, and worst of all, smile tolerantly (or even occasionally join in) at the somewhat flippant and not always respectful songs about the Queen and her "friendship" with her late ghillie John Brown. The trips were much enjoyed and it was late at night before some of them came home.

Those who stayed at home heard the bells ringing from the Old Church, and then as darkness began to fall, a few bonfires on the High Common and elsewhere appeared.

One local citizen donated his now-falling-apart and rot-ridden cart for the flames, as children danced round the fire singing a few of their favourite nursery rhymes.

It was a Friday night, and normally a half day was worked on a Saturday, but some (not all) business owners even gave their workers a holiday then as well!

May 25 1967

Arbroath was tonight like the aftermath of nuclear war between the hours of 5.30 and 7.30.

No-one was to be seen. Cars were parked in solemn silence. Cats walked unmolested in Keptie Street and elsewhere.

The few humans to be seen were hurrying somewhere and not in any sort of mood to discuss there they were going.

A bus came in and one or two people got off, but no-one got on. The beach was deserted apart from the seagulls.

No bowling or cricket or golf tonight. In houses, curtains were drawn, and although voices could be heard inside – sometimes excited, loud voices – no-one came out or went in.

Pubs were busy – but only if they had a flickering black and white television there and by 1967 most pubs did.

There was some sort of football match on, coming from Portugal, and someone said something about a European Cup final.

Round about 7.00 pm a loud noise was heard from all over Arbroath, and the noise rose and rose until "the first British team to win the European Cup" was heard oftener and oftener amidst cheers and green flags.

Doors suddenly opened into the bright spring sunshine and "We've done it" was heard with particular paeans of praise being uttered in honour of someone called "Jock".

It was a remarkable night and much celebrated by everyone in Arbroath and elsewhere. Sad to record, it has not yet happened again.

May 26 1904

The Arbroath Herald today contains a review of their reporter's visit to the new Epidemic Hospital which will shortly be officially opened.

It is situated on the Forfar Road on the outskirts of town so as to be well away from the centre of town.

There have apparently been "grumblings" about it, for it is twice as large as necessary according to *The Arbroath Herald* and has been far too expensive.

It is about five acres in area and surrounded with a wall six feet in height. The newspaper approves of there being a belt of trees to shield the hospital from public gaze, perceived as a "barrier to disease spreading", a somewhat optimistic statement, one feels!

There are four pavilions – one for observation, one for diphtheria, one for scarlet fever and one for typhoid. The reporter is particularly impressed by the fact that in the scarlet fever pavilion, it is possible for the nurse on night shift to be able to see all her patients, both male and female at the same time.

In addition, each room is rounded so that no dust can gather in the corners! Scarlet fever has 18 beds, typhoid fever 10 and diphtheria 6, reflecting, presumably, the relative incidence of each illness.

There is then a discharge pavilion with arrangement for washing and disinfecting clothing, and for those patients who are to "leave the hospital" in less happy circumstances there is a mortuary and friends are able to see, through a window, their loved one laid out on the slab!

May 27 1976

Today was born Darren Burnett, a man who has a claim to be considered the greatest sporting Arbroathian, a claim he must dispute with Bob Sievwright.

Both are bowlers – but of different kinds! Sievwright was of course a cricketing bowler and Burnett is a "bowling green" bowler, both outdoor and indoor.

His highest profile success was at the Commonwealth Games in Glasgow in 2014 (for which he had to ask permission to be released from his policing duties) when he won the Men's Singles at the Kelvingrove Lawn Bowls Arena by beating Ryan Bester of Canada, a man whom he would meet on many occasions.

On this occasion on August 2 2014, Burnett won 21-9. On three occasions he has been the Scottish National Men's Singles Champion in 1999, 2002 and 2005, and twice the British Isles Champion in 2003 and 2006, and the World Singles Champion of Champions in 2006.

But these are only some of the many honours won by this unassuming policeman who has done a great deal to popularise the sport both in his home town and elsewhere in Scotland.

In the same way that Andy Murray raised the profile of tennis, and Chris Hoy the profile of cycling, Darren Burnett has done a great deal to raise the profile of bowls which has struggled to throw off its image of an old man's game.

Burnett is a policeman and was involved in a bad accident to his arm in December 2020.

Darren Burnett

May 28 1929

Exciting times in Arbroath with the General Election now only two days away.

Tonight Bailie Tom Irwin, the Labour candidate, addressed a packed house at the Webster Memorial Hall while the Liberal/Unionist candidate and sitting MP Sir Robert Hutchison, who had also been very active in Arbroath, was tonight in Forfar.

Indications were that the result would be close. It was difficult to predict because now all women over the age of 21 could vote, not just the privileged few that were allowed to do so in 1924.

Sir Robert Hutchison

Irwin talked about what Labour were going to do to bring about a change in society, but was often on the back foot as regards war, for their leader Ramsay MacDonald had been a pacifist in the Great War.

Hutchison, on the other hand, had served both in the Great War and in the Boer War and spoke out strongly about the need for discipline. He was against soldiers being allowed a "trade union" and was very much in favour of shooting and executions for cases of cowardice and desertion.

Hutchison, from Kirkcaldy, had briefly been MP for that town between 1922 and 1923, but had served Montrose Burghs well since that time.

Irwin felt that he had to deal with a smear that Labour were going to reduce soldiers' pensions, saying that Labour was the only party that had always defended the rights of the soldiers.

When the results were declared, Hutchison won by 11,715 votes to 9,381, and was returned for Montrose Burghs, but the national result was a "hung" Parliament – exactly what no-one was really wanting.

May 29 1920

The conditions were not really all that conducive for cricket, but a large concourse of people turned up to see Aberdeenshire at Lochlands.

It was of course the first time that the men from the Granite City had been in town for six years, and that had been in totally different circumstances.

There were quite a few disabled spectators in attendance to indicate just what the last six years had been about.

The forecast was for conditions to deteriorate, so Aberdeenshire won the toss and decided to bat.

This decision exposed them at an early stage to Bob Sievwright to whom they had no answer. With the second ball of the innings, the famous Arthur Broadbent, one time professional of Uddingston, patted back weakly for an easy caught and bowled, and then Bob bowled Aberdeenshire's professional, a man with the unlikely name of Wildgoose, for nothing, leading to all sorts of jokes about geese and ducks.

Aberdeenshire subsided weakly for 70 all out with Sievwright taking 6 for 32. It did not look like all that difficult a task for the home side, with Ferrier of Brechin "guesting" for them.

They struggled in the difficult conditions against top class bowling, until Fairweather (a most inappropriate name for the conditions) managed to hit 16 to see Arbroath home by 4 wickets. Normally in the 1920s, a team "bats on" even after they have won, but the rain was now heavier, and the game finished whenever Arbroath got over the line.

May 30 1936

Today saw the opening of the United Free Church in the High Street, a building which has had an interesting history.

It was purchased by the congregation from the St Thomas Lodge of Freemasons. In its time it has been an Episcopalian Church, a Free Church, a masonic temple and now a United Free Church.

Church history in Arbroath, as everywhere else, is complicated, but the United Free Church in Arbroath had been formed in 1929, without however having a permanent home.

The Ceremony was conducted by members of the Dundee Presbytery at 3.00 pm this Saturday afternoon with the Rev Rhys Price of Montrose presiding.

At one point, the key was handed over by the architect to Mrs T J Howie, who formally opened the door, and a Dedication Service was then performed by Rev James Muir, minister of the congregation.

There had been some alterations necessary to transform the Church from a masonic temple into a place of worship, but these had been comparatively few and uncomplicated.

The Church now has accommodation for a congregation of 300 with pews of pitch pine oak to match the panelling on the walls.

The chancel contained three lettered panels featuring the Law and the Beatitudes which had been a feature in its original Free Kirk days. The pulpit, font, table and chairs were all gifts from the Congregation.

Interestingly, the Minister's room has its own door to the outside – so that he can escape in a hurry after a sermon that may have displeased some members of his Congregation!

May 31 1889

Today Arbroath Common saw a visit from Lord George Sanger's world famous English and Continental Circus now on tour of the provinces of Scotland.

Not the least of the attraction was the Great McIntosh or Waterproof Tent "as dry as your own parlour" which would have been capable of holding 20,000 people.

Prices were expensive from three shillings down to six pence with all the seats (apart from the six pence ones) carpeted and "free from draught".

Even those who could not afford the prices for the Big Top, could still see the Grand Procession which started at one o'clock and paraded through the town.

Attractions included The Gordon Arabs from Khartoum, Gladiators from Ancient Rome and a race with two men standing on bare-backed horses.

There was also a great Kangaroo Hunt, a great Ostrich Hunt with real ostriches, and Buffalo Bill and his Cowboys, as well as the best clowns who have ever appeared in public.

This was naturally a great attraction for the Arbroath public, and one would have liked to see the real ostriches, however much it would have offended modern ideas of cruelty and political correctness.

The advertisement stops short of saying real kangaroos, however, and this seems to have been a piece of comic entertainment.

No indication is given of how well attended the event was, but one suspects there might have been a few empty seats in the Waterproof Tent. Three shillings for 1889 was certainly somewhat exorbitant.

June

ARBROATH AND FORFAR.—15¼ Miles.

Sec., J. Macdonald, Arbroath. Manager and Super., Alexander Allen.
From Forfar to Arbroath, 7 and 10 a.m. 1¾, 4½ & 7 p.m.
From Arbroath to Forfar, 9 a.m., 12 10, 3½, 5¾ & 8½ p.m.
FARES—First class, 2s 3d; second class, 1s 9d; third, 1s 3d.

GLASGOW, PAISLEY, & GREENOCK.—22½ Mls.

Managing Director, Jas. Tasker, Greenock. Supt., Alex. Ross.
From Glasgow, at 8 and *10 a.m.; 12 noon: *1, *3, 4, *5, and *7 p.m.
From Greenock, at 8½, 9½, and *10½ a.m.; *12½, 1½, 3½, *5½, & *7½ p.m.
No trains on Sunday.
*Stop at the Houston and Bishopton Stations when required.
FARES between Glasgow and Greenock—third class, without seats, 1s.; third class with seats, 1s. 6d.; first class, 2s. 6d.
Light Goods Trains: from Glasgow at 6½ a.m. and 6 p.m.
From Greenock at 6¼ a.m. and 6¼ p.m.
Third class passengers will be conveyed by these trains, fare 6d.

PAISLEY AND RENFREW.

SUMMER.—From Paisley at 6 10 a.m., and ten minutes after every succeeding hour until 8 10 p.m.
From Renfrew at 6¾ a.m. and a quarter from every succeeding hour until 8¾ p.m.
WINTER.—From Paisley, 6½ a.m. and every hour from 8¼ a.m. until 6¼ p.m.
From Renfrew, from ¼ before 9 a.m. until ¼ before 7 p.m.
FARES.—First class, 6d; second class, 4d.

DUNDEE AND ARBROATH.—16¾ Miles.

Secretaries, Shiell and Small, Dundee. Engrs. Grainger & Millar, Superintendent, Geo. Pattullo.
From Dundee 7 45 and 10½ a.m. mail, 1½, 4½, 6½, and 8¼ p.m., (9½ p.m. to Broughty Ferry only.)
From Arbroath 8½ and 10¼ a.m. mail, 1½, 4½, 6½, and 8¼ p.m., (9¾ p.m. from Broughty Ferry.)
FARES—Dundee to Arbroath, 2s.; 1s. 6d.; 1s.—Mail, 2s. 6d.; 2s.; 1s. 6d.
The trains will stop at Deyhouse on Tuesdays and Fridays twice.
The mail trains will stop at all the stations when required.

Bradshaw's railway timetable for June 1846

June 1 1939

There seems to be no limit to modern technology these days!

Today a police car has been touring Arbroath and indeed all of Angus showing its radio which can actually be used to receive and transmit messages even when the car is actually moving!

The benefits of this can be immense. Reception was good on the coast although it was less satisfactory around the Brechin area.

It is indeed a far cry from the days when the only way that policemen could communicate with each other was by a whistle.

There is little doubt that radio is the medium of the future, both through the BBC and now this way of being able to communicate with each other while actually moving.

Perhaps even the day will come when everyone will have their own communication with them – a sort of mobile telephone and what an advantage that would be in the case of accidents and emergencies!

We all know that for the past three years there has been a television service around London where you can actually watch in your own house something that is happening elsewhere, a football match for example.

Yes, the possibilities for the future are immense, but in the meantime there is a very large elephant in the room which we have to deal with, and it is called Hitler.

We are surely not going to have to go through another war again, only twenty years after the last one?

June 2 1953

It was definitely "chilly for June" today, but it was a special day for the town. It was the day of the Coronation of Queen Elizabeth II in London.

The town had been well decorated for months with all sorts of patriotic bunting and flags all over the place.

The day itself was one of the coldest days for the time of the year that anyone could remember and it was particularly cold near the coast.

There was a variety of parades, tea parties and other activities, but they were less than a total success because of the unpleasant weather.

There was a 21 gun salute at Springfield Park by members of Q Battery, Arbroath, of the 276 Field Regiment RA (TA) under the command of Major Howard Graham.

After this, Provost James Kydd Moir was invited to toast the Queen's health at Battery Headquarters at East Abbey Street.

Some youngsters who had looked forward to this day for years were just a little disappointed that the Queen had chosen to get crowned in a place called London rather than Arbroath!

A more pointed objection, particularly appropriate for Arbroath, was the question why she was called Elizabeth II, when there had never been an Elizabeth I of Scotland?

But the main thing was that it was a holiday, the pubs were open, the picture houses were open and there was a bonfire at night!

In some ways it was looked upon as a symbol that the bad old days of unemployment and wars were over, and that a new age was dawning.

June 3 1922

The sun was hot today as Lord Inchcape unveiled the War Memorial this Saturday afternoon on High Common.

It has been erected by public subscription, and on the Memorial were inscribed the names of 490 men and one woman from Arbroath and District who had made the ultimate sacrifice in the Great War.

The crowd was huge and special seats had been laid aside for the relatives of those who had died, as well as for the ex-Service men, some of whom appeared wearing their service medals.

The platform party contained people like the Earl of Strathmore and Provost Anderson and a variety of local Ministers. Much tribute was paid to the fallen from Arbroath and the surrounding villages and farms in the area, and the simple solemnity of the occasion impressed everyone.

It is rare for such a large crowd to be sombre but the mood reflected the occasion. Everyone in Arbroath had known at least one of the fallen.

There was a certain amount of jingoism in the air, and little sympathy was expressed for defeated Germany, but there were also quite a few people in the crowd who would have wondered why it had ever happened.

The memorial itself was an impressive one on the hill overlooking the town looking at the sea, the harbour, Gayfield football ground and other symbols of Arbroath.

All those who were at this ceremony were very impressed with it, and would have remembered it all their life.

War Memorial Unveiling ceremony.

June 4 1850

It is clear from the pages of *The Arbroath Guide* that the condition of the "working classes" is one which affects a lot of people in Arbroath.

In the first place the Parochial Board (although the attendance was described as "thin") met in the Town Court to determine the rate for poor relief.

They decided that the assessment should be £2,220 and that the rate should be 8d in the pound.

And then we find that the newspaper is full of praise for the Dundee and Arbroath Railway who have decided to offer "every facility for the working classes for enjoying pleasure excursions at a cheap rate".

The massive reduction in fares on a Saturday between Arbroath and Dundee is evidence and proof

> "of their desire to see the working man and his family, after the labours of the week, placed in a position in which he may be enabled to enjoy rational recreation and the invigorating influence of pure air".

It is clear that, although there is still a residual distrust of organisations like the Chartists with their absurd demands for "universal manhood suffrage", there is also a desire to see an improvement in everyone's lot because last week "a greater degree of drunkenness and dissipation in both sexes" has been seen than in many previous weeks.

The repeal of the Corn Laws a few years ago, although not directly affecting Arbroath as much as other parts of the country, is looked upon as having been a good thing.

June 5 1995

Today, for the first time ever, an Arbroath man became the Secretary of State for Scotland!

This was Michael Forsyth.

He had been given several minor jobs before then under Margaret Thatcher, and now John Major had given him the big job.

Forsyth had been born in Montrose in 1954, but had been educated at Arbroath High School from 1966 to 1972 and then St Andrews University from 1972–1976 where he had involved himself in right wing politics, becoming the President of the Conservative Association of the University.

He won the Stirling seat in the Conservative landslide of 1983, and soon made progress in Scottish Conservative circles.

Being a Conservative in Scotland has its good and bad side – the good side is that there aren't too many Tories around, so progress and promotion are quite easy for an ambitious man, but the downside is that you are always unpopular and even occasionally seen as inflicting an alien culture and set of beliefs on your nation.

Forsyth was elected in Stirling in 1987 and 1992 on reduced majorities before he eventually lost his seat in the Labour landslide on 1997.

He was given a lot of credit for his part in getting the Stone of Destiny restored to Edinburgh Castle (possibly Arbroath Abbey might have been a better choice!) but he was associated with unpopular causes as well like School Boards and the Poll Tax, and he was generally not liked in Labour Scotland.

It would be fair to say that Michael did not always enjoy universal popularity in Arbroath!

June 6 1841

The 1841 Census for Scotland was taken on the night of 6 June 1841. The population was 11,211.

The following information was requested:
  Place (name of village, street, square, close, etc.)
  Name of each person that had spent the night in that household
  Age*
  Sex (indicated by which column the age is recorded in)
  Profession or occupation
  Where born**

*The ages of people over 15 years old were usually rounded down to the nearest 5 years. Therefore, someone who was actually 24 years would have their age listed as 20, and someone who was actually 27 years old would have their age listed as 25. If people lied about their ages, or if their real ages were not known or reported correctly, the gap between the rounded age recorded on the census and their actual age may be quite significant.

**The "Where Born" column only asked two questions - 1) whether born in same county, and 2) whether Foreigner or whether born in England or Ireland. Possible answers and abbreviations to question #1 include: Yes (Y), No, (N), or Not Known (NK). For question #2, the following abbreviations were used: England/Wales (E), Ireland (I), and Foreign Parts (F).

George Salmond, aged 12, lived with his parents, William - a coal merchant - and Isabella, and siblings Ann, David - a surgeon, William, Joseph and Patrick in Shorehead, Arbroath. Isabella Hutton was a servant.
By 1851 George was married to Jessie, and a flax dresser in St Vigeans.
In 1861 he was a Grocer's salesman, and living in Bank Street, with sons George Burns and William and daughter Jessie.
By 1871, and living in 19 Allan Street, he was established as a baker and grocer, employing two men and two boys, possibly his sons George and William.
Still in Allan Street in 1881, George has eight children still living at home.
His son George, now a Foreman Baker, has moved out, and is living with his wife Eliza and sister-in-law Ellen Fettes in 8 Stanley Street. By 1891 this generation have three children - Jessie, Isabella and George.

June 6 1944

It had of course been no secret that the invasion was coming.

Soldiers had been given a few days leave then moved to somewhere in the south of England, nurses had been transferred from Stracathro to hospitals in Portsmouth or Southampton, and everyone knew why.

It had been meant to be Monday June 5 but had been postponed for 24 hours because of bad weather, but today it happened.

People who had listened to the 7.00 pm News on the BBC Home Service were able to come to their work with the news, and by about 9.00 pm there was no-one in Arbroath who did not know.

"All going to plan, and what a plan!" said the Prime Minister in the House of Commons, later in the morning. Everyone rushed home for their lunch and to listen to the 1.00 pm news.

The *Evening Telegraph* arrived and newsagents were quickly sold out.

Arbroath saw people in groups of twos and threes on benches near the beach and in public parks poring over the newspaper with its map which showed that the landing was in Normandy near Bayeux and Caen.

Details were still sparse, but there was a certain euphoria in the town which soon however gave way to anxiety among those whose sons and husbands might have been involved.

The main problem was that one simply did not know. Was he already on the beaches? Was he on a ship? Was he still waiting in Portsmouth?

The absence of news was good news, but everyone now feared, more than ever, the sight of the red Post Office motor bike carrying the man with a telegram.

June 7 1832

This was the day that the Reform Act received Royal Assent from King William IV and became law.

The news was greeted with a certain amount of enthusiasm in the town for it brought an end to an iniquitous system whereby Arbroath had been part of Aberdeen Burghs which contained 5 electors!

In 1830 the Tory James Carnegie had defeated the Whig Horatio Ross 3-2.

In 1831 for some reason Horatio Ross had been returned unopposed, but now Arbroath would be in a much smaller constituency called Montrose Burghs, and there would be laws laid down involving property and so on about who could actually vote.

The Reform Act had been passed after much agitation and not a little disorder in the town, and it was certainly a step forward. But Arbroath's celebration were somewhat muted for there was an outbreak of typhus in the town.

The Fife Herald warns its readers

> "Arbroath — We regret to say that typhus fever in its most virulent form is at present very prevalent in this place. For the last four weeks, many of every age have been cut off by its malignity, neither the flower of youth nor the grey hairs being found fit to stem the onset of this mighty tyrant"

Plagues of diseases like typhus and cholera were by no means uncommon in the 1830s, but this one seems to have been a particularly bad one, with Arbroath, being a sea port, particularly vulnerable to diseases being brought in from foreign countries.

June 8 1935

Today the annual meeting of the Arbroath branch of the Scottish Society for the Prevention of Cruelty to Animals was held in the Erskine Church Hall on Saturday with Mr W O Brown presiding.

Mr David Littlejohn submitted the Committee report for the past year and was pleased to announce that cruelty to animals appeared to be on the wane, and that for the second year in succession, not a single case of animal abuse had been brought to the attention of the Arbroath police.

While this was a reason for happiness, there was no reason to be complacent and everyone was asked to be on their guard.

In 1935, of course, there were far fewer horses around than there had been in the pre-war days.

Motorised transport was slowly taking over, but horses were still employed by milkmen, coal deliveries, street cleaners and others, and were recognised and much loved by the population.

Prizes were then awarded to those from each school who had done well in writing on the topic "Why it is our duty to promote kindness and discourage cruelty to animals".

There followed a talk by Mr Brown on "Wild Animals – Their Homes and Habits" with particular reference to the animals who lived in Scotland, and the Angus Glens in particular.

Such creatures were not seen very often on the streets of Arbroath, but the 1930s was a great age of hiking, and he encouraged the youngsters to join a hiking club and they would then have the opportunity of seeing such animals on the hills.

June 9 1914

A bizarre and unusual offence – the first of its kind in Arbroath – came to light at the Police Court today.

James Middleton, a lorryman of 26 Helen Street, was charged with having obstructed four police constables in their duties in Millgate Loan, Arbroath by stopping a motor car and shouting to the driver "Ca canny, min, you are in a trap!"

Motor cars were now becoming quite common in Arbroath, and were known to go at excessive speed, sometimes almost 20 miles per hour.

This was a clear danger to the public, including children who were naturally attracted to the new brand of vehicle and could come too close to them.

The police had laid a trap involving policemen standing hundreds of yards apart and counting, to calculate just how quickly this car was travelling, but Mr Middleton had decided to warn the driver.

The accused had done this on the spur of the moment and had not even realised that he was committing an offence, and a very strong point in his favour was that the car had indeed slowed down.

Chief Constable MacDonald had been approached by Mr Middleton, a man of impeccable character, and was convinced that the man who had shown regret for what he had done and did not mean any harm by his action.

Bailie Alexander Mclaren Robertson agreed and dismissed Mr Middleton but not without telling him that he really should have been helping the police, and expressing his concern at the speed that these cars travelled sometimes.

June 10 1944

Gayfield was the scene of a Sports Carnival this sunny Saturday afternoon in honour of Arbroath's Salute The Soldier campaign.

The Carnival had been arranged some time ago, but as it turned out, it could not have been better timed, because of course Tuesday had seen the opening of the Second Front in Europe in what had become known as D Day.

News was of course scarce and naturally heavily censored but it did appear as if a successful landing had been made in Normandy and that progress was being made.

At Gayfield this afternoon, it was the main topic of conversation with the optimistic talking about the end of the war in a few weeks' time while the pessimists recalled the various "pushes" of the Great War in which everyone had talked about "Berlin in A Fortnight" but the reality had been a great deal different.

Meanwhile on the field, the Army won the competition with 25 points in various athletic events, beating the RAF and civilians who reached 24 and the Royal Navy 23.

Mrs Lamb, the wife of Provost John Lamb presented the prizes for events which included Athletics, Cycling, a Tug of War and a Marathon Race which had started in Carnoustie.

The joy and happiness of this occasion was spoiled to a certain extent by the thought that now that a front had been opened in France, some of these wonderful soldiers and servicemen who had charmed everyone in Arbroath, would soon be transferred to Northern France.

June 11 1901

John Street, Forfar, not far from the Station, saw today a terrible tragedy involving an Arbroath family when two year old Jeannie Soutar, daughter of engine driver Andrew Soutar and his wife Helen, of Cairnie Place, Arbroath was killed by a lorry.

The youngest of six children, she was accompanied by her mother and was in the County Town to visit some friends.

While amusing herself in the warm sunshine in John Street, which is very steep, the small child was attracted by the sight of horses pulling a lorry full of jute bales coming from Laird's Factory passing along Don Street at the bottom of John Street, and ran down to see the horses, but was unable to stop herself.

She fell under the wheel and before the driver could stop the horses, the lorry had run over her breaking her neck.

Death was instantaneous, and the remains were immediately removed while the distraught mother was comforted.

News travelled quickly and both towns were shrouded in mourning for some considerable time after that. It was a total accident and no blame could reasonably be attached to anyone.

It was simply one of these accidents that were simply far too common, but, other than impressing on children not to run too fast, and mothers to keep a hold of their children if possible, and lorry drivers to go at a reasonable speed, there was little that could realistically do done to prevent such accidents.

Fear was expressed about these "horseless carriages" that everyone kept talking about. Such accidents might be even more frequent then.

June 12 1893

Arbroath will have to get used to hearing loud bangs on a Monday night.

Today the Arbroath Artillery began their practice on the Common for their squads who intend to go to the Barry Camp later in the summer.

Having received orders from Dundee this morning, the Arbroath Artillery assembled on parade this Monday evening under the command of Captain Gordon, Captain and Adjutant Osborne RA, Lieutenants McBain and Dickson and 50 rank and file.

They then proceeded to practise their firing drill in preparation for the various competitions that will be held in the camp at Barry. The "Artillery" were looked upon with a sort of benign tolerance by most of the Arbroath population.

They were the prototype of the Territorial Army or the Home Guard ("Dad's Army" of the Second World War) and clearly enjoyed dressing up in soldiers' uniforms, marching about town and firing empty shells into the sea.

They might even be allowed to fire a shell or two on the occasion of the imminent Royal Wedding! They were paid a little for attending camps, but it would be difficult to imagine a situation when they would actually be required to go to the Crimea or the Sudan.

Many of them were ex-regular soldiers who had "served the Queen" in India and elsewhere, and it was basically a harmless way of spending time. And of course women of all ages always express a weakness for a man in a uniform!

June 13 1927

"Lord, mind Gavin Hamilton's deserts,
He drinks and swears and plays at certs!"

So says Holy Willie in his prayer in the works of Robbie Burns.

This is another Gavin Hamilton, but he is no less controversial a character in this discussion at Arbroath Town Council tonight.

The problem seems to be not entirely unconnected with the fact that he is a football player for Arbroath FC, but the main issue concerns the Gas Works where Hamilton is employed.

The letter was from William Masson and John Moyston who felt that they had been passed over for promotion (in spite of many years of hard work and loyal service) in favour of Mr Hamilton who had no special qualification for the job and was a "residenter" in town, having only recently arrived.

Attached to the letter was a testimonial from Mr Young, the Gas Manager. Yet it had been Mr Young who had appointed Hamilton!

Oh dear, just what was all this about? Are we talking here about "jobs for the boys"? Was Mr Young a great Arbroath FC fan who wanted to retain Hamilton so that he would not ask for a transfer to some other club?

Were the two complainers guilty of xenophobia because Hamilton was an "incomer"? It didn't really matter, because the Town Council agreed to take no action.

One suspects however that Masson and Moyston did not go to Gayfield very often next season to cheer on Mr Hamilton!

June 14 1947

A disappointing reply was received by the Town Council from Bertram Mills Circus who have turned down the opportunity to come to Arbroath Common for a two or three day visit in July and August.

It was felt that the Circus would enhance the town and bring more visitors in the summer months, but the Town Clerk had received a letter from Mr Bernard Mills having to decline the invitation. The Circus reluctantly said "No".

The main problem seemed to be transport. Before the war, the policy had been to transport their bulky equipment including their Big Top and their wild animals by road.

Now they moved everything by train, and the railway company felt that it would be unable to guarantee this in the current circumstances of labour shortages, and the paucity and poor quality of rolling stock.

In addition, it would prove to be prohibitively expensive to have visits for only two or three days. In such circumstances they had reluctantly to say no to Arbroath's request, although they stressed that things might be a great deal different next year as the financial situation improved, and the country recovered from the war.

In the meantime, they stressed that the Circus would be in Dundee for a whole month from July 2 until August 2, and they hoped that Arbroath people would avail themselves of the opportunity to visit the Circus when it was there.

Arbroath would have to rely on its other attractions to bring in the tourists this year, and it was hoped that the good weather would encourage holidaymakers in spite of this word that everyone kept using in 1947 — "austerity".

June 15 1962

Today was a great landmark in education in Arbroath when a new secondary school, Arbroath Academy, was officially opened.

For some time, for many decades in fact, it was obvious that Arbroath High School, a fine building with a great tradition of education, was simply not really big enough.

A new building was needed to cope with an increasing number of children in the town, the "baby boomer" generation, i.e those born immediately after the Second World War, particularly with the building of new houses in the northern part of the town.

The new school was opened today by Sir William Arbuckle of The Scottish Education Department at a ceremony presided over by Lieutenant William Scott of Letham, Chairman of the Angus Education Committee, and attended by the local MP James Duncan.

The first Headmaster or Rector was Mr Crawford. The school was originally designed to be a Junior Secondary School which catered for those pupils who had failed their "Control" examinations (as they were called in Angus, the equivalent of the 11+ in England).

Some 10 years later, this clearly iniquitous system was abolished and replaced by the comprehensive system which, for all its faults, did give children more of a chance to develop at their own pace.

In 1972 came ROSLA (Raising of the School Leaving Age) when all pupils stayed on until they were 16. Since then, there have been many changes to education and expansions to the school, which no-one could have foreseen in 1962.

June 16 1954

The absurdity of the Laws on gambling were highlighted again today at Forfar Sheriff Court in a case involving Arbroath man David Spink of 4 Addison Place.

Technically all betting with bookmakers was illegal (and would remain so until 1961), but everyone knew that it was going on and the police normally turned a blind eye to it, except now and again, when they had a spectacular raid on a known bookmaker's shop on a day like Derby Day.

On Derby Day, Mr Spink happened to be in Forfar and had the misfortune to walk into a betting shop while a police raid was actually still going on!

Police Sergeant Gibb had just closed the door, most punters having taken the hint and scampered, when Spink pushed the door open, walked in right up to the counter and asked if he could put a bet on here.

There was no reply, for everyone was so "flabbergasted" according to Sergeant Gibb, and Mr Spink was then escorted to the Police Station to be cautioned and charged.

Mr Spink was thus certainly guilty of extreme folly, but most people in 1954 (let alone in the 21st century) would struggle to find anything bad or evil in what he did.

He told Bailie Lakie that he was not a man who normally bet on horses, but as it was Derby Day, he fancied a bet. He was fined £1.

June 17 1935

A new attraction in Arbroath has just appeared in the form of a Miniature Railway.

It is in the West Links Park and has been erected by Mr Matthew Kerr of Balfield Farm, Dundee and it has already proven to be a success with the children.

Hopefully it will become more so in the holiday season, now that Arbroath is going out of its way to make itself a major tourist centre.

The Miniature Railway has the advantage of being close to the "big" railway line between Aberdeen and Dundee and therefore clearly visible to passengers.

The line, built during the previous winter, runs 250 yards, and is capable of carrying 12 to 20 passengers (depending on how big they are) but there are intentions to expand both the length of the line and the rolling stock.

The gauge is 7.5 inches, but this is generally agreed to be too narrow and it will be widened in the following winter. One of the engines is a miniature version of the celebrated 1923 locomotive 4472 *Flying Scotsman*.

From such humble beginnings, Mr Kerr could hardly have imagined just how popular the railway would become.

The next few summers would see huge queues at the Miniature Railway, especially during the Glasgow Holiday week.

Although the Second World War curtailed things to an extent, the 1950s and the 1960s saw tens of thousands of people, from all over the United Kingdom and beyond, flock to Arbroath so that the children could have their "shottie" on the "wee railway"!

It eventually closed in October 2020.

Kerr's Miniature Railway

June 18 1928

Auchmithie has not been associated with much in the way of boating accidents but this proud record was brutally shattered today when a couple of local men failed to return from a crab and codling fishing.

The curious thing about this incident was that both men, although unrelated, were called David Cargill.

The elder one was aged 76, a fisherman, now a widower, but the younger one, aged 35 was married, to Robina Spink Cargill.

The two men had recently hired what used to be a pleasure boat called *The Blossom* from Mr Stewart Marnie of Arbroath and had set out in very pleasant conditions at 6.00 am in the company of about 10 other boats.

Having finished their operations, the boats set out for home at about 10.00 am in the morning, *The Blossom* being one of the last boats to decide to return.

What happened next is a mystery and no-one saw what happened. When the boat had not returned by lunch time, there was no particular cause for alarm, it being assumed that the two men had decided to do some more codling fishing.

It was only when tea time arrived and there was still no sign of them that the alarm was raised.

Motorised life boats and fishing boats then went out to search, aided by aircraft from Leuchars in Fife, but nothing was found except an oar which no-one could say for certain was from *The Blossom*.

It was only on the following morning that the boat was found under the water with the jacket of one of the two men, this sad discovery being made by yet another David Cargill, the father-in-law of the younger man. Cargill was a common name in the area.

The bodies were never recovered.

June 19 1918

Latin scholars are familiar with the phrases "res ad triarios venit" and "usque ad triarios" which means that the third line soldiers are now involved in the battle and that it is going on to the bitter end.

These phrases are very appropriate to Arbroath in this apocalyptic summer of 1918 as every single man who is considered able to be serving his country is being "combed out" as the saying goes.

It was often said that it was the Regular Army in 1914, the Territorials in 1915, the Volunteers in 1916, the Conscripts in 1917 and "what was left" in 1918.

Tribunals were being held in the Town Hall under the Chairmanship of Provost Rutherford Thomson to decide whether anyone was entitled to an exemption.

They decided on 20 cases today, some of them as old as 43, and men who frankly would be doing a better job for the war effort at their trades and blacksmiths, bakers etc rather than being reluctant soldiers.

There were various criteria for exemption like "being in sole charge of a business", "being in sole charge of children", as well as illness and infirmity, but there were quite a few fine lines that had to be decided on.

Some were given a temporary exemption, others a conditional exemption but most were told that they had to join up. In the meantime casualties are still being reported, but it now seems that the German advance of the spring has at least been stalled.

June 20 1889

The Victorian age is often considered an age of progress with the idea that the novel Oliver Twist, for example, is a caricature of what actually happened.

Maybe not.

The Arbroath Herald today prints advice from "The Board of Supervision" with reference to what one should do with the problem of vagrants.

The advice is that in the first instance, the Poor House should be used. It is "always the safest and most expedient form of relief", and it is the best place to deal with those who are unable to look after themselves. They would be adequately cared for there.

It is "highly objectionable" to give them a ticket for a local boarding house, and even worse to actually put money in their hands.

Only in extreme cases when the Poor House is full and there is a huge quantity of vagrants, should the Inspector consider "billeting" them in lodging houses, only for one night at a time and a plain meal of 4 ounces of oat meal converted into porridge or brose.

Clearly Mr Bumble would have been proud of such advice, but one would not like to have been a pauper in Arbroath in 1889!

This being midsummer, it is no uncommon sight to encounter families of poor people sleeping in the beach or the cliffs, and then coming into town to beg for food.

It is a practice that Arbroath Town Council and the various Churches would like to have stopped, for it is believed that such families spread diseases and commit crimes!

June 21 1837

News travels quickly in 1837, and a little more than a day after it happened in London, Arbroath knew that the King was dead.

Arbroath being on the coast often got news early, but experience told you that you could never trust it, until it was verified.

This morning a boat came into the harbour saying that "someone in Dundee" had said that King William IV had died yesterday.

This afternoon, the official communication from London reached the Town House when a courier arrived on horseback from Dundee.

Naturally such news travelled quickly round the town – for when was it ever easy to keep a secret in Arbroath? – but there was a distinct lack of grief, for no-one had ever seen him, or knew what he looked like!

He was called "silly Billy", not without cause, but his reign from 1830 had seen things like the First Reform Act and the abolition of Slavery in the British Empire. More interest centred on his successor.

He had no legitimate offspring (loads of illegitimate ones, however!) and the throne now passed to his niece, Princess Alexandrina Victoria, who was only 18!

What chance did she have of controlling the vast British Empire?

Apart from anything else, she would be the first Queen since before the Jacobite rebellions of a hundred years ago. And had there been a Queen of Scotland since Mary, Queen of Scots?

Such topics were much discussed in Arbroath that bright midsummer's day. At least the Coronation (whatever that was) might see the magistrates grant Arbroath a public holiday when it happened. Would they?

June 22 1900

Nearly every week letters from soldiers at the Front have been appearing in the *Arbroath Herald* and have been read with deep interest.

Mourning over the dead and wounded has been heard in not a few homes in town.

The death of the Earl of Airlie in battle on 11th June sent a thrill of sorrow throughout the whole of Angus ; but no death touched more deeply Arbroath and district than that of Lieutenant Walter Garnet Rait, who died of enteric fever at Wynberg on 22nd June.

A memorial service, attended by the Provost and Town Council, was held in the Old Church on 1st July; and from all classes there came expressions of the deepest sympathy with Colonel Rait and the Anniston family in the irreparable loss of their gallant son.

Lieutenant Walter Garnet Rait

June 22 1935

In splendid weather and before a huge crowd, Arbroath United won, in the last over, the local derby v Strathmore at Lochside Park, Forfar, thereby retaining their place at the top of the Strathmore Union.

Games at Forfar were often spicy and well attended with loads of Arbroathians attending by train. Unlike the football which was next door to Forfar Station, Lochside Park was a good mile away but the walk through the town was leisurely and punctuated with a few stops at hostelries where supporters could indulge in good natured banter with the locals.

Each team had a Scottish Internationalist in their team – Bob Sievwright for Arbroath at cricket and Strathie had Dave McLean at football.

They were great rivals, and although good friends after the game, not above giving each other the verbals on the park with occasionally an audible expletive heard by the crowd on a still, quiet day.

Today however it was Bob's son, young Bobby who scored 40 as Arbroath reached 120, a competitive total. And then old Bob had the misfortune to dislocate his spinning finger and was out of action to his intense disappointment.

However in spite of some lusty blows from McLean who reached 39 before being caught, Myles, Nolan and Ramsay all bowled well for Arbroath and Strathie were all out for 94 in the last over.

It was a cheerful walk through the town to get the train home with some Arbroathians even magnanimous enough to contribute to the Benefit Fund for Len Halstead, the Strathie professional.

Presentation of Strathmore Cricket Union Trophy by the Earl of Strathmore to R.W. Sievwright, Captain of Arbroath United Cricket Club, in 1934. In the background, R.L.Lang and C.C.Moir.

June 23 1919

In fine weather this Monday evening, an open air meeting was held in support of the Victory Loan, a scheme by which everyone was asked to lend the Government some money with the idea of getting it back on some future occasion.

It was basically just an extra form of taxation and a continuation of the War Loan scheme.

Speakers included Provost Rutherford Thomson, Bailie David Wilson and the MP for Montrose Burghs Mr J Leng Sturrock.

The Pipe Band under Pipe Sergeant Soutar was in attendance as well, and a large attendance gathered.

It was an opportunity to see again the men who had been overseas, the men who had returned badly injured, and to console and comfort the many war widows, still trying to come to terms with their loss.

Leng Sturrock commended the scheme to the good people of Arbroath, but like everyone else, was in no forgiving mood towards the Germans.

On Saturday, the German fleet interned at Scapa Flow in the Orkneys had scuttled itself as the German sailors deliberately sank their own ships to prevent them falling into the hands of the Allies under the terms of the Versailles agreement that was now on the point of being signed.

Mr Sturrock described this as "the nefarious Hun playing exactly the same sort of trick that might have been expected of him" and he hoped that the Government would make sure they were adequately compensated for their wickedness.

In these circumstances the Victory Loan was all the more necessary.

June 24 1902

No, it couldn't be true!

Rumours had spread round the town all this midsummer afternoon that it was all not going to happen!

How could this be? The town was all agog for the event scheduled for June 26, the first Coronation for over 60 years, and it was going to be postponed!

This evening the news was confirmed. Edward VII had gone down with appendicitis and needed an immediate operation, and he was eventually persuaded to postpone his Coronation.

He had spent his 60 years in dissipation with food, drink and women, so illness was hardly surprising. But what did this mean for Arbroath?

Almost immediately, all the decorations, flags and bunting were taken down and all parades, bonfires and sports events were immediately cancelled. The sense of disappointment was tangible as the workmen were seen at the Town House and the High Street dismantling everything.

It would fair to say that the disappointment at the loss of the holiday was greater than any concern for the health of the King, but there were a few events connected with the Coronation that were kept on.

Apparently in accordance with the wishes of the ailing King, the meal for the poor people in the Corn Exchange went ahead, as indeed did the entertainment and treat for the Poor House and the Dale School.

It was a great disappointment, but the King eventually recovered and the Coronation of King Edward VII and Queen Alexandra went ahead on August 9.

June 25 1855

The Arbroath Guide is a little annoyed that a very sensible suggestion made last year by Mr John A Anderson to the Police Commission has still not been acted upon.

Mr Anderson has suggested that it should be made compulsory that all streets should be named and all houses given a number.

In a small town like Arbroath most people know each other and a letter addressed to "Mr Smith near the foot of the High Street" would have a good chance of reaching its intended recipient, but it cannot be guaranteed as more and more newcomers have arrived in the town, and more and more new houses are beginning to make an appearance.

There are also a lot more letters these days. Since the introduction of the Penny Black stamp by Rowland Hill in 1840, it has been a lot easier to send letters, even just personal ones to relatives in Dundee or Forfar for example.

If every house was numbered and every street named concisely and accurately, not for example "near the end of the High Street" or "the house close to the Abbey" things would become a lot easier for the courier/postman.

Some letters could be very important, bringing for example news from the Crimea where things do not appear to be going very well at all these days.

Some towns already have a system like this, and it is clearly desirable that improvements are made as quickly as possible, and *The Arbroath Guide* is right to get upset about things.

June 26 1396

This is the day on which we are told John Gedy, Abbot of Arbroath Abbey was "granted the mitre".

What this exactly means we do not know, but we do know that Arbroath Abbey became one of the most famous in all Scotland.

John Gedy was probably the "Abbot of Aberbrothock" who features in the poem "The Inchcape Rock" by Robert Southey.

The Inchcape Rock lies about eleven or twelve miles off the coast of Arbroath and was a notorious place for shipwrecks, with even a hint in medieval times that there was something supernatural and evil about the way that so many ships were lured to death and destruction.

The good "Abbot of Aberbrothock" decided to do something about this. In the medieval world there was no electricity, so a lighthouse was not feasible, but the Abbot decided to place a bell on Inchcape Rock, the thinking being that it would ring with the wind on a dark and stormy night and warn ships to stay away.

To what extent this worked we do not know, but one day, Ralph The Rover, a notorious pirate, saw the bell and stole it.

Such wickedness got its just deserts when some time later when he was coming to Arbroath one dark night, Ralph's ships hit the Inchcape Rock (because there was no bell to warn him) and he, his crew and his ship all perished.

Southey's poem, first published in 1802, is a good one, showing how the wicked get their just deserts, but no-one can say how much truth there is in this legend.

June 27 1925

It may be that the "Roaring Twenties" have arrived in Arbroath!

Never has the town been so busy and so animated as today, with the railway station a particularly busy place.

It is of course the busiest day of the year for Sunday School picnics and other outings, with the Abbey Church leaving town with about 500 parents and children!

They were soon replaced by an arrival of an equally large group from Kirriemuir Old Parish Church all bound for the seaside.

What made everything so pleasant was the pleasant summer sunshine, and ice cream, bottles of lemonade and sandwiches were all clearly visible.

But there was also a bustle and a happiness that had not been around for a while, as it seemed that the economic depression of the few years after the Great War was now at last on its way out to be replaced with an era of progress.

This was of course illusory as events in the coal mining industry would soon show, but at the moment things were fine.

Behaviour was generally good, although quite a few elderly Church going ladies would have been shocked by the deportment of some of the younger ladies with their loud voices, nylon stockings, lipstick and their rather too obvious attempts to indicate to men that they were "available".

But then, of course, women were in the majority with war widows (still young and pretty in many cases) a common phenomenon. But that war was now over. There must never be another one!

June 28 1913

A strange event occurred at the Market Cross in the High Street this Saturday afternoon.

It was strange but it was not unprecedented for a similar thing had happened last year.

It was a Public Sale or a Roup of some property of Miss Alexina Jessie MacGregor of Abbethune House just outside the town.

Always considered an eccentric, the rich Miss MacGregor, born in Calcutta in 1847, had identified with the cause of Women's Suffrage to the extent of refusing to pay her taxes.

This had clearly brought her into conflict with the Commissioners of Income Tax and Inhabited House Duties who had last year seized one of her Rembrandt paintings and sold it.

This was a warning which she did not heed. Now, a year later, a silver tea urn was being sold by auction in front of a large and noisy crowd while she herself stood with some friends in a dignified silence watching and enduring the coarse insults of some of the crowd, mainly men.

The urn was eventually sold for £85 and bought by Mr Low of the Town House. The price was excessive, especially as she owed only £6 15 shillings and 10 pence in tax!

When the crowd dispersed, Miss MacGregor and her two supporters, both called Miss Grant and both from Dundee, held a protest meeting in which after enduring a certain amount of heckling, she won a certain amount of support by her reasoned arguments.

All this happened just a matter of weeks after the incident at the Derby when Emily Davison had thrown herself in front of the King's horse.

June 29 1920

At the meeting of the Schools Management Committee of the Education Authority, the Rector of Arbroath High School moved that there should be no more exemptions from school to allow children to take part in the potato harvesting.

This had been allowed during the War years and was totally justified then, and the children had played a large and heroic part in feeding the country.

Surrounded by fish and potatoes, Arbroath had never suffered from any serious food shortages. But times had changed.

Not only were all the soldiers now back from the war, but the town like the rest of the country, had a serious unemployment problem and there was an ample supply of labour which could do their bit in lifting the potato harvest.

There was a case still for closing the country schools, but there was no need to allow this to happen in the Burgh Schools. There were disadvantages in the "potato holidays" because education could become badly disrupted with pupils then showing a reluctance to go back to school in November.

Not only that, but they could learn "uncouth language and habits" from the farm hands! (Although, there were also some pupils, mainly girls, who could teach the farm labourers a thing or two!)

The Rector's views were supported by those of the socialist persuasion on the Education Committee, for there was an element of "fat cat" farmers getting cheap labour from young boys and now girls.

On the other hand, as far as poor families were concerned, a supplementary income was useful for the horrendous price of winter boots!

June 30 1961

The end of the school term saw the usual spate of Prize Givings in the town.

The Director of Education Mr John Eadie gave the address and his wife presented the prizes to pupils of Arbroath High School at the Webster Memorial Hall.

Mr Eadie said that there would be changes in education coming very soon, and there would have to be, not least because of the increase in school numbers as a result of the rising birth rate since the Second World War in what was called the "baby boomer generation".

The Rector, Mr D D Wilson gave his report on the year, mentioning that this was actually the centenary of the school which had begun in 1861, and there had only been five Rectors.

It was a school with a great tradition and a great reputation and one which had produced many fine pupils for every walk of life.

He then congratulated all his prize winners, particularly Robert G Baird who won the Dux Medal and the English, Latin and Greek Medals and had won a major scholarship for the University of St Andrews, as had David Buchanan and John Florence.

It was also the retirement of Miss Jennie Entwhistle of 56 Cairnie Street who had taught at the school for 40 years. She had been born in China, the daughter of a Missionary, and graduated MA from Aberdeen University.

It was appropriate that the service ended with the hymn "Lord, Dismiss Us With Thy Blessing".

In this year
Traders in Arbroath in 1915

YEAR BOOK ADVERTISEMENTS.

C. Y. MYLES,
Ladies' and Gentlemen's Tailor,
21 James Street & 112 High Street.

We hold a Stock of the Famous

BURBERRY
WEATHERPROOF
GARMENTS

For Ladies and Gentlemen.

Patterns on Application.

Burberry's Copyright

C. Y. MYLES,
21 James Street and 112 High Street.
Telephone 109.

Established a Quarter of a Century.

Moncur's Aerated Waters

Are all Guaranteed Pure, being Manufactured on Principles which Ensure a Thorough Purification of all Waters and Absolute Purity in all Essences, Syrups, &c., used

D. Moncur & Co.,
Aerated Water Manufacturers,
HELEN STREET, ARBROATH.

Make certain when Ordering Aerated Waters that you get **MONCUR'S**.

Vans Visit all Towns and Villages in the District.

HELEN STREET, ARBROATH

JAS. PETER

High-Class Ladies' and Gent's Tail[or]

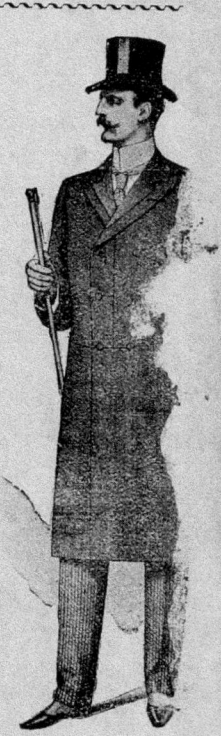

Tweed and Worsted Suitings.

Scotch and English Trouserings.

Serges, Vicunas, Coatings, in Black and Blue.

Overcoatings in all the Newest Materials.

Shirts, Braces, Ties, and Hosiery.

A SPLENDID SELECTION CAN ALWAYS BE HAD.

Customers may rely on all Goods being thoroughly Up-to-Date.

24, 26 & 28 COMMERCE STR[EET]
ARBROATH

Established 1868.

J. EDDIE,

**Practical Watchmaker,
Gold and Silver Smith.**

Our Stock is Large and Comprehensive, including Watches, Clocks, Jewellery, Silver, Electro-Plated Goods, All Soundly Made and of Best Quality

Special Stock of MARBLE and WOODEN CLOCKS, Suitable for Presentation. Generous Terms to Committees.

We have always New and Exclusive Designs in Silver and Electro Table Appointments.
Engagement and Dress Rings and 9 ct. and 15 ct. Pendants a Speciality

*Personal Supervision of all Repairs. Skilled & Prompt Attention at Moderate Charges.
We Specialise Watch and Clock Work because they have been our Special Study. High-Grade Chronometer and Repeating Watches Carefully Cleaned and Adjusted.*

Clocks Wound and Kept in Order by Contract.
Estimates Given for Special Work, Public Clocks, &c.

105 HIGH STREET, ARBROATH

(Opposite Town House.)

YEAR BOOK ADVERTISEMENTS.

TELEPHONE No. 89

J. & R. W. SIEVWRIGHT

Joiners and Contractors,

Lordburn Joinery Works
ARBROATH.

Jobbing Promptly Attended to.

Estimates and Sketches
GIVEN FREE.

Some Special Lines !

Splendid Selection of Pocket & Presentation Bibles in a Variety of Bindings.
Hymnaries with Music—Staff and Solfa.
Scottish Hymnals—Words and Music.

GIFT & REWARD BOOKS
Suitable for all Purposes.

Pocket Books. Autograph Books
PHOTO FRAMES.

Fountain and Stylo Pens.
Gent's Purses and Wallets.

Ladies' Handbags and Purses.
All the Latest Artistic Designs in
Serviettes, D'Oyleys, and Sweet Cases.

Any Magazine or Newspaper Supplied and Promptly Delivered on Arrival.

The Bible and Stationery Warehouse,
10 BROTHOCK BRIDGE.

YEAR BOOK ADVERTISEMENTS.

JOHNSTON'S EMPORIUM

ARBROATH.

THE SPOT FOR PRESENTS

All Kinds of Household Hardware.
China and Glass Wares, Fancy Goods.
Emporium always Crammed Full with every Novelty.
Everything in Cooking Utensils.
Everything for Baking at Home.
Baskets in Great Variety.
Abbey View Ware, Plaques, &c.
Presentation Goods of Various Kinds.
The Great Place for Cheap Travelling Bags, Travelling Trunks, Ladies' Hand-Bags, Purses, Combs, &c.

FINEST OLD
HIGHLAND WHISKY.

Carefully Selected from the Best Distilleries.

Guaranteed to be Thoroughly Matured.

DUNCAN M'LEAN,
44 KEPTIE STREET,
ARBROATH.

YEAR BOOK ADVERTISEMENTS. 45

West Port Association

LIMITED  *Established 1834.*

2 and 4 KEPTIE STREET, ARBROATH,

IS NOTED FOR Attractive Shops,
Courteous Shopmen,
Clean Handling of Goods,
Best Quality and Low Prices.

£262,148 (over a Quarter Million Sterling) has been returned to Members of this Association in Profits during **40 YEARS**, and all Housewives should start participating in the Benefits of its **Automatic Saving System** at once.

PAYMENT OF 1s. 3d.

Entitles Members to all the Privileges and Advantages of the Association, and this Entry Money may be paid to any of the Branches.

BRANCHES:
54 and 56 LOCHLAND STREET, 59 EAST ABBEY STREET, and 46 CAIRNIE STREET.

OLYMPIA

The Home of Comedy.

The Theatre That is Always Up-to-Date.

7 AND 9

The Theatre That is Patronised By All!

CIVILITY
COMFORT
CLEANLINESS

PERFECT PICTURES
PERFECTLY PROJECTED,
With First-Class Music, Ensure a Night's Enjoyment.

Cultivate the Olympia Habit

YEAR BOOK ADVERTISEMENTS.

THE HOUSE FOR

Holiday Attire, Week-Day Garb,  School Suits, Working Clothes

And Outfits of every kind for Home and Abroad.

THE BEST AND CHEAPEST ESTABLISHMENT
For MEN'S, YOUTHS'. and BOYS' CLOTHING,
HATS, CAPS, TIES, &c., is

A. K. ADAMSON, 9 Keptie Street

Mourning Orders have Special Attention

Far ye Save 5s a Pound a' the Year Round.

The POPULAR STORES

(WHOLESALE and RETAIL),

35 HIGH STREET and 2 JOHN STREET.

GROCERIES and PROVISIONS all the Finest.

☞ MARVELLOUS 2s TEA.

Rare Old "Auld Kirk," Wines, &c., and the Famous Influenza Rum.
Shipping and Fishing Crews Supplied on Best Terms.

JAMES TURNBULL, Proprietor.

JAMES RUXTON,

Chemist, "Star" Pharmacy,

KEPTIE ANGLE, ARBROATH.

Telegrams—"RUXTON, CHEMIST, ARBROATH."

Prescriptions Dispensed.
Drugs and Sundries.
Photographic Requisites.
CHEMICALS.

SPECTACLES.

Sight-Testing to Suit all Sights.

W. B. SMART,

Monumental Mason,

72 GUTHRIE PORT, ARBROATH

Monuments, Headstones, Crosses, &c., made to Order from selected Granites, Marbles and Freestones.

Tombstones Cleaned, Painted, Re-Lettered and Gilded. Designs Submitted.
Estimates Given for all kinds of Monumental Work

Charges Moderate.

ALEX. WALLACE & SON

Wholesale & Retail Glass & China Merchants,

Have always on hand the Latest Patterns of Glass and China Goods in the Market.

Tea Sets,
Breakfast Sets,
Dinner and
Dessert Sets
Toilet Ware.

Big Selection
of Epergnes,
Vases,
Flower Pots,
&c.

Goods Given on Hire, with Cutlery, at Lowest Prices.

14 PANMURE STREET, ARBROATH.

Telephone 1Y1.   Established 1877.

Telephone No. 155.

J. MITCHELL & SON,

Slaters and Cement Workers.

Jobbing of every Description Carefully Attended to.
ESTIMATES GIVEN for all kinds of Slater and Rough Casting Work.
Chimney Heads Repaired and Pointed.

20 PANMURE STREET, Arbroath.

HOUSE ADDRESS—30 WEST KEPTIE STREET.

THOMAS GIRDWOOD, M.P.S.

Family and Dispensing Chemist and Druggist,

12 KEPTIE STREET, ARBROATH.

*Prescriptions Accurately Dispensed with Purest Drugs.
Only One Quality—The Best.*

Nursery and Toilet Requisites.   Photographic Goods.

'Phone No. 99

The Plough and Harrow

Finest Whiskies, Brandies, Rums.

Sparkling Beers, Nourishing Stout.

Montrose Road, Arbroath
JOHN N. SMYTH, Proprietor.

At J. R. GREIG'S.

Choice Goods: Newest and Latest on the Market.

Have a Look and Compare Value—Everything at Rock Bottom Prices, Marked in Plain Figures.

Blouses, Overalls, Aprons, Pinafores, Handkerchiefs, Gloves, Corsets, Skirts, Dresses, Jerseys.

Cashmere Hose, Embroidered Hose, Fingering Hose, Top Stockings, Socks, Ties, Scarves.

UNDERWEAR.

Chemises, Nightdresses, Knickers, Combinations, Spencers, Semmets, Camisoles, Slipbodices.

J. R. GREIG, 37 COMMERCE ST., ARBROATH.

Royal Oak Bar,
47 GUTHRIE PORT, ARBROATH.

Wines, Spirits, & Malt Liquors of Finest Quality.

S. D. HUTCHISON, Proprietor

Royal Exchange Assurance
Incorporated A.D. 1720.

For FIRE, SEA, LIFE, ACCIDENTS, EMPLOYERS' LIABILITY *(including Domestic Servants under New Act)*, BURGLARY, PLATE GLASS, MOTOR CARS, LOSS OF PROFITS, FIDELITY GUARANTEE, THIRD PARTY.

The Corporation will act as Executor of Wills, Trustee of Wills and Settlements.

Special Terms Granted to Annuitants when Health is Impaired

Dundee Branch, - 30 Meadowside.

J. A. TOMBAZIS, Manager.

Telephone, No. 2179 (Two Lines.)   Telegrams—"Foxhound, Dundee."

AGENTS IN ARBROATH:

W. H. ALEXANDER, Solicitor | ROLLO S. BLACK, Accountant
D. & W. CHAPEL, Solicitors.

Angus & Mearns Packet of Stationery
1d   Best Value in the Market.   1d

BRODIE & SALMOND, Herald Office, ARBROATH

YEAR BOOK ADVERTISEMENTS.

Hotel Telephone, No. 25.   Hiring Establishment Telephone, No. 125.

IMPERIAL HOTEL,

RAILWAY STATION, ARBROATH.

THE ONLY FIRST-CLASS MODERN HOTEL IN ARBROATH.

Families and Commercial Gentlemen will find this Establishment replete with every comfort. Convenient and Comfortable Accommodation. The House has been Renovated Throughout. Hot, Cold, and Shower Baths. Boots in Attendance at all Trains. Terms Strictly Moderate.

First-Class Restaurant and Dining Rooms in connection with the Hotel.

Soups and Joints from 12.30 to 3 p.m.
FAMILIES SUPPLIED.

Liqueurs, Wines, &c., all of the Finest Quality.
Posting in all its Branches.

S. BANKS, Proprietor.

St Ruth's Art Studio,

ARBROATH.

Also at ST NINIAN'S STUDIO, BRECHIN.

The Portrait taken at **A. C. MILNE'S** either by Electric Light or Daylight has always his Best Attention.

PHOTOGRAPHY AND PORTRAITURE IN ALL BRANCHES.
PICTURE FRAMING.

Enlargements Beautifully Executed.   *Prices Moderate.*

WILLIAM HIGH,
SIGN OF THE CLOCK,
222 HIGH STREET,
ARBROATH

Presents in Great Variety.

YEAR BOOK ADVERTISEMENTS.

JAS. KELLY-
(LICENSED BROKER),
Rag, Waste, and Metal Merchant,
4 WEST GRIMSBY, Arbroath.
(Close to Foot of West Port.)

Estimates given for every Quantity of Old Material.
Parties can rely on obtaining Highest Prices in District.
Old Metal, Lead, Copper, Brass, Ropes, Rags, &c.,
PURCHASED FOR CASH.
A Post-Card or other Message will ensure Prompt Attention.

NOTE ONLY ADDRESS:
4 West Grimsby, Arbroath.

The Ship Inn.  Opposite New Baths.

D. COWAN, 19-21 Marketgate, Arbroath
Is Noted for the Excellence of his OLD WHISKIES and RUMS, which are FINELY MATURED and PLEASANT TO DRINK.

Beers and Stouts in Prime Condition

Arbroath Burgh School Board

ARBROATH HIGH SCHOOL.

THE School provides a Complete Course of Education —Primary, Intermediate, and Secondary. Pupils are prepared both for the University and for Commercial life. The Class Rooms and Laboratories are provided with all Modern Apparatus and Accessories. Needlework, Woodwork, Gymnastics, Singing and Dancing are included in the Curriculum.

The School is a Junior Student Centre.

Bursaries and Scholarships are very numerous.

All Information may be had from the Rector.

A. & M. JENKINS,
CONFECTIONERS.

Shortbread   Confections

Pastry : :   Fruits : :

TEA ROOM.
FANCY BISCUITS.   FINEST CAKES AND SCONES.
Finest Table Bon-Bons and Dessert Chocolates.

26 KEPTIE STREET, ARBROATH
(Nearly Opposite Railway Station).

In these dull times, everybody has to practice rigid economy. You can have a Tasty Meal without Cooking and at little expense by going to

Kerr's Potted Meat Store
270 HIGH STREET (Opposite Abbey.)

A Specialty in Oatmeal Puddings—3 Varieties

All our Meats are Guaranteed our Own Make and Absolutely Pure.

WM. ROSS, St Thomas Bar, Towernook

Where the Very Best WINES, SPIRITS, PORTERS, and ALES are kept in Stock always in Prime Condition.

LESSLIE'S
DENTAL 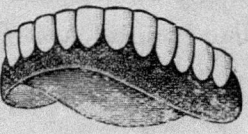 ROOMS,

Corner of Marketgate and Brothock Bridge,
ARBROATH.

Special for Eating and Speaking, and for Natural Appearance
Cannot be Surpassed.
OLD SETS Re-made and Repaired on the Shortest Notice.
Teeth Painlessly Extracted, Stopped, and Cleaned.
Country Patients Supplied Same Day.
LESSLIE'S ARTIFICIAL TEETH ARE THE BEST

VICTORIA CAFE
(Next Railway Line.)

Breakfasts, Dinners Teas, and Suppers at most Moderate Charges.

Commodious Hall and Rooms for Social and Wedding Parties, Club & Society Meetings Presentations, &c.

Soirees & Picnics
Purveyed for.

Ladies' Room
And all other suitable Accommodation.

MILLGATE, ARBROATH.
Misses MOLLISON, Proprietrix.

BELL ROCK TAVERN,

49 West Grimsby,
ARBROATH.

The Bell Rock Blend of Scotch & Irish WHISKIES Guaranteed well Matured.

WM. YOUNGER'S Edinburgh Ales always in Sparkling Condition.

Excellent Sitting Accommodation.

D. DINNIE,
Proprietor.

MEEKISON & JAMIESON

Peainters and Deorators,

5 Brothock Bridge, Arbroath

PAPER - HANGING MERCHANTS.

NOTICE TO PROPRIETORS, FACTORS, HOUSE HOLDERS.

We have the Largest, Cheapest, and Choicest Stock of Wall Papers in Town, at Prices to Suit all purposes.

Estimates Given for Every Class of Work.

Fred. F. Boath

HIGH-CLASS FAMILY BUTCHER & POULTERER,
24 KEPTIE STREET, Arbroath.

Home-Fed BEEF, Choice MUTTON, Finest PORK, &c.

Specialties: CORNED BEEF, PICKLED TONGUES, SALT ROUNDS.

We are Famed for PORK and BEEF SAUSAGES MUTTON and PORK CHOPS.

Try our Own Cured HAMS.

All Orders entrusted to us have Prompt and Careful Attention.

On receipt of Post-Card or Verbal Message, Assistants are despatched to any part of the Town

FRED. F. BOATH
(Nearly Opposite the Railway Station.)

YEAR BOOK ADVERTISEMENTS.

GENERAL ACCIDENT, FIRE & LIFE
ASSURANCE CORPORATION, LTD.

All Classes of Fire, Life, Sickness and Accident Insurance Effected,

INCLUDING

Workmen's Compensation ; Fidelity Guarantee ;
Driving Risks and other Indemnity ;
Live Stock ; Motors ; Burglary ; Plate Glass ;
Domestic and outdoor Servants ; &c.

AGENT:

NORMAN SCOTT MACKAY, Solicitor,
12 WEST PORT, ARBROATH.

COLIN P. M'CALLUM,
ST THOMAS DAIRY,
41½ MILLGATE LOAN, ARBROATH.

Dairy & Farm Produce.

Fresh Eggs & Butter Daily.

Home-Baked Scones and Pancakes our Speciality.

Dairy & Farm Produce.

FRESH MILK,
Twice Daily,
Delivered to any Address in Town

YEAR BOOK ADVERTISEMENTS.

THE YORKSHIRE INSURANCE COMPANY, LIMITED.

ESTABLISHED 1824

Accumulated Funds Nearly Four Millions.

Life Insurances issued, giving every advantage offered by any Insurance Company. Moderate Premiums. Liberal Conditions. Substantial Bonuses. Stringent Reserves. New Scheme combining Life Assurance and Old Age Pensions.

Fire Insurances effected by the Company on the most Moderate Terms according to nature of risk.

Employers' Liability.—Policies Issued covering full Liability under the Workmen's Compensation Acts 1897, 1900, and 1906; the Employers' Liability Act 1880, and the Common Law.

Personal Accident Insurance.—World-Wide Policies Issued, conferring Full Benefits at Moderate Rates.

Combined Accident and Sickness Schemes.

Burglary Insurances Transacted—Liberal Conditions, Low Rates. No Average Clause.

Live Stock Insurance Effected.—Accident, Disease, Foaling, Castration, and Stallion.

ANTHRAX (Horses and Cattle)—Insured Against under Special Policy.

Plate Glass Insurance.   Loss of Profits.

Dundee Office: Courier Buildings, 20 Meadowside.

D. GRANT REA, Resident Secretary.

Application for Agencies Invited.

Telephone No. 1167.   Telegraphic Address—"Yorkshire," Dundee.

GEORGE REID,
INSURANCE AGENT, ROYAL BANK, ARBROATH.

Motor Car, Live Stock and Anthrax Insurance Arranged on the most Favourable Terms.

Agent for the YORKSHIRE INSURANCE and other Companies.

YEAR BOOK ADVERTISEMENTS.

WINES, . .
SPIRITS, . .
BRANDIES,
RUMS . . .
Of only the
Finest . . .
Quality . . .

Comfortable
Sitting . . .
Rooms . . .
Clean, Cosy
and . . .
Cheery . .
Bar . . .

THE
VICTORIA
BAR

Sparkling .
BEERS . .
Nourishing
STOUTS .

Prompt .
and . .
Efficient .
Service. .

CATHERINE STREET
(Opp. Side Entrance to Railway Station.)
ROBT. GRAY, Proprietor.

JAMES R. COOK,

Plumber, Tinsmith, and Gasfitter,

36 MAULE STREET, ARBROATH.

JOBBING PROMPTLY ATTENDED TO.

MILK UTENSILS A SPECIALTY.

All Sizes, and to Measure.

Established Upwards of Fifty Years.

Telephone No. 24.

GEO. HARRIS,

Successor to DAVID HARRIS.

Wholesale and Retail

Family Butcher and Game Dealer,

29 MILLGATE & 36 HAMILTON GREEN, ARBROATH.

SPECIALTIES.

Prime Beef and Mutton—Always Large and Fresh Stock on hand.

VEAL AND LAMB IN SEASON.

Always in Stock, Salt Rounds, Plain & Spice Pickled.

Orders Promptly Delivered Daily by own Van in Town or Country.

Game and Fish Shop

23 MILLGATE.

Always on hand, Fresh Supplies in their Season.

FOR LATEST STYLES

In BLOUSES, SKIRTS, and GIRLS' DRESSES,
GLOVES, BELTS, and HATS, at KEENEST PRICES,

TRY EWING,

General Draper, 203 HIGH STREET, Arbroath.

YOU NEVER NEED TO WORRY

When Choosing a PRESENT for Weddings & Presentations.

J. M. MEFFAN,
33 MILLGATE,

Has always a Large and Varied Selection of all the Latest and Stylish Designs in Solid Silver, Silver Plate, and Jewellery.   Goods sent on Approbation.

OPTICAL PRESCRIPTIONS

Receive Special Attention, and Best Workmanship guaranteed in all Repair Departments.
We are Noted for Satisfaction in every detail.

JOHN M. MEFFAN,

Practical Watchmaker, Jeweller & Optician, 33 Millgate, Arbroath.

The Steeple Restaurant

140 High Street (Opposite the Steeple), **Arbroath.**

Teas at any time.   Nice and Comfortable Rooms.
Pies and Bridies every Friday and Saturday.
Finest Sweets and Chocolates.

Mrs A. S. POTTER, Proprietrix

FITZCHARLES & CO.,

DEALERS IN
Ancient & Modern Furniture,

HAVE always on hand a Large and Assorted Stock of Brass Dial Eight-Day Clocks and Desk Headed Drawers, Spinning Wheels and Reels, Corner Cupboards, Oak and Laburnum Chairs, Cruisie Lamps and other Furniture and Curios of all kinds.

Local Pictures in Oil and Water Colour, Old Engravings and Portraits.

An Excellent Selection of
Substantial Modern Furniture
To Suit all Classes.

WANTED
Antique Furniture
Of every description. Highest Prices given at the Recognised Curiosity Shop.

FITZCHARLES & CO.,
Modern and Antique Furniture Dealers, ::
64 GUTHRIE PORT
ARBROATH.

Waverley Temperance Hotel
ARBROATH.

(Within One Minute's Walk of Railway Station.)

13 Keptie Street

Visitors are Assured of Every Home Comfort.

WM. A. CRAIG,
Cabinetmaker and Upholsterer,
FUNERAL UNDERTAKER,
23-25 James Street, Arbroath

Maker of Artistic Furniture.
Original Designs for all sorts of Furniture in High Relief Carving.

No Reproduction of Original Designs.

Telephone No. 2y1.

James Law & Son,

MOTOR and GENERAL ENGINEERS,

East Grimsby, Arbroath.

CYCLE SHOP, - 5 BROTHOCK BRIDGE.

THE GOODS WE HANDLE ARE

Motor Cars.	Side Cars.	Motor Tyres.
Motor Cycles.	Cycles.	Petrol.
Oils.	Grease.	Accessories of every kind.

WE CAN SUBMIT ESTIMATES

For any Class of Car on the Market.
Also for Renewals and Repairs.

Motor Hiring Department

Close or Open Cars and Char-a-Bancs for any period.
Balls, Marriages, Concert Parties, &c.
Careful and Competent Drivers.

Give Us an Opportunity to Quote You

WHEN BUYING A MOTOR CAR,
MOTOR CYCLE, OR CYCLE.

YEAR BOOK ADVERTISEMENTS.

Established (1867) nearly Half-a-Century.

GEORGE SALMOND,

199 High Street, Arbroath.

Our Fairport Gingerbread

Is an Old-Established Favourite the length and breadth of the land. We make it with and without Fruit, and in Sizes to suit all.

Our OATCAKES

Thick and Thin, in Large and Small Tins, manufactured from the Finest Oats grown on the Braes of Angus. Our Oatcakes are well-known and highly appreciated.

TRY OUR FAMED SCOTCH SHORTBREAD.
FOR QUALITY IT EXCELS.

OUR VANS VISIT Carnoustie, Colliston, Forfar, Montrose, Friockheim, Carmyllie, Brechin, Inverkeilor, and Surrounding Country Districts Every Week.

☞ **FOR QUALITY IN WINES, SPIRITS, AND DRAUGHT ALES,**

TRY THE

EXCHANGE BAR

(Adjoining OLYMPIA.)

Large Room for Meetings, Presentations, &c.

Billiard Room.   **WM. HOVELL,** *Proprietor.*

WHITE HART HIRING
AND
Garage Company Ltd., Arbroath.

Furnished with the Latest Models of TAXI LANDAULETTES and TOURING CARS. Can be Hired by the Mile, Half-Day, Day, Week, or Longer Periods.

Horsehiring Department.

Up-to-Date and Smart Turnouts, with Stylish and Superior Traps. Carriages for Marriages, Pleasure Drives, and Picnic Parties arranged for, and have Special Attention.

Funeral Plant a Speciality.

Hearses and Funeral Cars and Mourning Coaches of the Most Modern Type.

CHARGES STRICTLY MODERATE.

All Orders have Personal Attention from

D. FINDLAY, Manager

TELEPHONE No. 111

Telephone No. 78

WILLIAM BRAND & SON,

SLATERS,

Slate and Cement Merchants,

30 DISHLAND STREET

ARBROATH.

Estimates Given for Granolithic Paving.

Chimney Heads Repaired and Pointed.

All Repairs Punctually Attended to.

James Kydd & Sons,

Joiners, Builders, Contractors, and General Wood Turners,

6 EAST MARY STREET, ARBROATH.

Every Description of Work Carefully and Promptly Attended to by Experienced Workmen, at Moderate Charges.

ESTIMATES GIVEN.

FUNERAL UNDERTAKING

Every Requisite Kept.   Day and Night Attendance.

House: 59 DISHLAND STREET.

Strachan & Farquhar,

Mourning Specialists and Furriers.

DRESS & COSTUME MAKING DEPARTMENT
UNDER NEW MANAGEMENT.

We have secured the services of Miss PETERS, who has had Large Experience in First-Class Establishments.

Mourning Dresses, Costumes, Rest Gowns, and Maternity Gowns

A Special Feature, at Very Moderate Prices.

FRENCH & ENGLISH MILLINERY

Always in Stock, and as we receive a Delivery of New Models from London every Month we are always Up-to-Date in the Latest Fashions.

Furs Altered, Cleaned, and Made Up into New Styles

AT

STRACHAN & FARQUHAR'S,
177 and 179 High Street.

ANDREW FIFE,

Builder and Contractor,

ARBROATH.

Yard, - - Reform Street
House, - - 29 Lindsay Street

All kinds of Jobbing Work Carefully Done.
Estimates Given.
Orders for Town and Country Promptly
Attended to.

D. Y. WALKER, Butcher

Corner of Millgate Loan and West Grimsby,
ARBROATH.

Prime Beef, Mutton, Pork, &c.   Every Joint we Sell is
Very Tasty and Appetising.   Try them.

Our Sausages at **9d** per Lb. are Delicious and Far-Famed.
Won many Golden Opinions.

Roast Beef and Braised Beef.   Rinded Fat, **3** Lbs. for **1/2**.
Poultry and Fresh Country Eggs.

Established 1859

JAMES SIMPSON,

Successor to ALEX. SCOTT,

Joiner, House Carpenter,
Building Contractor,

ST MARY STREET, ARBROATH.

UNDERTAKING.

This Department Receives Careful Attention.

House Address: SALISBURY PLACE.

High-Class Workmanship.

Mill and Factory Furnishings.

Jobbing Promptly Attended to.

Telephone No. 152

Calder Brothers

Builders and Monumental Masons,

84 KEPTIE STREET, ARBROATH.

Monuments and Headstones in Granite, Marble, and Freestone.

Memorial Brasses, Tablets, &c.

Tomb Railings in Wrought or Cast-Iron.

Designs and Prices sent on Application.
Inscriptions Cut in Town or Country.

Jobbing of every Description.   All Orders Promptly Attended to.
Estimates Given for all Kinds of Work.

Telephone 42.   D. R. CALDER, Licensed Valuator.

Albert Buick,

Waste and China Merchant,

11 NORTH GRIMSBY, ARBROATH.

All Sorts of Old Brass, Copper, Metal, Ropes, Sails, Rags, &c., Bought.—Highest Prices Given.

On Receipt of Post Card we will call and Quote Terms.

TELEPHONE No. 82

JAMES JACK,

Pharmaceutical Chemist,

Manufacturer of Aerated Mineral Waters,

HIGH STREET, ARBROATH,

Invites the attention of the Public to his

Aerated Mineral Waters

In the Production of which only the Purest and Best Materials are Employed.

The Various Beverages are of the Highest Quality, and are Supplied at Moderate Prices.

All Water Used is Carefully Filtered and Guaranteed Perfectly Pure.

To be had of all Licensed Dealers & Grocers.

ORDERS LEFT AT

102 HIGH STREET,

PROMPTLY ATTENDED TO.

GEORGE REID, F.S.A.A.,

Incorporated Accountant and Insurance Agent,

ROYAL BANK, ARBROATH.

BUSINESS:

Life Assurance. Fire Assurance. Annuities.

Personal Accident, Driving Accidents, Burglary, Workmen's Compensation (including Shop Assistants and Domestic Servants), Sickness, Fidelity Guarantee, Loss of Profits, Motor Car, Motor Cycle, Live Stock, Anthrax, &c.

COMPANIES:

NORTHERN ASSURANCE.   LIFE ASSOCIATION.
LONDON AND LANCASHIRE FIRE.
SCOTTISH TEMPERANCE.   YORKSHIRE ASSURANCE.
LONDON, LIVERPOOL, AND GLOBE.
HORSE, CARRIAGE, AND GENERAL.
VULCAN BOILER AND GENERAL.
GENERAL ACCIDENT.
CAR AND GENERAL CORPORATION.
THE EMPLOYERS' LIABILITY ASSURANCE CORPORATION.
NORWICH UNION FIRE INSURANCE SOCIETY, LTD.

And other Standard Companies.

Proposals Adjusted and Arranged under Most Favourable Terms on Application to

George Reid, Royal Bank, Arbroath.

THE
NORTHERN ASSURANCE COMPANY
LIMITED.
ESTABLISHED 1836.
Accumulated Funds, - £8,253,000

FIRE.
Burglary.
Fidelity Guarantee.
Plate Glass.
Third Party.
Drivers' Risks.
Property Owners' Indemnity.
Lift Accidents.
Transit Risks.

LIFE.
Annuities.
Personal Accident.
Sickness and Accident.
Workmen's Compensation
Domestic Servants.
Motor Cars.
Private Motor Cycles.
Live Stock.

Combined "Household" Insurances:
FIRE. BURGLARY. ACCIDENTS TO SERVANTS.

District Offices: Northern Assurance Buildings,
110 COMMERCIAL STREET, DUNDEE.

Directors at Dundee:

JAS. W. BARTY, Esq., LL.D. | C. C. DUNCAN, Esq.
J. ERNEST COX, Esq. | JOHN M. HENDRY, Esq.

Secretary—WILLIAM PRINGLE.

☞ Prospectuses and Proposal Forms may be had on Application from any of the Company's Agents.

Queen's Table Strawberry Jam

Fit for the Queen's Table

The Most Popular Preserve in Scotland.

☞ Sale Increased Threefold.

EVERY JAR IS LABELLED "QUEEN'S TABLE."

One of the Commanders of His Majesty's Navy Says:—
"I have never seen finer Jam than this in any part of the world."

"Marguerite" in the Evening Telegraph says:—
"Equal to the Finest Preserve which the most careful Housewife could turn out."

"Marie" in the Courier says:—
"This Jam shows the Art of Fruit-Preserving in Perfection."

MANUFACTURED ONLY BY

DUNDEE AND ARBROATH
Preserve Manufacturing Coy., Ltd.,
ARBROATH.

To be had from all Provision Dealers.

YEAR BOOK ADVERTISEMENTS.

FURNITURE MANUFACTURERS, UPHOLSTERERS, FUNERAL UNDERTAKERS.

TELEPHONE 106

J. P. Grewar & Son,

MAKERS OF

Hair, Wool, Fibre and Spring Mattresses,

Venetian, Duchesse, Linen and **other Blinds.**

Only First Class Materials and Workmanship Employed.

ESTIMATES GIVEN.

Corner Gravesend & Panmure Street
ARBROATH.

CARPET AND LINOLEUM FACTORS, FURNITURE REMOVERS AND STORERS.

YEAR BOOK ADVERTISEMENTS.

Mrs J. H. BROWN
Family Grocer, Tea, Wine & Spirit Merchant,
BROTHOCK BRIDGE, ARBROATH.
Agent for "Big Tree" Brand Californian Wines.

TEAS—Best Selection—1s 4d to 3s perLb.   WINES and SPIRITS.
MALT LIQUORS.   GROCERIES & PROVISIONS always Fresh.

Arbroath Gas Corporation.

GAS COKE.

FIRST-CLASS FUEL FOR BAKERS' OVENS.
INDISPENSABLE FOR "KEITH'S" FURNACES.
ECONOMICAL FOR HOUSEHOLD PURPOSES.
SPECIALLY USEFUL FOR GREENHOUSES.
50 PER CENT. CHEAPER THAN COAL.

Single Bags Delivered at **6d** Each.

Orders by Post Card to ARBROATH GAS WORKS will be promptly attended to.

When in MONTROSE Visit
THE PAVILION, Traill Drive
(OPEN APRIL TO OCTOBER)
GEO. CARNEGIE, Lessee.

TEAS.   ICES.   CONFECTIONS.
Motor, Driving, and Picnic Parties Catered for.

Also, 3 JOHN STREET, MONTROSE.

J. R. MACKENZIE'S

London Mantle House,

Where You will Find the Newest and Best.

LADIES' TAILORING

In Costumes, Coats, and Skirts to Order.

EXCLUSIVE STYLES.

BEAUTIFULLY TAILORED AND PERFECT FITTING.

THE READY-TO-WEAR DEPARTMENT

Of our Business has always on hand a Large Choice of

COSTUMES, COATS, WATERPROOF GARMENTS, SKIRTS, BLOUSES, &c.,

In Black and all the Fashionable Shades and Materials, Thoroughly Well Made and Perfect Fitting.

Smart Millinery and Dressmaking.

J. R. MACKENZIE'S

Ladies' Outfitting Establishment,

145 HIGH STREET, Arbroath,

And DUNDEE STREET, CARNOUSTIE.

THE CENTRAL
Coffee and Dining Rooms

19 MILLGATE, ARBROATH.

Breakfasts and Dinners.   Teas and Suppers.
Charges Strictly Moderate.   *Best Attention Given.*

Soirees, Picnics, and Marriage Parties Supplied.

HALL AND OTHER ROOMS TO LET FOR MEETINGS.

E. MANN, Proprietrix.

DAVID PIRIE
Watchmaker & Optician.

Presentation Goods — Tea Spoons, Jelly Spoons, Butter Knives, Knives and Forks—All in Neat Cases.

All kinds of Watches, Clocks, and Jewellery *PERSONALLY* Cleaned and Repaired. Spectacles and Eyeglasses to Suit all Sights. WEDDING, KEEPER, and ENGAGEMENT RINGS. Large Selection of Gold and Silver Brooches, Scarf Pins, Seals, &c. Second-Hand Watches taken in Exchange.

262 HIGH STREET, ARBROATH.

E. & J. MACLURE,
Arbroath Dye Works,
68 HELEN STREET, ARBROATH.

Thos. Muir, Son & Patton
LIMITED

Coal Merchants, Colliery Agents, Steamship Owners

TELEPHONE No. 4

Carting Contractors, Lime and Cement Merchants

BRANCHES:
Fairmuir
Lochee
Stirling
Bridge of Allan
Causewayhead
Dunblane
Crieff
Perth
Broughty Ferry
Carnoustie
Arbroath
Inverkeilor
Forfar
Justinhaugh
Montrose
Brechin
Edzell
Cupar-Fife
Wormit
East Newport
Monifieth
Nairn
Guthrie
Downfield

Are prepared to Supply from their Depots:

Best English Household Coal
Best Scotch Household Coal
English and Scotch Small Coals
Caking, Treble, and Wishaw Washed Nuts
Steam Chew Coal.   English and Scotch Cokes
Round Char, Anthracite or Blind Coal for Millers,
Bakers' Ovens, Greenhouses, and Heating Apparatus
CARBONITE—The New Fuel for Parlour Fires
FIREWOOD—Chopped and in Blocks

Special Quotations for Quantities and Waggon Loads at Railway Stations and Sidings.
Orders Booked and Prices Arranged at all their Branches and Depots.

TERM REMOVALS & GENERAL CARTING by Special Arrangement
Agents for Messrs JAS. STEWART & SON, Anniston Brick and Tile Works.

DISTRICT DEPOTS:
39 Helen Street & 69 West Grimsby, Arbroath
And at Railway Stations, Carnoustie and Inverkeilor.
REGISTERED OFFICE, - - 26 YEAMAN SHORE, DUNDEE.
Arbroath Agent : R. DAVIDSON.   House : Gordon Villas, West Newgate

CHARLES SKEA,

Salt and Whiting Merchant,

DICKFIELD STREET, ARBROATH.

STORES, - - -	DICKFIELD STREET
HOUSE ADDRESS, - -	19 HANNAH STREET

'PHONE No. 10

GRANT & LAING,

Family Bread, Biscuit and Pastry Bakers,

Have a Varied Selection of Plain and Fancy Tea Bread Daily.

CAKES OF EVERY DESCRIPTION.

Pies & Bridies.   Tea Biscuits & Oatcakes.

FINEST SHORTBREAD A SPECIALITY.
SENT TO ALL PARTS OF THE WORLD.

BROTHOCK BRIDGE, Arbroath.

J. S. CRUICKSHANK,

25 HAMILTON GREEN, ARBROATH,

HAS always in Stock LADIES' and CHILDREN'S UNDERCLOTHING, BABY FROCKS and GIRLS' SCHOOL FROCKS—*All Own Make*.

SERVANTS' CAPS, APRONS, CUFFS & COLLARS, WRAPPERS, and AFTERNOON DRESSES in Stock or Made to Order; also, Good Variety in PRINT OVERALLS, PINAFORES, and WORKING BLOUSES—*Good Washing Material.*

FANCY DRAPERY, HOSIERY, NECKWEAR, FANCY PINS, HAIR PADS and NETS, COMBS and PINS, &c.

BOYS' CAPS, KNICKERS, SHIRTS, &c., also in Stock.

ESTABLISHED OVER FIFTY YEARS.

James Soutar, Limited

(SIGN OF THE EAGLE),

104 High Street  108 High Street

ARBROATH   ARBROATH

Our Principal Departments

Are Household Drapery, Blouses and Underclothing, Dress and Costume Making, Millinery, Umbrellas and Gloves, Men's Outfitting and Shirtmaking.

We are Sole Agents in Arbroath

For The Jaeger Co.; Aertex Cellular Co.; J. & J. Cash, Ltd.; Viyella; Lincoln, Bennett & Co.; and many other First-Class Firms.

Gentlemen's Department:	Ladies' Department:
104 High Street	**108 High Street**
Telephone 73	Telephone 73

JAMES R. THOMPSON,

Carver, Gilder, Picture Frame Maker,
and Mount Cutter.

ENGRAVINGS CLEANED.

225 High Street, Arbroath.

ARCHIBALD DONALD, Sen., & SON
PLASTERERS.

Plain and Ornamental Plastering.

CEMENT WORK DONE.
TILE LAYING, MOSAIC.
LIME WATER SUPPLIED.

Orders in Town and Country
Carefully and Promptly
attended to.

ESTIMATES GIVEN.

House Address, Kelly Cottage.

EAST MARY STREET, ARBROATH.

YEAR BOOK ADVERTISEMENTS.

D. R. MACDONALD,
HATTER AND HOSIER,
TARTAN SPECIALIST.

FIT O' THE PORT,
AND

23 COMMERCE STREET, Arbroath.

FUNERAL UNDERTAKING.

W. A. LYALL

Every Requisite Supplied

Charges Strictly Moderate

Memorial Wreaths and Globes

4 DISHLAND STREET, Arbroath

Attendance at all Hours.   Night Address—8½ Dishland St.

All Orders Personally Attended to

Cabinetmaking, Upholstering, & General Jobbing

Under Careful, Personal Attention

UP-TO-DATE TAILORING.

Nothing adds more to a Man's Appearance that Well-Tailored Clothing. Come here for the BEST STYLE, FIT, and FINISH in all Branches of Modern Tailoring.

Ladies' Coats, Jackets, and Costumes Made to Order.   Perfect Fitting.

GEORGE DUTHIE,

Ladies' and Gent's Tailor, 45 Hill Street, Arbroath

Established 1809.

North British
AND
MERCANTILE
INSURANCE COMPANY,

In which are vested the Shares of the Railway Passengers Assurance Coy. and the Ocean Marine Insurance Coy. Ltd.

FIRE—LIFE.
ACCIDENTS OF ALL KINDS.

Personal Accidents.	Motor Car.	Annuity.
Accidents and Illness.	Lifts.	Marine.
Railway Accidents.	Burglary.	Transit of Securities.
Employer's Liability.	Fidelity Guarantee.	Loss of Profits.
Public Liability.	Plate Glass.	Live Stock.

Total Funds, - £23,600,000
Revenue 1913, - £5,630,000
Claims Paid, - £73,000,000

Prospectus on Application.

Chief Offices { EDINBURGH, ... 64 PRINCES STREET
LONDON, ... 61 THREADNEEDLE STREET, E.C.
DUNDEE BRANCH, ... **13 PANMURE STREET.**

AGENTS IN ARBROATH:

NORMAN M'BAIN, Solicitor. R. C. KINLOCH, Bank of Scotland.
REID, LORIMER, & MOON, Solicitors. W. J. ROLLO, Commercial Bank.
D. D. SANDEMAN, Jun., Solicitor. W. E. CRICHTON, C.A.

CHARLES GRAY,

Sale and Cover Maker,

22 NORTH GRIMSBY, ARBROATH.

TENTS and MARQUEES Made to Order.   ROPES, TWINES, &c.,
of all kinds.   SHOP SUNSHADES
Horse, Stack, Engine, Sail, or other Covers to Order.
'Phone 2y4.   *Estimates Given for all Kinds of Canvas Work.*

David J. Scott

GLASS MERCHANT & GLAZIER.

Dealer in Sheet, Polished Plate, Silvered Plate, Rough Plate, Figured Rolled, Cathedral Rolled, Muffled, Rippled, Opal, Muranese.

Memorial Windows, Church Windows, Domestic Windows, Glass Blinds, Glass Embossing, Glass Bevelling, Glass Brilliant Cut, Glass Bending.

Greenhouse and Roof Painting Done by Experienced Workmen.

Every Description of Plain and Ornamental Lead Glazing.
Special Designs and Estimates Submitted on Application.

BROTHOCK BRIDGE, ARBROATH.
And BANK STREET, DUNDEE.
Telephone 107.

PETER R. GOWANS

Stationer, Newsagent, and Tobacconist,

67 MARKETGATE, ARBROATH.

Newspapers and Periodicals Promptly Delivered.   Fancy Goods of Every Description.
All the most Famed Brands of CIGARETTES in Stock.

All kinds of Trout and Sea Fishing Tackle

Telephone No. 77.

James Robertson & Son

JOINERS, CONTRACTORS, UNDERTAKERS, AND LICENSED VALUATORS.

By the application of the most Up-to-Date Methods and Machinery, and the Careful Personal Supervision of all Orders, they are prepared to Execute all Work entrusted to them in the most Efficient and Economical Manner.

Special Attention given to

Church Furnishings, Office Fittings & Furniture, Shop Fittings, Show Cases, &c.

Jobbing Work Carefully and Promptly Attended to.

ESTIMATES GIVEN.

JOINERY WORKS,
MILLGATE, ARBROATH.

136　　　YEAR BOOK ADVERTISEMENTS.

Telephone No. 156

Ramsay & Gordon,

Builders and Contractors,

Yard,	- - -	FERGUS SQUARE
House,	- - -	51 ROSSIE STREET

ARBROATH.

Estimates Given for all kinds of Mason Work.

Jobbing of every Description Promptly Attended to.

SIGHT-TESTING

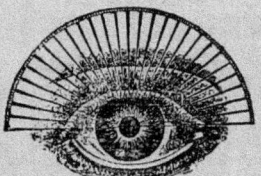 ### SPECTACLES
AND
EYE-GLASSES
No Charge for Testing.

HOWAT DUNCAN, M. Ph. S., D.B.O.A.

(Qualified Optician by Examination, London)

209 HIGH STREET, ARBROATH.

The 'Arbroath Herald' Sporting Page

Appeals to all "Red Lichties" at Home and Abroad.

Full and Brightly-Written Reports of all Games.　　Price One Half-Penny.

138　　　YEAR BOOK ADVERTISEMENTS.

PRACTISE ECONOMY　　　*Telephone No. 94*

And Buy your Butcher Meat at

JOHN LAMB'S

See Windows for Choice Selection.

A Trial Order Respectfully Solicited.

We are Supplying the FINEST BUTCHER MEAT at Prices to Suit Everybody.

Personal Attention, Efficient Service, and Prompt Delivery Guaranteed to all Orders.

HAMS.
Our Far-Famed Mild-Cured Ham, Specially Cured by our own process, makes a Delightful Breakfast.

SAUSAGES.
We make Sausages a Specialty. Finely Seasoned, and Guaranteed to give Satisfaction.

COOKED SPICED BEEF.
A Delightful Cold Meat for Breakfast, Dinner or Supper.

JOHN LAMB, FAMILY BUTCHER,
78 HIGH STREET, ARBROATH.

A. FERGUSON,

General Draper and Fancy Goods Warehouseman,

50 KEPTIE STREET & Corner of GOWAN STREET

ARBROATH.

AGENT FOR FAUDEL'S SEWING MACHINES.

Misses J. & C. GRANT,

BABY LINEN WAREHOUSE,

33 WEST PORT, ARBROATH.

Underclothing and Infant Millinery.

Infants' Robes, Pelisses, Millinery, Frocks, Pinafores, and every Requisite, for Infant Wear. SPECIAL LINES in Plain and Fancy Blouses, Belts, Neckwear, Underclothing, Hosiery, Corsets, Gloves, and Fancy Drapery. Leather Bags, Purses, Hand-Mirrors, Hair Brushes, &c. Servants' Caps and Aprons.

Agents for Pullars' Dye Works, Perth.   REGISTRY for SERVANTS.

The Baby Linen Warehouse,
33 WEST PORT, ARBROATH.

JAMES STEVENSON,

Grocer and Spirit Merchant,

53 LADYLOAN, ARBROATH.

LIQUORS of the Best Quality kept in Stock.

Norwich Union Fire Office

Founded 1797

With which is incorporated the *Norwich & London Accident Insurance Association.*

Head Offices: Norwich & London.

FIRE. ACCIDENT. MARINE.

Sickness. Employer's Liability. Third Party. Fidelity.
Burglary. Plate Glass. Property Owners. Hailstorm.
Motor. Loss of Profits following Fire. Live Stock.

PROMPT & LIBERAL SETTLEMENTS.

London Head Office (Temporary Premises): 126, Chancery Lane, W.C.

BRANCHES: 71 & 72, King William St., E.C.; 114, Cannon St., E.C.; Piccadilly (c/o St. James' St.), W.; and 26, Charles St., St. James', S.W.; 38, Cornhill, E.C. (Marine).

BRANCHES AND AGENCIES THROUGHOUT THE WORLD.

DUNDEE BRANCH:
Courier Building, 20 Meadowside.

J. R. WILSON, F.C.I.I., District Manager.

TELEPHONE, No. 172

AGENTS:

W. & J. MACKINTOSH, Solicitors, 107 High Street, Arbroath
A D. & A. C. ANDERSON, Solicitors, 21 Market Place, Arbroath
NEILL & GIBB, Solicitors, 93 High Street, Arbroath
C. M. DORWARD, Tea Merchant 67 Guthrie Port, Arbroath
JAMES WALLACE, Merchant, Panmure Street, Arbroath
JOHN STEWART, Letham Mill, near Arbroath

Established Over 40 Years.

ROBERT BROWN,

FAMILY GROCER,

Tea, Wine, and Spirit Merchant,

1 KEPTIE STREET,

ARBROATH.

FIRST-CLASS VALUE IN EVERY DEPARTMENT.

All Goods Guaranteed of Best Quality.

Arbroath Friendly Coal Society

LIMITED,

Coal Merchants and Colliery Agents.

Registered Office and Depot: **29 LADYLOAN, Arbroath.**

EDWARD SPINK, Manager.

Membership, 2530.   **Share Capital, £2381**

This SOCIETY has always in Stock, and is prepared to supply, all kinds of ENGLISH and SCOTCH HOUSEHOLD COALS and TREBLE NUTS of Best Qualities; also, PATENT FUEL BRIQUETTES.

FIREWOOD—Superior Firewood Cut into Short Lengths, 2s 2d per Cwt.

Orders sent by Post, or Left at Office, receive Prompt Attention.

Members Enrolled at any time.   Particulars on Application at Office.

Agents for the Co-Operative Insurance Society Ltd.

Alexander Reid,

Builder and Sculptor,

17 LINDSAY STREET,

ARBROATH.

Gravestones
AND
Monuments

Executed in Marble, Granite, and Freestone.

Designs Submitted for Approval.

Artistic Marble
AND
Granite Work

Old Stones Cleaned, Dressed, and Re-Lettered.

Additions Made to Present Stones.

Every Description of Pavement, Brick, and Stone Work.

Monumental Work.

Having a Thoroughly Experienced Sculptor, Special Attention is given to Every Description of Monumental Work.

Ladies' and Gent's Tailors.

ALL GARMENTS MADE BY

D. Thornton & Son

HAVE JUST THAT ENVIED DISTINCTION WHICH PUTS THEM IN THE FOREFRONT

261 High Street, Arbroath.

To Shopkeepers and Others.

The Arbroath Plate Glass

MUTUAL INSURANCE ASSOCIATION

Is the CHEAPEST and MOST CONVENIENT Medium for the

INSURANCE OF SHOP WINDOWS,

SCREENS, SHOW-CASES, MIRRORS, &c.

Low Rates.   Frequent Bonus Years

Premiums Quoted and other Information given on application to

WM. H. ALEXANDER, Solicitor, 62 High Street,
Secretary and Treasurer.

YEAR BOOK ADVERTISEMENTS.

ESTABLISHED 1824.

Scottish Union & National

INSURANCE COMPANY.

Assets, - - *Over £10,250,000*

Head Office: 35 ST ANDREW SQUARE, EDINBURGH.

Fire, Lightning and Explosion (including Loss of Profits.)
Life and Endowments.
Annuities and Pensions.   Accidents and Illnesses.
Leasehold and Capital Redemptions.
Employers' Liabilities.
Burglary and Theft.   Fidelity.   Transit of Securities.
Property Owners' Liabilities.
Third Party Liabilities.
Glass Breakage.   Motor Car Risks.
Horse Driving Accidents.   Marine.

All these Insurances Effected on the most Favourable Terms.

Please apply for a Copy of the Company's Prospectus containing Particulars of the Latest Schemes.

AGENTS IN ARBROATH:

W. & W. H. ALEXANDER, Solicitors, 62 High Street
J. & W. MACDONALD, Solicitors, High Street
A. T. MORRISON, Commercial Bank
NEILL & GIBB, Solicitors, 93 High Street
WM. SOUTAR, British Linen Bank

District Office: 41 ALBERT SQUARE, Dundee.

JAS. W. MUIR, Resident Secretary.

Telephone No. 46.   Telegraphic Address—"UNITATE," Dundee.

J. B. MARTIN,

Tobacconist, Stationer, and Newsagent,

46 KEPTIE STREET, ARBROATH,

Opposite the Railway Station.

Proof Against Vermin & Dry Rot

IS YOUR HOUSE DAMP?

It can be made PERFECTLY DRY and Quite Impervious to MOISTURE by the use of

ASPHALTE — The Initial Cost is Trifling, and the Additional Comfort and Health Derived is Evident.

ESTIMATES FREE BY POST, WIRE, OR TELEPHONE.

Prompt Attention to Orders.

W. BRIGGS & SONS, LTD., DUNDEE.

Wires—"Cement," Dundee.   Telephone Nos. 1767-1768.

MRS D. GALL,

Family Grocer, Tea, Wine and Spirit Merchant,

1 CULLODEN ROAD, ARBROATH.

Groceries, Spirits, and Malt Liquors of Finest Quality.

R. ANDERSON

(Successor to Robert Shepherd),

FAMILY GROCER,

Tea, Wine, and Spirit Merchant,

43 EAST ABBEY STREET,

ARBROATH.

GROCERIES AND PROVISIONS.

SCOTCH AND IRISH WHISKIES.
Purest and Fully Matured.
BRANDIES, WINES, AND CORDIALS.
ALES and STOUTS always in Prime Condition.

GEORGE KEITH

(Successor to JOHN KEITH),

SAIL, COVER, AND TENT MAKER,

5 EAST GRIMSBY, Arbroath.

House—7 ANN STREET.   Telephone 2y3.

VAN, ENGINE, SAIL, and other COVERS. SHOP SUNSHADES a Specialty. TENTS and MARQUEES Made to Order.

Estimates Given for all Kinds of Canvas Work.

M. MATTHEW & SON

THE LEADING
Ladies' & Gent's Tailors
AND
High-Class Dressmakers.

Marriage and Mourning Orders
IN ANY NUMBER
AT SHORT NOTICE.

Stylish & Charming Outfits.

EFFICIENT CUTTERS.

PERFECT FITTING.

The Latest London and Continental Styles.

226 HIGH STREET, ARBROATH.

A. G. PETRIE,
BLACKSMITH,
GRAVESEND, ARBROATH.

BASSINETTE and MAIL CART TYRES SUPPLIED.
WEIGHING MACHINES ADJUSTED.
ORNAMENTAL RAILINGS and GATES SUPPLIED.

TELEPHONE 101

T. R. GRANT,
Registered Plumber, Gasfitter and Electrician,
BROTHOCK BRIDGE, ARBROATH.

All Kinds of Garden and Suction Hose, Hot Water and Sanitary Appliances Supplied or Repaired.

Electric Light, Bells, and Telephones Fitted by Competent Electricians.

AGENT FOR BRAY'S INCANDESCENT BURNERS.
Large Selection of BURNERS, GLOBES, MANTLES, &c.
Full Particulars, Price-Lists, Instructions, &c., may be had on Application.

Telephone No. 150.

CHRISTIE & ANDERSON,
Builders and Contractors,

Yard: EAST MARY STREET, Arbroath.   House: 28 KYD STREET

ESTIMATES GIVEN for all kinds of MASON WORK.
JOBBING OF EVERY DESCRIPTION PROMPTLY ATTENDED TO

The British Law

FIRE INSURANCE COMPANY, LIMITED.

Head Office, - 5 Lothbury, London, E.C.

DAVID M. LINLEY, General Manager.

Subscribed Capital,	£1,050,000
Paid Up Capital,	150,000
Reserves,	273,000

= FIRE. =

Fidelity Guarantee.
Workmen's Compensation.
Employers' Liability.
Personal Accident & Sickness.
Burglary.
Third Party.
Motor Car.
Lift, Crane, and Hoist.
Boiler and Engine.
Property Owners' Indemnity.
Loss of Profits due to Fire.
Glass Breakage.
Live Stock.

Dundee Board
Chairman—JOHN OGILVIE, Esq. (Messrs J. & J. Ogilvie, Solicitors), Dundee.
JAS. A. GRAHAM, Esq. (Messrs J. A. & T. Graham, Solicitors), Dundee.
H. VICTOR NEILL, Esq. (Messrs Neill & Gibb, Solicitors), Arbroath.

Edinburgh Board
Chairman—ROBERT STRATHERN, Esq., W.S. (Messrs Strathern & Blair, W.S.), Edinburgh.

North of Scotland Board
Chairman—J. P. ROBERTSON WHITE, Esq., Advocate in Aberdeen (Messrs Hunter & Gordon, Advocates in Aberdeen), Aberdeen.

Branch Offices, { 34 QUEEN STREET, EDINBURGH.
{ 80 UNION STREET, ABERDEEN.

DISTRICT SECRETARY—JAS. H. M'ROBERT, A.C.I.I.

AGENTS IN ARBROATH:
NEILL & GIBB, Solicitors, 93 High St.

YEAR BOOK ADVERTISEMENTS.

DAVID KYD,

Dealer in Antique Curiosities and Furniture,

29 GRAVESEND, ARBROATH.

Large Variety of New, Second-Hand and Antique Furniture in Stock – Cheap. All kinds of Second Hand Furniture (Modern and Antique) Bought, Sold, and Exchanged. *Highest Prices. Enquiries Solicited.*

Established 1856.

DAVID COOK & SONS,

Registered Plumbers, Tinsmiths, Gasfitters, &c.

ELECTRIC and MECHANICAL BELLS; MALLEABLE IRON, TIN, LEAD, BRASS and COPPER in Sheets and Tubes always in Stock. Hot Water and Sanitary Appliances Supplied or Improved.

Estimates Given for all Kinds of Work.

CARRIAGE LAMPS.

LAMP GLASSES (Bevelled or Plain) Supplied & Repaired. SOCKETS, SPRINGS, CANDLES, and other Accessories for Carriage Lamps.

219 HIGH STREET, ARBROATH.

Established 1825.

ARCH. C. DONALD

(Son of the late Alex. Donald, Plasterer),

Plasterer, Cement Worker, and Tile Layer,

41 LINDSAY STREET, ARBROATH.

Whitewashing & Limewashing Done. Boilers, Steam Pipes, &c., Covered with Non-Conducting Compositions. Jobbing Work of every description receives Careful and Prompt Attention.

Estimates given on Application.   PURE LIME WATER.

YEAR BOOK ADVERTISEMENTS.

TELEPHONE No. 125

Arbroath Horsehiring Company
LIMITED,
12 DISHLAND STREET, ARBROATH
(OFF KEPTIE STREET.)

All Orders have the Prompt and Personal Attention of
WILLIAM CLARK, Manager.

TAXI-CABS:

The New "NAPIER" Landaulettes for Hire.

Cabs always in Readiness at Stables and Railway Station.

Brakes, Waggonettes, Dog-Carts, Covered Brakes, 'Busses, &c., on Hire.

SUPERIOR AND MOST CONVENIENT ACCOMMODATION — The Stalls Accommodate 100 Horses, and every facility is at hand The Premises are Central, and within a Minute's Walk of Station

SUPERIOR BROUGHAMS and LANDAUS.
To Suit all Classes and for all Occasions.
MEN ON PREMISES FOR NIGHT ATTENDANCE.

168   YEAR BOOK ADVERTISEMENTS.

Telephone 103.

William L. Grant & Son,
PAINTERS AND DECORATORS,
267 HIGH STREET, ARBROATH.

Ceiling and Wall Decorations in English and French Paper-Hangings, Lincrusta-Walton, Anaglypta, &c.

Mrs Geo. Urquhart
(Successor to the late Donald M'Lennan),

Grocer, Wine and Spirit Merchant,
38 BARNGREEN, ARBROATH.

Finest Old Blended Scotch and Irish Whiskies.
GROCERIES always Fresh and of Very Finest Quality.

Orders Carefully Attended to and Delivered to any Part of the Town

M. HOGG,
CONFECTIONER,
63 KEPTIE STREET, ARBROATH.

Chocolates of Superior Quality.   Cakes Fresh Daily.

ARBROATH
Electric Light & Power Co.
LIMITED.

Electric Energy has Many Uses
AND MANY ADVANTAGES.

The ELECTRIC MOTOR is Simple
The ELECTRIC RADIATOR is Convenient
The ELECTRIC COOKER is Cool
The ELECTRIC IRON is Clean
The ELECTRIC FAN is Hygienic
The ELECTRIC LAMP is Artistic
☞ **AND ALL ARE ECONOMICAL.**

For Particulars, Apply to

The Electricity Works,
SOUTH GRIMSBY, ARBROATH.
Telephone No. 136.

172   YEAR BOOK ADVERTISEMENTS.

D. YOUNG & SON,

Cartwrights & Joiners,

16 SOUTH GRIMSBY

ARBROATH.

Lorries, Vans, &c., Built to Order.
Jobbing Promptly Attended to.

HIGH-GRADE WORK.

Stevenson Bros.,

Art Dyers and Dry Cleaners,

THE EMPRESS HYGIENIC LAUNDRY

DUNDEE.

STEVENSON BROS., Proprietors.

Arbroath Office, - - - BROTHOCK BRIDGE.
Carnoustie Agent, Misses E. & M. Gardyne, High Street.

WILLIAM RENNIE,

Family Grocer, Wine & Spirit Merchant,

5 GUTHRIE PORT, Arbroath.

Finest Blends of Old Scotch and Irish Whiskies.
TRY MY FAMOUS RUMS, WINES, &c.
GROCERIES always Fresh.   *Trial Order Solicited.*

The Leading Drapery & Outfitting Establishments.

ALEXANDER HIRD'S,

28 KEPTIE STREET,
AND
258 HIGH STREET.

UNBEATABLE VALUE IN ALL DEPARTMENTS.

DRESS GOODS.	PRINTS.	CALICOS.
FLANNELETTES.	SHIRTINGS.	LININGS.
LINENS.	WINCEYS.	BLOUSES.
GLOVES.	SKIRTS.	HOSIERY.
CORSETS.	LACES.	UMBRELLAS.
NECKWEAR.	BLANKETS.	TABLE CLOTHS.
RUGS.	BEDCOVERS.	BATH TOWELS.
WAXCLOTHS.	TABLE COVERS.	KITCHEN TOWELS.
LACE CURTAINS.	FANCY NAPERY in Excellent Variety.	

BOYS' SUITS.   YOUTH'S SUITS.   MEN'S SUITS.

LAMBS'-WOOL AND CASHMERE UNDERWEAR.

SCARFS, COLLARS, HOSE, &c., &c.

28 KEPTIE ST. and 258 HIGH ST.
ARBROATH.

176   YEAR BOOK ADVERTISEMENTS.

IF YOU ARE IN WANT

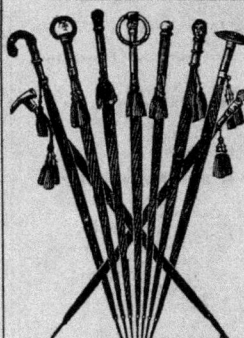

Of Umbrellas, Waterproofs, or Fancy Leather Goods

A Smart, Useful Week-End or Visiting Case

A Gladstone, Brief, Square or Kit Bag

A Saratoga, Cabin, or Overland Trunk

Suit Case or Travelling Rug

In fact, ANYTHING WHATEVER to make you Right for Travel at Home or Abroad, for Pleasure or Business,

Give Us a Chance to Meet Your Need.

We are confident our Value is beyond comparison for Soundly-Made Goods, and our Variety Unequalled.

Joseph Moffat

Umbrella Maker and Leather Goods Dealer,

32 KEPTIE STREET, ARBROATH

(Opposite Railway Station)

Robert Ballingall

Cycle and Motor Manufacturer,

DEPOT: 281 HIGH STREET, ARBROATH.

Works: 118 and 120 EAST HIGH STREET, FORFAR.

Our Specialty is "THE ELITE," Built to Order.

Agent for the GRAMOPHONE COMPANY.   Agent for the ROYAL ENFIELD CYCLES.

YEAR BOOK ADVERTISEMENTS.

The Arbroath Herald.

Every FRIDAY Afternoon

PRICE 1½d

Best and Cheapest Medium for All Classes of Advertisements.

No effort spared to make it the Fullest, Freshest, and most Readable Family Newspaper in the District.

Handy Time and Tide Table.

For Arbroath, Carnoustie, and District.

MONTHLY, 1d,

Contains Railway and Tide Tables, Calendar of Sporting Events, Postal Arrangements, Diary for the Month, Golf Scoring Register, &c.

"This Time Table, in addition to Arrival and Dispatch of all Local Trains, gives Carriers, Markets, Sporting Fixtures, &c., and is very useful to Commercial Men and the Public generally."

☛ Ten Thousand People use "Time & Tide" frequently every Month.

Neat Leatherette Cases to hold the Time and Tide Table, 6d each.

Eastern Forfarshire Directory.

And Arbroath Year Book.

ANNUALLY—2d, 6d, 1s, and 2s.
(Published on 1st January)

Crown 8vo, 250 pp.   40,000 Readers.

"The Completest, Most Interesting, and Popular District Directory in Scotland." —*Dundee Advertiser.*

BRODIE & SALMOND, Proprietors and Publishers.
Telephone 43.   Telegrams—Arbroath Herald.

Mrs R. L. Ross,

Wine and Spirit Merchant,

16 ROBERT STREET,

ARBROATH.

Established 1878.

George D. Fletcher

Italian Warehouseman, Family Grocer,
Wine and Liqueur Merchant,

18 Keptie Street, Arbroath

Only the Highest and Most Genuine Class of Goods procurable are Sold at the above Warehouse.

J. W. Harper's Tea Rooms

2 & 4 Guthrie Port—Opposite Abbey.

Finest Chocolates and Confectionery by Best Makers.
Try HARPER'S Celebrated Arbroath Rock.

ANDERSON & HEWIT,

Merchant Tailors,

128 HIGH STREET, ARBROATH.

A Large and Varied Selection

OF

Serges, Trouserings,

Tweeds, Vicunas,

AND

Overcoatings.

LADIES' COSTUMES
A SPECIALTY.

FIT and FINISH GUARANTEED

A Trial Order Solicited.

ANDERSON & HEWIT.

TEETH. TEETH.

IF your TEETH require attention consult me. I have made the Painless Extraction of Teeth my Special Study. Absolutely Painless Extractions **1s**; Complete Sets from **30s**; Repairs from **2s 6d**; Fillings from **2s 6d** to **£1 1s**.

W. H. M'PHERSON, ALSTON HOUSE, 86 HIGH STREET

(Near Town House), ARBROATH.

Hours—9 a.m. to 9 p.m. Sundays 1 to 3 p.m., 6 to 8 p.m. Also by Appointment.

The Oldest Scottish Office. Established 1805.

CALEDONIAN
Insurance Company.

FIRE.   LIFE.   ANNUITIES.

Personal Accident and all Illness

EMPLOYERS' LIABILITY.   BURGLARY.

Prospectuses Free on Application.

Dundee Office: 35 Albert Square.

Principal Agents in Arbroath:

W. & J. MACKINTOSH, Solicitors.   S. RENNY, Jock's Lodge.
DEWAR & WEBSTER, Solicitors.   W. J. ROLLO, Bank Agent.

THOS. CLARK, MOTOR AND CYCLE AGENT,

274 HIGH STREET (Corner of James Street), ARBROATH.

Agent for Star, Lloyds, Hopper, and other Leading Cycles.

All Accessories Kept in Stock.

Repairs Receive Personal Attention.

YEAR BOOK ADVERTISEMENTS.

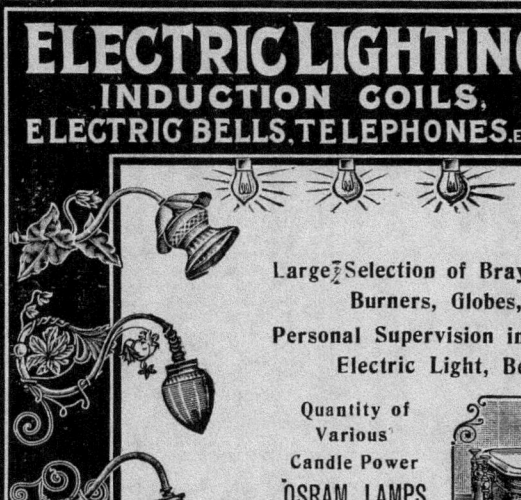

**ELECTRIC LIGHTING
INDUCTION COILS,
ELECTRIC BELLS, TELEPHONES, ETC**

Estimates Given for all kinds of Work.

Full Particulars can be had on Application.

Large Selection of Bray and other Inverted Burners, Globes, Mantles, &c.

Personal Supervision in Fixing Electric Light, Bells, and Telephones.

Quantity of Various Candle Power OSRAM LAMPS Always kept in Stock.

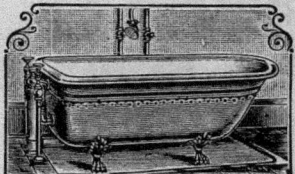

HERRON & COLVILLE,

'Phone No. 148

Sanitary Plumbers, Gasfitters, Electricians.

SHOWROOM: **56 KEPTIE STREET** - WORKSHOP: **56½ KEPTIE STREET**

LOCHNAGAR BAR,
COMMERCE STREET
(Below Sheriff Court-House.)

Wines, Spirits, Beers, and Stouts always in Perfect Condition.

Large and Airy Rooms for Socials, Presentation Parties, &c.

TOM SCOTT, Proprietor.

CROOK & WEBSTER,

(Successors to GEORGE RAYNE)

Registered Plumbers and Gasfitters,
35 GUTHRIE PORT, ARBROATH.

HYDRAULIC RAMS, WINDMILLS, and PUMPS of every Description Erected and Repaired.

Estate Water Supplies
Laid Out on Most Modern Systems.

Flush Closets, Baths, Heating, &c., for Town and Country Houses.

Estimates given.   Charges Moderate.

House Address, 7 Guthrie Port

WHITE'S SEMOLINA.
FOR PUDDINGS, PORRIDGE, &c.
HOME MANUFACTURED.
GUARANTEED THOROUGHLY GENUINE.

From Best Hard American Spring Wheats, which turn out **Semolina Unsurpassed for Quality,** and Superior to that made from any Wheat grown on the Continent of Europe.

OTHER SPECIALTIES:
REFORM MEAL and WHOLEMEAL.

John F. White, Ltd., Dundee Flour Mills.

MORRIS-OXFORD CARS.

Agent for Forfarshire and Kincardineshire.

Popular Model, £173 5s; De Luxe Model, £199 10s; Cabrioles Model, £255

HUMBER, RALEIGH, HILLMAN, MARLBOROUGH and any Make of Light Car.

DAVID ROBBIE

24 BROTHOCK BRIDGE, ARBROATH,

HAS always on hand a Fine Stock of the Best Makes of CYCLES and MOTOR CYCLES, embracing TRIUMPH, SUNBEAM, HUMBERS, and other High-Class Grades, ALL AT LOWEST PRICES.

SECOND-HAND CYCLE CARS Always in Stock.

FOR HIRE.

A Fine Stud of LADIES' and GENT'S MACHINES, by the Hour, Day, or Month, at Moderate Rates.

Full Assortment of Cycle and Motor Accessories.

Repairs by Experienced Workmen.

YEAR BOOK ADVERTISEMENTS.

C. L. BALFOUR
Family Bread and Biscuit Baker.

Shortbread Ornamented any Special Motto.
Dishes Covered on Shortest Notice.   HOT PIES, **1d & 2d.**
Real Forfar Bridies, every Friday and Saturday, 3d each.

Marriage and Supper Parties,
          Picnics and Soirees, Purveyed.

41 BARNGREEN & 41½ GUTHRIE PORT, Arbroath

ALEX. SUTHERLAND,
Some time with the late Mr Wyllie,
Monumental Mason,
8 BAKERS WYND, ARBROATH.
Yard : 1 Barngreen.

LETTERING :
Granite.   Marble.   Freestone.

Orders Promptly Executed at Moderate Charges.

The Job-Printing Department

Is Furnished with a Carefully-Selected Stock of the Best Productions of the Type-Founders' Art. The Machinery is Modern, and Fitted with every appliance for the Execution of Work of the Most Artistic Style.

Here are one or two Opinions upon Printing turned out at the ARBROATH HERALD OFFICE:

The Glasgow Herald says—"The Office of the *Arbroath Herald* may be congratulated on the handsome appearance of their books, which, in all respects, are QUITE EQUAL TO THE BEST WORK OF MOST OF THE LEADING LONDON PUBLISHERS."

The British Printer says—"Printing work of Messrs Brodie & Salmond exhibits a wide range of typograpy, from name cards up to books, all executed with good taste and workmanlike skill."

An H.M Inspector of Schools writes—"The pamphlet is a most excellent bit of letterpress work. I did not think that printing work so excellent in every respect could be done outside large cities."

Dr Moxey, the Distinguished Elocutionist, says—"The programme pleases me exceedingly. The arrangement is quite original in style, and altogether happy. The whole get-up is admirable."

The John o' Groats Journal says—"As pretty a pamphlet from the printers' point of view as we have ever seen."

If you want Printing of any kind Get a Quotation & see Specimens of Work

SENT OUT BY

BRODIE & SALMOND,

Proprietors,

"ARBROATH HERALD," BROTHOCK BRIDGE, ARBROATH.

YEAR BOOK ADVERTISEMENTS.

ESTABLISHED 1856

ANDREW SCOTT

195 HIGH STREET,

ARBROATH.

Old Port Wines a Speciality.

TELEPHONE 11

TELEPHONE No. 114

CARNEGIE SOUTAR,

Family Bread, Biscuit and Pastry Baker and Confectioner,

122 HIGH STREET, ARBROATH,

And at MILLGATE, FRIOCKHEIM.

SHORTBREAD A SPECIALTY

Picnic and Marriage Parties Purveyed for.
Vans Deliver Orders in Surrounding Country Districts.

Orders given in at ARBROATH or FRIOCKHEIM will be Punctually Attended to.

YEAR BOOK ADVERTISEMENTS.

TELEPHONE No. 17

SMITH, HOOD & Co. Ltd.

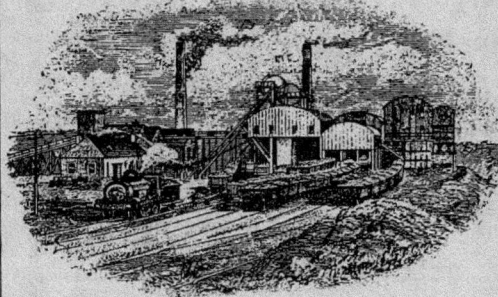

Largest
Coal Merchants
and
Colliery Agents
North
of the Forth.

Ship Brokers.

Registered Office, - - 48 UNION STREET, DUNDEE.

ARBROATH DEPOTS:
Railway Station, Chalmers St., & Letham Grange Station.

Office, - 53 KEPTIE STREET.

BRANCHES:

Bervie—Mr George Towns. *Broughty Ferry*—Mr J. Crawford. *Carnoustie*—Mr F. H Maconachie. *Forfar*—Mr A. Callander. *Inverkeilor* (N.B. Station)—Mr Wm. Robertson. *Montrose*—Mr Alex. Imrie. *Fairmuir*—Mr Peter Stewart. *Maryfield*—Mr J. Gray. *Stonehaven*—Mr R. V. Mitchell. *Brechin*—Mr D. C. Knowles. *Cupar-Fife*—Miss Cairns.

The following descriptions of BEST HOUSEHOLD COAL always in Stock:— Best Wallsend English Coals and Nuts; Stepend's Caking Coal; Dunfermline Splint Household Coal; Slamannan and Wishaw Nuts (for Kitchen Ranges); Anthracite or Blind Coal; Jewel Coal; Patent Fuel Briquettes; Best Coke for Vineries, Bakehouses, &c ; Small Coal for Mills and Factories. *FIREWOOD always kept in Stock.* Special Quotations for Waggon Loads.

For Prices, Terms, &c., apply to
A. P. LOWSON, Arbroath Agent.
House Address, - KEPTIE ANGLE.

200   YEAR BOOK ADVERTISEMENTS.

DAVID MACKAY & CO.,
FUNERAL UNDERTAKERS,
39½ WEST GRIMSBY, ARBROATH.

Every Requisite.   Night Attendance.
Charges Strictly Moderate.

Purity.   Strength.   Excellence.

STATION HOTEL and BAR

38 Keptie St.      **Jas. Malcolm**
ARBROATH.   PROPRIETOR.
(Opposite Railway Station.)   *(Under New Management)*

Whiskies, Wines, Brandies, Beers, Stouts, of Finest
Quality, all the Year Round.
Rooms for Socials, Presentations, Club & Society Meetings.

Private Orders form a feature of our Business, receiving Careful
Attention, and being delivered to any part of Town and District.
Country Customers are specially catered for. Large and
Comfortable Rooms.   Cycle Storage Free.
AIRY BEDROOMS.   Excellent Cuisine.   Moderate Charges

Telephone No. 124.

JOHN RAYNE,
Plumber, Gasfitter, Sanitary Engineer, and
Water Works Contractor,
11-13 WEST ABBEY STREET, Arbroath.

Estimates Given for Fitting up Electric Light Installations.
All kinds of Petrol Gas Installations Fitted up.
Orders from Town or Country attended to Promptly and Carefully.

YEAR BOOK ADVERTISEMENTS.

'Phone 84.   Wire—White Hart.

WHITE HART HOTEL,

163 HIGH STREET, ARBROATH.

This Old-Established Hotel is Unrivalled for its Comfort, Excellent Cuisine, and Moderate Charges, and is in the Most Central Business Part of the Town.

The Commercial and Coffee Rooms, Restaurant and Dining Rooms, are Fitted and Furnished in the Best Style.

THE WHITE HART HALL

Is Very Suitable for BALLS, MARRIAGES, and SUPPER PARTIES, and is Let on Very Moderate Terms.

*A*LEXANDER SMITH, *P*roprietor.

JAMES SHEPHERD

Family Bread and Biscuit Baker and Confectioner,

45 ST MARY STREET, ARBROATH.

Prize Winner at London Exhibition, 1910, and at Edinburgh, 1912, and Macclesfield, 1913, for HOVIS BREAD.

SHORTBREAD, Plain and Ornamented—any Special Motto. All Sorts of Plain and Fancy Tea Bread Daily. Hot Pies, 1d and 2d each. Real Forfar Bridies every Friday and Saturday. Marriage & Supper Parties. Picnics & Soirees Purveyed.

What no Visitor should be Without!

NEW SERIES OF
Illustrated Guide Books
For Arbroath and District.

1—**ABOUT ARBROATH: A CHATTY DESCRIPTION OF A** Walk through the Burgh, with Notes on Historical Events and the Principal Buildings, 28 Illustrations, to which is added "Some Notes on the Physiography of the District," by Dr T. F. Dewar, M.D., B.Sc. Paper Covers, 3d.

2—**GUIDE TO THE CLIFFS, CAVES, AND COAST SCENERY OF** the District between Elliot Links and Lunan Bay, with numerous Photographic Illustrations specially prepared for this Guide Book. The Guide also contains a Short Paper on the Marine Algæ of the District, by James Jack, F.L.S. Paper Covers, 3d.

3—**THE LAND OF THE ANTIQUARY: NOTES OF A TOUR FROM** Hospitalfield to Red Castle and back by way of Inverkeilor and Marywell, with Special Reference to Scenes and Incidents in "The Antiquary." Numerous Illustrations of places mentioned in the tale. Paper Covers, 3d.

4—**GUIDE TO CARNOUSTIE AND ITS ENVIRONS**—The Visitor, in a Series of Short Excursions, is not only made acquainted with the Principal Streets and Bye-Ways of this Popular Seaside Burgh, but is conducted to all the Places of Interest in the Vicinity. The Guide Book is Finely Illustrated with 34 Reproductions of Photographs specially taken for this Publication, and has Two Beautifully Engraved Maps, covering the District between Westhaven and Barry Church. Paper Covers, 3d

In addition to the descriptive matter, each of the Volumes is supplemented with carefully prepared Maps of the District, and a large number of Photographic Reproductions of interesting sights to be visited. They will be found not only entertaining and reliable Guides, but interesting Souvenirs of a District remarkably rich in Historic and Literary Associations.

To be had of all Booksellers, or BRODIE & SALMOND, Publishers.

Britannic Assurance Co.
LIMITED.

Chief Offices, = Broad Street Corner, Birmingham.

ORDINARY BRANCH.

Whole Life Assurances, with and without Profits.
Endowment Assurances, with and without Profits.
House Purchase, in combination with Life Assurance.

INDUSTRIAL BRANCH.

Adult Assurances, Whole Life and Endowment.
Children's Assurances, Whole Life and Endowment.

Over £9,800,000 Paid in Claims.

Particulars of many Attractive Assurances may be obtained at

Local District Office, 211a High St., Arbroath.
F. CAMERON, Superintendent.

Telegraphic Address—"Smart, Jeweller, Arbroath."

DAVID SMART,
Jeweller and Silversmith,
4 WEST PORT, ARBROATH.

A Complete Stock of
Sterling Silver & Electro-Plate
Always on hand.

New and Exclusive Designs in
Gold & Gem-Set Jewellery
To Choose from.

WATCHES OF EVERY GRADE KEPT IN STOCK.

REPAIRS of every description done on the Premises.

☞ Sole Agent for Arcadian Mounted Crest China.

LISTEN! 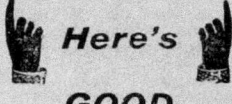 Here's GOOD News		Our Doorway is a Short Cut to Economy
The Popular Stores.		The Popular Stores.

Our Fresh Creamery Butter

Is simply Delicious—Quality Absolutely Perfect—Delightful Flavour Always Fresh, Price **1s 4d** per Lb. Please try it for yourselves.

For Cheese, Butter, Margarine, Teas, Hams, Bacon, Eggs. All Grades—All Prices.

Confectionery Department.

We Stock the Best of Everything in Chocolates, Caramels, Toffees, and Confectionery. You needn't pay more than **3d** per Quarter for the **Best Fresh-Made Chocolates.** Try them, and note the Superior Flavour.

Everything of the Best, at Popular Prices.

Cigarettes.   Tea Room.   Teas Daintily Served

Wiltshire Dairy Stores

29 MARKET PLACE, ARBROATH.

Johnston's GRAND Emporium

CROSS HOUSE, CARNOUSTIE.

The Spot for Household Hardware.
China and Glass Wares of Every Kind.

Special Attention devoted to all your requirements where Boarders are kept.

Dishes of the right sort. Goblets, Saucepans, Frypans, Stewpans that will last and give satisfaction. Odd Dishes, Teacups and Saucers in Half-Dozens. Plates to match all the different kinds. Teapots Galore

DISHES ON HIRE, with or without Cutlery, Spoons, &c.

Lamps, Gas Burners, Mantles, Gas Globes, Tumblers, Wine Glasses in Great Variety

Brushes, Brooms, Mats, Rugs, Tubs, Stools, Screens, Fenders, Trunks, Travelling Baskets, Bags, &c., all at Cut Prices.

TO FARMERS—We Stock Netting (all Sizes), Riddles, Spades, Shovels, Graips, Forks, Hoes, Scythes, Ropes, Twines, Handles, Roofing, Felt, Nails, Hammers, Saws, Files, and other Goods you require. What we do not keep in Stock can be procured in a few hours from Arbroath Warehouse

INSPECTION INVITED.

JAMES JOLLY,
PHOTOGRAPHER,
5 HIGH STREET, CARNOUSTIE.

Portraits, Groups, Wedding Groups.
Children's Photographs a Speciality.
Enlargements.   Picture Framing.   Outdoor Work of all Kinds.

Good Work Promptly Executed.
AMATEURS SUPPLIED WITH MATERIALS

216   YEAR BOOK ADVERTISEMENTS.

JAMES THOMSON,

Family Bread, Biscuit,
AND
Pastry Baker.

Country Orders Delivered by Our Own Vans Free.

GARDYNE STREET,
FRIOCKHEIM.

Established 1859.   *'Phone No. 23, Carnoustie.*

Carnoustie Co-Operative Association Ld.

General Grocers, Bakers; Drapers, Dressmakers, Tailors, and Clothiers; Bedding & Floorcloth Factors; Coal Merchants,

CENTRAL PREMISES—
Corner of DUNDEE STREET & FERRIER STREET

BRANCH AND COAL DEPOT—
BROWN STREET, CARNOUSTIE.

Co-Operators are Invited to Call and Inspect our Stocks. All Goods are of the Best Quality, and our Prices will compare most favourably with any in the District. **Bread Vans Call Daily.**

All Orders entrusted to us shall have our Prompt and Careful Attention. A TRIAL ORDER IS SOLICITED.

YEAR BOOK ADVERTISEMENTS.

TELEPHONE 42
E. W. MATHEWSON
Painter and Decorator.

PICTURE FRAMING Neatly, Expeditiously, and Cheaply Done.

Hand-Stencilled Friezes a Specialty.

Dundee Street, Carnoustie,
AND BROTHOCK BRIDGE, ARBROATH.

TELEPHONE 75
WILLIAM FERRIER
Ladies' & Gent's Tailor & Outfitter,
HIGH STREET, CARNOUSTIE.

Latest Designs and Novelties in Gent's Neckwear.

ANDREW HEGGIE,
Watchmaker, Jeweller & Optician,
THE CROSS, CARNOUSTIE.

Watches, Clocks, Jewellery, and Electro-Plated Goods. Spectacles and Eye-Glasses to Suit all Sights. Repairs Done in all Branches.

Brodie & Salmond, Printers, Arbroath

For Bright, Breezy Notes,
And all the Latest Topics of the Week,
READ THE SPECIAL COLUMN
Carnoustie Day by Day
IN
$\frac{1}{2}$d **The Arbroath Herald** $\frac{1}{2}$d
Every Friday Morning.

YEAR BOOK ADVERTISEMENTS.

Telegrams: Firemaster, Arbroath.

ROWLAND C. FARQUHAR,

Building Contractor,

Undertaker.   House Factor.

Contractor to H.M. Office of Works.

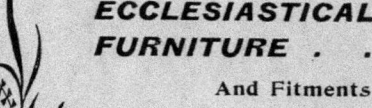

TECTONIC . .
DIPLOMAS , .
IN
General Building, =
Carpentry, Joinery,
Architectural - -
Design, Surveying,
&c.

PORTABLE . .
GREENHOUSES .
Cosy Summer = -
Houses & Shelters.

Quaint and Attractive
Cabinet Joinery.

ECCLESIASTICAL
FURNITURE . .
And Fitments.

JOINERY IN ALL
BEST STYLES .
(Ornamental & Artistic)

Bar, Shop, Office
And other Fittings
Executed.

Shop Fitter.
Show-Case Maker.

Estimates Given for all kinds of Work.

4 and 6 HILL PLACE, ARBROATH.

Established 1860.   Telephone 104.

July

SLEEPING CAR EXPRESSES

LIMITED SLEEPING ACCOMMODATION IS PROVIDED BY TRAINS RUNNING VIA THE "EAST COAST" ROUTE BETWEEN ENGLAND AND SCOTLAND AS UNDER:—

WEEK DAYS

		THE ABERDONIAN	E	THE NIGHT SCOTSMAN	MFO		FSX	FO	FSX THE TYNESIDER	FSO THE TYNESIDER
	a.m	p.m.	p.m.	p.m.	p.m.	p.m.	p.m.	p.m.	p.m.	p.m.
ONDON (K.C.) dep.	1 0	7 0	7 15	10 15	10‡20	10 35	10D45	11D0	11 35	11 45
				a.m.	a.m.	a.m.	a.m.	a.m.	a.m.	a.m.
terborough (N.) "	2 28	...	...		...	...	12D25	12D37	1 15	1 23
rantham "	...	9 8	9 26		12‡33	12 45	1D12	1D24	2 0	2 8
rk "	5 0	10 F56	11 B16		...	2 32	3D24	3D24	4 7	4†15
arlington arr.	5 46	...	...		...	3G20	4A12	4A12	4 55	5† 3
rryhill "	...	...	...		...	...	4 43	4 43	...	...
urham "	...	...	...		...	...	5 1	5 1	5 28	5†36
ewcastle arr.	6 40	a.m.	a.m		3‡44	4N8	5A29	5A29	5A55	6A†3
ewcastle dep.	...	12 F37	12 B57		...	...	...	...		
nmouth arr.	7 32	...	...		...	...	...	...		
rwick "	8 9	...	...		...	5N32	...	...		
rem "	...	...	...		...	C	...	...		
linburgh (Wav.) "	9 27	3 F11	...	6A15	6‡30	7AH1	...	...		
rt William ... "	...	...	10J2	...	...	...	...	...		
ndee (Tay B.) "	...	4 F52	...	8 Z33	...	...	...	...		
broath "	...	5 F24	...	...	...	...	...	...		
ontrose "	...	5KF49	...	...	...	...	...	...		
erdeen "	...	6KF47	...	...	...	...	...	...		

WEEK DAYS

	THE TYNESIDER	FO	FSX	E		MFO		THE NIGHT SCOTSMAN		THE ABERDONIAN	
	p.m	p.m	p.m.	p.m		p.m.	p.m	p.m.		p.m	p.m.
erdeen dep.		...	...	...	...	...	...	...	...	7 10	...
ontrose "		...	...	...	...	...	...	...	...	8 9	...
broath "		...	...	...	...	...	...	...	...	8 34	...
ndee (Tay B.) "		...	...	...	...	...	...	8 E35	...	9 6	...
rt William ... "		...	...	...	...	...	...	...	...		4 L40
linburgh (Wav.) "		...	...	...	...	10‡ 0	1020	10 40	...		...
rem "		...	...	8 27	...	...	...	...	...		...
nbar "		...	...	8 43	...	...	...	...	...		...
rwick "		...	...	9 31	...	...	1142	...	...		...
nmouth "		...	...	1021	...	...	...	...	...		...
orpeth "		...	...	1049	...	a.m.	a.m	...	...		...
wcastle "	1035	...	...	...	...	12‡43	1 7	...	...		...
nderland "	...	1055	10 55	...	...	...	...	...	...		...
est Hartlepool "	...	1126	11 26	...	...	...	...	...	...		...
ockton "	...	1152	11 52	...	...	...	...	...	...		...
rham "	11 0	...	...	...	...	...	...	...	...		...
rlington "	1134	...	...	...	...	...	...	...	...		...
	a.m	a.m	a.m.	a.m				a.m.		a.m	
rk "	1229	1253	1 27	...	...	...	...	...	...	...	...
antham arr.	2 12	2 44	3 36	3 36	...	3‡51	...	4 35	...	...	...
terborough (N.) "	...	...	4 20	4 20	...	...	...	...	...	5 28	5 58
ONDON (K.C.) "	4 35	5 5	6 5	6 5	...	6‡20	6 40	6 55	...	7 15	7 45

Arrival times—Tuesday to Sunday mornings inclusive

A Passengers arriving Darlington (F class only), Newcastle (Centr and Edinburgh (Waverley) in th Sleeping Cars may remain in the until 8 0 a.m.
B On Fridays departs York 11 25 p and on Saturday mornings Newca 1 6 a.m.
C Calls only when required at 6 31 a on Weekdays (6 37 a.m. on Sund to set down from King's Cross
D First class accommodation to Darli ton: Third class to Newcastle
E Except Saturdays
F On Fridays departs York 11 10 p. Newcastle 12 51 a.m. and arri Edinburgh 3 25, Dundee 5 4, Arbro 5 36, Montrose 6 1 and Aberd 6 59 a.m.
FO Fridays only
FSO Fridays and Saturdays only
FSX Fridays and Saturdays excepted
G Sunday mornings only
H On Sundays arrives Edinburgh 7 7 a
J On Saturdays arrives Fort Will 8 59 a.m.
K On Sundays arrives Montrose 5 and Aberdeen 6 53 a.m.
L On Saturdays departs Fort Will 5 15 p.m.
MFO Mondays and Fridays only
N On Sunday mornings arrives N castle 4 13, Berwick 5 37 a.m.
Z Sunday mornings excepted
† On Sundays departs York 4 35 a and arrives Darlington 5 23, Dur 5 56 and Newcastle 6 23 a.m.
‡ Third class accommodation only

SUNDAYS

	THE ABERDONIAN		THE NIGHT SCOTSMAN				THE TYNESIDER
	p.m	p.m	p.m.	p.m.	p.m	p.m.	p.m.
NDON (K.C.) dep.	7 0	7 15	10 15	10‡20	1035	10D45	11 30
		a.m	a.m.	a.m.	a.m	a.m.	a.m.
terborough (N.) "	...	...		...	...	...	1 8
antham "	9 8	9 26		12‡33	1245	12D37	1 53
rk "	1056	1116		...	2 32	2D57	3 50
rlington arr.	...	...		...	...	3A45	4 38
rryhill "	...	...		...	...	4 16	...
rham "	...	...		...	...	4 34	5 11
wcastle arr.	a.m	a.m		3‡44	4 8	5A2	5A38
wcastle dep.	1237	1257		...	...	...	
nmouth arr.	...	...		...	...	...	
rwick "	...	...		...	5 32	...	
em "	...	...		...	C	...	
linburgh (Wav.) "	3 11	...	6A15	6‡30	7A1	...	
rt William "	...	10 2	...	...	...	...	
ndee (Tay B.)... "	4 52	...	8 33	...	...	...	
broath "	5 24	...	...	...	...	...	
ontrose "	5 49	...	...	...	...	...	
erdeen "	6 47	...	...	...	...	...	

SUNDAYS

	THE TYNESIDER					THE NIGHT SCOTSMAN	THE ABERDONIAN
	p.m	p.m	p.m	p.m.	p.m	p.m	p
Aberdeen dep.		...	...	...	...	...	7
Montrose "		...	...	...	...	...	8
Arbroath "		...	...	...	...	...	8
Dundee (Tay B.)... "		...	...	...	...	8 35	9
Fort William "		...	...	...	...	...	
Edinburgh (Wav.) "		...	...	10‡ 0	1020	1040	
Drem "		...	8 27	...	...		
Dunbar "		...	8 43	...	...		
Berwick "		...	9 31	...	1142		
Alnmouth "		...	1021	...	...		
Morpeth "		...	1050	a.m.	a.m		
Newcastle "	1035	...	...	12‡43	1 7		1
Sunderland "	...	1055	...	...	...		
West Hartlepool "	...	1126	...	...	...		
Stockton "	...	1152	...	...	...		
Durham "	11 0	...	...	...	...		
Darlington "	1134	...	...	...	...		
	a.m	a.m	a.m			a.m	
York "	1229	1253	...	...	...	...	
Grantham arr.	2 12	2 44	3 36	3‡51	...	4 35	
Peterborough (N.) "	...	...	4 20	...	...	...	5
LONDON (K.C.) "	4 35	5 5	6 5	6‡20	6 40	6 55	7

Bradshaw's railway sleeping car timetable for July 1951

July 1 1914

Summer weddings always have a rare attraction for Arbroathians, particularly if the participants are well known in the town.

This glorious Wednesday afternoon, Arbroath saw the closest that it is likely to ever come to a society wedding in the United Free Church in the High Street.

Hundreds of people thronged the High Street with "oohs!", "aahs!" and "she's awfa prutty" as the bride and groom emerged from the Church after the service conducted by Reverend Tweedie.

The groom was George Robertson, classical master of Arbroath High School and many of his pupils, now on summer holiday, were there to see him.

He married Emily Hood, the only daughter of Mr and Mrs J Hood, the well-known bookseller of Keptie House, Arbroath.

There were over 100 guests and a reception was then held in the Imperial Hotel with *The Arbroath Herald* giving rich and lavish descriptions of what everyone wore on what was a very bright and happy occasion.

The happy couple were well wined and dined, and then escorted to the railway station to begin their honeymoon and their new life together. Everything seemed fine, the weather was almost perfect.

If anyone had noticed in his newspaper anything about an Archduke of the Austro-Hungarian Empire being shot by a Serbian fanatic a few days ago, he would have simply shrugged his shoulders and said that is that sort of thing that happens in that part of the world but it has nothing to do with us!

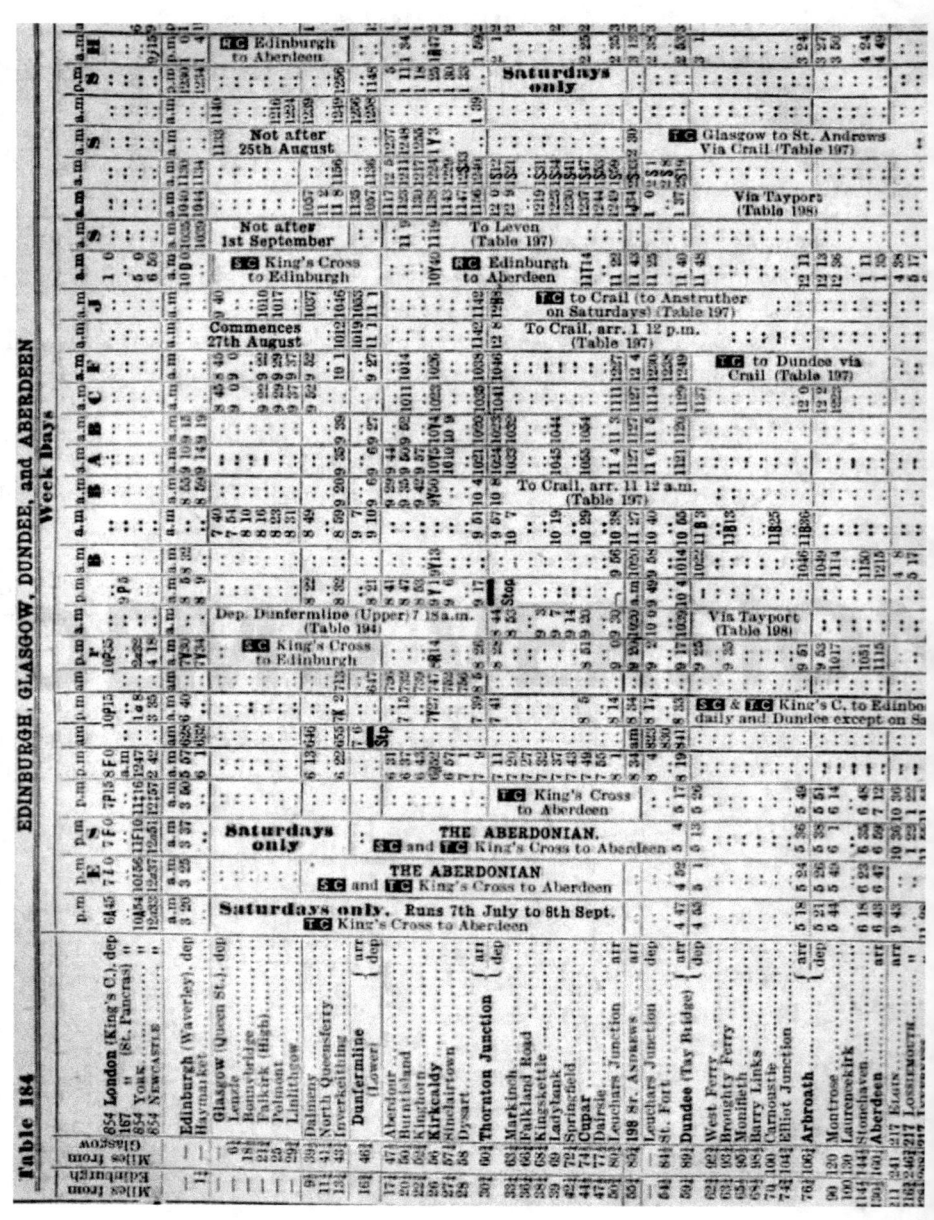

Bradshaw's railway timetable for July 1951

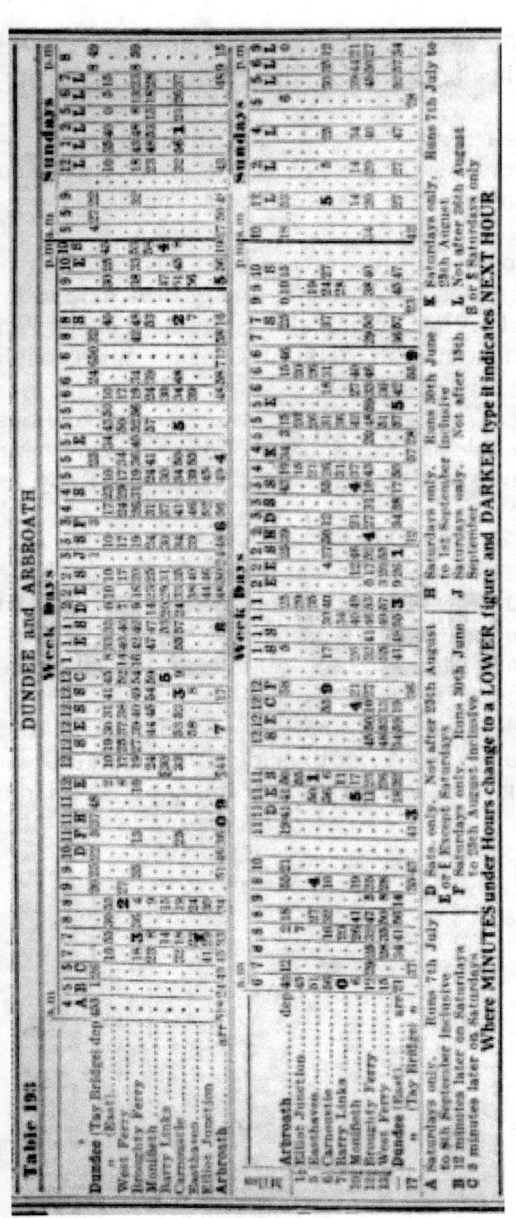

Bradshaw's railway timetable for July 1951

July 2 1924

One of the most striking differences between life before the war in the sporting world and after, has been the growth of tennis in Arbroath, particularly women's tennis.

Tennis is of course one of the few sports that women can participate in – football, cricket, rugby and others were more or less closed doors to women at this time, but tennis, in the shape of the Arbroath Ladies Tennis Club was flourishing.

There are plenty of role models – this year a British girl called Kitty McKane (later Kitty Godfree) won Wimbledon, thereby breaking the stranglehold of Suzanne Lenglen, the French star commonly called "La Divine", (The Goddess). This phenomenon had the effect of filtering through to local level.

The Arbroath Herald even asks the question of whether the facilities at the public tennis courts are adequate and quoted Town Treasurer Mr Robertson, who reported drawings from the tennis courts of £209 as distinct from £154 expenditure.

There is a certain amount of waste land near the tennis courts, and although it might be rather late this year to lay out more courts, it might be an idea to expand for next year, now that holiday makers are returning to Arbroath from Glasgow in even greater numbers every year.

In the meantime the Arbroath Ladies team continues to do well in the Midlands League, beating Carnoustie and Newport Ladies.

It is also another example of the increasing self-confidence and emancipation of women in the 1920s, one of the side effects of the Great War, although it is fairly obvious that women's tennis will remain a middle class sport for some time.

July 3 1920

Economic depression continues to be the order of the day with a few hints that after the summer holidays in early August, some more factories, particularly the flax making ones will have to put their workers on short-time working.

This is in addition to those already in that sad condition. There really does not seem to be any easy or quick solution to the problem, and in this context we cannot imagine the gloating of *The Arbroath Herald* about Provost and Mrs Anderson meeting the King and the Queen at Holyrood Palace going down too well in certain areas of the town!

But there was some good news.

Those who had been able to afford a trip to Broughty Ferry today would have seen a great performance from Arbroath's hero Bob Sievwright in the Forfarshire v Perthshire match, a game much talked about and discussed, for it was another sign of the return to normality after the War.

Forthill was crowded like never before and they saw Bob bowl from start to finish of the Perthshire innings, "trundling down" 25 overs with 12 maidens and taking 6 wickets for 42 runs, thus paving the way for a Forfarshire victory.

It is interesting to see that *The Arbroath Herald* in 1920 refers to Bob as a "veteran". He had another 27 years to run, and the best of his career was yet to come!

It was something at least for Arbroathians to be cheery about as they caught their train back home that lovely summer evening.

July 4 1890

There seems to be little doubt that this is the age of the railways.

There are still a few Arbroathians who can remember when there were no railways or when the Forfar line was born in 1839, but for most people, certainly most businesses, the railway has come to dominate their lives.

In March the Forth Railway Bridge was opened and quite a few people from Arbroath have gone to see this marvel, and even travelled across it, coming back to report what a scary experience it all was!

And now locally, a great deal of work is being done at Elliot Junction. A new waiting room was built a couple of years ago, and now the platform is being widened to bring it in line with the waiting room.

A retaining wall has been built on the links, alongside the station and the hole between the wall and the old platform has been filled up with carted earth.

The reason for this work and temporary inconvenience to rail travellers is quite simply the volume of traffic, for this small junction is a very busy place some mornings.

But the most striking difference is the small light iron footbridge which enables passengers to cross the line quickly and safely from one platform to the other.

The bridge has been finished this week, and there is still a certain novelty value for children being able to walk over the railway!

July 5 1906

Today was one of the best days of the year so far for weather.

Provost Alexander, Magistrates, Councillors and friends were treated by Mr A Smith of the White Hart Hotel to the annual "junket" or a trip to Lunan Bay.

It was the first outing of the Antiquary Coach from "Fairport" – a reference to *The Antiquary* of Sir Walter Scott in which Fairport used as a pseudonym for Arbroath.

The coach is described as having four bays and was followed by two large brakes, both splendidly horsed.

The journey was enlivened by "good natured banter" as they proceeded towards Marywell, Inverkeilor, Redcastle and the South Mains of Ethie.

Every now and again, children attracted by the spectacle of the horses and the carriage came to see them, and the Councillors were delighted to throw "sweeties" to them, thus sparking off a "scatter" of the likes that one sees at weddings.

When they reached the South Mains of Ethie, they were entertained by Mr Morgan on the lawn with loads of food and drink. Mr Morgan was soon to be married and he was wished all the best by the company, and it was a fair bet that the journey home was enjoyed even more than the outward trip.

Even when they arrived back in Arbroath at about 7.00 pm, the festivities did not end there, for they were entertained for tea and further drinks at the White Hart Hotel.

It was one of those days where it did not hurt in the slightest to be a Town Councillor of Arbroath!

July 6 1893

It would be fair to say that the response of Arbroath towards the Royal Wedding was mixed.

Generally attitudes towards the Royal Family were varied, but there was a certain affection for the Prince of Wales, who would never let you down by failing to provide another juicy scandal!

Today was the occasion of the marriage of his son, the Duke of York, the grandson of the Queen, to Princess May of Teck, at the Chapel Royal, St James Palace.

A certain amount of ridicule had been caused by the German Princess's willingness (some even said desperation) to marry George after a two-month engagement. Her original fiancé, George's brother — the louche, immoral and generally awful Prince Albert Victor Christian Edward, Duke of Clarence and Avondale — had died during a flu epidemic in only the previous year.

It was a case of "second time lucky" for Princess May! It also said a certain amount about the Royal Family's enthusiasm to get their hands on a young girl of royal blood who was still fertile and not a Roman Catholic!

Arbroath declared a Holiday, but amazingly some workers refused it! This was true in the Millgate Works and the Abbey Leather Works, for some felt that with the short time working that had been prevalent, enough money and orders had been lost!

Some enlightened employers closed at 1.00 pm and gave their workers a half day off with pay.

The public buildings were all decorated with bunting and flags, while in the afternoon there was a parade of all the uniformed organisations starting from Hill Street and ending up at the Town House where Provost George Keith had a cake and wine party.

There was then music on the Common and a bonfire at 10.00 pm, with the licensed premises given leave to stay open until 11.00 pm.

July 7 1934

Today, Arbroath's new Open Air Swimming Pool was opened before a large crowd of spectators.

It was opened by the Earl of Strathmore of Glamis Castle whose daughter Elizabeth is of course married to the Duke of York and has two lovely children Elizabeth and Margaret.

He was accompanied by Provost William Chapel.

The new pool, a great asset to the town's burgeoning hospitality industry, is open just in time for the influx of holiday makers from Glasgow next weekend.

The ceremony was followed by a Mannequin Parade and then a Beauty Competition.

There was also a demonstration of Diving by two Scottish Champions, then an individual swimming race won by Miss Nairn, then a team race won by Paisley with famous figures of Scottish swimming like Ellen King and Arbroath's own Ella Cargill also in attendance.

The new Pool's deficiencies became immediately apparent when a shower of rain came on! The platform party then adjourned to the Hotel Seaforth.

The cost of the pool was by no means cheap, but part of the thinking was to give unemployed people a job, and it is hoped that Arbroath will soon recoup the cost in the number of additional holiday makers coming to the town.

Certainly with an Abbey, the harbour, good railway connections, the beach and now an Open Air swimming pool, Arbroath seems ideally placed to take advantage of the slow upturn in trade which is becoming apparent now that the worst of the worldwide slump seems to be receding.

July 8 1912

Today at Raeburn Place, Edinburgh, on the first day of the Scotland v Australia three-day game, Arbroath's Bob Sievwright became the toast of Scotland with his 7 for 71.

The Arbroath Herald trumpeted that Sievwright had "laid the Kangaroos" low, and indeed it was a fine performance from the slow left armer who was able to move the ball both ways.

It was all the more impressive because he was not getting a great deal of help from the wickets, and the Scottish evening papers were full of admiration for the "wizard from Arbroath".

For this game against Scotland, Australia naturally enough rested one or two of their Test players, but even so 7 for 71 was a good return against the "Corncrakes" or the "Colonials", as they were called.

One of the victims was the great Charles Macartney, whom he had caught. Another was Warwick Armstrong, but the problem was that Armstrong had scored 149! Indeed, Sievwright's performance was the only good Scottish one for Australia finished with 295.

Had he been better supported, it might have been a far better day for Scotland. There was another Arbroath United man playing for Scotland in Maurice Dickson and he would make his mark on the game tomorrow with a classy 98 before he was bowled by Minnett.

Sadly, that was about all the good news for Scotland who then subsided to a rather heavy defeat, but it was not the fault of Arbroath!

Don Bradman and Bob Sievwright. The picture was taken in Edinburgh in 1930. Body language perhaps indicates that the famously sanctimonious and clean living Bradman disapproves of the vulgar Sievwright smoking a cigarette?

July 9 1916

It was becoming clear, in spite of military censorship, that the big "push" in France a week ago was no great success.

Although the newspapers were talking in vague terms about a "general advance" and "hitting Huns hard", there was a disturbing lack of detail about villages or towns that had been captured.

All the time lists of casualties were beginning to appear in *The Courier* including a few Arbroath boys mainly listed as "missing". However, today at least, the Somme casualties were not the main topic of conversation.

Of far more immediate concern to the Arbroathians this Sunday was the fact that the town was flooded, thanks to incessant heavy rain since about Thursday at midnight with frequent outbursts of thunder and lightning.

The water had entered some houses and factories with the area round about the Brothock Bridge said to be the worst of all with the offices of *The Arbroath Herald* suffering severe inundations, the likes of which had not been seen for forty years.

It was of course no laughing matter but there were a few jokes about some haddock being seen swimming along Keptie Street, and how there was something looking like a German Submarine or U Boat on Gayfield football ground.

From the Hume Street area of town, there came the true story of an elderly, ailing woman who refused to get out of her bed to go elsewhere, until she saw the water level reaching the bottom of her bed!

Even after the floods subsided, the amount of damage remained quite considerable.

July 10 1958

It is not very often that an Arbroath man gains a "Chair".

George Anderson has been appointed Professor of Old Testament Studies at Durham University, having been a Lecturer in the University of St Andrews in Literature and Theology of the Old Testament.

George was born in Arbroath in 1913, and was educated at Arbroath High School. His mother is still alive and lives at Gowanlea Cottages.

He won a Harkness Scholarship to St Andrews University where he studied Classics for four years, graduating with First Class Honours and winning the John Burnett Prize for Greek, and the Marshall Prize for Latin.

He also studied at Cambridge and at Lund University in Sweden where he became an expert in Semitic Languages.

He was ordained a Methodist Minister in 1940 and served in the Armed Forces for six years, three of them in the Middle East. Recently he has been back in town conducting services at St John's Methodist Church.

He remains a well-known and much loved character, being able to combine his gentle erudition with a sense of humour and of tolerance, free from the sanctimony and distance of so many clerics.

His appointment was heard with great joy among his friends in Arbroath, and he leaves St Andrews with the best wishes of all concerned.

And won't his widowed mother be proud of him?

July 11 1998

Arbroath United had an unusual player in their team for their Strathmore Union game against Meigle today.

This was no less a man than Derek Randall of Notts and England, now retired.

He had spoken last night at the club's Dinner and had been invited to play for the club today.

This innovative and original idea duly reaped its reward when a larger than usual crowd turned up to see the Test cricketer.

Known as "Arkle" after the famous racehorse, he was a character in the field but his antics did not prevent him bringing off some brilliant run outs.

He also hit two famous Test centuries in Australia – 174 in the Centenary Test of 1977 against Dennis Lillee and 150 against Rodney Hogg in 1979.

Now 47, he had been retired for a few years but he spoke brilliantly at the Dinner on the Friday night and today hit 105 for Arbroath.

This was not enough, however, to stave off defeat by Meigle, who thus could tell everyone that they had beaten Randall's Arbroath.

Randall was charming to everyone throughout the weekend, but felt that the defeat had possibly been due to some of the guys having too good a time of it the night before!

He added however that the future for Arbroath was for bright for "there seemed to be thousands of kids about the place all day and their enthusiasm was fantastic".

July 12 1947

Tragedy occurred today at Lochlands.

Arbroath's greatest ever cricketer in Robert Willis Sievwright, while batting at the wicket along with his son Arthur, collapsed and died.

It was a Strathmore Union game against Perthshire XI and Sievwright, now aged 65, really ought not to have been playing, but the club, which had lost so many players since 1939, were struggling to put a team on the field.

He came out to bat at about 5.05 pm with the team fighting to save the game. He was never a great batsman but managed to edge the last ball of the over for a three.

He had thus run 66 yards and had to face the first ball of the next over. To the horror of the crowd, he made no attempt to play the ball which passed harmlessly by, but then collapsed, probably dead before he hit the ground.

He had played more than 40 years for Arbroath United, regularly taking over 100 wickets a season with his slow left armers and "chinamen".

He took a grand total of 2,242 wickets in his career which lasted from 1905 until 1947. He played 18 times for Scotland against great players like Jack Hobbs of England and Warren Bardsley of Australia.

He was the proprietor of the Lordburn Joinery Works in Arbroath.

His funeral the following Tuesday, conducted by the Reverend David Crombie of Arbroath Parish Church, was one of the biggest that Arbroath had ever seen and was attended by representatives from most cricket clubs in Scotland.

July 13 1947

The Sunday Post
PRINTED AND PUBLISHED EVERY SUNDAY MORNING.

SUNDAY, JULY 13, 1947. RADIO—Page 4. PRICE TWOPENCE.

Morning Special

"Sivvy" Dies At The Wicket While Batting With His Son

PRINCESS ELIZABETH REFUSED ADMISSION TO ASCOT ENCLOSURE!

R. W. Sievwright, famous Scottish cricketer, collapsed and died while batting at Lochlands, Arbroath, yesterday.

He was partnered at the wicket by his son Arthur when the incident occurred.

Mystery Explosion In Dundee House—Two Injured

CAR OVERTURNS NEAR DUNDEE

Nylons Vanish At Docks

Germans' Freedom Dash To Eire

A Great Bowler

Remarkable Feats

Keen to the End

British Soldiers Chloroformed And Kidnapped

Rough Seas Too Much For Channel Swimmer

RUSSIA CHALLENGES BRITAIN AS PARIS TALKS OPEN

THE DEFICIT

To-Day's Weather

July 13 1932

Today saw the death of John Petrie of Cairnie Street, a Town Council Employee at the "coup" or "dump" in Montrose Road.

This was the famous Jock, Jockie, Jeck or Jack Petrie, who scored 13 goals (some say he scored more than that) in the famous win of Arbroath against Aberdeen Bon Accord in 1885.

The funny thing was that he was not even a centre forward that day. He was playing on the right wing and cheerfully admits to losing count of the goals he scored!

He was a well-known figure in the town and was much mourned in the world of Scottish football.

He was a shoemaker to trade, working in Dundee for a spell, but left, after a shoemaker's strike, to go to Belfast for and to play for Distillery in the 1890s.

When he returned to Arbroath, he became the trainer for 29 years and was always willing to play in benefit games and training sessions, sometimes coming back to Gayfield at night and practising on his own.

The story goes about the time when some East Fife supporters in the old stand at Bayview started saying things about Arbroath, ridiculing smokies, lighthouses and Abbeys and pouring scorn on the 36-0 game saying that it was not possible and how could anyone possibly score 13 (or more) goals?

An Arbroath lady then stood up and introduced the man she was sitting beside. It was Jockie Petrie himself, the world record holder!

The Fife men duly apologised, humbled to be in the presence of this great man.

July 14 1789

Today is what history has called the Bastille Day.

Little evidence exists that Arbroath had any direct involvement in it, but there can be little doubt that once the story broke, a few people began to ask a few questions.

Arbroath had been at peace since the Jacobite rebellion of nearly 50 years ago now, but the involvement of the town on the defeated side meant that there was always a military presence not far away, just in case.

The Americas had shown that it was possible to break the hold of the corrupt British government, while some Arbroath sailors who had worked on ships involved in the slave trade had come home asking questions.

Meanwhile a fellow in Ayrshire with family connections in Montrose was writing poetry asking questions about why wealth was so badly distributed.

The rising in France saw an intensification of the military presence of Dragoons in the town and now every fishing boat was examined when it came into the harbour just to see if there were any French spies being smuggled in to the town on board!

Some brave people even ventured to suggest that as Arbroath had once been the centre of rebellion against King Edward, could it not become the same again against King George?

These were uneasy times in the town, and every one suspected that war might not be far away. And where did local man George Dempster of Dunnichen fit into all this?

July 15 1957

Today in Forfar died Fred Mann, born in Arbroath in 1892 and a man much loved in both towns.

He was until 1955 Principal Teacher of Classics at Forfar Academy, a position from which he retired because of ill health.

He grew up in Arbroath and was educated at Arbroath High School before graduating with First Class Honours in Classics at Edinburgh University.

He played cricket for Arbroath United (alongside men like R W Sievwright) and also football, tennis and badminton.

The First World War then got in the way of his career, but he served with the Royal Army Field Ambulance in Egypt and France. He then taught at George Watson's in Edinburgh, at Kelso High School before being appointed to Forfar Academy in 1929 where he continued the fine Forfar tradition of producing scholars for St Andrews University.

He was an Elder at the Lowson Memorial Church in Forfar, and was well known as a violinist, being a member of the Forfar String Quartet for many years.

His heart still lay in Arbroath, and under the pseudonym of "Cypher" he wrote for *The Arbroath Herald,* in particular a brilliant satire called the Ballad of The Stone of Destiny.

He was also sometimes "The Drummer" for *The Forfar Dispatch*, and was well loved by his pupils and fellow members of staff for his kindly disposition and sense of humour, often joking that he did not like New Year's Day for he did not know who to support – Arbroath or Forfar – for he loved them both, in the same way as both towns loved him.

July 16 1920

For the past two weeks, advertisements have been appearing for recruits to join the 5th (Angus) Battalion of the Black Watch.

It is very much a local Battalion with Lieut-Col Hon M Bowes-Lyon of Glamis Castle, the Commanding Officer, with The Earl of Airlie Second in Command.

It is stressed the recruitment is open to both ex-Servicemen and men with no military experience. Men aged 18 to 38 were invited to apply as long as they were over 5 feet 2 inches in height. There would be a camp every September, and during that time soldiers would receive £1 Bounty.

If they were called out for any other camp or "embodiment" they would be paid at the same rates as the regular Army. Recruitment was going well because this was an era of heavy unemployment, but nevertheless it was a little surprising that so many men, having survived a horrible war, were willing to have another go.

The nation was of course at peace, but there was no guarantee that the peace would last, and in any case there was a civil war going on in Ireland, for which they might be deployed.

And it was fairly obvious that there might soon be trouble in the mines and on the industrial front, and soldiers might be needed to quell difficult outbreaks of disorder.

But it was clear that this was no deterrent for young men. The Drill Hall in Marketgate was a busy place these evenings!

July 17 1909

There was certainly no lack of things to do in Arbroath this glorious summer Saturday afternoon!

Apart from the usual sporting pursuits of cricket, golf, bowls and tennis, there was the swimming gala of the St Thomas Swimming Club and Humane Society held at the West Dock. This attracted a huge attendance of both local people and Glasgow holidaymakers.

The races started from the fishing boat Hesperus which had been kindly lent for the occasion and the swimmers headed to the shore. But there was another attraction as well – a novel one of a Sand-Building Competition!

High tide was between two and three o'clock, but by four the tide had receded sufficiently to allow a start to the competition on the vast area of Arbroath Sands. For a long time, the area was a scene of frenzied activity with all the categories well laid out and everyone allocated their plot.

The sheer diversity of things being made astonished the judges, but it was generally agreed that the model of St Vigean's Church and churchyard made by Emily Eaton, aged 12, of 6 Princes Street, was the best for its detail and similarity to its original. Emily won the silver bangle for the 9-14 Girls category.

The other two categories were won by brothers James, aged 12, and Norman, aged 9, Johnston of 18 Hannah Street. The trouble was, of course, that you could not take your models home with you!

And sooner or later, they would be washed away. But photographs were taken of what was really a very happy occasion.

July 18 1844

This Thursday saw the annual Saint Thamas's market.

For some reason, there has been a decline enthusiasm in the town for this event, possibly because there are now increasing possibilities of going out of town for a day's holiday, now that the railway has given everyone the opportunity to go to all the places on the line to Forfar, and to Forfar itself.

Today's holiday did not start very well, for it rained heavily all morning with the noise of the rain falling even drowning out the cries of the sweetie wives.

At about one o'clock an improvement in the weather was noted and at the same time, the *Tarbert Castle* steamer made her appearance from Montrose, bringing a fair number of passengers to mingle happily with the local citizens.

The High Street from the Post Office to Horner's Wynd was well lined with stands, and much animated activity, although *The Arbroath Guide* was of the persuasion that not as much trade was done as in previous years.

At about five o'clock the *Tarbert Castle*, which had been to the Bell Rock, returned and picked up its Montrose passengers, and things more or less came to an end.

The indifferent weather this year did not help, but things used to be a great deal better. But tomorrow would be a holiday for most Arbroath people, and everyone was preparing for a trip inland to the country, or possibly a sail.

July 19 1936

The weather is splendid and Arbroath is busy and full of holiday makers.

There are clear signs that the economic depression has gone, and this Sunday afternoon, catching the mood, the Arbroath Town Mission holds an open air service on Low Common.

There is a distinct international flavour to this meeting as the main speakers were Mr A McKellar of Johannesburg, South Africa and Mr A Lindsey of Lancashire, both students of The Bible Training Institute in Glasgow.

They were currently travelling round the country (on bicycles) doing work for the Scottish Evangelistic Council.

The worship was supplemented by a clutch of soloists from Glen Mavis in Lanarkshire and from Glasgow itself. If there was a certain west of Scotland bias in all this, then the audience would have felt at home, for there was a large contingent of Glasgow holiday makers in Arbroath at the moment.

The Glasgow Fair had started on Friday, and Saturday had seen the Station a very busy place, as trains disgorged passengers with thick Glaswegian accents!

In the evening there was another open air meeting in the Wynds.

This time a feature of the meeting was the number of people who came out of their houses with chairs so that the elderly could get a seat!

Little seemed wrong with the world that fine Sunday night, the only fly in the ointment being the news that some serious political disturbance, like a military coup, was going on in Spain

July 20 1930

A local Arbroath man has done very well for himself and Scotland at the Rifle Shooting at Bisley.

This is John Eddie, a jeweller and member of the Miniature Rifle Club, who was one of the team which won the National Challenge Trophy for Scotland.

The scores were Scotland 1919, England 1915, Ireland 1874 and Wales 1840.

The conditions were: teams of 20, seven shots per man fired at 200, 500 and 600 yards.

The leading score for Scotland was Lieutenant Eccles was 98 made up of 32, 32 and 34. Sergeant Eddie from Arbroath had a score of 94 – 31, 32 and 32, which was not far behind.

In the Alexandra Competition – seven shots each at 500 and 600 yards, he had a score of 62 while in the King's Prize, he aggregated 130.

His work at Bisley has been most creditable, and is a tribute to all the hard work he has put in practising over the winter at the Miniature Rifle Club.

It is not a sport that has a great following in Arbroath. For obvious safety reasons, it can never be a major spectator sport, but it does have its following.

It is strictly controlled by licences etc. and strict precautions have to be taken against rifles falling into the wrong hands!

It was very popular in the years immediately after the Great War among ex-Servicemen who had learned how to shoot in the Army, and it is always good to see success for a local man.

July 21 1846

A major political demonstration was held today in Arbroath in favour of Free Trade.

This was the age old argument against Protection. Free Trade meant that food could be brought in from abroad without paying tax, and it meant cheaper food.

The Protectionists felt that the stress should be laid on British food which should be "protected" by high taxes on imported food.

Free Trade was very popular but Prime Minister Robert Peel had just committed political suicide by repealing the Corn Laws to allow cheap imported food, particularly in Ireland where the potato crop had failed.

He was probably too late in Ireland, but he did make some attempt. He was immediately deposed from office by the rest of his Tory Party who were naturally supporters of the interests of farmers and landed gentry who were more interested in their own profit than they were in feeding the masses.

Today the now deposed Peel was much feted in a huge demonstration in a parade that started at the Convent Churchyard and ended up at the Town House where they were addressed by Provost James Gibson.

All the trades – Bakers, Tailors, Shoemakers, Shipwrights and others (including the Total Abstainers, who were hardly a trade, but nevertheless claimed to show the advantages of an abstemious lifestyle) took part.

The Arbroath Guide is extremely impressed, saying that there can be few towns which have shown their appreciation of Free Trade measures more than "our burgh".

July 22 1919

Arbroath's Carnival, organised by the Merchants' Association, is in full swing, and it is clear that there is a determination of Arbroathians to enjoy themselves as much as possible after the dark days of the last few years.

The Carnival has not been on the same scale as pre-war occasions – how could it be? – but there were nevertheless a fair selection of hobby horses, swing boats and so on, and the occasion has been marked with good weather and a reasonable number of visitors from the west, although not yet on the scale that there used to be.

There is of course the lack of young men, and the melancholy sights of women with several children in tow, smiling and trying to make the best of it.

Other young men are being pushed around in bath chairs; yet others are being escorted, because they are blind, by a proud but broken hearted mother.

Trains are still arriving at the station bringing home men who had now been demobilised, glad to be home but uncertain of their future.

At least with the lovely summer weather, the flu epidemic seems to be in at least temporary and hopefully permanent recession.

There is talk now of a Housing Scheme being built with houses with large kitchens and indoor flushing toilets! Such luxury!

But *The Arbroath Herald* wonders and worries about where all the money is going to come from.

July 23 1889

The weather has been marvellous, but Arbroath Station was once again the scene of angry criticism this Holiday Week.

The Arbroath Herald happened to be there this morning at about 10 o'clock and describes a scene of confusion, crush and occasionally panic with some passengers, unable to actually get through the crowds to their train, understandably turning very angry.

Although the station was fine in the days when it was simply a matter of local trains to Forfar or Dundee, the rail network has now expanded to an almost incredible extent.

The building of the high profile Forth Railway Bridge (due to open next year) is likely to increase railway traffic even further.

The problem is that the station is simply far too small with not enough Waiting areas. Provost Anderson has raised this matter on many occasions with the railway companies, so far with no success.

It is intolerable that the Holiday Week, which should be relaxing and restorative, is a cause of more stress being added to people.

It is now an age where "everybody is going somewhere" and the railway companies, who are making an absolute fortune out of this, really have to take some responsibility.

At the moment the state of Arbroath Railway Station is an absolute deterrent for people travelling.

Worse still, it has been the subject of some sarcasm in *The Forfar Herald* with jokes about "single file" travelling and the biggest place in the station being the "conveniences" etc.

July 24 1922

It was the Monday of the Holiday Week, so where else was there to go on a day of splendid weather but to the Steele Park, Forfar, for the Forfar Games, the mecca for athletics for all Scotland?

Half of Arbroath, it seemed, crammed onto the morning trains for the county town with time to go shopping, visiting friends and relatives, even visiting a public house or two before the games which *The Courier* claimed to have attracted a crowd of 15,000!

If this is true, it was one and a half times the whole population of the town of Forfar. But it was a great day, although Arbroath was not as well represented in the events as it used to be in the great pre-war days.

But there was Johnny Hadden, the cyclist and Jimmy Hogg the "hop, step and jump" man, both of whom ended up second in their events. There was an Arbroath team in the Five-A-Side football, but they did not shine.

Nevertheless, there was some great entertainment in the Dancing and the Horse Trotting.

For those who tired of the Games, there was the chance to climb Balmashanner Hill (vulgarly known as Bummie!) to see their very impressive and quite stunning War Memorial, which had been unveiled last year, as well as a spectacular view of the Grampian Mountains.

Then time to go home with some of the men what is commonly known as "the waur o the ware" after having spent rather too long in Jarman's Hotel bar just opposite the Forfar Station.

Arbroath v Forfar Tennis Club. 1889

July 25 1962

Mr Fred Mosely, aged 54, of 64 Seaton Road, Arbroath and an attendant at the Swimming Pool, is fast becoming a local hero.

For the third time this summer, he dived into the pool to rescue someone.

This time it was Marjory Nicoll, aged four, of 7 High Street, Arbroath, the only child of Mr and Mrs G Nicoll, attending an event with her friend Linda Black of Strathmore Avenue.

She had been at the pool to watch the weekly "Miss Arbroath" competition, and just as the competition was coming to its end, she fell fully clothed into the pool in an area where it was seven feet deep.

As shouts of alarm went up from the crowd filing away from the pool seats, Mr Mosely ran to the side, dived in, still wearing his tracksuit, and brought the little girl to safety to the cheers and applause of the crowd.

The day ended happily for little Marjory, for she was given a hot drink in the attendants' room and then take home in a taxi, none the worse for her escapade, and still determinedly clutching in her hand a few pennies which she had not released even when she was in the water.

Mr Mosely said that there were times when one just had to do things without thinking. It was a not infrequent occurrence with all these excitable children around, but fortunately there had not, in recent times, been anything serious happening.

July 26 1945

Arbroath, like the rest of the country, is reeling today at the General Election results.

Depending on one's viewpoint, one is either despondent or ecstatic for the country has delivered a landslide victory for Labour.

Voting was actually carried out three weeks ago, but the results have been delayed to allow the "soldiers vote" to be brought home and allocated to their constituencies.

So many soldiers, sailors and aircraft men are still in uniform and this may have helped Labour in that "anti-Officer" feelings might be translated into working class v rich people.

The result for Montrose Burghs was announced from the steps of the Caird Hall, Dundee, and it was a majority for John MacLay, the National Liberal (an umbrella term which included Conservatives), of 3,000 over the Labour candidate Alex MacNair.

That was no surprise, although it was a reduced majority, but elsewhere Labour swept to power in a landslide victory, and Mr Churchill was now the Leader of the Opposition.

The vote was really a protest against the awful living conditions that people had suffered before the war, and the hope was now expressed that if Labour delivered on its National Health Service promise, very soon a completely new and better world would emerge.

Not everyone in Arbroath saw it this way, or course, and for many middle class people, there was a real fear that Labour were going to take everyone's money away from them!

July 27 1917

There is little to be happy about these days, but it is still the holidays. Even if you work in the Munitions industry, you still get your holidays.

In fact, holidays were encouraged because it was good for morale, and there was also the undeniable fact that, unemployment having disappeared and men (and now women) working in the Munitions industry earning loads of money in overtime, there was actually quite a lot of money about.

Arbroath therefore thrived with restaurants, pubs and hotels all doing well, as the town still attracted some Glaswegians and of course soldiers and sailors on leave.

It was an odd time, as everyone tried to enjoy themselves while they could, for news of casualties kept filtering back to the town.

It was probably true that everyone in Arbroath knew personally someone who had been killed or wounded, and the carnage did not differentiate by social class.

Rich or poor did not seem to matter, and although there was a certain amount of truth in the stereotype of the Officers sitting in a chateau sending Privates to their death, it was not universally the case.

But there was some good news as well with local men being promoted or decorated. Today, for example, there was news of Major M R Dickson being mentioned in dispatches on Salonika.

Major Dickson had been captain of the Arbroath United Cricket Club before the war and had captained Scotland as well.

But there was still no sign of an end to it all, and it was no coincidence that one of the favourite songs was the fatalistic "We're here because we're here because we're here…"

July 28 1939

The Arbroath Herald reports in a new craze which has hit the town recently and "spread like a fever".

It is a game called "Hi-Li". It consists of a table tennis bat with a piece of elastic attached to it and at the end of the piece of elastic there is a rubber ball.

The skill consists in being able to control the ball, but that is very difficult because the elastic stretches unpredictably and uncontrollably.

It came to town with the first Glasgow holiday makers a few weeks ago, but of course there is nothing really new about it because it used to be called "Dingbat" when it was played in the Victorian age.

It is not really dangerous but there is always the chance that the ball might bounce back and hit the player on the face.

Two young men have already given demonstrations of how to do it. One is Danny Cole, the world champion who is on tour and gave a demonstration at the Bathing Pool, and the other is Arbroath man Duncan Ross who is based at the New Savoy Cinema in Glasgow and who is organising competitions in Arbroath and Carnoustie.

Shopkeepers have sensed the market and have sold scores of Hi-Li sets.

It is now no uncommon sight in the town to see boys and girls walking along the road, engaging in the earnest conversation that adolescents indulge in and balancing their Hi-Lis at the same time!

July 29 2009

Tonight an Arbroath girl made her debut for Scotland Under-15s.

This was Kelly Clark. The game was in Germany and no-one would want to be reminded of the score, for it was Germany 6 Scotland 1.

But this was just the start of Kelly's International footballing career, for she went on to play 19 times for the Under-17s and 12 times for the Under-19s.

Born in 1994, she had grown up with a love of all sports, attending Gayfield with her father, who was a season ticket holder, and watching him play in pub games. (He also played cricket for Arbroath United).

She began to play for Inchcape Strollers as early as 2001 and in 2006 she played and scored in the Inverbrothock Watters Cup Final team. In 2010 she moved to Forfar Farmington, and she was still only 15 when she made her first team debut.

In 2013 she would move to Stirling University to study to become an accountant, and then she joined Celtic, for whom she has now played 200 times and become captain.

She talks at length about the problems that she faced in trying to get a chance to play football as a young girl and all the hurdles of prejudice and stereotyping that she had to face. She is a defender, and has done a great deal for club and the town. She now works part time on Celtic TV.

Kelly Clark

July 30 1914

Just what exactly is going on in Europe these days?

Here we are in sunny Arbroath in the loveliest weather we have had for many years. The town is full of tourists, everyone is spending money in cafes and restaurants, playing cricket, golf and tennis, walking along the cliffs, swimming in the sea and generally enjoying themselves ... and in Europe they are talking about war!

Austria and Serbia are already at war – but that is hardly unusual because there have been many wars in the Balkans, but now these awful men, the Kaiser of Germany and the Czar of Russia are picking sides and looking likely to join in!

They are cousins of each other and cousins of King George V, and their grandmother was old Queen Vic of Great Britain!

Sadly she has been dead for a while now, otherwise she would have banged their heads together!

And the really horrible thing is that we in Great Britain seem to have some sort of alliance with the Czar – why? – and we might even be drawn into the war that these two spoiled brats seem to want.

But no, that cannot be allowed to happen! Leave us here in sunny Arbroath! Is there any cricket on Saturday? When does the football season begin?

There is a cheap railway excursion to Edinburgh advertised for next week, and how do you fancy one of these new motor car things? A wee bit expensive, I fear!

But what's this I hear about the reservists being called up, and the terries (the Territorial Army) being put on reserve? What is it all about?

July 31 1961

A remarkable attempt at a world record was begun to day in the Red Triangle Hut at 10.00 am this morning.

Apparently the record for non-stop playing of the piano was 133 hours, and it was calculated that anyone who started to "tinkle the ivories" at 10.00 am would reach his/her target at 11.00 pm on Saturday night.

This was what Sandy Strickland ("Syncopating Sandy") from Bolton was attempting to do. The record holder was a German from Dusseldorf called Heinz Arntz who had played 132 hours.

Sandy Strickland's playing was very versatile from classical stuff to Sir Harry Lauder's "Keep Right On To The End Of The Road" to an "Arbroath Tango" that he had composed himself.

He welcomed visitors and was able to do things like eat and drink with one hand while still playing with the other, and the prurient wondered how he coped with the toilet!

He remained cheerful throughout, always saying that more than half of the battle was being won simply because he was enjoying what he was doing.

Eventually at 11.00 pm on Saturday August 5 he reached 133 hours and achieved his goal. Crowds had gathered throughout the day to watch him and to cheer him on.

The wonder was that he didn't even seem tired as the Ambulancemen lifted him from his chair to carry him to a taxi to take him to his hotel!

It was some achievement! And he was very grateful for the help he had received from the good people of Arbroath!

August

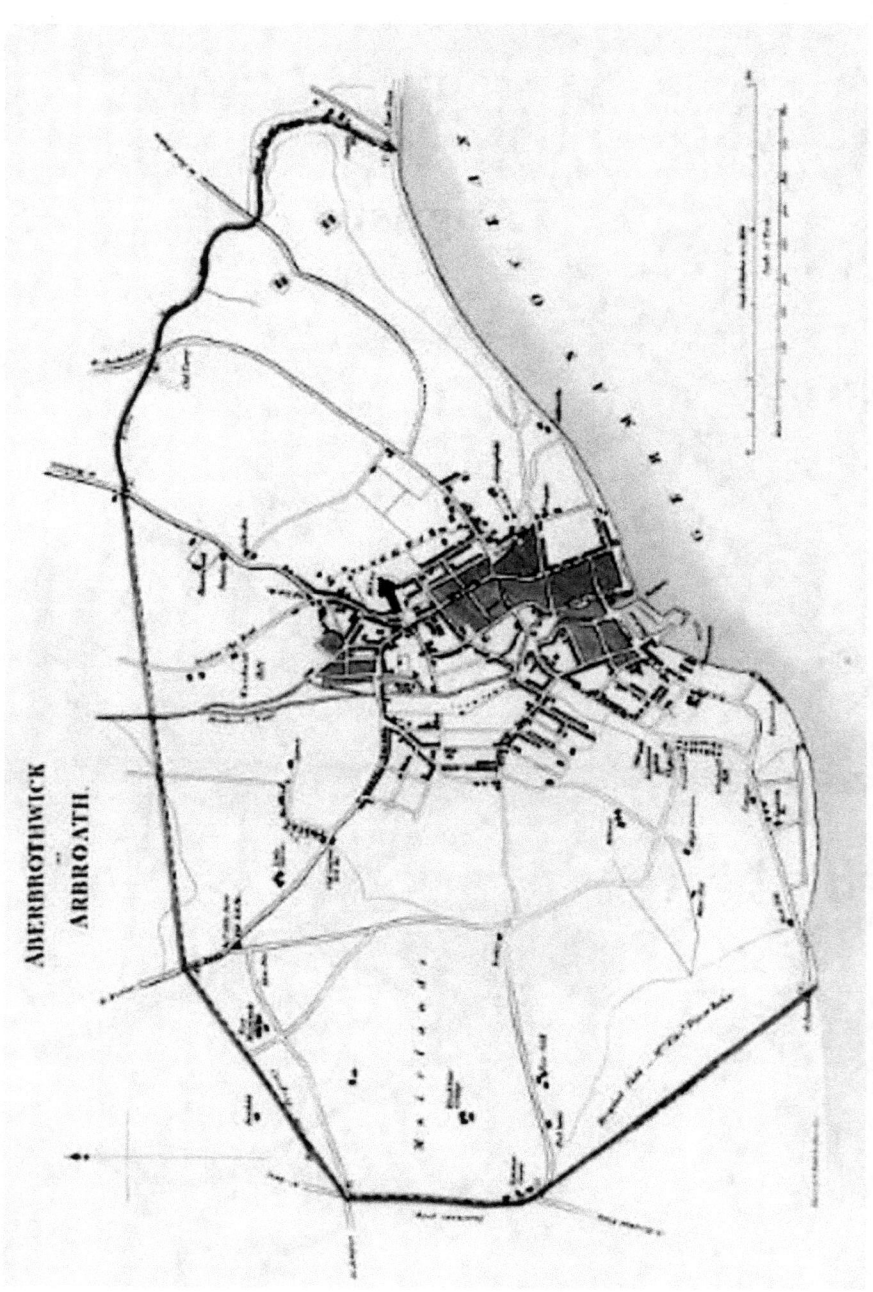

Arbroath 1832

August 1 1914

No-one was oblivious to the deteriorating international situation and there was the realisation that we might soon be at war because of what was happening in the Balkans.

Nevertheless Arbroath United took on Cupar at Lochlands and lost.

Captain Maurice Dickson was injured with a bad foot, and Bob Sievwright was acting captain, making, according to some spectators, a bad mistake when he took himself off the bowling and gave the ball to a young lad called G C McLeod.

The young man was promptly savaged by Cupar batsman A W Douglas who hit him for 20 in the one over. As Arbroath were defending a meagre total of 94, these 20 runs were crucial.

Clearly "Savant" the reporter of *The Arbroath Herald* is thinking about the imminent war, with imagery "like a French navalman popping away at a German cruiser" and "the enemy's shells seemed to misfire" when Sievwright came on to bowl.

Meanwhile the Junior Football season had also started with Parkhead beating Ardenlea at Low Common.

But there was no mistaking the fact that everyone was talking about what seemed inevitable. It was even looked forward to, for it was a new concept to more or less everyone except those who had served in South Africa.

A war in Europe seemed to symbolise adventure and thrills, plus the undeniable pleasure of young men getting to wear kilts, a prospect which seemed to excite young men and young women alike!

August 2 1930

Today was a great day at Gayfield football ground, for the town was graced with the arrival of Lord Baden Powell, founder of the Boy Scout movement and hero of the Boer War of 30 years ago.

But it was a damp squib and the day almost collapsed in disarray altogether. The weather was foul with intermittent heavy rain.

The hero of the hour did not arrive at the time specified. He was due to arrive at 10.45 am and hundreds were at the station to see him, but the train which arrived was the local one from Forfar.

The distinguished visitor was arriving in the County Town by a later train, which did not have a suitable connection with Arbroath. A car had to be sent to Forfar Station to meet him and he duly arrived at Gayfield two hours later than he should have.

Once there however he impressed everyone with his speech, making jokes about how he had sent the bad weather to test the mettle of the Angus Scouts and to see whether scouting could be carried out in fair weather and foul!

The ideal was the three h's – to be healthy, happy and helpful citizens. Several displays by the various troupes of Scouts from all over the County were carried out, and the National Anthem was sung before the distinguished visitor left.

It was a day that, in spite of the unfortunate things that happened, would be long remembered in Arbroath and Angus.

August 3 1892

A certain amount of interest has been created in town by the discovery yesterday of some human remains at Hospitalfield.

The Angus Agricultural Show will be held there and a small pit was being dug in which to install a pole for a marquee, when the spade struck something which sounded like bones. That was what they turned out to be, and there was no doubt that they were human.

There is a raised mound or plateau in Hospitalfield, not unlike the "square" or the "wicket" on a cricket field, and it is now believed that this was a burying area. Apparently other bones have been discovered there in the past. But nobody seemed able to say with any certitude just exactly how old they were.

Today the bones were reburied, even though several museums in the area would have liked them. It is possible that this was near the "hospitium" of Arbroath Abbey – not a hospital in our modern sense of the word for people who are ill – but more like a workhouse or a poorhouse, funded by the Abbey, for people with no homes, and even also acting as a primitive hotel for travellers as well. This is why it is called Hospitalfield.

The Angus Agricultural Show organisers did not seem in any way concerned about this unusual discovery on where their show was going to be held – in fact, if anything, it added to the attraction!

August 4 1914

Arbroath, like everywhere else, is in a ferment of excitement today.

War will be declared at 11.00 pm tonight if the Germans do not vacate Belgium — which they are giving no signs of doing.

Already some detachments of the Naval Reserve have left town, destination uncertain, and the local press has already been gagged by Government restrictions.

This morning, a German schooner called *The Behrend* sailed into Arbroath Harbour with a cargo of linseed oilcake.

It had come from St Petersburg in Russia some 24 days previously. The captain and crew, apparently unaware of the international situation, had indeed been amazed at the amount of warships they had seen in the North Sea.

The Chief Customs Officer and the Chief Constable boarded the vessel, talked to the captain, and put the vessel and its crew under arrest.

There were a few doubts about the legality of this high-handed action as the countries were not yet at war, but the orders seem to have come from the War Office.

A large crowd gathered to see the schooner, and although the crew were not allowed to go ashore, they waved to the locals before starting to help unload the cargo.

It is difficult to find out what eventually happened to the German crew. One hopes they were repatriated. They knew nothing about the war, and in any case, it had not yet started!

August 5 1929

The "talkies" have come to Arbroath!

Tonight at the Palace Theatre in James Street, a "talkie" picture was shown for the first time, and was pronounced a great success by those who had come to see it.

The film was called, funnily enough for Arbroath's first talkie, "The Barker" with Milton Sills and Dorothy Mackaill, and the sound system was good enough for all to hear even though the actors all spoke in an American accent.

There had been cinema in Arbroath at various places since well before the Great War, but if one had wanted to see a "talkie", one had to take a train to Dundee to do so.

Previously, there has been writing on the screen to indicate what a character was saying, and a local pianist would play romantic music when appropriate or fast music when someone was travelling by train or when there was a car chase.

The arrival of the "talkies" (by about 1935 most cinemas would be "talkies") brought about a change in the cast of the films because not all actors were good speakers.

It also obliged The Palace to raise prices to 9d, 1/-, 1/3d and 1/6d but that was only a slight increase, and in any case, the influx of customers soon paid for the installation of the sound facilities.

The Arbroath Herald does not claim to know how it all works, but is very impressed by the new system and commends it to the readers, while the Palace in its advertisements stresses that you can "Hear and See" at the Palace and mentions attractions like the sound of a waterfall or a battle in the Great War.

August 6 1937

Arbroath has been very lucky this year to have a variety group called the "After Tea" entertainers with their regular performances at the Webster Hall.

They are on most evenings and sometimes belie their name by putting on a matinee performance in the afternoon.

They are "variety" in the true sense as well, for each performance is totally different in the sense that one of the "regular" audience could attend a show on Monday and Tuesday and see a different programme!

The comedians are Tommy Loman and Lex McLean, both full of Glasgow patter, which of course goes down very well with the many Glaswegians on holiday in the town.

Peggy White sings Scottish songs and Ted McAdam sings many songs of the American plantations. Such songs are now in the 2020s not considered acceptable but were perfectly respectable in the 1930s.

There is a man called Tom Douglas who does accordion and piano solos, and another pair of young comedians. And there is a smart dancing group called the "After Tea Girls".

Next week, the group is to further diversify with a pantomime of "Babes In The Wood". Loman and McLean will be the bold bad robbers, and a few other artistes have been brought it as well specially for this week.

There can be little doubt that their performances are a great enhancement to the town, and provide something to do for the holiday makers when the weather isn't so good, but the artistes will be as aware as anyone that the days are shortening, the schools are going back and the football season is about to start – all signs that the summer is fast disappearing.

August 7 1945

It was with mixed emotions that the good people of Arbroath read in this morning's *Courier* "New Wonder Bomb Blasts Japan"

Yesterday the city of Hiroshima had been annihilated by what came to be known as an Atomic Bomb, dropped by the Americans.

The surrender of Japan would follow a week later, but no-one knew that at the time, and what if the Japanese had a similar bomb and retaliated?

The war in Europe had been over since May and many Arbroath soldiers and seamen were now home, not necessarily demobbed completely but certainly enjoying some leave.

The dropping of the bomb at least absolved the Allies from the necessity of launching an invasion of Japan next year, something that might have produced even more casualties than the bombing of Hiroshima and later Nagasaki did.

On the other hand, those who had died were all civilians. But there was now at least some hope that the prisoners held in these awful camps (and no-one as yet knew the full horrors of them) might be home some time – and that included quite a few young Arbroath men who had been compelled to surrender at Singapore in 1942.

The Arbroath sense of humour, even in these direst of circumstances did not fail, and questions were asked about an Atomic Bomb landing in Arbroath.

Would the fish all fry in the harbour? Would the Round O would still be there even though all the other buildings were destroyed?

An old lady was heard to remark, that if it happened to Arbroath, "There would be naebody left in Arbroath bar the country fowk"

August 8 1898

This Holiday Monday is what the writer of *The Arbroath Guide* calls St Tammas Market Day.

He is nostalgic as he talks about the old days in Arbroath on St Tammas Market Day when

> "the High Street of the good old town was crowded with sweetie stands and the Abbey Green with penny shows, merry go rounds and hobby horses and when we youngsters stood wi' gapin mou's and witnessed what to our minds were the wonderful and grand plays of Rob Roy, Robin Hood and Gilderoy etc, or set off to the merry go rounds or the shogin boats"

But that was in the past by 1898.

Now he is distressed by the number of people, old and young, who desert the town (presumably because they can now afford the railway fare!) and travel on excursions as they fly away "into the pure and balmy air of the country".

Our good writer reflected that there was no point in staying in a deserted Arbroath and decided to take a railway trip to the berry lands of Blairgowrie instead, leaving on the 5.30 am train from the Arbroath Station.

It was a good trip, he tells us, meeting some Dundee factory workers who "wrocht" in a Blairgowrie factory, but were now going back to Dundee for their holidays, as well as a slightly snobby middle class family from Forfar.

He returns to Arbroath still lamenting the decline of St Tammas Day in Arbroath.

August 9 1920

The Town Council resumed its meetings today after its summer holidays, and Treasurer Duncan painted a very black picture indeed.

The basic problem was that the country is "bust" and therefore so is the Town (and indeed very town in the kingdom).

There is very little money available to be spent on the necessary things, let alone any fresh development.

The problem was of course brought about by the colossal spending on the Great War which had now been over for nearly two years, but still has its effect.

Trade has slumped because there is no market for goods, and although the world will recover, it will take a long time.

In the meantime, the message from the Treasury is to curb all "reckless spending", but Arbroath is now heavily in debt or "overpaid balance" as it is euphemistically described.

In spite of all this, there have been a few improvements with tarmacadam being spread over some of the High Street, and near the Police Station.

There are still tremendous problems caused by the Brothock Bridge, which has been a source of anxiety and frustration since long before the war, and now needs fairly urgent attention.

Many people criticise the Council for what they have done or not done, but some balance needs to be shown for times are not easy. Unemployment remains high, although there is some good news in that the flu pandemic seems to be largely in retreat.

August 10 1935

A famous Arbroath man and well known character died tonight.

This was George Edward, physical education instructor for all Arbroath schools, a position from which he very reluctantly retired in 1928 and only because he had reached the age limit.

He was a native of Brechin and in 1882 enlisted in the Scottish Rifles where he served for over ten years and developed such an enthusiasm for physical education that in May 1895 he was appointed to his post in Arbroath and stayed there the rest of his life apart from his service in the Great War.

He was wounded at the Battle of Loos, from which he recovered and was eventually discharged in 1919.

He was involved with the 1st Arbroath Boys Brigade and the local YMCA gymnastic club, his finest hour being when his team won the Dundee and District Junior Gymnastic Association Shield in 1901.

He was a member of the British Legion, the Arbroath Golf Club and a frequent attender at Gayfield, where on several occasions he watched a player who had learned the rudiments of the game at his hands!

He was also an office bearer at Hopemount Church. His funeral was held at the Eastern Cemetery and was very well attended because so many people had happy memories of having been taught by him.

He was survived by his widow, two sons and five daughters. He was 72.

August 11 1928

Today was officially opened Inchcape Park, near Ladyloan, the home of Ardenlea Junior Football club.

The pavilion was all festooned in bunting, and the ceremony was performed by Bailie and Mrs Chapel and consisted of a white tape being cut where the pitch was separated from the new dressing room accommodation.

Bailie William Chapel was welcomed by Mr Cargill, the President of the club, and he congratulated Ardenlea on their "pluck, energy and enterprise" in going ahead with the idea of having their own ground, something that was not always very common in Junior circles.

Bailie Chapel then said that there used to be a "college" in Arbroath in Montrose Road called "Damley" which turned out some very fine Scottish football players not least the immortal Jockie Petrie who scored his 13 goals in the famous 36-0 win in 1885.

A few other possibly apocryphal stories were told like Rangers protesting about Gayfield being two inches short after being defeated (that one was actually true!), an Arbroath player walking to Dundee to play in a team that beat Dundee then walking back again, and on a cold day players arrived at the ground with football strip already on underneath their normal clothes which they put on again after the game!

"We were quite hardy".

There was then a good natured friendly game between Ardenlea and Maryhill Hibs, the current holders of the Scottish Junior Cup. It ended in 3-3 draw.

August 12 1945

The war in Europe has now been over for three months and news of the Japanese surrender is expected any day now following the news of the bombs that had been dropped on Nagasaki and Hiroshima.

This Sunday night, the Webster Memorial Hall saw a concert given by the band of the 4th Infantry Division of the Polish Army in aid of the Welcome Home Fund.

The large and enthusiastic audience showed unstinted appreciation of the performance of the band and orchestra in their programme of light and classical music.

Thanks were accorded to Captain Ruzyllo of the 12th Ambulance Unit of the Polish Unit, stationed at Windmill House, for having arranged this entertainment.

It was rather ironic that it was in aid of the Welcome Home fund for Arbroath, because, for most of the Poles, a return home was doubtful because Poland had been "liberated" by the Soviet Union, not necessarily a step in the right direction, to put it mildly.

Some of the Poles would decide to remain here in Great Britain. They had proved to be welcome visitors, sometimes too welcome for there had been a few pregnancies – but such things happen in war!

There were more respectable relationships as well, for quite a few marriages of local girls to Polish soldiers resulted, and many people in Arbroath to this day have Polish surnames.

There was also the apocryphal story of an Arbroath girl who had delivered a wooden baby. Wooden? Aye, she was marrit tae a pole!

August 13 1909

Mr Howie's farm at Beechwood was the scene of a demonstration of a new invention today.

It was a new potato digger, now on the market and sold by Martin's Cultivator Company Ltd of Stamford.

A large crowd assembled, mainly farmers and farm labourers, to watch the digger in action.

The main benefit seemed to be that fewer potatoes were lost or damaged by the blades and that no screen or heck was required, and that the potatoes were deposited more evenly thus making life easier for the gatherer.

The potatoes were dislodged in the usual way with a steel share and then spread with revolving forks, the prongs of the digger catching the potatoes in such a way as to ensure that they had less chance of being bruised or buried in the earth.

After the potatoes had been gathered, the ground was gone over with the "graip" or the harrower to make sure that the ground was "clean" of loose potatoes.

Everyone who saw it was convinced that it was the way forward for the potato harvest, but the only problem was of course the price.

The local agent was James Cuthbert and he was on hand to discuss terms with any farmers who wanted to know more.

This demonstration came at the right time, for the potato gathering had just started for the season and would go on until October.

Potatoes of course were, more or less, the staple diet of Scotland, and Arbroath would always have an ample supply of fish and chips.

James Cuthbert

August 14 1960

Arbroath United's professional Doug Greasley, who had also been professional at Brechin at one point, hit his highest score of the season when he knocked up 132 against Cupar in a friendly on Sunday at Lochlands.

Yesterday's game against HMS Condor was abandoned because of thunder storms but the weather was fine today.

Arbroath's popular professional entertained his fans by hitting 15 boundaries including one glorious six. Arbroath reached the mighty score of 218 when the innings closed with the next highest score being Ron Kidd on 23!

In spite of the high score, Cupar professional John Dennis finished with 8 for 84, the duel between professional and professional being the highlight of the innings.

After tea time, Arbroath were unable to force a win as Cupar held out for a draw with Dennis with 62, keeping spin bowler Joe Vannet at bay. Vannet finished with 5 for 54.

But the day belonged to Doug Greasley who has now scored 1,000 runs for the season. Can he however complete the double for the season by taking 100 wickets?

Only a few games of the season remain, and he has now taken 92 wickets. As always in cricket, a lot will depend on the weather.

It had been a reasonable season as far as weather was concerned, but Arbroath had not done so well in the Strathmore Union which would be won by Perthshire XI this year.

August 15 1896

Mary S. Young

August 15 1896

St Mary's Episcopalian Church today in splendid weather had its annual outing and picnic to Kinblethmont Estate, the home of Mr and Mrs Lindsay-Carnegie.

The party was about 300 in all and included children from the Sunday School, the Bible Class and Park Street Mission. The children all met at the Church at 2.30 pm and were then conveyed in horse driven lorries to Kinblethmont, preceded by the Boys Brigade and pipers.

The children were under the supervision of the Rev C E Little, Miss Young and Mr J White. When they arrived at the extensive grounds of the estate, no effort was spared to make the children all feel welcome.

Swings were erected, races were instituted and games of football and cricket were arranged. Everyone entered into the spirit of things and a great time was had by all.

Tea was served at 5.00 pm. After that games continued in the fine weather until it was time to go home.

Three cheers were called for Mrs Lindsay-Carnegie who not only gave them the use of the grounds but also supplied milk and fruit gratis for the children.

The company arrived back in Arbroath at 9.00 pm, everyone having had a good time. It was a particularly valuable experience for children of a poorer background who did not always get as many opportunities for travel away from home as other children did.

Of course, this being mid-August, the spectre of "going back to school" was not far away.

Mrs Lindsay-Carnegie

August 16 1921

A member of staff of *The Arbroath Herald* had cause to visit the library and met an old acquaintance who had been born in the town but now no longer lived there.

They had not seen each other since long before the War and after catching up with what had happened to them and their families, the exile launched a tirade about why the art room in the library did not have a single picture of a local artist?

James Watterston Herald, who died in 1914, for example, and W Lamont had all won fame outside their home town and were well known in art circles, but there was no sign of any of their works in the town where they had been born, and where they had learned the rudiments of painting and art.

Why did local people not have the chance to enjoy the works of these men? Indeed there was every chance that many Arbroathians were unaware of such talented local men.

The gentleman had a point, but the answer was the obvious one that there was a lack of money in these straitened times for such "luxuries" as works of art certainly were, and there was simply not that amount of money in the town at the moment.

The Arbroath Herald then appealed to any "leal hearted" Arbroathians (and those with plenty money) to consider this sort of thing, even in legacy and bequests.

The library, a fine building with good staff, was doing a great job lending free books in these difficult times, and needed to be supported.

August 17 1935

Today was a disappointment for the 5,600 spectators, a more than respectable attendance who made their way to Gayfield for Arbroath's first home game in the First Division of the Scottish League.

The season had opened last week with a trip to Ibrox and a fairly predictable hammering, but no-one would hold that against the newcomers to the top League.

Today however was a different matter – it was against Albion Rovers at Gayfield. Albion Rovers, never a rich club and always under the shadow of the big two in Glasgow, were a respectable outfit.

Nevertheless, Arbroath were expected to win, but lost 1-2 and *The Arbroath Herald* is in no doubt about what the problem is "the forward line is still a minus quantity" (one suspects that the writer is a Maths teacher in his day job!) and "there is not a shot in the Gayfield locker as at present furnished".

The defence and the midfield are good enough. But the forward line of Lowe, Johnstone, Flucker, Jamieson and Carver were not up to scratch, and it is not difficult to work about the terms of abuse that were hurled at the centre forward!

But captain Colin McNab, a Scotland International who played most of his career with Dundee, is a reliable influence even though he is slowing down a little, and he has time on his side as he and Manager McGlashan try to steady the ship.

Next week's game is against Clyde at Shawfield, and that will be a difficult but by no means impossible assignment as long as there is an improvement in the forwards. It is good to be among the big boys though, with derby games against Dundee and Aberdeen to be looked forward to.

August 18 1926

In the death of "Muckle Meg", Arbroath lost one of its greatest and best known characters.

This was Mrs Margaret Swan, 25 Union Street East, who died at the age of 84, although some claimed that she was older than that.

She was a fishwife in the true sense of the word, and much loved for her kindly nature, although there was a hard side to her as well.

She was widowed many years ago and was left with a large family to bring up on her own.

Taking up the business of the curing and selling of fish, she was frequently seen about the town with her creel of fish.

By sheer hard work she was able to ensure that each member of her family got off to a good start in life, and she continued working at her trade until a very advanced age.

She was described euphemistically as a "tall, robust woman" and much respected even outside the town among summer and holiday visitors who knew that they would not be cheated if they bought their fish from "Muckle Meg".

Her youngest son James now ran her business from 32 Barngreen, and many others of her extended family were employed in the fishing industry in the town.

Her funeral was a busy and well attended one, for she was so well known. Her passing marked the decline and possibly the end of a special breed of Arbroath fishwife.

August 19 1890

A bizarre and unfortunate accident occurred today to Mary Murray, 56, the wife of John Murray, the market gardener of Dishland Hill.

Mrs Murray was leading a cow to pasture on Dishland Hill accompanied by her dog. The dog ran at the cow, barking loudly.

This infuriated the cow which then attacked the dog, which then ran from it and took refuge behind Mrs Murray. The cow then collided into Mrs Murray, knocked her onto the ground and trampled on her.

This was seen by one of Mrs Murray's daughters, who screamed and attracted the attention of William Simpson, of Millgate Loan Cottage, the Coachman of Edwin Charles Cumming of Green Bank House.

Mr Simpson ran to the assistance of Mrs Murray and was able to beat off the cow. Mrs Murray was then conveyed home in Mr Cumming's Coach and Dr Dewar, of Hill Terrace, was sent for immediately.

He at once managed to reassure Mrs Murray that no bones were broken and that everything else seemed to be in good working order. Mrs Murray however was severely shocked and traumatised and had to be confined to bed for several days before eventually recovering.

Mr Simpson deserved a great deal of credit for what he had done, for without his prompt and courageous action, things might have been a great deal worse for Mrs Murray.

No record exists of what happened to either the dog or the cow, but presumably Mr Murray made sure that they were kept apart in future!

August 20 1940

This event could not be reported officially at the time because of censorship regulations, but, Arbroath being Arbroath, stories spread and the truth came out gradually.

The Battle of Britain was raging in the skies of Kent, and it was widely expected that an invasion would occur after the defeat of the RAF.

Arbroath beach was of course heavily fortified to thwart a possible invasion there, but a great deal of aerial reconnaissance was being done by the enemy.

Today a German Heinkel 11 5C with a crew of three based in Stavanger, Norway crossed over Arbroath but crashed on Fauldiehill, near Arbirlot.

Whether it had been shot down by Fighter Command or whether the pilot had simply lost his way, no-one really knows, but two of the German crew were killed and the other one was badly injured.

A local farmer rescued the man, Lieutenant Tonne, from the burning aeroplane and took him to Arbroath Infirmary where he eventually recovered from his injuries and became a prisoner of war.

Such incidents were by no means uncommon at this stage of the war, but details could not be leaked to the public by the Press for fear of causing panic and alarm. Public morale was considered a vital thing.

The Arbroath Herald would normally try to get round this obstacle by talking in a vague and roundabout way about an "incident in the East of Scotland".

Captured German Heinkel aircraft, 1943

August 21 1947

Tonight was held in Arbroath Abbey the first ever pageant to commemorate the famous signing of the Declaration of Arbroath in 1320.

It will be held on the next two nights as well. It was organised on behalf of the Overseas Fund of the YMCA, and contained a cast of 112 local people with a commentary provided by Mr F W A Thornton who asked his audience to appreciate "the spirit and dignity which must have been evident in that far off day".

The pageant opened with a short opening service led by three local ministers, and then Bailie Robert McGlashan introduced Lord Kinnaird who declared the pageant open. The pageant began with the entry of cowled monks following the Lord High Abbot with the Bishops of St Andrews, Brechin and Dunkeld.

There was then a fanfare of trumpets to announce the arrival of Robert the Bruce flanked by Lord Douglas and Lord Randolph.

The Declaration was then signed. After this part of the evening, there was a display of dancing by local performers, and a clachan scene performed by Arbirlot WRI while the pipe band of the Arbroath British Legion provided music.

Considering these were times of austerity and that some clothing was still on the ration, the costumes were very impressive.

There would be more lavish pageants in future years, but this was a good start, and in future years, the Pageant would attract large crowds.

August 22 1902

Today at Arbroath Police Court, James Stewart, ship master of Hannah Street was charged with having, at the junction of Ladyloan and West Grimsby, assaulted Thomas Dalgety, a flaxdresser, with a stick on the face and head to the effusion of blood.

What seems to have happened is that Dalgety, a well-known scrounger and general pest commonly known as "Digity" (a corruption of Dalgety) had been pestering Stewart, a reasonably wealthy man, asking him for money (for drink, presumably) and trying to "mouch" off him.

Stewart had said no, Dalgety had persisted, insults had been exchanged and eventually Stewart had hit him with his stick.

Dalgety had then been conveyed to a local chemist's shop at the West Port, where his wounds had been dressed.

He was then sent home but was later admitted to Arbroath Infirmary not because of the seriousness of the wounds, but because Dalgety's wife, herself an invalid, was not able to look after him.

There was a funny side to this as well, because one could imagine Dalgety milking the situation hoping to arouse pity and compassion from the bystanders, and it also transpired in Court that Stewart, a tall well-built man, was actually 78!

It was possibly not a record age for an assault case, but it was certainly unusual for a man of that age to be prosecuted for this offence.

Bailie William Alexander said that there had been no need to hit Dalgety with a stick, but as the wounds were not all that serious, he limited the fine to 10 shillings six pence with the alternative of 14 days "breed and watter".

August 23 2015

The greatest day in the history of cricket in Arbroath when Arbroath United, with a surprising degree of ease, won the Scottish Cup by beating Grange by 93 runs at New Williamfield, Stirling.

Arbroath, with a team of three Carnegies, two Burnetts, a Ford, Willemse, Waller, Petrie. Ramsay and Hurst won the toss and decided to bat and with Fraser Burnett scoring 104 not out, finished on 217 for 7 after 50 Overs with Grange's somewhat wayward attack surprisingly conceding 21 wides.

It was the other Burnett, Calvin who took 3 for 21 in the Grange reply which lasted only 39 Overs as they were bowled out for 121.

This result was greeted with great joy among the many supporters of Arbroath at the game, and was a great tribute to the club which is very proud of its local traditions and had for a long time punched above its weight among the rich teams of Edinburgh

Arbroath United innings			**Runs**
BNW Ford	bowled	Blain	7
JS Waller	caught	Pyne-James bowled Blain	11
FWG Burnett	not out		104
E Willemse	caught	Goudie bowled McCallum	14
+HG Carnegie	caught	Aslam bowled McCallum	8
CG Burnett	caught	Pillai bowled McCallum	22
*MJ Petrie	caught	Blain bowled McCallum	3
BA Carnegie	caught	McCallum bowled Aslam	1
BC Carnegie	not out		15
C Ramsay	did not bat		
MR Hurst	did not bat		
Extras	(5 b, 6 lb, 21 w)		32
Total	(7 wickets, innings closed, 50 overs)		217

Grange		**Runs**
NAG Farrar	bowled Ford	8
*R Flannigan	caught and bowled Willemse	31
HG Munsey	bowled Ford	3
NFI McCallum	caught FWG Burnett bowled Ramsay	27
IG Worth	bowled CG Burnett	5
G Goudie	bowled Ramsay	10
AR Pillai	lbw bowled Waller	12
+KW Pyne-James	caught Petrie bowled CG Burnett	6
H Aslam	run out (BA Carnegie)	1
RT Routray	not out	4
JAR Blain	caught Ford b CG Burnett	3
Extras	(1 b, 5 lb, 8 w)	14
Total	(all out, 39.1 overs)	124

August 24 1932

A big event today in The Picture House when Sir Harry Lauder appeared for his Jubilee Concert, as he called it.

He was not born in Arbroath, but he did live for two years there when he was young, and was proud to call himself an Arbroathian.

He was born in Portobello in 1870, but when his father died in 1882, his mother and the children moved to Arbroath to be beside her family who now lived there.

He was a "part timer" as far as education was concerned attending the school of the ferocious "Stumpie Bell", while working the rest of his time at Gordon's Mill where they made flax.

It was in Arbroath that he made his first public appearance as a singer at the Oddfellows Hall where he won a prize in a competition, the prize being a watch.

It was also in Arbroath that he picked up his rich Scottish accent which he never lost and which made him famous wherever he went all over the world.

Tonight in front of a large and very appreciative audience he sang all his famous songs like "Keep Right On To The End Of The Road", "She Is My Daisy" and "Roamin In The Gloamin", and he made it clear that he was glad to be at home with this "ain folk".

Some people still remembered him from his days in the town and he was delighted to be able to speak to them.

Sir Harry Lauder's Jubilee Lunch

August 25 1926

An unpleasant case of assault occurred today and it all seemed to have something to do with the Arbroath and District Whippet Club.

"Whippeting" was a form of greyhound racing which was apparently legal but had a bad reputation because it was associated with illegal bookmakers and betting and also with ill treatment of the dogs themselves.

What happened was that George Carrie Masson of 33 Leonard Street struck Allan Scott on the right eye with his clenched fist and rendered him unconscious.

The accused pleaded guilty. Masson, apparently had been the Secretary of the Whippet Club, but Scott had been asked to do the job (possibly because of some irregularity in the accounts) on a pro tem basis, and had approached Masson about this on the street.

The two had "had words" on the subject, and in the course of the discussion Masson had punched Scott and rendered him unconscious.

Masson's side of the story was that he had resigned as Secretary but refused to hand over the books until they had been properly audited.

An argument ensued and Masson, previously known as a well behaved man and with no criminal record, had punched Scott.

Provost Alexander Robertson's reaction to all this when it came to the Police Court was a little surprising and remarkably lenient. He had known Masson since he was a child, and had been a friend of his grandfather.

He dismissed Masson and told him to give up "whippeting", which he blamed as the source of this whole business.

August 26 1907

Arbroath was sad this Monday morning to note the death of Forfar man George Young, the tenant farmer of Panlathy Farm on the Dalhousie Estate and a well-known local citizen.

He was 63, and had farmed at Panlathy since 1884. His health had been described as "far from satisfactory" for a while, but his passing was sudden.

He had at one point trained as a lawyer, something which gave him a great insight into the practicalities of running a farm. He was well known and respected for his knowledge of agricultural matters; in 1904 when the Angus Show was in Arbroath, Mr Young had been one of the main organisers.

He was an Angus County Councillor for many years, being usually returned unopposed to serve Arbirlot, and he was also a Justice of the Peace and a keen supporter of the Liberal Party with its Progressive approach. Of course, he was delighted that the Liberal Party were now in power in Westminster carrying out a raft of much needed reforms.

He was also Session Clerk of the United Free Church of Barry, and had served under no fewer than six Ministers there, bring a particular friend of the present incumbent Reverend Campbell.

He was much loved by all for his genial disposition and kind and sympathetic approach to most things. His funeral to Barry Churchyard a couple of days later was very impressive, even in the heavy rain, with the whole village pulling its blinds down and closing all shops for the duration of the funeral. He left a widow, Jeannie, but no children.

August 27 1960

There was a new sporting heroine in the streets of Arbroath this Saturday night, and she was called Anita Lonsbrough.

This Saturday night, a fine one after some recent rain, saw Arbroath enjoy a British Gold Medal in the 200 metres Breaststroke at the Rome Olympics, and they were able to do so, thanks to the modern miracle of television.

These TV sets were now well within the pockets of almost every family. They could be hired from Grant's or the Co-operative at about 10/6d per week.

They opened up a new world to so many people, with 1960 being the first opportunity that Arbroath people had to watch the Olympic Games. The previous games had been held in Australia in 1956, and that was just too far away for an outside broadcast, but this year the Olympics were in Rome and that was well within the reach of Eurovision.

Tonight many people forsook the cinema and even by-passed the dancing and the amusement park to watch the TV. Some pubs even had the wit to install a TV in their bar so that the punters could watch the sport.

The highlight today for the Arbroath sporting public was not the victory of Arbroath United over Dundee HSFP at Lochlands, nor the draw that Arbroath got at Falkirk, but the victory of the girl from Huddersfield who persuaded TV Commentator David Coleman to burst a gut describing her victory, shattering the calm of an otherwise placid late summer Saturday evening.

August 28 1914

The country has now been at war for more than three weeks, and already the British Army is in the field at Mons with a few Arbroath men apparently involved.

The town is still in a fervour with words like "patriotism" and "service" in the air as young men are constantly pressurised to join up.

Many are indeed attracted by the idea of a chance to get away from their mundane, hum-drum jobs, and no one as yet talks about trenches, casualties and death.

A few however do pause and wonder. But *The Arbroath Herald,* like most provincial newspapers in 1914, very jingoistic and imperialist, is urging people to join and has decided to employ a very subtle form of emotional blackmail by composing a Muster Roll of all those who are currently in uniform, so that those who are not will be asked the question "Why not?"

It is acknowledged that this will involve a serious depletion of the local labour force – Shanks Foundry have now lost 79 men to the Forces, Fraser 72 and Keith and Blackman 31. The Post Office has a total complement of 27, and 16 of them have now joined up.

It was a remarkable time in history, and it is very easy with the considerable benefit of hindsight to deplore the "rush to slaughter" etc. but no-one really realised just what they were letting themselves into.

It was going to be "over by Christmas", or even "over before the leaves fall" so let's all get a piece of it before it disappears!

August 29 1948

The time was (and not all that long ago) when any entertainment on a Sunday night, apart from what the Church had organised, was frowned upon, but it was clear that in recent years the power of the Church had waned.

Cricket matches on a Sunday were now commonplace and tonight in the Webster Memorial Hall a capacity crowd saw the Burgh Instrumental Band present a Grand Variety Concert featuring all the artistes who had taken part in "Arbroath Follies in 1948".

Councillor J K Moir proposed the Vote of Thanks to the various people who had taken part – comedians Johnny Rae, Bert Williams and Ike Freedman, tenor Alasdair Dick, soprano Sadie Stevens, dancers Dean and Denton, troubadours Douglas and McEvoy, and Betty Attwell and her Music Makers.

Musical items were provided by the Instrumental Band, conductor Mr A Whyte. Bert Williams acted as compere and the show was produced by Alasdair Dick.

It was clear that the town was now recovering nicely from the Second World War. New houses were being built and more were being planned .

The revolutionary National Health Service had started recently.

At least as important as all that was the fact that this looked like as if it were going to be an era of full employment with everyone in work and able to attend concerts like this.

True, rationing was still in force but more and more things were becoming available, and although people talked about "austerity", it was something that could be endured, and was a great deal better than the depression after the last war.

And we could now enjoy Sunday!

August 30 1939

Arbroath is in an advanced state of readiness for what now seems inevitable.

All the Air Raid Patrol services are at full strength, although there are a few vacancies in the Auxiliary Fire Service.

Air Raids are the biggest worry, but the traffic lights at the junction of Keptie Street and Lochlands Street have been screened.

White chequered lines have been painted at the corners of streets to help if lighting fails.

The entrances to the Railway Station in Keptie Street have been painted white.

Some of the Black Watch C Company have already been mobilised and a large crowd gathered in the Drill Hall in the Marketgate to see their departure.

The ARP have been practising sending messages. All fishing boats were tied up in the harbour by order on Tuesday of this week but they are now allowed to operate if they have permission for certain areas.

Emergency procedures have been practised for the evacuation of patients from Arbroath Infirmary and the local branch of the British Legion (veterans from 1918, mainly) are forming a Home Guard.

Preparations are also being made for the reception of evacuees from Dundee, as many as 2,000, it was claimed, but it is difficult to make any concrete preparations until such time as they see how many actually come. Some are expected as soon as Saturday.

There are still those who are going around saying that "It may not happen", but to most people it seems pretty inevitable.

ARP Wardens

August 31 1961

Norman Crawford, the local librarian, delivered an interesting talk to his fellow members of Arbroath Rotary Club on "the Language and Lore of School Children".

This was at the weekly meeting at Goodfellow and Steven's restaurant. He said that no matter how uncouth and uncivilised children seemed to be, they were still tradition's greatest friends, for their vocabulary and culture scarcely seemed to change from one century to another.

In their self-contained community, they were respecters, even venerators, of custom with the same jokes being cracked as had been in the time of Queen Anne, and the same riddles as in Henry VIII.

"Halves" was called out in Stuart times for something that had been found so that it could be shared, and warts could be cured in the same manner now as they had been in the time of Francis Bacon.

The song "ring a ring of roses" was now sung by children unaware that they were singing about the Great Plague of London.

A draw in a game of bowls was called "peels", and it was still common in some part of Great Britain to call for a truce in an argument of a fight by saying "barley".

Just imagine, said Mr Crawford, the amount of bother that could be saved at Arbroath Town Council or in the Houses of Parliament if someone could just, at an appropriate moment, shout "barley"!

Mr Crawford's talk was well received by his audience. Councillor Goodwillie presided and Mr W Robertson proposed the Vote of Thanks.

September

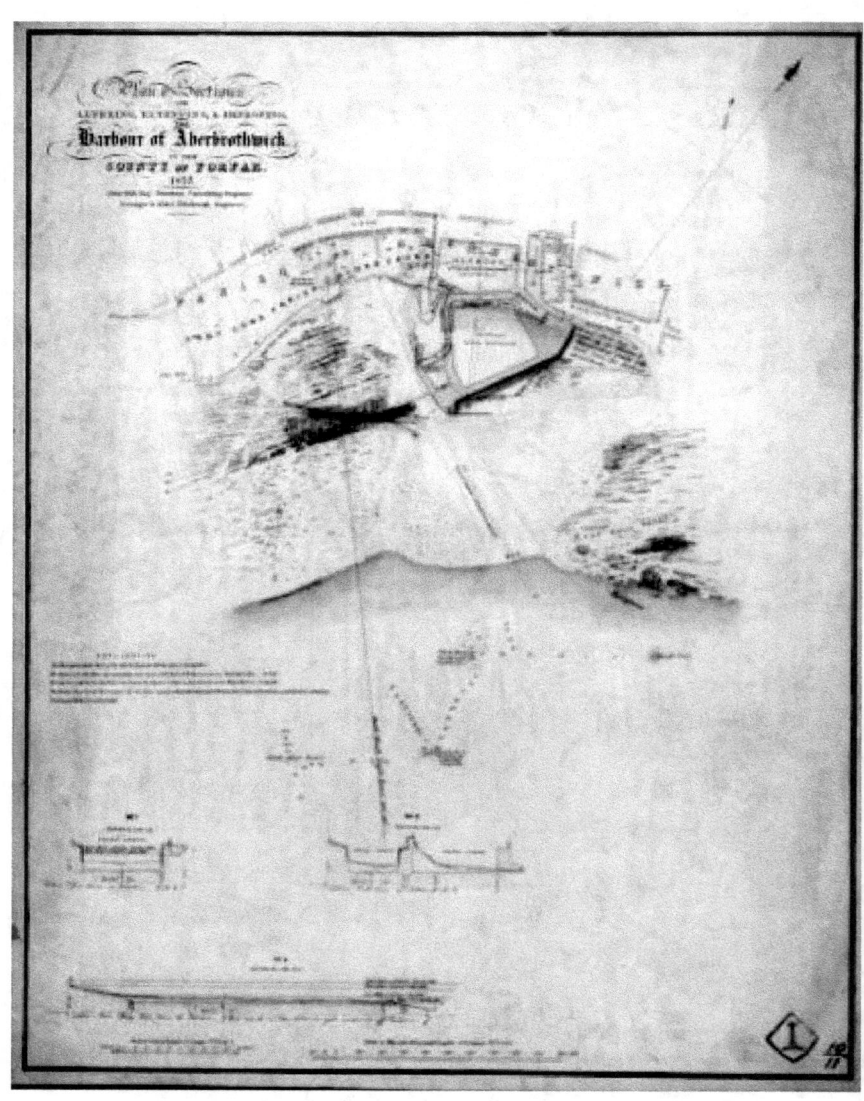

Arbroath Harbour 1837

September 1 1906

This Saturday morning, a group of local boys, pupils of Arbroath High School, committed a daring and outrageous deed.

They managed to climb over the fence at Arbroath High School and played a game of football on the field!

They were of course duly removed, because that had been expressly forbidden.

The Rector's reaction was rather surprising, albeit perhaps for the wrong reason.

He did not necessarily want them to be totally prevented from playing on the High School grounds because he feared that, such was their love of football, they might go the Common to play the game where they would have "intercourse" (sic) (in the 1906 sense of the word, one hopes, meaning "friendship"!) with the rough and ready "common" boys (common in more senses than one, suggests *The Arbroath Herald*).

It is not hard to detect a fair amount of snobbery and social divisions here, but the local press seems to find it rather funny.

The local, common, boys might introduce the High School boys to some undesirable habits, whereas the High School boys might show a little "side", a word meaning a patronising and arrogant attitude to people who are perceived to be of a lower social order.

So where do we go from here? Social divisions seem to run deep in 1906 Arbroath, but of course, the original cause of the problem, a game of football might actually cross class lines!

It might also lead to more er – "intercourse" (1906 sense of the word, of course!) between the patricians and the plebeians, the bourgeoisie and the proletariat, the rich and the poor.

September 2 1901

Amidst a great fanfare of metaphorical trumpets, Arbroath Theatre was opened tonight in James Street where the Victoria Hall used to be.

With Provost Colin Grant in attendance along with the Magistrates and the Town Council, the Theatre hosted its first ever play when "The Penalty of Crime" was put on by Miss Blanche's players all the way from St Albans in Hertfordshire.

On Saturday there was to be another play from the same company — "Shadows Of A Great City" and this time the management and players of Arbroath Football Club were invited.

The Theatre had been equipped in the latest style,

> "no attempt being spared to make it one of the best and most comfortable in the provinces. The Lessees trust that by engaging first class companies, they will have the support of the public in the town and the district"

said the advertisement. There was no doubt that a great deal of work had been going on all summer, and those who went there were very impressed by the comfortable seats, the lighting and the "rest rooms" — that wonderful euphemism for the toilets.

Certainly great artistes, like Edmund Tearle and Kate Clinton, had been engaged to perform plays like "Hamlet" and "Jeanie Deans".

Plays had been performed in Arbroath theatres for more than a hundred years — *King Lear* in 1793, for example — but a major test would await the new theatre at the end of the month when "Calder's Famous Cinematograph" would come to the Arbroath Theatre — the cinematograph being that subversive new invention of the new century and seen as a threat to the traditional theatre.

September 3 1939

It was a far from a normal Sunday in Arbroath.

The expected announcement duly came over the radio as the ultimatum expired.

Great Britain was once again at war with Germany.

Many people were in Church when the declaration was made. It was hardly unexpected news. The country had expected it a year ago but Mr Chamberlain had managed a deal at Munich.

Not this time, though. The main fear was attack by air, and that was something that people, having seen newsreels in the cinema of what had happened in Spain, were aware that there was no real escape from.

In Arbroath the main talking point was the arrival of the evacuees from Dundee. It could hardly be described as a total success. No-one had really thought out the huge cultural differences for children living in Dundee slums (sometimes in awful poverty) adapting to life in a coastal town.

In any case, was Arbroath with its docks and harbour really any safer than Dundee?

Everyone, with very few exceptions, was now seen walking about carrying a box. This was a gas mask – because "you never know", and the Station now began to see a steady stream of departures of young men and women to training bases in England and elsewhere.

All young men now awaited the call, but unlike 1914 where there was a certain excitement in the air, the prevailing mood was one of resigned acceptance of one's fate, and, surprisingly, a lack of opposition to the Government's decision to go to war.

September 4 1948

The town was devastated tonight with the news of a fatal road accident which occurred near Dundee.

A woman from Brechin was killed and an Arbroath man was left seriously injured in hospital.

The injured man was Albert Tomlinson, aged 55, an engineer with the Northern Tool and Gear Company, living at 10 Wallace Street, Arbroath; he sustained head and leg injuries.

His companion, Mary Craig, Manageress of the Brechin Laundry Company, was killed instantly. Mr Tomlinson was unmarried and they were clearly a middle-aged couple going to the cinema in Dundee.

It happened near Balmossie Bridge on the Arbroath to Dundee Road, when three Limited Stop buses full of holiday-makers approached and the leading bus skidded on the greasy surface straight into the approaching car.

There was no possible chance of avoiding it. Three women on the bus sustained minor injuries, and one of the passengers, who was a nurse, was able to give First Aid to Mr Tomlinson.

This did nothing to persuade people that road travel was any safer than railway travel, but in truth the real problem is the road itself which was made for horse and cart travel rather than the fast cars that are more and more common today.

Buses too, although they have been around for a long time now, are still too unwieldy for the narrow roads.

September 5 1962

The Territorial Army is on camp at Barry this week.

"C" Company of the 4/5th Battalion (Territorial Army) of the Black Watch was well represented on Sunday at the North Inch in Perth.

The Queen Mother, who has been Colonel in Chief of the Black Watch for 25 years, inspected the troops, presented a few medals and was cheered off by the men.

It was a great honour for some of the men to see the ex-Queen at close quarters, for of course she was associated with the County of Angus, being the daughter of the Earl of Strathmore.

Today they were visited by Sir Bernard Fergusson, leader of the Chindits in World Two, who came to camp to say good bye to the men. He was about to become Governor General of New Zealand.

Other activities at the camp involved drill, marching, training and army manoeuvres. The Territorial Army were still looked upon as a fairly important part of the nation's defences.

Although people still saw National Service, now gone, as some sort of simplistic answer to the problem of juvenile delinquency, most military men were not so keen on training reluctant conscripts.

For this reason, enthusiastic semi-professionals were looked upon as a valuable auxiliary service to the regular Army, even though it was becoming more and more obvious that if there was to be a Third World War, it would be a nuclear one rather than a conventional one with soldiers from the Black Watch.

September 6 1957

There seems to be little doubt that the Open Air Bathing Pool is bringing in the cash.

Now that the summer season has passed, Councillor A M Keith, convenor of the Public Baths Committee, was able to announce at the Town Council meeting that 116,345 people had paid to enter the Baths, an increase of over 15,000 from last year.

It is generally agreed that that had a lot to do with the fine weather, but it also had to do with the fact that news got round about the excellent facilities at Arbroath Bathing Pool.

The number included spectators, and the amount of swimmers was 84,856 compared with 75,181 from last year. Income was £2689, as against £2449, and the catering had similarly brought in an increased profit of £2337.

There was similarly no doubt that the weekly Miss Arbroath beauty parades drew attendances as well with 20,853 coming in.

The Pool was a great resource for the town and there were as yet no objections either from Churches or from women's groups about the exploitation of female flesh that these weekly beauty competitions seemed to involve.

Nor were the girls themselves unhappy about being leered at by lecherous men. In fact they rather enjoyed the attention. It would be another decade or so before the Women's Liberation Movement began to complain about this enslavement of women's sexuality to male eyes.

In 1957 it was all just harmless fun, and clearly as far as the town of Arbroath was concerned, profitable fun as well!

Open air pool

September 7 1893

Bailie Colin Grant had a rather tragic case to deal with this morning at the Arbroath Police Court, and it affected a woman!

It concerned Elizabeth Forsyth or Grady, millworker of no fixed place of residence who

> "within the public house at Fisheracre occupied by Ann Taylor assaulted the said Ann Taylor by beating her with her fists and knocking her down, and then assaulted William McLennan, flaxdresser, Ponderlaw Lane by assaulting him with a bottle 'to the effusion of blood' and behaved in a disorderly manner and committed a breach of the peace."

When asked to plead, the accused said that she had had so much liquor that day that she had no clear recollection of what had happened.

The two victims then gave evidence with Mr McLennan saying that he had needed to summon the doctor to attend to his head wound.

What the dispute was all about is not recorded, but clearly alcohol is a vicious ingredient to some occasions, and it would not be unreasonable to assume that the lady in question had possibly had dealings with Mr McLennan in the past on a personal basis, or even perhaps on a "professional" basis.

Bailie Grant, who presumably was experienced in dealings with cases of this kind, said that it was a very serious offence but that he would "modify" the fine to 7 shillings and 6 pence, with the alternative of seven days in prison.

He possibly felt that a higher fine might be unrealistic for Elizabeth to afford.

September 8 1921

A rare day for Arbroath when they were visited by Royalty in the shape of Queen Mary and her daughter the Princess Mary.

Their main port of call was Arbroath Abbey where they inspected the ruins and were told of the historical significance of the Abbey.

They also travelled to Annesley House for lunch, where they were entertained by Mrs Lindsay Carnegie.

They arrived by car from Forfar and came into town past Lochlands cricket ground, down by Keptie Street and the West Port, along Millgate, Commerce Street and the High Street to the Abbey, cheered by crowds, mainly of schoolchildren, all the way.

The weather was splendid and described as "royal weather for a royal occasion", and everywhere they went, they were cheered to the echo, proving what *The Arbroath Herald* said that the House of Windsor (as they were now called) was a very popular one in Great Britain.

There were always fears of security for everyone was aware of what had happened in Russia in 1917 to the King's cousin, and behind the apparent servility of the flag waving public, there was a certain discontent about the poverty that the War had brought.

Queen Mary in particular had needed to work hard to gain popularity, for no amount of propaganda could hide the fact that she was German and that her native language was German.

The Princess was pretty and charming, however. Where the King was that day, no-one seemed to know and no-one had the courage to ask.

Queen Mary in Arbroath in 1921

September 9 1924

Today, probably for the first time ever, a serving British Prime Minister appeared in Arbroath.

This was J Ramsay MacDonald, the first ever Labour Prime Minister, an unpretentious Scotsman from Lossiemouth, a town that had so many similarities to Arbroath.

He had agreed to attend a ceremony for the late Arbroath artist Mr J W Herald, for whom a plaque was unveiled.

MacDonald was given a great reception, but sadly because of the uncongenial weather, the ceremony had to take place indoors in the Arbroath Public Library, thus depriving quite a large number of Arbroathians from hearing him.

He came across very well, far from the revolutionary figure in the pay of the Bolsheviks (as he was sometimes portrayed) but also a little short of the demigod that so many factory workers and fishermen imagined him to be.

He was quite simply a nice man, who could very easily have been "ane o us". His Government did not have very much longer to run. It was in any case a minority Government heavily dependent on Liberal support, and had only been in existence since January.

Its achievements were not insignificant, especially the encouragement for Council Houses and the good relationships established with the Soviet Union.

A huge crowd gathered in the rain outside the Public Library just to catch a glimpse of the great man, and rather disturbingly for some people, strains of "The Red Flag" were heard in certain quarters!

Ramsay MacDonald in Arbroath in 1924

September 10 1932

A remarkable day to end the cricket season!

Brechin had played all their games and their record was played 14, won 9, drawn 2 and lost 3, making 20 points.

Arbroath had been less lucky with the weather and had played 12 games for 18 points.

The last Saturday of the season (September 10) was reached and Arbroath had games against Downfield at home and Mannofield XI at Mannofield outstanding.

They made the astonishing decision to play both games on that day, captain Bob Sievwright being keen to play up all the games rather than leaving one of them unplayed because of weather.

If Arbroath won one of these games, they would have shared the Championship with Brechin, but if they won them both, they would be champions outright.

So Arbroath split their resources, and made the mistake of sending the talismanic Bob Sievwright to Aberdeen, on the grounds presumably that Aberdeenshire might play some of their County players.

In the meantime the professional Williams stayed at Lochlands to deal with Downfield. The ploy failed and Arbroath lost both games!

Sievwright for once failed to deliver at Mannofield where D B McPherson scored a century for the Aberdeen side, and Williams was out for 5 at Lochlands.

Sievwright did take his 100th wicket for the season, but it was not enough. At Lochlands, Downfield easily surpassed Arbroath's undemanding total of 64.

The Arbroath Herald quotes loads of supporters, who are wise after the event, but *The Brechin Advertiser* sheds a Pecksniffian tear and says, tongue firmly planted in cheek, that "Arbroath are to be sympathised with".

Arbroath United Cricket Club were league champions in 1932. Back row: R.G. Sievwright, A. Angus, S. Duncan, R. Gleig. Middle row: T. Littlejohn, F. Millar, G. Anderson, A. Sievwright, N. Sievwright. Front row: C. Alexander, J. Ford, J. Counie, J.

September 11 2001

A car load of teachers came out of Arbroath High School heading to their cars after their day's work.

They were moaning (as teachers do) about their Headmaster, excessive workloads, impossible demands and disruptive pupils when a pupil shouted at them "America's on fire".

When questioned about this rather strange statement, the pupil (not one of the brightest, it would have to be conceded) softened a little and said "Well, there's twa muckle towers and somebody has been fleein aeroplanes at them...and they're oan fire!"

He was of course referring to what has become known as "9/11", the attack on the USA by Islamic extremists. The general consensus was that, no matter what the USA had done in the past, this was outrageous.

And of course, the world changed that day, and those responsible have been brought to justice in a terrible revenge.

It was one of the few days in Arbroath's history that national and international affairs took precedence over local affairs like football matches, discos and the price of fish.

But there was still the local angle to it with people going around saying that they hoped that it wouldn't happen here, and one Arbroath lady of a venerable age was heard to remark as she went into the supermarket to do her shopping that "At least there were nae Arbroath fowk there".

Although the final death tally was never found with any degree of accuracy, this claim seems to be true.

September 12 1885

Arbroath 36 Aberdeen Bon Accord 0 is still standing as a world record score.

There have been other higher scores in various parts of the world but there have been mitigating factors like a team deliberately scoring own goals or a failure to keep an accurate account of the goals.

It was a Scottish Cup game, and it may be that, as the cricket season was still going on, Bon Accord may have travelled south under the impression that they were to play cricket.

The game was played at Gayfield in continuous downpour and Arbroath were 15-0 up at half time. There were in fact more goals scored but referee Mr Stormont disallowed at least 5.

18 year old Jocky Petrie scored 13 goals, and although the opposition was poor, nevertheless it was a Scottish Cup tie and full credit must be given to Milne, Collie and Salmond; Rennie, Milne and Bruce; Petrie, Tackett, Marshall, Crawford and Neil for the achievement, which has seen Arbroath appear in all football record books.

By an odd coincidence on that very same day in Dundee, Dundee Harp beat another Aberdeen side, Aberdeen Rovers, 35-0. Again there was a dispute about the score.

The referee said 37, but Dundee Harp insisted it was only 35, so Arbroath's 36 is the record. Arbroath went on to beat Forfar 9-1 and Dundee East End 7-1 before succumbing to Hibs 5-3.

Queen's Park won the Scottish Cup that season.

September 13 1951

A historic day!

For the first time, television pictures are picked up in Arbroath!

Don Whitson and Ian Lindsay who work in the Radio Department of the Arbroath Co-operative Society were able to pick up test pictures from the new television transmitting station called Holme Moss near Huddersfield in Yorkshire.

This is clearly the start of something big, but very few people in 1951 would have been able to predict how big or indeed just what the next ten years would bring.

It was still hard to imagine pictures being transmitted to a box in this way to people's living rooms! BBC Television had started in 1936 from Alexandra Palace, but because of costs, it had been restricted to the London area, and even then only to the very few people rich enough to own a receiver.

When the war came along in 1939, television was scrapped and it only began again in the late 1940s.

The idea was to bring television to Scotland in 1952 with the building of transmitters at Kirk O'Shotts, near Glasgow, and Old Meldrum, near Aberdeen.

The progress of television was slow for a few years, although the Coronation of 1953 and the World Cup of 1954 did give television ownership a boost.

But then in the prosperous years of the late 1950s, things took off, and by 1961, television ownership was more or less universal, especially when commercial television arose to give some competition to the BBC.

September 14 1907

The Angus Volunteers may well be looked upon as an anachronism by many people in these days of professional armies and the building of Dreadnought ships, but not by the Arbroath and Forfar detachments of the Angus Rifles.

There was a certain amount of talk in the newspapers about the imminence of a war between Great Britain and Germany – nonsense of course, because the King was the Kaiser's uncle! – but in any case, the Army would always need good riflemen.

The shooting teams met for their annual shooting match at Cunninghill Ranges near Forfar today in fine autumn weather under the supervision of Major J Moffat, Forfar and Lieutenant Wilson, Arbroath.

For the match, everyone had to take 7 shots each at each of the 200 yards and 400 yards ranges, 12 men to fire in each team with the highest ten scores to count.

Record scores were recorded as Arbroath beat Forfar 62 – 60. Arbroath's average of 62 out of 70 was the best ever recorded at the Cunninghill Range, but Forfar's score of 60 was also highly credible.

The best individual shot was 65 and four men, two from each side, managed to get that, Arbroath's best scorers being Sergeant Calder and Corporal Matthews.

It was a very congenial and convivial occasion, and after the shooting was over, the Forfar men entertained their Arbroath equivalents to a meal and a few drinks before the Arbroath men got the last train home in a considerable state of intoxication, one would have thought!

September 15 1920

An examination in life saving was held tonight in Arbroath Public Baths under the Chairmanship of Mr A W Joyce of the Midland Counties Swimming Association.

Ten young members of the St Thomas Swimming Club had recently been under instruction from Mr A C Hogg for the past two months. Eight of the ten members passed their test to gain the Proficiency Certificate of the Royal Humane Society, while the other two were granted their Elementary Certificate.

In addition Mr Hogg himself was examined for the teacher's certificate and for this he gained the excellent result of 100%, with Mr Joyce expressing himself totally happy with what he had seen.

There were six girls: Misses Kennedy, Boath, Stirling, Hood and two Miss Pattersons (sisters presumably), and four boys: Messrs Carrie, Garden, Gordon and Bruce.

Mr Joyce congratulated Mr Hogg on what he had done, and the young people for what they had achieved. He hoped that they would make further progress in the higher awards of the Royal Humane Society.

It was of course one thing to "save the life" of a dummy in an indoor pool.

It would be something totally different to dive into the Harbour, for example, if someone, a non-swimmer perhaps, had fallen in, and one had to deal with all sorts of things like panic, currents, weather conditions etc.

Nevertheless, the foundations had been laid, and Mr Joyce was confident that these young people would be able to deal with any problem that might arise.

September 16 1950

The rugby season opened today this fine crisp autumn Saturday.

The main local game was played at the Air Station between HMS Condor and an Arbroath High School Former Pupils team denied of the services of some of their regulars, who were not yet available. Condor won 35-11.

It was also obvious that the School Former Pupils had not really had much opportunity to train together and were still a little "rusty".

Condor on the other hand were far better organised with three XVs in the field, not all of them *bona fide* sailors and soldiers at the base, for they were more or less an "open" team.

Today they were very impressive. Rugby had always been a poor second to football in Arbroath, who boasted of many junior, juvenile, amateur and school teams, but the hope was expressed that now that the cricket season was over, more men might be available to play the game.

Rugby struggled with the perception that it was a "rough" game, and it was certainly very much a regional game in Scotland in 1950. It was strong in the Borders, Edinburgh and to a lesser extent, Aberdeen and the posh parts of Glasgow, but the rest of Scotland didn't really understand the game.

Television had not yet arrived to show people Rugby Internationals, but just now and again, one saw a glimpse of the game on the Pathe or Gaumont News at the cinema.

September 17 1953

The flags were out today at 13 Townhead Road for the return of Private Frank Morrell of the Black Watch.

Frank had been serving in the Korean War and had been a prisoner of the North Koreans since last November. He was one of 530 POWS who docked at Southampton on Wednesday and he arrived in Arbroath early on Thursday morning.

His mother had gone to meet him, and naturally was overwhelmed to have him back. He was looking quite well after his experiences in captivity in a North Korean village, where he had met some American Marines and they had been allowed to cook their own food, heavily rice based.

The diet had been Spartan but adequate and there was no evidence of ill treatment, although they had done some ditch digging and road making.

Not everyone in Arbroath or indeed Great Britain in general saw the point of the Korean War, and no one was upset when it finished after some appalling casualties. It had lasted from 1950 to 1953.

One of the main objections to the war from the British point of view was that many of the soldiers serving were, like Frank, conscripts. Frank had been on National Service since July 1951.

Before that, he had been a butcher with the Arbroath Co-operative Society. He was due two months' leave after his prolonged stay, and had not yet made up his mind whether to take it all at once

September 18 1943

Junior Football is often a haphazard business at the best of times, but in war-time, it was even more so.

It was by no means unusual for a young man who had turned up to watch the game to be asked if he wanted to play, and anyone who had ever refereed a football match at any level was much sought after to take over the whistle.

Footballs were difficult to find sometimes, and often a ball used for schoolboys football had to be pressed into service, while strips all had that faded look, for clothing was severally rationed. And yet the show kept on the road.

Today for example Arbroath Victoria (the Vics as they were commonly known) were without the services of Vannet and Smart. Both had been called up to the Services since last week, and the half back line of Bell, Murphy and Mellor were entirely made up of Services personnel, whether local men on leave or men who just happened to be stationed in the vicinity and were available for a game.

Crowds were large, however, and usually very appreciative of the efforts made to provide a game of football.

Several hundred were at Gayfield today to see the First Round of the Forfarshire Junior Cup between the Vics and East Craigie.

They saw a good game, albeit somewhat lacking in sophistication, in which the local team were 0-3 down at half time, but recovered to win 6-3 with centre forward Kemp scoring five goals.

Anchorage had less luck than the Vics, losing 0-1 to Carnoustie.

September 19 1937

There is something that can bring light and cheer to the Autumn "fast" or Holiday Weekend when the town is less populated than normal.

Some early morning swimmers off the Ness brought back reports that they had seen a shark, some 20 feet long, in the sea.

Sightings of sharks in the North Sea are rare, it has to be said, and the swimmers often had a certain difficulty in making people believe them!

"You shouldna go swimming in the sea when you have a drink in you" was a common reply.

On Tuesday the crew of the *Floreat III*, a local fishing boat, said that they too had seen a shark off Lunan Bay and had passed only 50 feet away from it.

The crew of the *Annie Smith* claimed to have seen the same creature jump out of the water and back in again near Montrose.

It was certainly a talking point in the town for a few days, and although one can never really rule out an elaborate "leg pull" or "wind up", there does seem to have been a large fish in the area.

Whether it was a shark or not, we do not know, but it was enough to deter a few people from swimming in the sea for a few days!

In the meantime everyone enjoyed their Holiday Weekend with quite a few people away for the weekend, now that the economic recession was over and that everyone was back working.

September 20 1911

Not for the first nor the last time did the vexed question of Swimming Baths come up before Arbroath Town Council.

It has been an issue which has simmered on for some time, but one suspects that something that is playing a large part in the minds of the Town Councillors is that Forfar now has swimming baths, dedicated and paid for by Dunfermline's own Andrew Carnegie.

The argument has always been that Arbroath does not need swimming baths because it has the sea, but anyone who has tried to swim in the North Sea in February will appreciate the need for an indoor pool!

There are several points to be addressed. Where should Baths be situated? The site of the old Corn Exchange seems to be a good one.

What kind of water should they have? Fresh water from one of the local rivers like the Brothock, the Noran or the Esk?

Or salt water of which there is a never-ending supply piped in from the North Sea? It would distinguish Arbroath from other swimming pools, certainly.

And finally, the most important question would seem to be, "Do we approach Andrew Carnegie?"

We could say that he has done a great job in Forfar, and that we would like the same. We could point out that there are loads of people called Carnegie living in Arbroath, and that he is bound to be connected to some of them? Such things were discussed at the Town Council...but no decision was reached.

September 21 1889

Today on a fine day saw Forfar Athletic at Gayfield for a close game of football which Arbroath eventually won narrowly 4-3, although *The Arbroath Herald* is happy to concede that the "Stripes" (Forfar wore navy and black stripes) had hard luck.

The Forfar team and their supporters arrived at 2.20 at the Station, disembarked and carried their hamper all the way to Gayfield. Their arrival attracted a great deal of interest.

There was of course a certain amount of mild hostility with a few local insults being exchanged, but there was also, this year, a certain amount of what was called in the fish trade "speerin the guts oot of the Farfar leds".

Just what was going on in the County Town these days?

There was to be a strike in the jute factories starting on Monday! There had been strikes before but this one looked more serious, and already there had been appeals for money from jute, linen and flax workers in Arbroath.

It had been discovered that Forfar jute workers were being paid less than their Arbroath and Dundee equivalents, and the local Union was trying to redress the balance, but were getting nowhere, and the owners were refusing to go to arbitration.

Clearly there was a stand-off here, and life was going to get more interesting in Forfar and the local area.

However for the moment, passion was confined to the football field and everyone saw a good game today with Forfar scoring fewer goals than Arbroath in the same way that their jute workers brought home fewer pennies than the Arbroath ones did!

September 22 1912

At about quarter past midnight this Sunday morning, George Simpson, the signalman at Elliot Junction, was taking in his lamps as the last train had passed for the night when he made a gruesome discovery.

He discovered the trunk of a man's body lying on the railway line about 20 yards east of the bridge which spans the Elliot burn.

He immediately went to get Mr Carnegie, the Station Master, and the pair of them with torches found two legs a few yards away.

Sergeant Edward of the Constabulary was summoned and later in the morning it was established the remains were those of Robert McPherson, an asphalt worker.

He was identified by Alexander Paton with whom he lodged. He had been in Arbroath for the night and simply decided to take a short cut over the railway line.

But perhaps he had a drink in him and did not notice the approach of the Edinburgh express which left Arbroath at midnight?

When the train reached Dundee, there were traces of blood on the engine, but the driver was unaware that he had hit Mr McPherson.

His body was then taken back to his widowed mother in the High Street. There are a few unanswered questions about this, for example, why did Mr McPherson "lodge" with Mr Paton rather than stay with his mother?

There does seem to be an answer, but in 1912 not only was it illegal, but no-one seemed to be prepared even to acknowledge that it occurred at all.

September 23 1841

The Perthshire Courier reports a case in the Court of Justiciary in Perth involving Arbroath and resulting in three women — Helen Murray, Helen Robertson and Mary Sutherland — each being sentenced to 18 months imprisonment in Arbroath Gaol.

We wish that we could find out more about this case, for there are gaps, and the punishment for what they had done seems to be extraordinarily draconian.

Apparently last July 19th or 20th, they had assaulted and feloniously taken from the person of George Aird, a quarrier residing with John Carrie, Arbroath, a one pound banker's note.

Admittedly a one pound banker's note in 1841 would have been a considerable amount of money but the sentence does seem to be harsh.

But we do not know the circumstances of the assault. Did it happen in the house of Mr Carrie? Or was it in an alehouse? Or on the street?

The Jury found "the panels" (sic) guilty of robbery but recommended them to the leniency of the Court in consequence of what a Police Officer had said to them before they made their declaration.

So what was this all about? As likely a scenario as any is that Mr Aird had employed one of the girls for "services" but had failed to pay.

The aggrieved lady had then approached two of her friends, and the three of them had set upon Mr Aird, who was far from being an injured innocent. Even so, 18 months is a long time for such an offence, but life was unforgiving in 1841.

September 24 1903

Today *The Arbroath Herald* reports and encourages a rumour to the effect that a new golf club may be formed in Arbroath.

The newspaper talks about an Artisan Golf Club for the town, and the context is the subject which no-one likes to talk about in 1903 – social class!

The existing Arbroath Golf Club has been around for a long time, and the newspaper is full of praise for the benefits that it brings in terms of health and income to the town.

The problem seems to be that Arbroath Golf Club charges an Annual Subscription of £1, and 10 shillings as an entrance fee for new members.

In fact, this is not an outrageous fee and compares well with other local clubs in other towns. In addition, the recently built club house has to be paid for.

Considering that many Arbroath workmen earn considerably less than £1 per week, this is way beyond the pockets of most people in the town. Hence the idea to start a club with less of a financial outlay.

The Arbroath Herald is all in favour of this idea. It is after all, an age in which people, in new organisations like the various Socialist and Labour Parties, are beginning more and more to challenge and question the idea that healthy sports are the prerogative of the wealthy.

It is, after all, in the interests of everyone to have a healthy working class!

September 25 1905

Mr George Neave, missionary of the Arbroath Branch of the Scottish Coast Mission, reported that the work of the Mission in the past year had been carried out systematically and vigorously and had been productive of very satisfactory results.

Attendance at meetings had improved, and there had been a three weeks' series of special "evangelistic services which had quickened and stirred the hearts of the people and had evidenced a greater thirst for spiritual truths".

In the past year, open air preaching services had been held in Arbroath and Auchmithie, and they had been well attended.

Visitation was his main weapon, and he had distributed many tracts which had been greatly appreciated by people, particularly by fishermen coming home to port after a few difficult days at sea.

Donations had been made and the money had been used to distribute food and clothing to necessitous families, for example, those who had lost their breadwinners.

Mr Neave did not quite say this in explicit terms, but everyone knew that the big problem in the fishing community was strong drink, and Mr Neave's evangelical preaching was, quite rightly, directed at the evils of drink.

For this reason, meetings were often held on a Saturday night, and Mr Neave singled out for praise the ladies who had made the Mission Hall such a welcoming place with cups of tea etc. now that a kitchen with water supply had been installed, the cost having been met, to a very large extent, by voluntary contributions.

September 26 1922

In tough times, as the early 1920s certainly were, there was all the more need for the Co-operative Society, without any doubt one of the bulwarks of the poor and clearly one of the great successes of the Labour movement.

Not everyone liked trade unions, and certainly not everyone voted Labour in Arbroath, but everyone was happy to admit that he or she patronised the Co-op, the Sosh, the Store or whatever name was applied to this huge non-profit making concern.

Tonight the Arbroath High Street Co-operative Society held its quarterly general meeting in the Good Templar Hall and announced a decrease in sales and profits from earlier in the year, but still, after all deductions had been made, declared a dividend on 1 shilling 8 pence in the £1 for members and 10 pence for non-members.

This meant was that if you had spent, say £10 on your groceries, you would get 10 x 1 shilling and 10 x 8 pence back – something close to 17 shillings. (In decimal terms, 83p; a return on investment of 8.3%) It did not sound like very much, but it could make a huge difference to some families, and it was far better to see the profits being ploughed back to customers rather than see them accruing to private individuals. There were currently 2133 members.

A few donations were made to worthy causes like the Arbroath Infirmary and the Local Lifeboat Fund, and the Committee were unanimously re-elected for another year.

September 26 1989

This view looks across the Outer Harbour towards the town from the Breakwater on a windy day. The nearer of the two big boats on the left, with the two lifebuoys above the wheelhouse, is Telstar AH63. Its hull was a fairly strong blue colour, somewhere between cobalt and ultramarine. It had been built at Macduff on the Moray Firth in 1962, with the name Telstar and the Banff registration number BF291. This continued right through to the mid-1980s when it came to Arbroath, retaining the original name, but taking the Arbroath number AH63.

September 27 1949

At 5.00 am this morning the fishing boat *Silver Cloud* was re-floated at last after having run aground at Victoria Park, near the Ness.

This brought to an end a fairly alarming experience for the crew, even though they were subject to a certain amount of gentle ribbing for being "dry land sailors" and people wondering if they saw the "highway cod" on the road.

They had left Arbroath Harbour 24 hours earlier to go fishing at Johnshaven in the company of other boats, but then a thick fog rolled in and they ran aground.

With the tide receding, they could not move and were reduced to burning rags saturated with paraffin.

They were then spotted by the rest of the fleet, and the crew were able to scramble ashore a couple of hours later, having refused the offer of a line and a tow, fearing the boat might capsize and suffer damage.

The lifeboat and the coastguard were unable to help. The boat had to be left all day as the tide was out, but during the night, local shipwrights were able to jack up the boat and remove her from the spur of rock, on which she had settled, on to a lower bed.

When the tide came in, the boat was successfully re-floated but was then towed back into Arbroath Harbour to be inspected for damage.

It turned out that any damage was fairly minimal and in a day or two, *Silver Cloud* was back fishing.

September 28 1909

Law and order is not a serious problem generally in Arbroath.

Normally everyone, even from the poorest of backgrounds, respects law and policemen, and can behave themselves even under the influence of alcohol.

But there are exceptions. Clearly Thomas Waddington is a major local menace. This young man, a burly and powerful character by all accounts, is only 22 years of age but this is his seventh appearance in the Police Court.

Today he appeared before Bailie Robertson on three charges of malicious mischief, assault and disorderly conduct.

He had been in the St Thomas Bar on Saturday night but had become obstreperous and the services of a "chucker out" had to be requisitioned in order to escort him from the premises.

Waddington then hung about outside until closing time or "skailing time" as it was known as in 1909. He then rushed the door, damaged the door, struck the proprietor Mr Ross in the face and used foul language.

The police were then summoned and Mr Waddington was removed. Inspector Pyper was also in court and said that it was very difficult for publicans to keep law and order when there were people like Waddington around, particularly a man of such strength, and that something serious needed to be done about it.

Bailie Robertson was clearly in agreement and saying that the days of fines and warning were now over, and sentenced Waddington to 30 days in prison – what was commonly known in Arbroath as "breid and watter" in 1909.

September 29 1938

Arbroath like every other place in the world held its breath today as Prime Minister Neville Chamberlain met Adolf Hitler in Munich.

At stake was European and world peace, for Hitler was demanding a large slice of Czechoslovakia called the Sudetenland which contained German speakers and German sympathisers who had been taken away from Germany at the Treaty of Versailles.

Tension had risen in the town over the last two weeks, and although the verdict of history has not been favourable to Mr Chamberlain, the people of Arbroath today waited, wondered and would not be nearly so critical of the man who, for all his aloofness, was no warmonger.

It was just 20 years since the last war and Arbroath still contained plenty of evidence in the shape of men, still middle aged, with one leg, one arm or blinded, of just exactly what modern war could do.

No-one really wanted that again if it could possibly be avoided, for the sake of what Mr Chamberlain called "a faraway country".

Tonight, the town talked of little else with everyone hurrying home anxiously. The news broke on the radio early the following morning that an agreement had been reached, the feelings of relief were tangible, and the spring in the step of everyone in Keptie Street, the High Street and down by the harbour was clearly visible.

The Arbroath Herald, while sharing the happiness that there would not be any war, nevertheless asked the pertinent question "But is this peace?"

September 30 1961

Grampian TV comes to Arbroath!

There had been commercial television in Scotland before in the shape of Scottish Television which was broadcast from Glasgow, and Arbroath was just a bit too far away to receive a satisfactory reception.

Dundee and Forfar and certainly Perth were able to enjoy STV, albeit with patchy and unreliable reception, but you had to be very lucky in Arbroath to pick up a good picture.

But tonight changed all that, for Grampian was based in Aberdeen and the "picture" and "sound" were good, even better than BBC.

Grampian TV officially opened at 2.45 when Sir Ivonne Kirkpatrick, Chairman of the Independent Television Authority pressed the switch.

There then followed Horse Racing from Catterick and the sport that would soon come to rival football on a Saturday afternoon – Wrestling.

Very soon the names of June Imrie, Jimmy Spankie and Douglas Kynoch would become household names in Arbroath, as indeed would the programmes that Grampian made themselves like "Bothy Nichts" and the buttock-clenchingly amateurish quiz programmes which offered you a star prize of an LP record if you could tell them that Paris was the capital of France.

Advertisements were local as well and various local fish merchants took advantage of this new medium to advertise their goods. Local artistes too occasionally appeared on local variety shows.

The real attraction was of course the network programmes like Bruce Forsyth's Beat The Clock from the London Palladium, and the soap opera which had started in December last year and would dominate Arbroath's social life for the next few decades – Coronation Street.

October

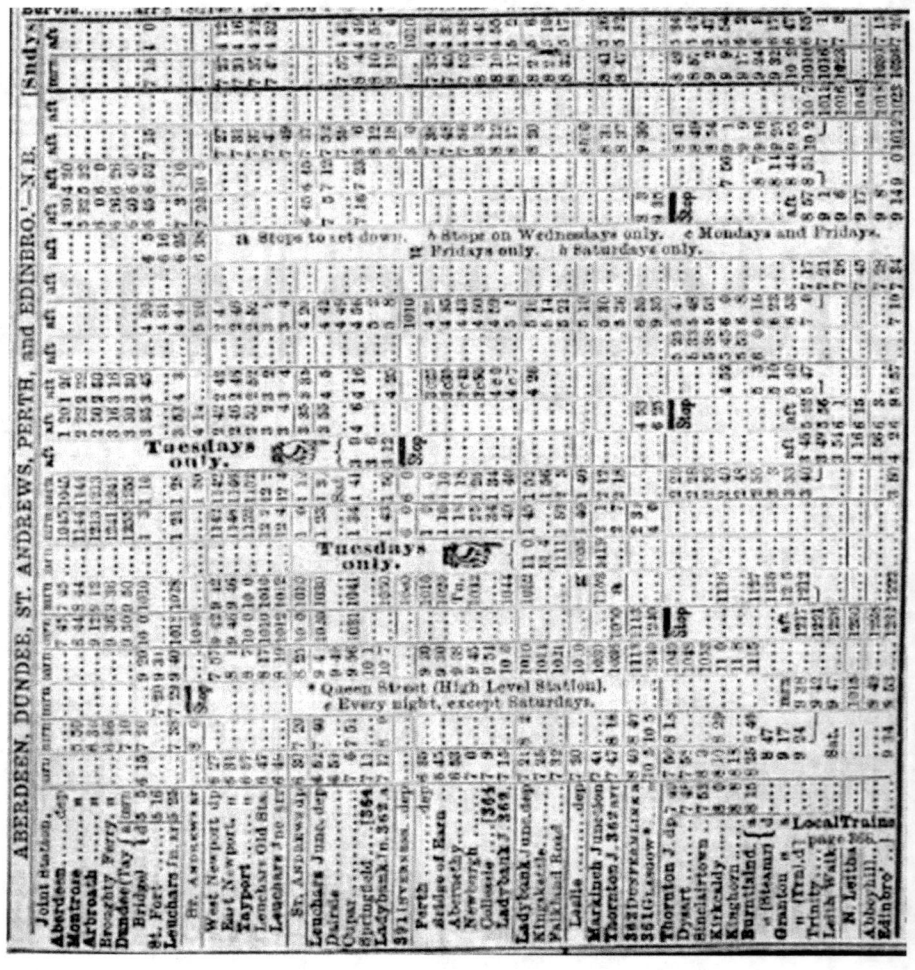

Bradshaw's railway timetable for October 1888

October 1 1903

Today's *Arbroath Herald* gives strong encouragement for local people to join the "Continuation Classes" as provided by the Arbroath School Board.

There is a uniform fee of 2/6d per student.

It is accepted that this might be a major obstacle for some families, but as the classes will run all winter, the money is a great investment.

Classes will be held at Arbroath High School, Keptie Public School and Ogilvy Place School.

Subjects to be taught will include Latin, French, German, Chemistry, Millinery, Nature Study, Book Keeping, Ambulance, Dressmaking and Singing.

Although the starting of the "night school" classes is a sad indication that the long summer nights have passed and that winter will soon be upon us, *The Arbroath Herald* stresses that education must not stop at school.

The most important time of a young man's life, it says, is after he has left school and before he settles down with a wife and family.

It is important that he has the education to be in a position to make the best use of opportunities that will present themselves to him. Not only that, but it is a patriotic thing to be educated.

This nation need fear no-one thanks to the Army and Royal Navy, (a reference to the recent successful war in South Africa) but no less important is her ability to make the right decisions and to have many people in a position to help her to an informed choice.

October 2 1934

A drama group calling itself the Arts League of Service Players put on Three One Act plays in the Webster Memorial Hall with some "remarkably fine acting".

The plays were "Lucrezia Borgia's Little Party", "Ivan, Anna and George" and "James Carrick".

They all went down well with the audience, who enjoyed the performances of Eleanor Elder, Ann Pichon, Dorrie Argyll, Mary Thornley, Alwyn Brown, Andrew Cruickshank, Dennis Hutchison, Clement McAllin, Hugh Mackay and Sydney Young.

One name stands out here – and that is Andrew Cruickshank, an Aberdonian who did various provincial repertory jobs in the locality before moving on to higher things, notably Dr Cameron in "Dr Finlay's Casebook" in the 1960s.

By the time that he became well known, he was generally typecast into playing crusty but likeable authority figures such as politicians, judges or doctors. It would have been interesting to have seen Andrew Cruickshank tonight.

Various other songs and dances were performed as well to supplement the programme.

The dances were "When she was bad, she was horrid" and "Lotus Land", and the songs were "Songs of the Hebrides" and "The Wee Cooper of Fife".

The players were thanked by the Master in Charge, the Rev W E Gladstone Millar and wished all the best in the future.

The audience was a good one and very appreciative of a rare treat of live theatre in Arbroath, which many people were beginning to fear was now losing out to the cinema, particularly as they now had "talkies".

October 3 1959

If there was ever the slightest doubt that Arbroath were going to struggle in football's First Division, today's result would confirm it.

From early on this Saturday, buses and trains had come in from Glasgow disgorging their passengers on a fine autumn day, as they had a walk round the harbour and sampled the hostelries.

The town of Arbroath was already well known to some of them who had spent holidays here.

A hard working Arbroath team were put to the sword by a youthful and enthusiastic Celtic team who beat them 5-0.

While Celtic's Bobby Evans and Bertie Peacock were in Belfast playing in the Northern Ireland v Scotland International (which Scotland won comfortably 4-0), youngsters Billy McNeill and John Clark were given a chance. It was Clark's debut.

Here at Gayfield, in front of a large and well-behaved crowd of about 8,000, the Arbroath team of Williamson, McLevy and Young; Wright, Fraser and Davidson; Shirrefs, Brown, Easson, Hay and Quinn fought well.

However, they were overwhelmed by a green-and-white tide, in which Steve Chalmers, who would score the winning goal in the 1967 European Cup final, scored twice.

This result left Arbroath at the bottom of the League table with only one won and one draw for six games, but Celtic Manager Jimmy McGrory praised the Angus team for their efforts and said "you never know in football" because the corner might be turned someday.

October 4 1947

It is not often that Arbroath has the treat of a play put on by professional actors, but tonight at the Webster Memorial Hall, they had the opportunity to see "The Lady From Edinburgh" produced by John Summer put on by Dundee Repertory Theatre on their tour of Angus, Fife and Perthshire.

In the same way as attendance at football matches and cinemas soared after the end of the war, so too did drama, both amateur and professional, enjoy a boom in the times that for some strange reason, people called "austerity".

The play had very little action in it in the sense that there were no murders or dramatic encounters with people from one's past, and therefore it relied to a great extent on the quality of the acting.

It concerned a widowed lady from Edinburgh living with her married sister in London and the effect that this had on the household.

It was one of these plays which worked very well in 1947, when there was a lot of enforced house-sharing going on, because of bomb damage and general disruption as a result of the war, but might not have been so successful 10 or 20 years later.

The audience appreciated the gentle humour and the nuances of the differences between Edinburgh and London life.

Drama at amateur level was now looking to take off after the war.

It had been popular enough during the war with Church groups etc. although the lack of young men had been a problem. Now that everyone was home, drama and opera were about to enjoy a boom.

October 5 1963

It's "tattie" time again! One thing that the county of Angus does not lack is potatoes.

The stable diet of so many people since someone brought them back from the Americas several centuries ago, and the supplier to the many fish and chip shops for which Arbroath is famous, potatoes still need to be gathered from the fields as no efficient machine has as yet been invented to do the job.

This means that Arbroath schools have a two-week holiday to allow children to earn some money.

Politicians who concern themselves about such things talk of calling them "the autumn holidays" rather than "the tattie holidays" in that the latter title tends to imply exploitation of young labour.

Young people, themselves, however have no feeling of being exploited. With wages upwards of £1 per day and a whole lot of fun with friends (and oh! the things that one can get up to in the dinner hour!) in the fresh air, these holidays are much looked forward to.

It isn't always fun, though. It can rain, and one gets a sore back with all the bending, at least on the first day.

There can be little doubt that the money earned is a welcome boost to everyone, no doubt with delicate negotiations between mother and offspring about how much must be given "to the house" and how much can be kept.

And a blind eye is turned to potatoes being taken home! After all, there are, literally, millions of them!

October 6 1920

A strange case appeared before Sheriff Gordon today.

It concerned Alexander Watt, a fish merchant, 22 High Street, Arbroath who was on a charge of

> having failed within 10 days after 5 May 1914, to exhibit to the Registrar a certificate of the vaccination of his child Lily who was born on 27 October 1913.

Alex Smith, Registrar of Births, stated that the law required parents to send a certification of vaccination to the Registrar within six months of the birth.

This had clearly not happened here, but there were several unusual features.

One was that, although Watt was not registered as a conscientious objector against vaccination, he had seven other children, none of whom had been vaccinated either, so the authorities would be obliged to prosecute him for them as well.

Another issue was that Watt had been called up for military service in August 1914, and he thought that the whole business had been forgotten about.

He also said that he was innocent from a legal point of view because the Registry Office could not prove that he had not sent a vaccination certificate.

It was not clear what Watt was arguing here. He was certainly happy more than once to try some emotional blackmail by mentioning his military service.

It raised the obvious question of why he did not get himself classified as a conscientious objector about vaccination.

The Sheriff was not impressed, imposing a fine of 2/6d on him with 30 shillings expenses. Mr Watt indicated his desire to take legal advice and to appeal.

October 7 1931

Today an Arbroath restaurateur was fined £3 with the alternative of 30 days in prison by Sheriff McDonald on a rather unusual charge.

Robert Parker Ralley, of 12 West Port, was charged under Section 1 of the Shops Act of 1912, for having, on every day between January 8 and July 25 1931, employed Ella Cargill 55 High Street as a shop assistant after half past one.

It did not seem to be the most heinous of offences, if it were even an offence at all, and Miss Cargill did not seem to object.

The problem was that he did not give Miss Cargill a half day, and the Shops Act insisted on this, unless he was prepared to pay her double time or overtime rates.

His first plea had been guilty, then he changed it to not guilty when he understood exactly what the charge meant.

His premises were closed on a Sunday, except during the Glasgow and Dundee holidays, and he was reluctant to give Miss Cargill an afternoon or evening off because most of his work was at night.

He stressed that Miss Cargill didn't seem to mind. Indeed her total number of hours was not excessive. But this, of course, ignored the thinking behind the law which was to protect the workers and to guarantee that there would be at least one afternoon when they had some leisure.

Sheriff McDonald duly enforced the law giving Mr Ralley a week to pay up. And in future, Miss Cargill would have an afternoon off!

October 8 1889

A mass meeting was held in the Corn Exchange tonight in support of the Forfar jute workers, some of whom were on strike and others had been locked out by their bosses, Craik and Don.

The meeting was presided over by John Quinn of Arbroath but was mainly addressed by representatives of the Forfar Union, Tommy Roy and Adam Farquharson and the Reverend William Cowper, Minister of the Forfar Baptist Church.

The problem lay in the notorious 12/9 wage paid to many male workers with families to support while Arbroath, Brechin and Dundee workers all earned 19 shillings.

Don, the biggest employer in town had made a profit of £31,000 last year.

The Forfar men outlined all these grievances and thanked Arbroath people who had already contributed £40 3/6 with the Burnside Works in particular contributing over £7.

The Forfar men were given a rousing reception by the Arbroath people, and hope was expressed that things could soon be resolved in favour of the workers, because it was believed that an attack on the working and living conditions of Forfar workers would very soon become an attack on Arbroath workers as well.

There were distinct similarities to the Ben Tillett Dock Labour dispute in London of that year, and Arbroath could be affected by that as well.

Arbroath continued to support Forfar until the issue was resolved by arbitration and agreement at the end of November.

Tommy Roy in his moment of triumph was very proud to acknowledge the support given to him by his fellow workers in Arbroath and elsewhere.

October 9 1927

Culloden Farm — no connection with the infamous battle in the Highlands — just outside Arbroath attracted large crowds this Sunday, in that Berkshire Aviation Tours Ltd were offering flights in the air for local people.

This was, apparently, the first time that this had happened and naturally people were afraid, yet fascinated.

It was like the first time that anyone travelled on the train to Forfar in 1839, or took a trip in a "horseless carriage" at the turn of the century.

Aeroplanes were a new method of transport which had first been seen in 1903 at Kitty Hawk in North Carolina when brothers Wilbur and Orville Wright flew for the first time.

Bleriot had flown the Channel in 1909, aviation had received a massive boost in the Great War and very soon there would be commercial flights all over the world.

Today some delighted passengers enjoyed a take-off, then a short flight over the town to see the Harbour, the Abbey, Lochlands and Gayfield with a view of Dundee, Forfar and Montrose in the distance.

The flight was pleasurable but expensive. There was also a demonstration by Captain Rimmer and Captain Nash of spiralling and looping the loop, even with some passengers inside.

Concern was expressed that the passengers might "fall out", but no, everyone was assured, we would all stay friends!

The Sunday afternoon coming would be even more spectacular for Captain Holmes was going to walk on the wings of an aircraft when it was travelling at 90 miles per hour.

October 10 1974

No-one ever thought that it would happen, but it happened today!
Arbroath at last turned the Conservatives out!

South Angus, once a byword for tipping the forelock (or simply, crawling!) to the aristocracy of the Strathmores and Airlies at last voted for someone else, in this case for a man called Andrew Welsh, a 30-year old teacher who stood for the Scottish National Party.

Welsh had worked very hard in Arbroath throughout the campaign, and had been helped by tactical voting on a huge scale.

Labour and Liberal voters, the penny having dropped, voted for the immediately likeable and sincere Welsh.

The election had been called because the minority Labour Government in power since March needed an overall majority, which it got – just.

So Harold Wilson returned as Prime Minister to a country which faced huge problems of inflation and industrial unrest.

It was tempting for the Scottish Nationalists to believe that Scotland, with all its oil (and that, of course, intimately affected coastal North Sea towns like Arbroath, Montrose and Aberdeen) could go it alone without England.

It was not as simple as that, but Welsh, riding on these sentiments, managed to poll 17, 073 votes, nearly 2,000 votes more than the sitting Tory, Jock Bruce-Gardyne, with the other two parties nowhere.

Welsh himself went out of his way to thank everyone who voted for him and promised to work for everyone as the SNP (hitherto treated as something of a joke) tried to carve out a credible future for themselves and Scotland.

October 11 1993

Andy Stewart died today at his house in Arbroath.

He was not yet 60 and had suffered health problems for many years.

He had been born in Glasgow in 1933 but had moved to Arbroath where his father taught Science at Arbroath High School, the school that Andy attended as a pupil.

He took part in the Arbroath Abbey Pageant in 1950, something that perhaps encouraged him to think of entertainment as a career.

He developed his skills in comedy, singing and impersonations and his big breakthrough came when he landed the job as the compere on the White Heather Club in the late 1950s.

He very soon became a national institution for hosting New Year programmes in the early 1960s, and his first real song which made his name was "A Scottish Soldier" which made him well known in Australia, USA, Canada and New Zealand.

He also sang "The Muckin O Geordie's Byre", "The Road And The Miles To Dundee" "Donald, Whaur's Yer Troosers" and many more songs, to add to his brilliant impersonations of Scottish characters.

He was a Rangers supporter all his life, something that perhaps explains his reluctance to sing Irish songs, at which he would have excelled.

He died of a heart attack the day after he had performed in a concert at the Usher Hall. His funeral service was held at St Andrew's Church, Arbroath and he was cremated at the Parkgrove Crematorium Friockheim.

He may have been born in Glasgow, but his heart lay in Arbroath.

Andy Stewart

October 12 1921

Today at Arbroath Sheriff Court a petition was presented to Sheriff Gordon for the removal of a tenant called Donald MacLennan, chauffeur, from the house at 7 Hannah Street.

MacLennan's defence was that he was not a monthly tenant (what that means, we cannot be sure, nor can we see what real difference it makes in any case) and that he was lodging a counter claim against his landlord Frank Matheson for expenses for a situation which he had lost, through having obtained a conviction at Arbroath Sheriff Court. He stated that he held Matheson partly responsible for this conviction.

MacLennan admitted that he was in arrears with his rent, but he had been out of work for 18 months and the only way he could pay off his arrears of £6 4 shillings would be by paying instalments.

Mr Webster, representing Matheson, replied that he was not really all that bothered about the money, but that he was wanting the removal of MacLennan from the premises, as MacLennan had been a constant source of annoyance and concern and would never pay anything.

They really only wanted to get rid of him. The Sheriff "granted the petitioner's crave" and gave MacLennan until the end of the month to remove himself from the premises.

There was clearly a great deal more to this case than what was now coming out in court, with "history" on both sides.

October 13 1912

It would not be the first time, one imagines, that Arbroathians have described their Town Council meetings as a "real load of, er, excrement"

But on this occasion, excrement has become a major issue in the town with particular reference to the Danger Point sewer.

Victorians had not been slow to spot a link between untreated effluent and diseases, but they had definitely been slow to do anything about it.

Now 12 years into the new century with clear (but minimal) improvements in other areas of life, the Town Council agreed that something had to be done about it.

By 12 votes to 6 the Council agreed to spend £500 on a "screening chamber and a short extension of the sewer".

This was too little too late in the view of *The Arbroath Herald,* which ventures the opinion that if Rip Van Winkle had wakened up after 20 years, he would not have been surprised to find that the topic was still under discussion.

A recent and very damning report of the Medical Officer of Health had left them with no option but to do something, but this was only about one eighth of what really needed to be done.

Councillor Wilson was certainly of the opinion that the problem really needed to be tackled wholeheartedly.

Certainly those who lived near there reported that the assault on their nostrils every time they opened their door was quite something, but, as one local philosopher put it,

"There is no money to be made out of ......"

October 14 1939

Today two young Arbroath men, next door neighbours, became the town's first casualties of the war.

They were George Shepherd and Robert Ritchie of 7 and 9 Airlie Crescent. Neither was married.

Slightly more fortunate was Edward Stewart of 2 Maule Street who had a wife and four children.

He was rescued from the sinking *Royal Oak*, but the other two went down. All three had been fishermen and had joined up as Naval Reservists.

Stewart had been a member of the crew of *Girl Jean*. All three had left the town on the outbreak of war and had been on board the *Royal Oak*, which had been lying at anchor in Scapa Flow in the Orkneys when a German U Boat had penetrated the defences and torpedoed the ship with loss of about 800 men, although 424 had survived.

This was a major blow to the idea of British naval invincibility, and caused serious concern to the First Lord of the Admiralty, Winston Churchill.

It was the first piece of really bad news to hit Arbroath since the outbreak of war. Unlike the First War where casualties had been heavy and immediate, the Second War had got off to a slow start with men leaving town in large numbers for bases in England for training.

A few were already in France guarding the Maginot Line, but little had been happening on the Western Front. This news therefore came as all the more of a shock to the families of the men.

October 15 1931

A General Election has been called for the end of the month, and today the Electoral Role has been made up.

The total number of voters will be 11,443, an increase of 141 from last time. Women outnumber men by 6,598 to 4,711.

This is quite astonishing considering that it was only 1928 that total enfranchisement was granted to all women, and it proves in some ways that the fears of the anti-Suffragists that women "would take over" were not entirely without justification.

There are several reasons for this, of course. One is that women tend to live longer than men anyway, but the other was the very tragic one that it was only 13 years since the end of the Great War which had caused the deaths of so many young men, and the sexual imbalance had still not worked its way through.

The sexual imbalance had advantages for young men in that they had a wider choice of sexual partner, and it might have meant that there were more chances of a job in more normal times, but in this respect, life was far from normal.

It was the time of the economic depression – the second such depression since the end of the war — and one of the things that the National Government was asking for a mandate for was its "Doctor's Remedy" of creating more unemployment.

Critics claimed of course that unemployment was no remedy; it was an illness. One way or other, however, politicians would have to take into consideration the views of the women.

October 16 1940

A German bomb was today dropped on Lochlands cricket ground!

For reasons of censorship and morale, this incident was merely hinted at and generally minimised in the newspapers, but people couldn't help noticing!

The noise was more like a door closing rather than an ear-splitting crack, according to those who saw and heard it, and it was fortunate that the bomb hit the outfield rather than the pavilion or indeed the nearby houses.

Children working at the potato harvest got a good view of it.

The following day, people took a walk up to see the damage, such as it was, with Bob Sievwright holding court and making jokes about the Germans doing more damage to Arbroath than Brechin ever did. The damage was soon repaired.

What it was all about, no-one seems to have been able to work out. It was probably a German bomber on a diversionary raid being chased by Fighter Command and dropping a bomb to make more speed to escape over the North Sea.

At this stage of the war, London was certainly being pounded but it was generally believed that the threat of an invasion had passed, at least for 1940, but it was still an uncomfortable reminder that the war was not too far away even from a peaceful East coast town like Arbroath.

The problem with air raids was that there was no real way of preventing them, it would appear.

October 17 1914

James Watterson Herald was born in Forfar on 29 July 1859 and died in 1914 in Arbroath.

The son of a shoemaker, William Herald, and Mary Watterston, he attended Forfar Academy, then enrolled at Dundee High School where he was awarded a prize for excellence in drawing. James Watterson Herald later became a renowned artist, known mostly for his watercolours and pastels.

After a short spell in Edinburgh and about 10 years in Croydon, James Herald took up residence in Arbroath around 1902, remaining there the rest of his life.

Content to earn no more than a living and judged by contemporaries as a recluse, Herald worked in his Commerce Street studio or his home in Bank Street.

He expressed no interest in personal wealth, giving away sketches in return for meal.

He died on 17 October 1914 aged 55, following a bad fall and a long period of ill health, and was buried in the Western Cemetery in Arbroath.

Ramsay MacDonald. MP, at the unveiling ceremony of the Memorial to J W Herald in Arbroath Public Library.

October 17 1910

Arbroath had a distinguished visitor tonight in Sidney Webb, one of the founders of the Fabian Society, along with his wife Beatrice.

He was now a London County Council member for Deptford and a well-known champion of social reform.

He had a large audience tonight as he addressed the problem of Unemployment under the auspices of the Society For the Prevention of Destitution. The platform party consisted of people like Provost Alexander and MP Vernon Harcourt.

Webb spoke well and eloquently stating that unemployment was nothing other than a disease. Like many diseases, it was preventable and all it really needed was a concerted effort on the part of all political parties to ensure that it did not happen.

For an unemployed person, there were not only the financial implications of not being able to support one's family, but also the consequences of moral deterioration that a life of idleness brings to anyone.

The important thing to realise was that it was not the fault of the unemployed person. There were several causes for unemployment, one of them being seasonal variations.

At the moment, for example, there was the harvest, particularly the potato harvest, and in the summer the fruit harvest, but the important thing was to ensure that work was available all the year round.

A minister from the audience talked about "wastrels" and "won't works", but Webb stated that it was important to ensure that such misapprehensions were not to be encouraged. Unemployment was a disease.

October 18 1961

Diamond Weddings are not very common.

To be married for 60 years to one person is no mean feat, and it is even more remarkable when the two people concerned are both Arbroathians and have lived here all their lives.

The celebration was held tonight for the convenience of family and friends, but it was actually on October 25 1901 that Andrew Blair married Mary Ford in Tuttie's Neuk Hall, the service being carried out by Reverend Dr Henry Angus of Erskine Church.

Andrew is now 86 and Mary 84. Andrew has now been retired for 18 years, but was previously employed as a tenter for 20 years at Baltic Works (Andrew Lowson's) and 30 years at Alma Works (Francis Webster and Sons Ltd.).

For many years he was a rock fisher and made his own tackle and rods, still enjoying his hobby until four years ago. He was also a very enthusiastic amateur gardener, a member of the Old Men's Club and of the Masonic Lodge Panmure (No.299).

The marriage had its ups and downs, no doubt, but considering that the Boer War was still in progress when they were married and that two huge and horrendous wars passed in the meantime, the couple have seen a lot together.

Blessed in the main with good health, and having learned that the success of a marriage is all done to tolerance and acceptance, they have been rewarded with happiness, their longevity being put down to contentment and the healthy sea air of Arbroath!

October 19 1927

The arrival of mains electricity in Arbroath may well be coming a step closer.

Electricity does of course exist in Arbroath but is dependent on generators and batteries, but the day may not be all that far way when every house will have electricity at the tap of a switch.

There are still those who think that idea is ridiculous and ask what is wrong with gas.

Tonight Mr George Balfour, at a meeting of the Dundee and Broughty Ferry Tramways Association of which he was Chairman, said that the Grampian Electricity Scheme, of which he was also Chairman, had plans in place to extend their electric cables from Broughty Ferry to Carnoustie, Arbroath.

From there they would cut inland to Friockheim and Forfar, and keep moving north to Montrose, so that very soon all parts of East Forfarshire would have access to electricity.

An area like Forfarshire which was quite sparsely populated in comparison with some other parts of Scotland, was one of the more difficult places to supply electricity to.

This announcement did seem like progress, although there were, as always, those who distrusted anything new. But electric lights apparently were far more powerful than gas ones could ever hope to be, and it would even be possible, some day, for an electric fire to replace a coal one.

This all seemed fantastic to people in 1927, but all those who had seen electricity working swore that is was something to behold and far better than anything that had been seen so far.

October 19 1991

On Saturday 19 October 1991, here are Marigold A52 and Sapphire AH79 together with a fine smaller boat on the right. The drawing was done from the road beside the Breakwater, looking towards the town.

October 20 1918

Cautious optimism seems to be the order of the day in Arbroath.

News from Europe seems to be good, and yet the good people of Arbroath have been fed so many lies over the past few years about "pushes" and "next stop Berlin" that it is difficult to get too optimistic.

There is in addition, the flu epidemic which is hitting Arbroath hard, and Primary Schools in particular.

This Sunday is Harvest Thanksgiving Sunday, a particularly important occasion in the context of 1918, for it is so vital, given the U Boat menace in the Atlantic, that Arbroath pulls above its weight in the production of corn, potatoes and "the harvest of the Ocean" – fish.

Arbroath has risen magnificently to this challenge, but at St John's Methodist Church, it being Young People's Day, Pastor Farmhill is worried.

He fears that some people may be unconsciously giving young folk the idea that spiritual and moral welfare is less important than physical and intellectual welfare.

He makes a direct appeal to parents to augment in the home the teaching given to children in the Church and Sabbath School.

He is probably aware that the war has loosened the hold that Churches have had over young people, who have grown up in a strange and even unprecedented situation of seeing so many young men disappearing and not returning.

Now even women are becoming involved in industry "wearing dungarees, smoking cigarettes and using foul language"!

October 21 1891

It was a big occasion in Arbroath today when the new premises of the Young Men's Christian Association were opened in the High Street.

The weather was disagreeable and severely affected the attendance at the opening ceremony.

Mr C. W. CORSAR.

Mr Charles Webster Corsar of Seaforth, Dundee Road, the Flax mill owner, who presided, had himself done a great deal, financially and otherwise, to facilitate the provision of these new premises to the YMCA.

There had been a YMCA in the town for many years, since 1858 according to one report, but they had always been handicapped by the lack of premises for their social, spiritual and sporting development.

Now they had something that would be the envy of other branches of the organisation in neighbouring towns and larger cities.

It was often one of the criticisms that the YMCA encouraged young men to focus on that institution to the exclusion perhaps of working for their own Church, but the argument against that was that you can never get enough of Christianity, and that the YMCA in any case was a non-denominational institution.

The formal proceedings were followed by a Dinner in the nearby Hall of the YWCA, then some "physical jerks" entertainment in the gymnasium, then what was called a Conversazione or Concert in the New Public Hall with many musical elements in it.

It was a fine start to the new premises and the YMCA was fated to play quite a large part in the social life of Arbroath for many years in the future.

October 22 1846

The year's potato harvest has been a disaster.

It would cause untold suffering (and long term implications) in Ireland where the potato was more or less the only crop, at least in the west of the country, but the potato blight also affected other parts of Great Britain as well not least the county of Forfarshire.

It had been the habit in previous years for people from the town to hire in the spring strips or patches of land to grow potatoes with a view to storing and keeping them for the winter or even perhaps to sell them on.

Normally, it would be a source of pride and happiness to walk out and watch the progress of the potatoes, but not this year, for disease has destroyed all but a very few potatoes.

The Arbroath Guide however is pleased to report that the landowning fraternity have made life easier for those who have rented the land.

They have either remitted rent altogether or reduced it to half rate. The good thing is that, although many people have lost a great deal of money, no-one has actually starved because there are so many other vegetables and of course (in the case of Arbroath at least) fish around.

At this stage it is not yet clear whether potatoes will ever grow again, although the balance of opinion is that they probably will because the blight was not universally bad and there have been diseases like this before.

The mistake in Ireland, of course, was to be totally reliant on potatoes.

October 22 1984

"Quirky Twists", *The Arbroath Herald* reported, "in Abbey Theatre's Gripping Thriller".

It requires the utmost concentration to keep abreast of what we are told is happening has happened, or is about to happen. There is not much real action, and actions, we are told sometimes speak louder than words. We might have heard better had we seen more!
The producer, Neil Fyffe, has overcome great difficulties of space in the little theatre, in presenting a play that requires three settings. These are cleverly designed and speedily changed.

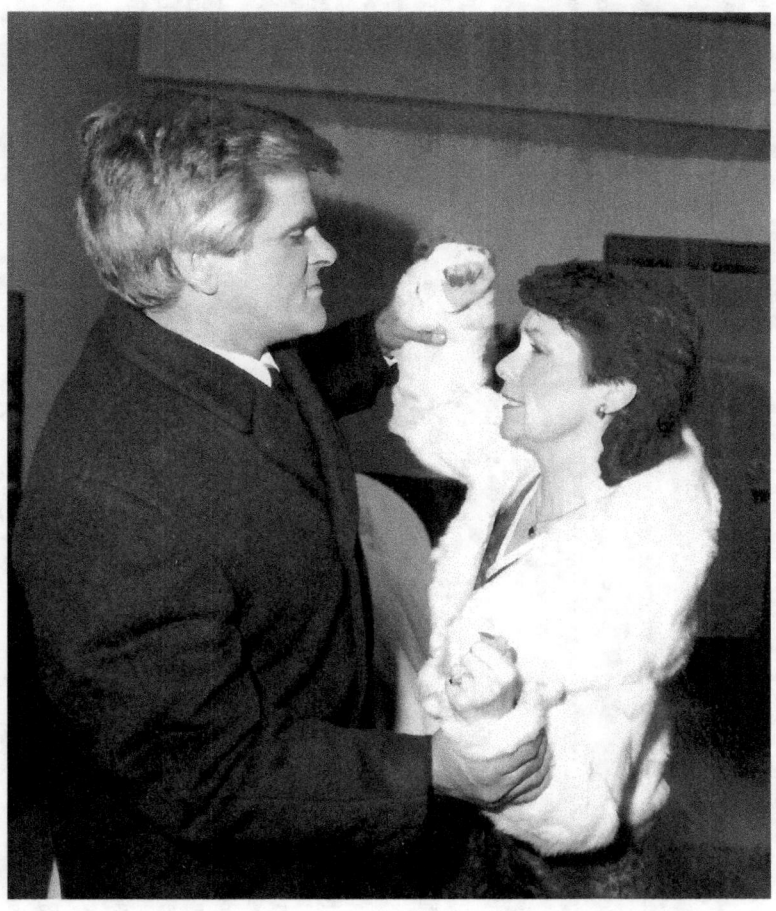

Brian Bruce and Irene Stott

October 22 1984

THE ABBEY THEATRE
Presents
" WHO SAW HIM DIE? "
by Tudor Gates

CAST

Superintendant Pratt	Brian Bruce
John Rawlings	George Milne
Dr. Adcock	Michael Christie
Christine	Irene Stott
Sergeant	Michael Clark
Mick Jennings	Steven Proctor

PRODUCED by NEIL FYFFE

Set Designed by	Neil Fyffe
Set Painted by	Bob Chaplain, Douglas Middleton & Michael Clark
Set Built by	Allan Gillies
Lighting Set by	Ken Heathfield
Lighting Operated by	Brian Gamble and Brian Naylor
Prompt	Glenda Moir
Assistant Prompt	Carol King
Stage Manager	Margaret Mitchell
Assistant Stage Managers	Claire Hill and Kate Hill
Front of House	Frank Moir
Catering	Irene Manders and Theatre Members

****

Playing at the ABBEY THEATRE from Monday 22nd October to Saturday 3rd November 1984.

SYNOPSIS OF SCENES

ACT ONE   Scene One - Dr. Adcocks Surgery early evening.
           Scene Two - The same, a few minutes later.

INTERVAL

ACT TWO - A flat in Willesden several weeks later, late afternoon.

INTERVAL

ACT THREE - A Cellar.

****

ART EXHIBITION in the Coffee Lounge by -
JOHN F. GRAHAM, Montrose.
****

NEXT PRODUCTION - 17th to 22nd December The Pantomime
" HUMPTY DUMPTY "
in the Webster Theatre
****

558

October 23 1934

Tonight at the Wesley Guild of the Methodist Church a fascinating lecture was given on "Songs Of The Negroes".

The lecture was given by the Reverend Joseph Brice of Montrose, and it was an enthralling lecture given by a man who had been to Africa and America and who clearly knew what he was talking about and who clearly enjoyed talking about it.

The highlight of his talk was his gramophone records, his gramophone being "manipulated" (as *The Arbroath Guide* puts it) by his wife.

The approach of the Negroes to worship was of course radically different from that of the white man, and the missionary had to work hard sometimes to counteract the effect of witch doctors and other wrong influences which could affect the Negro.

But yet the Negro was not entirely unaware of the beauty of God, and some of the songs that were played on the gramophone indicated this.

There was a certain emphasis on refrains with a lead singer or a group of singers singing a line and then it being repeated, either in song or in speech, by another group.

There were also many Negro songs on a non-religious theme about lost loves, and people who have gone away, either dead or enslaved.

In the 1930s in the United Kingdom there were already a group of people who were beginning to question at least the value of Mission to foreign countries.

Many were beginning to see it as an attempt to patronise and even to keep in subjection the black people and to curb their legitimate aspirations.

October 24 1962

Arbroath was living in terror these days!

Like every other place, the town was dominated by the thoughts of nuclear war.

This was the time of what history calls the Cuban Missile crisis when the Americans told the Soviets to remove their missiles from Cuba and the Soviets said "No".

Perhaps in retrospect, there was a little bit of "armchair soldiering" and "Boys Own" stuff going on here.

It was alarming at the time with the BBC and the newspapers showing their ability, not for the first or last time, to terrify the world.

Those who went to Dundee tonight to see Dundee playing Sporting Lisbon in the European Cup at Dens Park were terrified they might never come back.

The town seethed with rumours about how Arbroath because of HMS Condor and the American base at Edzell were going to be the first to be wiped out.

Besides, was there a better place than Arbroath beach for the Russians to land and launch their invasion of Scotland?

People who should have known a lot better talked about boarding up their house and living in their cellar.

A public information film shown in schools told you that if the bomb landed when you were out on your bike, you should immediately dive into a hedge and cover yourself with ferns.

Little hope was held out for anyone seeing Christmas ... but then of course, it all went away as quickly as it had arrived!

October 25 1900

MR CHARLES CORSAR.   MRS CHARLES CORSAR.

The marriage of Mr Charles Corsar to Miss Marion R Hutchison, daughter of Rev. D. Hutchison, D.D., ex-Moderator of the United Presbyterian Synod, was the occasion of several interesting ceremonies, the whole of the employees in the mills, factories, and bleaching works of the firm of Messrs D. Corsar & Sons uniting to do honour to their young master on the happy occasion

Mr Corsar was presented with a splendid marble clock and bronze vases, and on all sides the heartiest good-wishes for his happiness were expressed. The marriage took place in Rev. I)r Hutchison's Church, Bonnington United Presbyterian, Leith, in the afternoon, and that evening there was a festival in the Public Hall, Arbroath, presided over by Major Corsar and Mr Wm. Ducat.

The festival was largely attended, and representatives of all departments in the firms works expressed keen hopes of happiness for the newly married couple

The non-commissioned officers of the local Companies of the 1st F.V.A. enjoyed supper, in the White Hart Hotel; and the indoor and outdoor servants at Seaforth and Rosely were also appropriately entertained.

October 25 1957

It was probably an exaggeration to say that the Queen visited Arbroath today – in fact it wasn't true at all! – but Arbroath's royalist sympathisers were able to get a quick glance of her as she was driven in a car out of the gates at RNAS Condor.

Why she didn't insist on coming into Arbroath was a matter of some puzzlement to the good people of Arbroath (who all pay their taxes like everyone else!) but when she landed at RNAS Condor, she was immediately driven to Drumkilbo, the house of her cousin Lord Elphinstone.

The Earl and Countess of Airlie were there to meet her as well. She was just back from Canada and the USA in a tour which was described as "triumphal" and this was a private visit.

She would be met by her husband, the Duke of Edinburgh, who had been to the atomic power station at Dounreay.

Feelings towards Her Majesty in Arbroath were generally quite sympathetic, in spite of this apparent snub. She had only been Queen for five years and had a couple of charming children who had not yet disgraced her.

She had connections with Angus, for her mother was of course Lady Elizabeth Bowes-Lyon, the daughter of the Earl of Strathmore of Glamis Castle.

She had a dreadful upper class English accent but at least her youth seemed to symbolise a new age of life in the 1950.

It was as if the 1950s were seeing the start of a new Britain – young, cheerful and positive. Pity she didn't come into the town, though!

October 26 1910

Some people were happy about this, others less so, but it appears that this year there will be no election for the Town Council.

Mr W K Macdonald, the Town Clerk announced that in the three wards – High Street and Millgate, Lochlands and Keptie, and Abbey and Guthrie Port, the vacancies were all filled.

The only change was in Lochlands and Keptie where David Littlejohn wished to retire and would be replaced by Charles Milne.

There still was what was called the "greetin meetin" where all candidates said what they wanted done – the old hardy annuals of demolishing slums, building new houses, clearing up the streets and the need for swimming baths.

The baths issue was a sore point because nearby Forfar had persuaded Andrew Carnegie to cough up some money for baths – but there was little innovative or revolutionary stuff.

It was possibly good to have a rest from politics because in October 1910, Arbroath, and indeed the whole country, was in between General Elections over the vexed question of the House of Lords. It had now been compelled to accept the "People's Budget" of Lloyd George, and the Liberals were now trying to emasculate for ever the powers of the House of Lords.

Arbroath, as part of the Montrose Burghs Parliamentary constituency, tended to support the Liberals on this issue.

They had voted for Robert Vernon Harcourt in January and it looked as if there would have to be another General Election soon, so possibly it was a relief not to have a Town Council one!

October 27 1953

This must go down as one of Arbroath's saddest ever days when six members of the lifeboat The Robert Lindsay capsized in stormy weather just outside Arbroath Harbour.

They were returning at about 6.00 am after a fruitless search for a vessel in distress when they were overwhelmed with waves about 20 feet high, according to some reports.

The boat was swept along the side of the west breakwater and capsized onto the rocks in front of Inchcape Park.

One man, Archie Smith, survived by holding on to a rope thrown by watchers on the land, but the others David Bruce, Harry Swankie, William Swankie, Thomas Adams, David Cargill and Charles Cargill were all killed in the disaster.

The brothers David and Charles Cargill were both due to be married before the end of the year.

In a small community like Arbroath, everyone knew everyone and the sense of loss was felt by all.

The survivor Archie Smith was taken to Arbroath Infirmary and was badly bruised but his wife was allowed to see him later that day.

The funeral was held in the Old Church on Saturday October 31 and conducted by the Reverend Angus Logan, and then the interment was in the Eastern Cemetery.

It was estimated that over 10,000 lined the streets of Arbroath in pouring rain and a bitter east wind in total silence for the brave men who had perished.

The lifeboat itself was recovered fairly quickly and restored, and the lifeboat service continued.

October 28 1920

Life was not easy for anyone in 1920, not least in Arbroath.

Most towns had suffered terribly during the Great War (as it was now termed) but it was now time to pick up the pieces and move on.

Housing was generally agreed to be dreadful but one of the ideas coming from the central Government of Lloyd George was the building of Housing Schemes of good quality houses.

They were all to have running water and indoor toilets, and were to be built for the working classes as part of the Prime Minister's idea to make a country "fit for heroes to live in" and to take the sting out of the new Labour Party which had been advocating these ideas.

Tonight, a few days before the Municipal Elections, Bailie David T Wilson in the Panmure Masonic Hall defended his Convenership of Housing Scheme.

He was clearly on uneasy ground here, for so far, no houses had as yet been produced and the Housing Scheme had been constantly under attack from the local Press and other quarters.

The opposition was of course spearheaded by local landlords who saw a potential Housing Scheme, run by the Town Council, as a threat to their livelihoods.

There were other problems as well – shortage of raw materials, shortage of money from Westminster (even though it had been promised) and the multiple labour problems and strikes which had resulted from the end of the War – and little progress had been made.

Yet everyone agreed, said Bailie Wilson, that houses were urgently needed.

Too many Arbroath families were still living in damp, unhealthy houses and having to share outside toilets with other families.

October 29 1896

This was a great age for the expansion of the railways.

A generation or two ago had seen the start of the railway, then looked upon as the height of luxury and pretentiousness.

But the railway lines to Forfar and Dundee had been a very obvious success, and now everyone was keen to get into the act, including the good people of Arbirlot and Carmyllie.

Tonight a meeting was held at the Old Schoolroom in Arbirlot to demand the opening of a branch line to Carmyllie which might then run on as far as Letham and even into Forfar, thus supplying a rival line to the existing one.

A similar meeting was also held at Carmyllie.

Various ministers (very important people in 1896) were on the platform demanding a passenger service. At the moment a "feasibility study" was being undertaken by the Caledonian and the North British Railway line.

This meeting was being called to put maximum pressure on the engineers and the accountants to assure them that the line was not only viable but even essential for those heavily populated parishes who deserved a railway line just the same as anyone else.

Support from the aristocracy and the landed gentry had been sought in the shape of the Earl of Dalhousie and Colonel Ouchterloney, and this had been forthcoming.

The meeting ended in a spirit of optimism that it would soon be possible to travel by rail between Arbirlot and Carmyllie.

October 30 1930

Today was the first appearance in public of Princess Margaret, born a couple of months ago in Glamis Castle, the daughter of the Duke and Duchess of York and granddaughter of the King and Queen.

The fact that she was born not only in Scotland, but actually in the county of Angus, less than 20 miles away from Arbroath fills *The Arbroath Herald* with joy and pride.

Questions are asked about whether she was Scottish or English, and even a little speculation about whether, as she was born in Scotland, she might one day be Queen of Scotland!

The baby is actually fairly far up the pecking order for the throne of Great Britain.

There is the Prince of Wales, as yet unmarried (although, goodness knows, there have been many stories about him and women!), her father the Duke of York, then her sister Princess Elizabeth and then the baby herself.

She is certainly cute and lovely, and many Arbroath women get all "clucky" about children when they see her, and there is a general desire of the matronly Arbroath middle aged ladies to look after and cuddle her loveable but ailing father.

There tends to be less love expressed for the pushy and sometimes too gushing Duchess (who even claims that she comes from Forfar!), and as for the baby itself, well, maybe it was a blessing that they did not know just exactly what the future was going to bring for "Mad Meg"!

October 31 1956

There is a certain anxiety among all the "guising" and "dookin for apples" this Hallowe'en, for it seems that Great Britain has taken military action against Egypt in an attempt to regain possession of the Suez Canal.

This is the era of National Service, where young men were taken away from their homes, families, careers and girl-friends for two years and compelled to join the Army, whether they wanted to or not!

It was incredible that it still went on but it meant that Britain had a huge Army with the capacity to get itself involved in foolish adventures like this.

Therefore it is a fact that several Arbroath boys will be involved in this action, some of them unwillingly.

The Dundee Courier portrays all this in a spirit of jingoism and talks about the "pride" that Arbroath should have in its boys who were serving as soldiers and sailors.

The reality was totally different, with anxiety the main emotion. The townsfolk recalled the dark days of little more than a decade ago when young men left Arbroath Station and no-one was really all that sure if they would see them again.

As it was, all reservists were on stand-by and some had already left.

Fortunately, this turned out to be a colossal British military fiasco.

The American allies and the Labour Party (and indeed the United Nations) eventually persuaded Prime Minister Eden of his folly, and Britain withdrew with a massive loss of pride and prestige but a minimal loss of life ... and the boys came home!

**In this year
Traders in Arbroath
in 1925**

Established Over 50 Years.

FOR VARIETY AND SOUND VALUE

IN

GENERAL DRAPERY AND OUTFITTING

VISIT

Alexander Hird's

DRAPERY AND OUTFITTING
—— ESTABLISHMENTS ——

28 KEPTIE STREET

AND

258 HIGH STREET

ARBROATH.

Telephone No. 82.

JAMES JACK

Pharmaceutical Chemist,

Manufacturer of Aerated Mineral Waters,

102 HIGH STREET, Arbroath

Invites the attention of the Public to his

Ærated Mineral Waters

In the production of which only the Purest and Best Materials are employed.

The Various Beverages are of the Highest Quality, and are supplied at Moderate Prices.

All Water used is Carefully Filtered and Guaranteed Perfectly Pure.

To be had of all Licensed Dealers & Grocers

ORDERS LEFT AT

102 HIGH STREET

PROMPTLY ATTENDED TO.

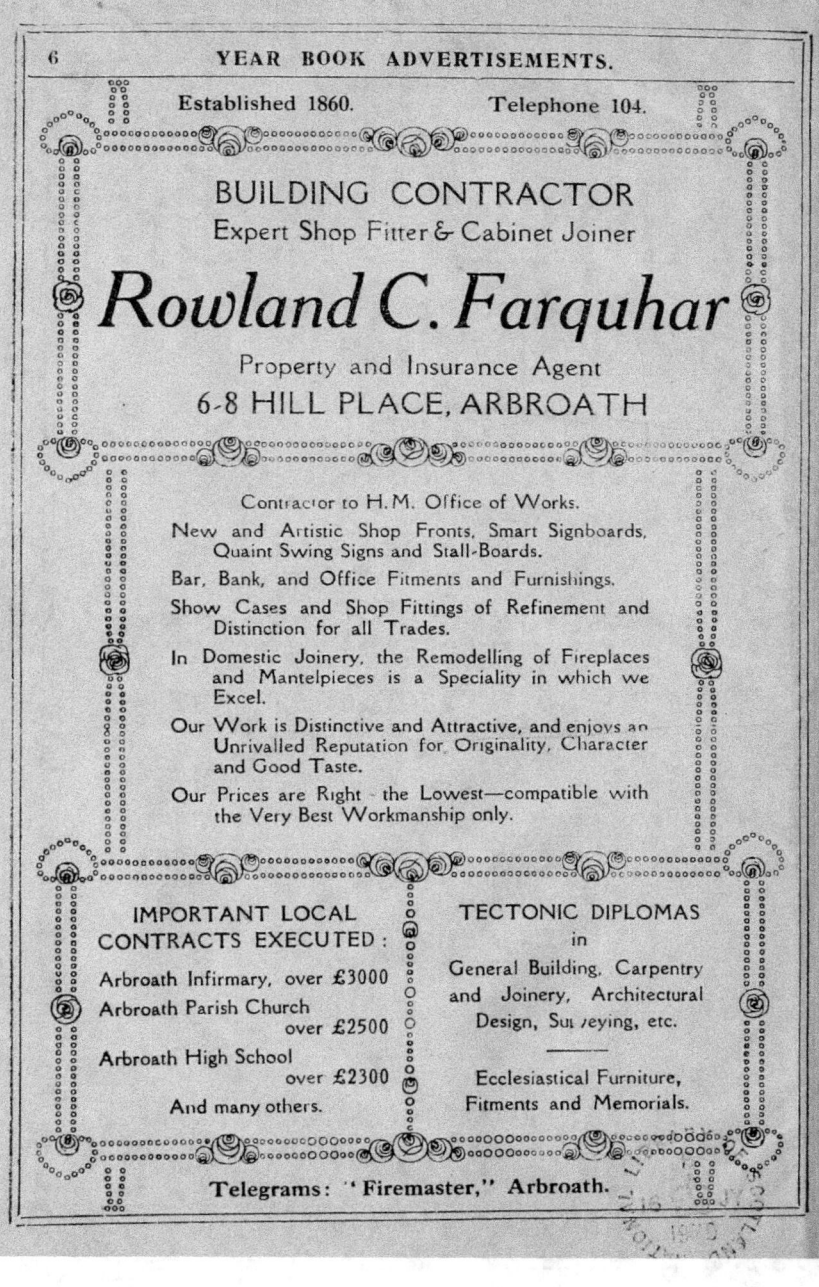

Established Upwards of 100 Years

Where to Do Your Shopping
AT
GEO. HARRIS'

Family Butcher, Game Dealer and Poulterer

29 Millgate, Arbroath

Telephone No. 24  Telephone No. 24

SPECIALITIES.

PRIME BEEF and MUTTON—Large and Fresh Stock on hand at all times.

VEAL and LAMB in Season.

Always in Stock, SALT ROUNDS—Plain and Spice Pickled.

POULTRY—Neatly Dressed—Ready for Table.

Large Supplies of RABBITS in Season.

SPECIAL DEPARTMENTS.

Rings, Watches, Stainless Cutlery, and Silverplate.

Silver Plate is one of the Special Features of our Stock. Tea Sets of from Three to Six Pieces, from 40/- to £25. Teapots from 15/- to 85/-.

Special Stock of Diamond Rings from £5 to £30. Diamond & Ruby or Sapphire, 30/- to £10.

We have large Stocks of all kinds of Watches but specialise in Gold and Silver Wrist Watches of Guaranteed Reliability. Gold 50/- to £12. Silver 17/6 to £4 10/-.

High-Class Watch, Clock & Jewellery Repairs.

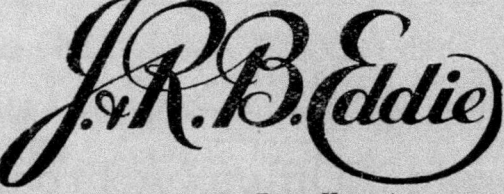

(Opposite the Town House.)

Furnish the Home At PERT'S

No matter what kind of Furniture and Furnishings you require, we can supply them at prices which defy competition. We have always on hand a Splendid Selection of Chesterfields, Bedroom Suites, Drawing Room and Dining Room Furniture, Kitchen Furniture, &c., &c. It is a good plan to come and compare the values at PERT'S before making a purchase of Furniture.

PERT'S

The House Supreme for Quality Furniture

14, 16, 18 APPLEGATE and 178 HIGH STREET
Also at 29 LORDBURN ———— ARBROATH
Telephone No. 44

YEAR BOOK ADVERTISEMENTS.

Arbroath's Premier Picture House:

THE PALACE

JAMES STREET, ARBROATH.   'Phone 212.

Proprietors—The Scottish Cinema and Variety Theatres Limited.

THE RESORT of the Elite.

The Prettiest And Best Equipped Theatre In the Provinces.

Our Aim, As Always, To Entertain To Elevate To Amuse

Mr R. B. STEWART, Manager.

THE HOME Of Good Entertainment

THE HOME Of Good Music

THE HOME Of Good Pictures

THE HOUSE Of Distinction

Always an Up-to-Date Programme

You are sure of a Pleasant Evening at the Palace.

Continuous Performance, 7 to 10-30.   **Saturday, 6-30 and 8-30.**
Doors Open at 6.30.   Doors Open at 6 and 8 20.

People's Popular Prices. Seats may be Booked in Advance, 3d extra.

Children's Matinee every Saturday at 2-30.

Doors Open at 2 o'clock.   SEND THE BAIRNS.

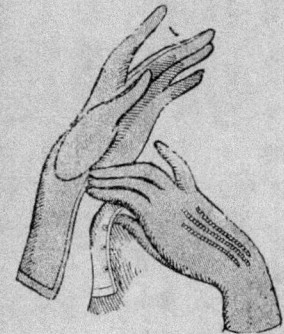

GLOVES
FOR
CHILDREN
LADIES AND
GENTLEMEN

BEST MAKES Kept in Stock

Red Lichtie Collars
Red Lichtie Caps
Red Lichtie Shirts
Red Lichtie Underclothing

Registered.

All Guaranteed.

Handkerchiefs, Braces, Ties, Scarves, Golfing Jackets, Sweaters, etc., etc.

D. R. Macdonald

Hatter, Hosier, Glover, and Tartan Specialist

Fit o' the Port and 23 Commerce St.,

Telephone No. 250.   ARBROATH

18   YEAR BOOK ADVERTISEMENTS.

LIGHT IN THE HOME

You can now Light your House by Electricity with a First-Class Plant at a Really Low Price.

The Armstrong Whitworth

Electric Lighting Set, as illustrated above, is Cheap and really Reliable. We can give you Expert Advice.

Contractors for Complete Electric Lighting, Heating, Power, Telephone, and Bell Installations.

Wireless Sets and Components.

F H. ATKINSON

Electrical, Mechanical, and Motor Engineer,

20-22 MILLGATE, ARBROATH

'Phone No. 281.

DO YOUR SHOPPING
AT

The Premier Butcher Poulterer and Game Dealer in this District

One Quality Only—THE BEST.

JOHN LAMB
Corner of Commerce St. & High St.
ARBROATH.

Telephone No. 94.   Established 1820.

Arbroath's Greatest Attraction!

Winton's Arbroath ROCK

THE LAST WORD IN PURITY AND EXCELLENCE.

SOLE MAKER:

JAMES WINTON

MANUFACTURING CONFECTIONER,

31 West Port & 59 Guthrie Port

ARBROATH.

YEAR BOOK ADVERTISEMENTS.

Arbroath's Leading Family Picture House.

COMBINING EDUCATION WITH AMUSEMENT.

Resident Manager—W. W. MITCHELL.

OLYMPIA
PICTURE THEATRE.

TELEPHONE No. 197.

CONTINUOUS PERFORMANCE
6-30 to **10-30** Each Evening.

SATURDAY—TWO HOUSES, **6-30 & 8-30.**

An Olympia Theatre Presentation is a Guarantee of Quality.

For Good & Suitable Music, Cleanliness & Comfort, Unbeaten Anywhere.

Seats may be Booked without any Extra Booking Fee.

Children's Matinee—Saturdays, 2-30.

Red Lion Bar  2-4 Barngreen

WHISKIES, BRANDIES, RUMS and
WINES of the BEST VINTAGES.

DRAUGHT and BOTTLED BEERS
always in SPARKLING CONDITION.

WILLIAM B. PEDDIE
Wine and Spirit Merchant
2 & 4 BARNGREEN, ARBROATH.

DAVID J. SCOTT
Glass Merchant and Glazier

Dealer in Sheet, Polished Plate, Silvered Plate, Rough Plate. Figured Rolled, Cathedral Rolled. Muffled, Rippled, Opal, Muranese Memorial Windows, Church Windows, Domestic Windows, Glass Blinds, Glass Embossing, Glass Bevelling. Glass Brilliant Cut, Glass Bending.

Greenhouse and Roof Painting done by Experienced Workmen.
Every Description of Plain and Ornamental Lead Glazing.
Special Designs and Estimates Submitted on Application.

Brothock Bridge, - Arbroath
And BANK STREET, DUNDEE.
Telephone 107.

The Delight We Find

In selling good shoes is only equalled by the comfort you will find in wearing them. We are Agents for the following Makers of Highest Grade Footwear.

"Lotus and Delta."   "Moccasins."
"Grenson."   "C.R." & "Scot."

Call and Inspect our Stock.

Singer & Booth
FOOTWEAR SPECIALISTS,
39 COMMERCE STREET, ARBROATH.

THE LOCHLANDS BAR
14½ LOCHLANDS ST., ARBROATH

———◆———

WHISKIES, BRANDIES, RUMS, WINES, all of the Best Vintages.

———◆———

DRAUGHT BEER always in Sparkling Condition.

———◆———

BASS'S BEER in Bottle.
COOMBE'S STOUT & TENNANT'S STRONG ALE.

———◆———

SITTING ACCOMMODATION.

WM. McLEAN, Proprietor.

A. BRUCE,
Bookseller, Stationer, and Tobacconist.

Splendid Selection of Toys, Games, and other Goods at Reasonable Prices.

8 WEST PORT, ARBROATH.

Telegrams—"Royal Hotel, Arbroath."

Excellent Service. *Charges Moderate.*

ROYAL HOTEL,
HIGH STREET, ARBROATH.

Entirely Remodelled and Redecorated, and is now one of the Leading Hotels in the District.

First=Class Family and Commercial.

MRS MARGARET CALDER, Manageress.

T. C. PATON,
General Draper and Outfitter,
63 HELEN STREET, ARBROATH.

Goods of First-Class Quality Only Stocked. Prices Moderate.

D. JAMIESON & SON
Plasterers and Cement Workers
4 Gravesend, Arbroath, & Kinloch St., Carnoustie

PLAIN and ORNAMENTAL WORK a Speciality. Cement Work, White Washing and Lime Washing done. Jobbing of all Descriptions in Town and Country Carefully and Promptly attended to. Special Quotations for House and Factory Proprietors, Factors, etc. Fireproof Fabric Plaster made to order on the Premises. Estimates Given.

House Address - 2 MARKET PLACE, Arbroath.

DAVID HUTCHISON
Draper and Milliner
1 WEST PORT, ARBROATH

Black and Coloured Silks, Dress Stuffs, Household Napery. Blankets, and a Large Assortment of Beautiful Down Quilts, at Very Moderate Prices.

Always in Stock, a Splendid Assortment of the Famous "St Margaret's" Blouses.

SPORTS COATS, JUMPERS, AND HOSIERY.

Mey's La Cybele Corsets, Nuvo Corsets, St Margaret's Corsets.

MILLINERY

PROVISIONS of Quality at Keenest Prices.

Charles Porter
Grocer and Wine Merchant, CAIRNIE STREET

Bottled Beers & Stout always in Splendid Condition.

86　　　YEAR BOOK ADVERTISEMENTS.

ARBROATH
Equitable Co-operative Society
LIMITED
GUTHRIE PORT - - AND BRANCHES.

In Every Department of our
.. Business our Axiom is ..

QUALITY & SERVICE

Come to the Equitable for all your Household and Personal Requirements—the Selection is Without Equal.

Arbroath Equitable Co-operative Society
LIMITED

James Swan
Wholesale and Retail Fish Merchant

32 BARNGREEN
ARBROATH

Fresh Fish in Season

Arbroath Smokies Our Speciality.

Large or Small Quantities Supplied.

Terms Moderate.

WILLIAM BOOTH

(Late of F. & J. SELBY)

High - Class Tailoring
FOR
Ladies and Gentlemen
ALSO,
Ladies' and Gent's Outfitter

3 MILLGATE, ARBROATH.

The Shakespeare Bar

187 HIGH STREET
ARBROATH

Wines and Spirits of the Finest Quality.
Our Whiskies are Old and Thoroughly Matured.
Draught and Bottled Beers always in Prime Condition.
Guinness' Stout and Bass's Ale.

ALEXANDER JEFFREY, Proprietor.

All Classes of Joinery Work

Carried Out Promptly & Efficiently.

J. R. Anderson & Co.

JOINERS AND CONTRACTORS,

7-11 St Mary Street, Arbroath.

ESTIMATES FURNISHED
For all Classes of New and Alteration Work.

Alexander Addison

CYCLE AND MOTOR AGENT,
279-281 HIGH STREET
ARBROATH

46   YEAR BOOK ADVERTISEMENTS.

JAMES LAW & SON

Motor and General Engineers

Brothock Bridge - Arbroath

Works Adjoining—At EAST GRIMSBY

'Phone 193.

THE PLOUGH & HARROW

Finest Whiskies, Brandies, Rums.   **Sparkling Beers, Nourishing Stout**

Montrose Road - - - Arbroath

JOHN W. STEWART, Proprietor

WILLIAM HIGH

Sign of the Clock

222 High St. - Arbroath

PRESENTS in Great Variety.

T. & D. SAVEGE

PAINTERS & DECORATORS,

257 HIGH STREET, ARBROATH.

Established 1875.   Telephone No. 105.

For Ladies' Coats, Costumes, Furs, Gent.'s Suits and Overcoats.

D. Thornton & Son

Drapers and Milliners

261 High Street, - Arbroath

J. MITCHELL & SON

SLATERS AND CEMENT WORKERS.

Jobbing of every description carefully attended to. Estimates given for all kinds of Slater and Rough Casting Work. Chimney Heads Repaired and Pointed.

PANMURE STREET, Arbroath.   *Telephone 155.*

House Address—30 WEST KEPTIE STREET.

Thomas Clark

Cycle and Motor Dealer and Repairer,

274 HIGH STREET———ARBROATH

All the most Reliable Cycles and Accessories in Stock.
Highest Satisfaction Guaranteed in all Repairs.
Charges Moderate.   Call and obtain my Latest Prices.
All Wireless Necessaries Kept in Stock.

C. N. ANDERSON

Wine & Spirit Merchant,

"THE STAG,"

WEST PORT, Arbroath

Begs to call attention to his Stock of OLD SCOTCH WHISKY, much Famed for its Mildness and Delicious Flavour. Matured in Sherry Wood.

BRANDIES, RUMS, PORTS, and SHERRIES
of Highest Class.

DRAUGHT & BOTTLED BEER of the Best Quality,
Procured from the Best Brewers.

BEST LONDON STOUTS.

Furnish the Home at FERGUSON'S

Real Good Value in Furniture and Furnishings is our maxim. We buy in the best markets, and give our customers the benefit. The Low Prices we charge is convincing proof of this. When you want Value, come to **FERGUSON'S**. If you have any **LEFT-OFF CLOTHING** we will be pleased to buy it. We pay the Highest Price within reason. Second-Hand Musical Instruments. Violin and Mandoline Strings a Specialty.

FERGUSON'S, 11 AND 13 APPLEGATE, ARBROATH.

George Keith

Sail, Cover and Tent Maker

22 N. GRIMSBY  **ARBROATH**

Motor Car Hoods Re-Covered or Repaired. Bonnet Covers Made to Order. Van, Engine, Sail, and Other Covers. Shop Sunshades a Speciality. Tents and Marquees Made to Order.
Estimates Given for All Kinds of Canvas Work.

Highest Satisfaction Assured in
:: All Work Undertaken ::

JAMES CUTHILL

Slater and Cement Worker

5 HAMILTON GREEN, ARBROATH

Estimates Given. House Address—
1 HAYSWELL ROAD.

NORAH H. WOOD

Dressmaker and Costumier

64½ KEPTIE STREET, - ARBROATH

Agent for Messrs W. & J. BOWIE, Dyers, Glasgow.

J. BLACK,

Bookseller, Stationer, and Confectioner,

10 BROTHOCK BRIDGE, Arbroath.

Bibles, Books, Stationery, &c.

All the Daily Papers.   *Circulating Library.*

Best Confections only Stocked.

Good Quality Pianos

Reliability the one Great Note

Into our Instruments is embodied all that is best in Construction, Finish, and Resonant Tone Qualities.

Write for Catalogue and Prices.

Paterson, Sons & Co., Ltd.

MUSICSELLERS,

145 HIGH STREET, ARBROATH.

D. Y. WALKER, Family Butcher

BEST QUALITY

 Prime Beef, Mutton & Pork

Kept in Stock.

POULTRY AND EGGS.

CORNER MILLGATE LOAN & WEST GRIMSBY,
Telephone 115.   ARBROATH.

DAVID KYD,

Dealer in all kinds of General, Modern & Antique Furniture,
29 Gravesend & 23 Spink Street, Arbroath.

Established a Quarter of a Century—the Oldest and Largest Second-Hand Business of its kind in Town. Always in stock, every description of Household and Office Furniture; also a large stock of General, Antique, and Modern Goods on hand. The Cheapest and Largest Selection in Town. Furniture, &c., &c., bought, sold, and exchanged. Highest Prices Given.

CROOK & WEBSTER

Registered Plumbers and Gasfitters

35 GUTHRIE PORT, ARBROATH

Hydraulic Rams, . . .
Windmills and Pumps
of every description .
Executed and Repaired.

Flush Closets, Baths,
Heating, &c., for Town
and Country Houses.

Estate Water Supplies
Laid out on most . .
Modern Systems.

Estimates Given.

CHARGES MODERATE.

House Address—7 Guthrie Port, Arbroath

DAVID PIRIE, WATCHMAKER AND OPTICIAN

PRESENTATION GOODS—Tea Spoons, Jelly Spoons, Butter Knives, Knives and Forks—all in Neat Cases. All Kinds of Watches, Clocks, and Jewellery *personally* Cleaned and Repaired. Spectacles and Eyeglasses to suit all sights. Wedding, Keeper and Engagement Rings. Large Selection of Gold and Silver Brooches, Scarf Pins, Seals, &c.

Silver Name Brooches a Speciality.

262 HIGH STREET, ARBROATH

TAILORING
— FOR —
LADIES AND GENTLEMEN.

MATTHEWS offer to Ladies and Gentlemen a service which is satisfactory from every point of view.

At Matthews, Tailoring has reached a high standard rarely met with, in which both Ladies and Gentlemen of discernment can place their confidence.

It is our experience, the skill of our staff, the materials we work with, the care, the effort, the desire to produce garments of which you and we will both be proud—these are the things that have made our service so reliable and our productions so satisfactory.

And at all times prices are reasonable.

MATTHEWS
Tailors and Outfitters ::
226-228 HIGH STREET, ARBROATH.

The British Law
Insurance Company Limited.

HEAD OFFICE, - 5 LOTHBURY, LONDON, E.C.2.

FIRE

Fidelity Guarantee
Employers' Liability
Personal Accident
Burglary
Third Party
Motors
Marine
Executor and Trustee

Lifts
Boilers
Property Owners' Indemnity
Solicitors' Indemnity
Loss of Profits Due to Fire
Glass Breakage
Live Stock

DUNDEE BOARD

Chairman—Jas. A. Graham, Esq. (Messrs J. A. & T. Graham, Solicitors), Dundee.
H. Victor Neill, Esq. (Messrs Neill & Gibb, Solicitors), Arbroath.
Thos. K. Douglas, Esq. (J. & J. Ogilvie, Solicitors), Dundee.

EDINBURGH BOARD

Chairman—David Lyell, Esq., W.S. (Messrs Horne & Lyell, W.S.), Edinburgh.

NORTH OF SCOTLAND BOARD

Chairman—James Johnstone, Esq., Advocate in Aberdeen (Messrs Hunter & Gordon, Advocates in Aberdeen), Aberdeen.

Branch Offices { 34 Queen St., EDINBURGH
                 80 Union St., ABERDEEN

District Secretary—JAS. H. McROBERT, A.C.I.I.

AGENTS IN ARBROATH:

NEILL & GIBB, Solicitors, 93 HIGH STREET.

Arbroath Burgh School Management Committee.

ARBROATH HIGH SCHOOL.

THE School provides a COMPLETE COURSE of Education—Primary, Intermediate, and Secondary. Pupils are prepared both for the University and for Commercial life. The Class Rooms and Laboratories are provided with all Modern Apparatus and Accessories. Needlework, Woodwork, Gymnastics, Swimming and Singing are included in the Curriculum. The School is a recognised Centre for the training of Students intending to become Teachers. Bursaries and Scholarships are very numerous.

All information may be had from the Rector.

JOHNSTON'S
GRAND
EMPORIUM

Commerce Street
and High Street

The House for Everything and Everything for the House. : : : :

Specialists in Ironmongery, Hardware, Glass Wares, and Fancy Goods. : :

The Spot for Presents

Everything in Enamelled Ware.
Everything in Aluminium Ware.
Everything in Hardware.

Presentation Goods of Various Kinds.

The Great Place for Inexpensive :
Travelling Bags, Travelling Trunks,
Ladies' Hand-Bags, Purses, Combs, &c.

All Travelling Requisites.

Note Addresses—

Commerce Street & High Street
ARBROATH.

YEAR BOOK ADVERTISEMENTS.

H. L. C. RUST
Boys' and Gent.'s Outfitter
KEPTIE STREET, ARBROATH

FOR ALL that is RELIABLE and UP-TO-DATE in ——

Boys' and Men's Wear

SATISFACTION GUARANTEED
—— in all Purchases made from ——

H. L. C. RUST
KEPTIE STREET   -   -   ARBROATH

TELEPHONE 12.

WILLIAM THOMSON

Butcher and Gamedealer

148 High Street, Arbroath

(Opposite Kirk Square)

Corned Beef and Pickled Tongues.
Prime Beef, Mutton, Pork, &c., always on hand.
Cooked Meats a Speciality.

Orders Called for and Promptly Delivered.

148 HIGH STREET, ARBROATH.

YEAR BOOK ADVERTISEMENTS.

Telephone No. 17.

Smith, Hood & Co. Ltd.

LARGEST COAL MERCHANTS AND COLLIERY AGENTS NORTH OF THE FORTH————————SHIP BROKERS.

Registered Office,   -   48 UNION STREET, DUNDEE

Arbroath Depots:
At Railway Station,
Chalmers Street,
and
Letham Grange Station

Office:
53 KEPTIE STREET.

BRANCHES—**Bervie**, Mr George Nicoll; **Carnoustie**, Miss C. S. Milne; **Broughty Ferry**, Mr J. Crawford; **Forfar**, Mr MacFarlane; **Inverkeilor**, Mr William Robertson; **Montrose**, Mr A. Imrie; **Maryfield**, Mr John Gray; **Stonehaven**, Mr R. V. Mitchell; **Tayport**, W. M. Young; **Cupar**, Miss B. Cairns; **Newport**, Mr Tough; **Brechin**, Provost James Addison; **Johnshaven**, Mr George Towns; **Inchture**, Mr Simpson; **Wormit**, Miss Gilmour.

The following Descriptions of Best Household Coal always in stock—Best Wallsend English Coals and Nuts; Dunfermline Splint Household Coal; Anthracite Coal; Jewel Coal; Patent Fuel Briquettes; Peat Briquettes; Best Coke for Vineries, Bakehouses, &c.; Small Coal for Mills and Factories.

FIREWOOD ALWAYS KEPT IN STOCK.

SPECIAL QUOTATIONS FOR WAGGON LOADS.

For Prices, Terms, &c., apply to:—

A. P. LOWSON, Arbroath Agent.

House Address—KEPTIE ANGLE.

At J. K. Moir's

Sweet Lavender and Chilprufe Underwear for Children.

See the Selection we are able to place before you.

J. K. MOIR,
177-179 High Street, Arbroath.
'Phone No. 240.

YEAR BOOK ADVERTISEMENTS.

Servants' Registry. *Agent for Pullars' Dyeworks, Perth*

MISS STEWART

Ladies' and Children's Underclothing. *Smallwares and Fancy Drapery.*

33 WEST PORT, ARBROATH.

Charles P. Whitton

26 HIGH STREET and
2 LADYBRIDGE STREET, ARBROATH

for VALUE in

Groceries, Provisions, Wines & Spirits.

George Cooper, M.P.S.
Family and Dispensing Chemist.

12 KEPTIE STREET,
ARBROATH. 'Phone No 182.

D. YOUNG & SON

CARTWRIGHTS AND COACH PAINTERS,

16 SOUTH GRIMSBY - ARBROATH

LORRIES, VANS, &c., BUILT TO ORDER.

Telephone No. 117.

W. B. WILLIAMSON,

FAMILY BREAD AND BISCUIT BAKER AND CONFECTIONER.

Sole Maker of the Famous Ducat Shortbread.

ABBEY BAKERY, ARBROATH.

TELEPHONE 103.

W. L. Grant & Son

PAINTERS AND DECORATORS,

267 High Street - Arbroath

Shepherd's Morning Rolls

—PAR EXCELLENCE

Are favoured by those who can appreciate good quality. If you have not yet tried them make a point of having them on the breakfast table without delay and you will be delighted with their superiority.

SHEPHERD'S VAN will Call EVERY MORNING on request

BRONZE MEDAL at Glasgow Exhibition of 1924 for Morning Rolls.

DIPLOMA OF MERIT at Aberdeen in 1923 for French Bread.

PRIZE WINNER at Edinburgh in 1917 and London Exhibition, 1910.

Shortbread, Plain and Ornamented—any Special Motto. All sorts of Plain and Fancy Tea Bread Daily. Hot Pies and Bridies every Friday & Saturday. Marriage & Supper Parties. Picnics & Soirees purveyed.

James Shepherd

FANCY BREAD AND BISCUIT BAKER AND CONFECTIONER,

45 ST MARY STREET, ARBROATH

The Kiddies are Always Happy

WHEN YOU GIVE THEM SWEETS FROM OLYMPIA CHOCOLATE STORES.

All the Best Makers are represented in our Selection.

Chocolates, Caramels, Toffees, &c. You needn't pay more than **6d** per Quarter for the Best Chocolates—Freshly Made. Try them, and note their superiority.

The Leading Brands of Cigarettes are Kept in Stock.

Olympia Chocolate Store

MARKET PLACE, ARBROATH.

You Can Depend

On the Quality of the Fish you Buy at BEATTIE'S.

Our Supplies come Daily from Arbroath Harbour, and are sold direct to the Public at Keenest Market Prices.

ORDERS CALLED FOR AND DELIVERED.

Beattie's Fish Depot,
BROTHOCK BRIDGE, ARBROATH.

Waverley Temperance Hotel, Arbroath

Within One Minute's Walk of RAILWAY STATION.

13 KEPTIE STREET

VISITORS are assured of EVERY HOME COMFORT

THE NORTHERN
Assurance Company Ltd.
ESTABLISHED 1836.

FIRE
Burglary.
Fidelity Guarantee.
Plate Glass.
Third Party.
Drivers' Risks.
Property Owners' Indemnity.
Lift Accidents.
Transit Risks.

LIFE
Annuities.
Personal Accident.
Sickness and Accident.
Workmen's Compensation
Domestic Servants
Motor Cars.
Private Motor Cycles.
Live Stock.

Comprehensive "Household" Insurances:
FIRE.   BURGLARY.   ACCIDENTS TO SERVANTS.

District Offices: Northern Assurance Buildings
110 COMMERCIAL STREET, DUNDEE.

Directors at Dundee:

JAS. BARTY, Esq., LL.B.
J. ERNEST COX, Esq.
J. A. KYD, Esq.
C. C. DUNCAN, Esq.
ANDREW HENDRY, Esq.
C. H. MARSHALL, Esq., S.S.C.

Secretary—ROBERT BUTTER.

Prospectuses and Proposal Forms may be had on application from any of the Company's Agents.

FOR LUNCH OR TEA

Visitors will find the Service and the Cuisine all they could desire at the

Central Dining Rooms

MILLGATE, ARBROATH

NOTE.—We cater for Dances and Weddings, and have Special Facilities for carrying through the work with promptitude.

Ask Us for Quotations

'Phone 183.

D. M. BUCHANAN, Proprietor.

The VICTORIA CAFE

(NEXT RAILWAY LINE.)

Millgate   -   Arbroath

BREAKFASTS, LUNCHES, TEAS, &c., &c.,
MODERATE PRICES, SMART SERVICE, FINE CUISINE.

Commodious Hall and Rooms for Social and Wedding Parties, Club and Society Meetings, Presentations, &c.

SOIREES AND PICNICS PURVEYED FOR.

Ladies' Room and all other suitable Accommodation.

D. M. Buchanan

Telephone No. 183   PROPRIETOR

T. R. GRANT

Registered Plumber and Heating Engineer

BROTHOCK BRIDGE

ARBROATH   Telephone 101.

Grant & Laing

Family Bread, Biscuit and Pastry Bakers

HAVE A VARIED SELECTION OF PLAIN & FANCY TEA BREAD DAILY.

Cakes of every description.
Pies and Bridies.   Tea Biscuits and Oatcakes.

FAMED SHORTBREAD
:: Sent to All Parts of the World. ::

Brothock Bridge, Arbroath

J. B. MARTIN

Tobacconist, Stationer & Newsagent

46 KEPTIE STREET, ARBROATH

Opposite the Railway Station

A. W. PORTEOUS

AT **162 HIGH STREET, ARBROATH**

Where only the Best is Sold of

Cakes, Biscuits, & Confectionery

Brown Bread.   TEA ROOM.   Vienna Bread.

JAMES THORNTON

JOINER,

8 LOCHLAND ST., ARBROATH

Estimates Given.   Highest Satisfaction Guaranteed in all Work undertaken.

R. T. Butchart

CABINETMAKER———UPHOLSTERER.

NOTE NEW ADDRESS:

25 James Street, Arbroath

(Opposite "The Palace.")

Telephone No. 3.
Telegrams—Stewart, Butcher, Arbroath.

George Stewart

FAMILY BUTCHER AND GAME DEALER,

173 High Street - Arbroath

Mrs M. Scott

HIGH-CLASS CONFECTIONER,

286 HIGH STREET - ARBROATH

The Finest Confections from all the Best Makers kept in Stock.

286 High Street - Opposite the Abbey

YEAR BOOK ADVERTISEMENTS.

At 19 Guthrie Port, Arbroath,

You will find everything in the Crockery Line that the Housewife requires AT KEENEST PRICES compatible with Good Value. **You should do your Shopping here.** In Town and Country I call regularly for any waste that you may wish to dispose of. Goods may be had in Exchange, or Cash if desired. My Selection of TOYS is well worth your attention.

JAS. SWORD, China Merchant
GUTHRIE PORT, ARBROATH.

STEVENSONS
LAUNDERERS,
Artist Dyers and Dry Cleaners,
DUNDEE.

Arbroath Office - **BROTHOCK BRIDGE.**

CARNOUSTIE AGENTS—
Misses E. & M. GARDYNE, High Street
Miss E. B. CROWE, 37 High Street.
Send P.C. for Van to Call.

132   YEAR BOOK ADVERTISEMENTS.

WHEN IN NEED OF
RELIABLE FOOTWEAR
INSPECT THE STOCK OF
MACLAREN BROTHERS
29—COMMERCE STREET—29
ARBROATH.

Famed for almost Half-a-Century for Footwear of the Highest Quality and Style.

Smart Garments
for the Children and their Elders.

All the year round we have a large stock of well-made Garments which we sell at very reasonable Prices. Make your purchases from the Stock of M. ANDERSON—Dependable Drapery Goods, Fresh Stocks of Groceries, High-Class Confectionery.

M. Anderson
Merchant,
CORNER OF HELEN STREET & LOCHLAND ST., Arbroath.

Chas. Moonlight,

LADIES' AND GENT'S TAILOR
:: AND PRACTICAL FURRIER ::

All Branches of the Fur Trade Undertaken From the Curing to the Finished Article.

CLEANING AND DRESSING

7 BROTHOCK BRIDGE, ARBROATH

ASPHALTE WORK
IN ALL ITS BRANCHES.

BRIGGS' READY ROOFINGS

ARE SUITABLE FOR ALL CLASSES OF BUILDINGS AND EVERY TYPE OF ROOF. SEND FOR SAMPLES AND PRICES.

Prompt Attention to all Orders and Enquiries.

William Briggs & Sons, Ltd.
5 COWGATE, DUNDEE.

A. G. PETRIE,
BLACKSMITH,
GRAVESEND, ARBROATH.

Bassinette and Mail Cart Tyres Supplied.
Weighing Machines Adjusted.
Ornamental Railings and Gates Supplied.

YEAR BOOK ADVERTISEMENTS.

MRS J. H. BROWN,
FAMILY GROCER, TEA, WINE & SPIRIT MERCHANT,
BROTHOCK BRIDGE, ARBROATH.

Finest Blends of Teas.   Wines and Spirits.   Malt Liquors.
Groceries and Provisions Always Fresh.

Make a Habit of Coming to Knight's for Bread.

All KNIGHT'S SPECIALTIES are made from the Finest Ingredients and represent the Best Value in the Bakery Trade. Knight caters for Picnics, Socials, and Wedding Parties at Charges which are most reasonable.

ROBERT KNIGHT, Jr.
BAKER AND PASTRY COOK,
KEPTIE STREET - ARBROATH

DAVID MACKAY & CO.
FUNERAL UNDERTAKERS,
39½ WEST GRIMSBY - ARBROATH

Every Requisite.   Night Attendance.
Charges Strictly Moderate.

Norwich Union Fire Office

Founded 1797

Head Offices: NORWICH & LONDON.

Fire. Accident. Marine.

FIRE and Consequential Loss, Accident and Sickness, Fidelity, Employer's Liability, Third Party, Motor Cars, Property Owners, Burglary, Engineering and Boiler, Plate Glass, Live Stock.

Branches and Agencies Throughout the World.

DUNDEE BRANCH:

COURIER BUILDING,

20 MEADOWSIDE.

W. S. WHYTE, *District Manager.*

Telephone No. 4372.   Telegrams—"NUFAM."

Thos. Muir, Son & Patton

LIMITED

COAL MERCHANTS.

LOCAL BRANCHES—ARBROATH, 39 Helen Street (Telephone 4); 69 West Grimsby (Telephone 4); and at the following Railway Stations— Carnoustie (Tel. 2); Inverkeilor (Tel. 4); Cauldcots (Tel. 4).

WE ARE

Coal Merchants, :: Colliery Agents
Lime Merchants, Carting Contractors

Specialists in all Classes of Industrial and Household Fuel, both Wholesale and Retail.

BUNKERS—Finest Navigation and Steam Coal——Foundry Coke—— Smithy Coal—— Malting Coke —— Tractor Coal —— Gas Coke.

Our advice is at your service, and a Post Card will bring a Prompt Reply regarding anything in which we may be able to serve you.

Registered Office, Nethergate House, Dundee.
Telegrams—"Muir," Dundee.   Telephone, 744 (4 Lines.)
ON ADMIRALTY LIST.

Arbroath Gas Corporation.

GAS COKE.

FIRST-CLASS FUEL FOR BAKERS' OVENS.
INDISPENSABLE FOR "KEITH'S" FURNACES.
ECONOMICAL FOR HOUSEHOLD PURPOSES.
SPECIALLY USEFUL FOR GREENHOUSES.

CHEAPER THAN COAL.

SINGLE BAGS DELIVERED.

Telephone No. 78.

WM. BRAND & SON

Slaters and Plasterers, : :
Slate and Cement Merchants,

30 DISHLAND STREET, Arbroath.

ESTIMATES GIVEN FOR GRANOLITHIC PAVING.
CHIMNEY HEADS REPAIRED AND POINTED.

ALL REPAIRS PUNCTUALLY ATTENDED TO.

— YOUR —
FRENCH CLEANING
AND
ART DYEING WORK

NOW DONE IN ARBROATH.

Our Building has been Specially Built for this Purpose.

Our Machinery is of the Latest and Up-to-date Description.

Our Works are Efficient in all Departments.

Our Prices are Cheaper than out of Town.

Our Work is Satisfactory.

A Trial Order will Convince You.

The Arbroath French Cleaning and Art Dyeing Works,

GALLOWDEN, ARBROATH.

'Phone 228.   DONALD L. MANSON, Proprietor.

James Kydd & Son

JOINERS, BUILDERS, CONTRACTORS, GENERAL WOOD TURNERS,

16 South Grimsby, Arbroath.

Every Description of Work carefully and promptly attended to by Experienced Workmen at Moderate Charges.

Estimates Given.

| FUNERAL UNDERTAKING. |

TO SHOPKEEPERS AND OTHERS

The Arbroath Plate Glass

MUTUAL INSURANCE ASSOCIATION

Is the Cheapest and Most Convenient Medium for the

INSURANCE OF SHOP WINDOWS

SCREENS, SHOW CASES, MIRRORS, &c.

LOW RATES.

Premiums Quoted and other information given on application to

Wm. H. Alexander, Solicitor, 62 High Street.

Secretary and Treasurer.

The Yorkshire
Insurance Company
Limited

Established 1824. **Assets Exceed 8¼ Millions.**
Claims Paid Exceed £21,000,000.

Life Insurances issued, giving every advantage offered by any Insurance Company. Moderate Premiums. Liberal Conditions. Substantial Bonuses. Stringent Reserves. New Scheme, combining Life Assurance and Old Age Pensions.

Fire Insurances effected by the Company on the Most Moderate Terms, according to nature of risk.

Employers' Liability.—Policies issued covering Full Liability under the Workmen's Compensation Act, 1897, 1900, 1906, and 1923, the Employers' Liability Act, 1880, and the Common Law.

Personal Accident Insurance.—World-Wide Policies issued, conferring Full Benefits at Moderate Rates.

Combined Accident and Sickness Schemes.

Burglary Insurances Transacted. — Liberal Conditions. Low Rates. No Average Clause.

Live Stock Insurance Effected. — Accident, Disease, Foaling, Castration, and Stallion.

Anthrax (Horses and Cattle).—Insured against under Special Policy.

Plate Glass Insurance.   **Loss of Profits.**

Motor Car.—Special Scheme for Private Cars at Lowest Rates.

Motor Cycle and Side-Cars.—Full Benefits at Low Rates.

DUNDEE OFFICE—44 REFORM STREET.

D. GRANT REA, Branch Manager.

Applications for Agencies Invited.

Telephone No. 5467.   Telegraphic Address—"Yorkshire, Dundee."

R. S. SWEET, Insurance Agent, Royal Bank, Arbroath.
Agent for the Yorkshire Insurance Company, Limited.

Established 1850.

Peter Herron & Sons

ENGINEERS AND OXY-ACETYLENE WELDERS,

AND

GENERAL BLACKSMITHS AND HORSESHOERS,

22 PONDERLAW STREET,

AND

10 SOUTH GRIMSBY,

ARBROATH.

SPECIALISTS IN

ACETYLENE WELDING, STEAM, GAS, AND OIL ENGINES, WINDMILLS,

Ornamental Gates and Railings.

WE ARE ALSO BUYERS OF ANY OLD MACHINERY, SCRAP, &c.

Estimates Given.   Telephone 143.

JAMES RUXTON

CHEMIST,
"STAR" PHARMACY,

Keptie Angle - - Arbroath

Telegrams—"Ruxton, Chemist, Arbroath."

PRESCRIPTIONS DISPENSED.

DRUGS AND SUNDRIES.

PHOTOGRAPHIC REQUISITES.   CHEMICALS.

SPECTACLES.

SIGHT-TESTING TO SUIT ALL SIGHTS.

Archibald Donald & Son

Plasterers, Cement Workers, and Tile Specialists, - - -

East Mary Street, - - Arbroath.

'Phone No. 257.

ORDERS IN TOWN AND COUNTRY PROMPTLY AND CAREFULLY ATTENDED TO.

BREEZE BLOCKS MADE TO ORDER FOR PARTITION WALLS.

ESTIMATES GIVEN.

YEAR BOOK ADVERTISEMENTS.

Winners of Gold Medal and Diplomas for Bread Making.

Arbroath, No. 114———TELEPHONES———Friockheim, No. 2.

Carnegie Soutar & Sons,

FAMILY BREAD, BISCUIT, and . . . .
PASTRY BAKERS and CONFECTIONERS

118 HIGH STREET———————ARBROATH.

And at MILLGATE, FRIOCKHEIM.

SHORTBREAD AND BRIDESCAKES A SPECIALTY.

Picnic and Marriage Parties Purveyed for.

Orders given in at Arbroath and Friockheim will be Punctually Attended to.

HERRON & COLVILLE

PLUMBERS, GASFITTERS, ELECTRICIANS,

56 and 56½ KEPTIE STREET,

ARBROATH.

JOBBING OF EVERY DESCRIPTION PUNCTUALLY ATTENDED TO.

ESTIMATES GIVEN.   Telephone No. 148.

A REPAIR SERVICE THAT SATISFIES

If you require repairs, large or small, to your motor cycle or car let us have the opportunity of demonstrating our ability to do the work satisfactorily. Charges are most moderate. Any make of car or motor cycle supplied. All Accessories, Petrols, Oils, Greases.

Lochland Street Garage

W. DOYLE, Proprietor.

Where You Get Good Service.

THE OLDEST SCOTTISH OFFICE—ESTABLISHED 1805.

CALEDONIAN
INSURANCE COMPANY

Claims Paid, - £19,843,000.

FIRE, LIFE, ANNUITIES.   PERSONAL ACCIDENT AND ALL ILLNESS.
EMPLOYERS' LIABILITY.   BURGLARY.
MOTOR, MARINE, AND GENERAL.

The "Caledonian" Comprehensive Policy covers all Ordinary Risks to which a Householder is liable.

Prospectuses Free on Application.

DUNDEE OFFICE: 35 ALBERT SQUARE.

PRINCIPAL AGENTS IN ARBROATH:
W. & J. MACKINTOSH, Solicitors.   JOHN H. SIM, Bank Agent.
CLARK, OLIVER, DEWAR & WEBSTER, Solicitors.
G. TILLOTSON, Bank Agent.

YEAR BOOK ADVERTISEMENTS.

Telephone No. 150.

CHRISTIE & ANDERSON

(Sole Partner—GEO. K. SKEA).

BUILDERS AND CONTRACTORS.

YARD:
East Mary St., Arbroath.

HOUSE:
17 Jamieson Street.

Estimates Given for all Kinds of Mason Work.
JOBBING OF EVERY DESCRIPTION PROMPTLY ATTENDED TO.

William Morrison

Plasterer and - Cement Worker

17 Green Street, Arbroath

Estimates Given on Request and Highest Satisfaction Guaranteed

---

SEND YOUR FRIENDS ABROAD
A COPY OF

"The Arbroath Herald"

EVERY WEEK. The Charge for Posting Direct from the Office is **3/3 per Quarter.**

A GIFT that is better than a FIVE POUND NOTE to "Red Lichties" abroad.

ARBROATH HERALD LTD., Herald Buildings.

Joseph Moffat

Umbrella Maker and
Leather Goods Dealer

32 Keptie Street, Arbroath

WE SPECIALISE IN

Umbrellas, Travelling Requisites,
and Fancy Leather Goods.

SEE WINDOWS.   INSPECTION INVITED.

We have 30 Years' Reputation behind us
FOR
QUALITY, VALUE, & SERVICE.

Joseph Moffat
32—KEPTIE STREET—32
ARBROATH.

JAMES A. THOMSON

WHOLESALE AND RETAIL
IRONMONGER AND SEEDSMAN.

Household Furnishings.
Farmers' Accessories.
Tools for All Trades.

Ranges, Grates, and Tiles.   Guns and Ammunition.
Bee Keepers' Supplies.

Engineers', Joiners', and Blacksmiths' Furnishings.

134 HIGH STREET, ARBROATH.
'Phone No. 116.

Established 1856.   Telephone No. 11.

On the Breakfast Tables of the Best Families in Town or County.

OUR PURE TEAS AND COFFEES.

ANDREW SCOTT,
195 HIGH ST., ARBROATH.

Telephone No. 77.

James Robertson & Son

Joiners, Contractors, Undertakers and Licensed Valuators.

By the application of the Most Up-to-Date Methods and Machinery, and the Careful Personal Supervision of all Orders, they are prepared to execute all work entrusted to them in the Most Efficient and Economical manner.

SPECIAL ATTENTION GIVEN TO

OFFICE FITTINGS AND FURNITURE
SHOP FITTINGS, SHOW CASES, &c.
CHURCH FURNISHINGS   -   -   -

JOBBING WORK CAREFULLY AND PROMPTLY ATTENDED TO.

ESTIMATES GIVEN.

Joinery Works,
MILLGATE   -   ARBROATH.

The Station Cycle Works

HELEN STREET, ARBROATH.

We are Experts in Every Branch of the Construction and Repairing of Cycles and Motor Cycles, and can Re-plate and Overhaul any make of Machine. Stove Enamelling, Re-plating, Brazing. Accessories of every description. Moderate Charges. Expert Workmanship. Let us Repair your Mangle. New Rollers Fitted at Moderate Price.

Manufacturer of the Famous Fairy Polishes

D. FAIRWEATHER, Proprietor.

You will find that FISH only of the FINEST QUALITY are kept at

Stephen's Fish Mart

(WHOLESALE AND RETAIL).

15 Keptie Street - Arbroath.

Telephone No. 170.

Finnans, Smokies and Kippers a Specialty.
Orders by Post or 'Phone Receive Strict Attention.

MRS D. KERR,

POTTED MEAT MANUFACTURER,

44 BARNGREEN - ARBROATH.

One Quality Only—THE BEST.

ELECTRICITY

The Simplest Means
of obtaining

LIGHT
HEAT
and
POWER

.. Switch It On ..
.. That's All ..

ARBROATH ELECTRIC
LIGHT & POWER CO. LTD.

SOUTH GRIMSBY - ARBROATH

Telephone No. 136

170   YEAR BOOK ADVERTISEMENTS.

Tested Garden Seeds - *Guaranteed Farm Seeds*
EVERYTHING FOR THE GARDEN.
CATALOGUES ON APPLICATION.

Rose Bushes | *Vernon's* | Bulbs
Fruit Trees | | Seeds
Bedding-Out | 84 KEPTIE STREET | Garden Tools
Plants | | Insecticides
All in Season | ARBROATH | etc., etc.

WREATHS, CROSSES, etc., at Shortest Notice.
Selected Poultry and Pigeon Foods.
Re-Cleaned Bird Seeds.

Bell Rock Tavern

40 WEST GRIMSBY, Arbroath

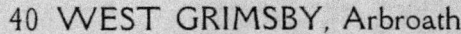

The Bell Rock Blend
Of Scotch and Irish Whiskies
Guaranteed Well Matured.

DRAUGHT BEER
always in Sparkling Condition.

Excellent Sitting Accommodation.

D. DINNIE, Proprietor.

YEAR BOOK ADVERTISEMENTS.

Chas. P. Mitchell

Family Grocer,
Tea, Wine and Spirit Merchant,

66 Keptie Street, Arbroath.

Only the Highest and Most Genuine Class of Goods Sold.

All Orders Receive Prompt Attention.

Mrs DUNLOP

CONFECTIONER,

26 Keptie Street, Arbroath

(Nearly Opposite Railway Station).

Fancy Biscuits	Shortbread.
and	Fruits. . .
Finest Cakes	Confections

Finest Table Bon-Bons and Dessert Chocolates.

A SPECIAL LINE IS OUR HOME-MADE CONFECTIONS:
Peppermint, Horehound, Cinnamon, and Clove Balls.

ESTABLISHED OVER 100 YEARS.

Scottish Union & National
Insurance Company.

ASSETS - £13,000,000.

Head Office - 35 ST ANDREW SQUARE, EDINBURGH.

Fire, Lightning and Explosion
  (Including Loss of Profits)
Life and Endowments.
Annuities and Pensions.
Accidents and Illnesses.
Leasehold and Capital Redemptions.
Employers' Liabilities.
Burglary and Theft.
Fidelity and Court Bonds.
Transit of Valuables.
Property Owners' Liabilities.
Third Party Liabilities.
Glass Breakage.
Motor Car Risks.
Vehicle Owners' Liabilities.
Householders' Consolidated.
Boiler Explosion.
Machinery Risks.
Lift Accidents.
Marine.

All these Insurances Effected on the Most Favourable Terms.

Please apply for a Copy of the Company's Prospectuses containing Particulars of the Latest Schemes.

AGENTS IN ARBROATH:

W. & W. H. ALEXANDER, Solicitors, 62 High Street.
CLARK, OLIVER, DEWAR & WEBSTER, S.S.C., N.P., Brothock Bank House.
McBAIN & ANDERSON, Solicitors, 15 Hill Street.
J. & W. MACDONALD, W.S., 7 Hill Street.
NEILL & GIBB, Solicitors, 93 High Street.
JOHN STEWART, British Linen Bank.
WILLIAM WALKER, Commercial Bank.

District Office: 13 PANMURE STREET, Dundee.

JAMES W. MUIR, F.C.I.I., Resident Secretary.

Telephone No. 4446   Telegraphic Address—" Unitate," Dundee.

T. Savege & Co.

Painters and Decorators :

219 HIGH STREET,
ARBROATH

Established Over Half-a-Century.

GEORGE SALMOND

BAKER,
199 HIGH STREET, Arbroath.
Telephone 164.

Our Fairport Gingerbread, Tea and Paste Biscuits, and Cakes are Favourites wherever used.

OUR LOAF BREAD

Is a line we pay particular attention to, and from our long experience in the selection and manipulation of the different materials, with the aid of the most up-to-date machinery, we supply to the public the principal article of dietary to please the most fastidious taste.

Van Deliveries in all Parts of the Town Daily.

G. R. HUNTER

Practical Boot and Shoe Repairer
200 HIGH STREET, ARBROATH

REPAIRS of every description at shortest notice. Charges Moderate. Always on hand Large Stock of Footwear Requisites

Punctuality is the Politeness of Kings!

The Horsehiring Co.
Always up to Date and Always up to Time.

Whether it be a Comfortable Taxi or Brougham or a Luxurious Landaulette: whether it be to pay a call, to meet a train, to attend a wedding, or to make a whole day tour through Bonnie Scotland, we can give Service—THE BEST POSSIBLE SERVICE.

The Features we offer :—

Our Taxis await every Train at the Railway Station.
Our Premises are Central & near the Railway Station.
Our Staff is Courteous and Obliging.
Our Powerful Austin Cars will take you any distance.
All Orders are given Prompt and Personal Attention, at whatever time of day or night.

Superior Funeral Service.   Coach Painting.
Motor Engineering Work Carried Through.

Arbroath Horsehiring Company Ltd.
12 DISHLAND STREET, ARBROATH.

Telephone No. 125.   WILLIAM CLARK, Manager.

GEORGE BLACK

JOINER AND CONTRACTOR,

Ernest Street Joinery Works.

Property Repairs carried out under Personal Supervision at Keenest Rates. Send your Enquiries. Incubators, Brooders, Sectional Poultry Houses, &c., at Keenest Rates.

Estimates Given for all proposed New and Reconstructional Work.

NOTE ADDRESS:

ERNEST STREET, ARBROATH.

Nothing but the Finest Home-Fed Beef, Mutton, and Pork, kept in Stock.

ROBERT GLASS

Butcher and Poulterer  2 Brechin Road Arbroath

Orders Called For and Promptly Delivered.

YEAR BOOK ADVERTISEMENTS.

Telephone No. 124.

JOHN RAYNE

PLUMBER, GASFITTER, SANITARY ENGINEER, AND WATER WORKS CONTRACTOR,

11-13 West Abbey Street, Arbroath.

Estimates Given for Fitting Up Electric Light Installations.
Orders in Town or Country promptly attended to, and carried out with the greatest care.

All Garments made by

REID & CUTHILL

Have that envied distinction which puts them in the forefront.

We always have on hand a Wide Range of the Finest Cloths in Harris and Shetland Tweeds, Worsteds, Serges, and Vicunas, &c.

Only the Finest Materials are used, and Customers may rely on all our productions being thoroughly Up-to-date in Style and Finish.

Personal Attention given to every Order, and Satisfaction Guaranteed.

REID & CUTHILL Tailors for Ladies and Gentlemen

BROTHOCK BANK, ARBROATH

R. A. MacFarlane

MOTOR ENGINEER,

ABBEY GARAGE, ARBROATH.

Any Make of Motor Car or Cycle Supplied.
Charabanc for Hire at Reasonable Rates

'Phone No. 211.

BUIST & CO.

Specialists in Linen and other Goods made in Scotland

LINENS of QUALITY

Price Lists on Application

BUIST & CO.
38 Guthrie Port —— Arbroath

David D. Barnett

WINE & SPIRIT MERCHANT,

3 MILLGATE LOAN, Arbroath

(FIT O' THE PORT).

Barnett's Special Scotch Whisky

Is the Finest and most palatable obtainable. Highly recommended for Invalids It is the same Fine Old Whisky that Sir Ralph the Rover and the Abbot pledged their bond of friendship on the deck of Sir Ralph's ship.

Barnett's Famed Scotch & Irish Whiskies

Pure Mellow Spirits—A Treat to Drink.
Specially Old Demerara Rum.
Very Old Brandies and Wines (Port and Sherries) kept in Stock.

Barnett's Beer always in Sparkling Condition

The same as used at the Court of Mary Queen of Scots.
Combe's Stout and Bass's Ale in Prime Condition.

DAVID D. BARNETT

3 MILLGATE LOAN.

The Rendezvous of Arbroathians returning home from all parts of the World.

Royal Exchange Assurance

INCORPORATED A.D. 1720

Royal Exchange, London (Head Office)

Fire, Life, Sea, Accident, Motor Car, Plate Glass, Burglary, Employers' Liability, Fidelity Guarantees, Third Party, Lift, Boiler, Machinery, Live Stock. Trustee and Executor.

Dundee Branch - 51/53 Meadowside

J. A. TOMBAZIS, Manager.

AGENTS IN ARBROATH:

W. & W. H. ALEXANDER, Solicitors, 62 High Street.
D. & W. CHAPEL, Solicitors, Market Place.
CLARK, OLIVER, DEWAR & WEBSTER, Solicitors, Brothock Bank.
THOS. W. P. GOURLEY, Solicitor, 82 Marketgate.
W. & J. MACKINTOSH, Solicitors, 1 Hill Street.
A. L. ROBERTSON, M.R.C.V.S., 40 Hill Street.
JOHN H. SIM, Bank of Scotland, High Street.
JOHN STEWART, British Linen Bank, Brothock Bridge.

190   YEAR BOOK ADVERTISEMENTS.

In Every Department of Motor Car Service

We can advise you in a practical and helpful way. IT PAYS TO COME TO ROBBIE'S before purchasing a Car, because there are no regrets afterwards.

We are prepared to undertake all classes of Repairs, and to execute the work satisfactorily and with promptitude.

The Leading Makers of Motor Cycles are represented in our Agencies.

Our Taxi Service is equalled by none in Town or Country.

D. ROBBIE & CO.,
MOTOR ENGINEERS,
Dishlandtown St. & Brothock Bridge
ARBROATH.

'Phone No. 129.

ANDERSON & HEWIT,

MERCHANT TAILORS.

128 HIGH STREET,
ARBROATH.

ALEXANDER REID

BUILDING CONTRACTOR,
17 LINDSAY STREET, ARBROATH.

Gravestones and
Monuments
Executed in Marble,
Granite and
Freestone.

We Specialise in
Artistic
Marble and Tile
Work.

All Classes of
Building Construction
Executed in
Stone, Brick, or
Reinforced Concrete

Designs Submitted
and Estimates
Given.

Furniture Manufacturers,
Upholsterers,
Funeral Undertakers

Telephone 106.

J. P. Grewar & Son

MAKERS OF

Hair, Wool, Fibre and Spring Mattresses,

Venetian, Duchesse, Linen and other Blinds.

ONLY FIRST CLASS MATERIALS AND WORKMANSHIP EMPLOYED

Corner Gravesend & Panmure Street

ARBROATH.

Carpet & Linoleum Factors, Furniture Removers and Storers

196　　　YEAR BOOK ADVERTISEMENTS.

PATRONISED BY THE NOBILITY.

Telephone No. 84.　　　　　Telegrams—"White Hart."

White Hart Hotel

HIGH STREET, ARBROATH

THIS Old-Established Hotel, unrivalled for Comfort, Excellent Cuisine, and Moderate Charges, in the Most Central Business Part of the Town, and adjacent to all the Banks and Public Buildings, has been entirely Re-Modelled and Re-Furnished. The Commercial and Coffee Rooms, Restaurant, and Dining-Rooms are Fitted and Furnished in the Best Style.

ALEXANDER SMITH keeps nothing but a Very Superior Class of Spirits and Beers. The Hotel Cellars contain an Excellent Stock of Very Old and Superior Wines.

THE WHITE HALL

Is very suitable for Balls, Marriages, and Supper Parties, and is Let on Very Moderate Terms.

ALEXANDER SMITH, Proprietor.

HOWAT DUNCAN

M.Ph.S., F.B.O.A.,

209 HIGH STREET, - - ARBROATH

REGISTERED BY THE JOINT COUNCIL OF QUALIFIED OP-TICIANS for Sight-Testing, the Dispensing of Hospital and Oculists' Prescriptions, and the Supply of Glasses to Insured Persons under the National Health Insurance Act.

R. Anderson & Co.,

208 HIGH STREET, ARBROATH.

FRESH FISH IN SEASON.

Arbroath Smokies a Specialty.

FINNANS OUR OWN CURING.

All Orders Promptly Attended To.

208 HIGH STEET, ARBROATH

Telephone No. 42.

CALDER BROTHERS,

Builders and Monumental Masons,

22 ELLIOT STREET, - - ARBROATH.

Monuments & Headstones in Granite, Marble, & Freestone. Designs and Prices sent on application. Inscriptions Cut in any Cemetery. Makers of Concrete Blocks and Slabs. All Kinds of Concrete Work Executed by Experts in Concrete Construction.

Jobbing of Every Description Promptly Attended to.

If you have ELECTRICAL WORK to be done

Ask us for Quotations before coming to a decision. We do only First-Class Work, and our Prices compare favourably with others—moreover, personal attention is given to every job. Electricity stands for—

CLEANLINESS, CONVENIENCE, & ECONOMY.

Allow us to make your Installation. WE SPECIALISE in RADIO WORK, and will be pleased to give Practical Demonstrations by arrangement.

J. D. CAMPBELL

Electrical Engineer,

15 ALLAN STREET, ARBROATH.

YEAR BOOK ADVERTISEMENTS.

Telephone, No. 66

ROBERT BROWN

*Grocer, Tea, Wine
& Spirit Merchant*

Italian Warehouseman

3 Keptie St., & 2 Bridge St.

ARBROATH

Goods Delivered in Town and District by Motor.

YEAR BOOK ADVERTISEMENTS.

Do you help to organise Whist Drives?

Because if you do, you should certainly see the value we are at present offering in serviceable

WHIST CARDS

Our prices are the Keenest in the trade, and we give very prompt delivery of all orders. Get the "Herald" to print your Whist Cards.

Arbroath Herald
LIMITED
BROTHOCK BRIDGE, ARBROATH.

ARCHIBALD DONALD & SON

Plasterers, Cement Workers, and Tile Specialists.

35 HIGH STREET, Carnoustie

'Phone No. 257 Arbroath.

Orders in Town and Country Promptly and Carefully attended to.
Breeze Blocks made to order for Partition Walls.

Estimates Given.

Arbroath Office and Yard—EAST MARY STREET.

STATIONER AND TOBACGONIST,   **A. WILL**   THE LEADING HOUSE AGENT.

34 HIGH STREET, CARNOUSTIE.

LISTS ON APPLICATION.

All the Latest Books by the Most Popular Authors.

Fancy Goods, Leather Goods, Crest China.   Circulating Library.

Specialist in Crayon Drawings and Miniatures.

R. WILSON ASTBURY

Artist Photographer,

(5½ Years Manager for Valentine & Co., Ltd., Dundee.)

Photography in all its Branches.

THE STUDIO, HIGH STREET, CARNOUSTIE.

Read the Arbroath Herald

EVERY FRIDAY.   **PRICE TWOPENCE.**

— TO —
Shopkeepers, Merchants
TRADESMEN, &c.

We are in constant touch with the pick of the Largest Paper Manufacturers in the Country, and are thus able to supply the products of their Mills of any Grade or Quality on the very best terms possible.

IF IN WANT OF PAPER

of any kind, Plain or Printed, let us quote you. It will cost you little, and save you much.

WRAPPINGS OF EVERY DESCRIPTION,

All Sizes and Weights. Grease-Proof Papers for Grocers, Butchers, and Dairy Produce Dealers, in Various Grades. Grocers' Grey, Kraft, and Glazed Brown.

BAGS OF EVERY KIND AND SIZE.

We hold a Large Stock of all Sizes and Various Qualities in use by Bakers, Confectioners, Seedsmen, Tobacconists, &c., at Makers' Prices. Any Special Make Quoted for and Supplied on Shortest Notice.

TWINES

Cotton, Hemp, and Manilla, suitable for Parcelling and other purposes.

Arbroath Herald Limited
PRINTERS and STATIONERS.

Awarded Highest Diploma Glasgow Exhibition.

THE
D. & A. Preserve Co.
LIMITED

Were Awarded **HIGHEST DIPLOMA** for
. . their Exhibit of High-Class . .

Jams, Jellies, Marmalade and Peel
AT THE 1922

Bakers, Grocers and Allied Trades Exhibition in Glasgow.

This is only another Testimony to the unbroken record for Purity and Excellence which these Preserves have so honourably held for Half a Century.

PROCURE A SAMPLE OF OUR
"QUEEN'S TABLE" PRESERVES
And you will unhesitatingly confirm this verdict.

D. & A. Preserve Co. Ltd.
Preserve Works, Arbroath

KELTIC BOOTS
TREAD THE WORLD

Selling Agents
IN
South Africa,
New Zealand,
Australia, Canada,
West Indies,
China and the East.
And Throughout
Britain and Ireland.

SOLE MANUFACTURERS:

S. FAIRWEATHER & SONS, LTD.
ABBEY WORKS, ARBROATH.

RETAIL SHOPS:
213 HIGH STREET and 20a KEPTIE STREET

C. Y. MYLES & SONS

Distinctive Overcoats

All our garments are hand tailored by men of long experience, and customers can always rely on the cut of our clothes being in the first of fashion.

PRICES MODERATE

There is no comparison between the hand-tailored garment and the machine-made article; besides, why not keep trade in our own town?

Agent for Burberry and Aquascutum Weatherproofs.

C. Y. Myles & Sons
Ladies' and Gentlemen's Tailors,
19-21 James St. & 112 High St., Arbroath.
Telephone No. 109.

November

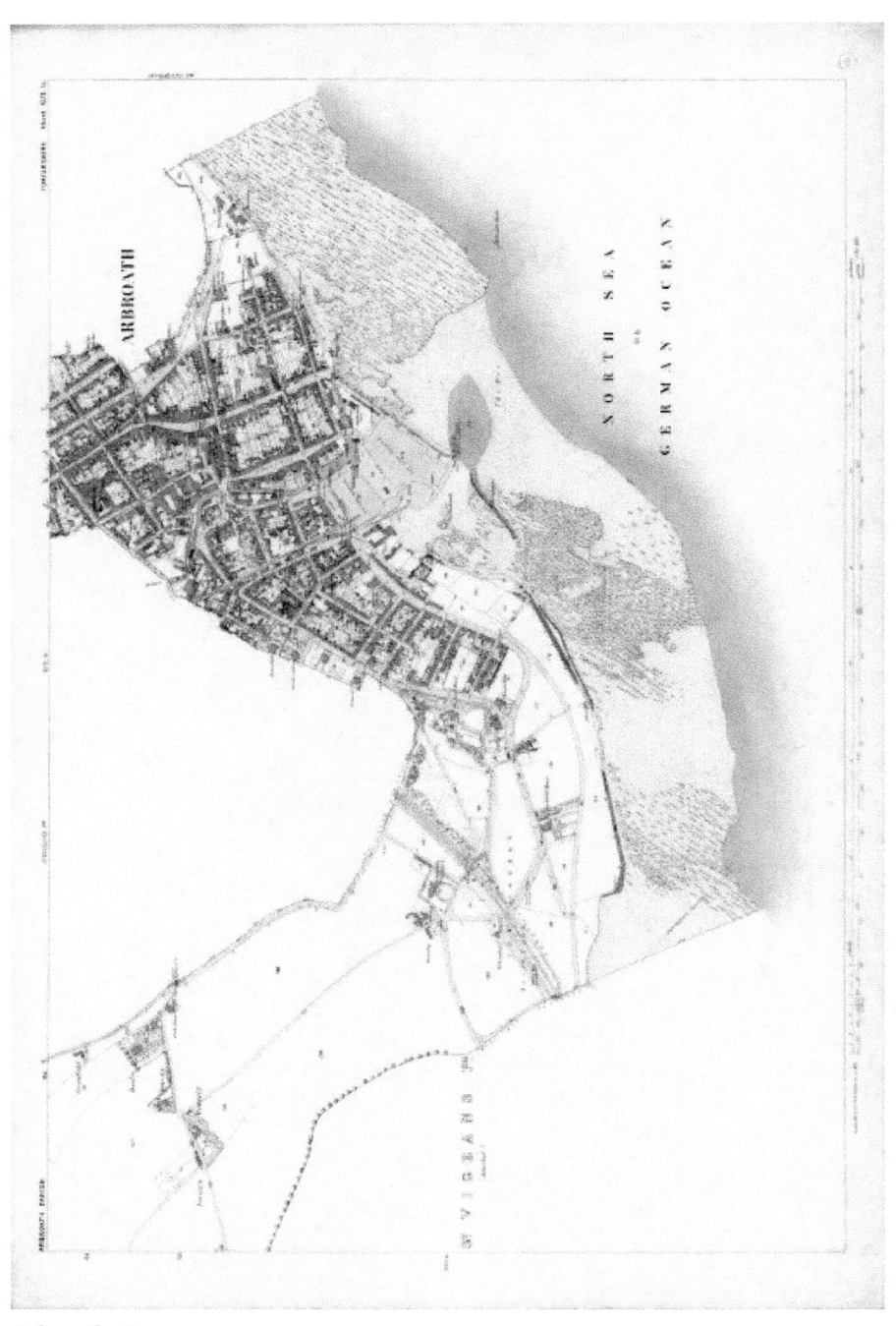

Arbroath 1839

November 1 1901

Bailie Robert Melvin was a busy man at the Arbroath Police Court this morning dealing with a couple of his "regulars", it would appear.

Mary Spink, millworker of Hope Street was fined two shillings and sixpence with the alternative of 24 hours imprisonment.

She pleaded guilty to the charge of being drunk and incapable after she had met a man called Craig who took her to several pubs and "filled her fou" and then left her.

One suspects that there was a little more to this story than she was prepared to tell, and the next "client" for Bailie Melvin was no less a person than one Alexander Craig, aged 39, a grocer of 2, Abbey Park.

Mr Craig pleaded guilty to having last night in Chalmers Street behaved in a violent and indecent manner by cursing and shouting.

He was in the company of the previous prisoner, Mary Spink, and when the police came to apprehend Mary, he began to interfere, telling the policemen to leave her alone.

He was fined 10 shillings with the option of seven days in prison.

This incident seems to contradict Mary's story for he clearly had not abandoned her, as she claimed, although there seems to be little doubt that he had indeed "filled her (and himself) fou".

One would like to know what happened to these two poor souls.

It seems unlikely that they would have been able to afford these fines, so a spell "inside" appeared to beckon for the pair of them.

November 2 1920

Today was Election Day in Arbroath (and indeed the rest of Scotland) but it was an Election with a difference.

There was the Election for the Town Council, something that aroused no great attention other than in the Abbey and Guthrie Port Ward where John Souttar was standing on a Labour ticket.

He didn't succeed, unlike his friend William Whitton in Forfar who was luckier, but his presence made it interesting and it was an indication of what would happen in the future.

What was far more interesting was the National Poll about alcoholic drink. The background was the appalling amount of drink that was consumed – as any Monday morning in the Police Court would indicate.

Everyone remembered that licensing and restrictions needed to be introduced in the munitions industries during the war.

This poll gave the electorate the opportunity to vote for No Licence, No Change or Limited Licence.

Churches backed No Licence, "the Trade" (ie publicans, hotel keepers and brewers) naturally went for No Change.

Surprisingly in Arbroath, only 91 voted for the middle option, but the 1053 who were in favour of No Licence were decisively outvoted by the 4521 who were in favour of No Change.

Presumably, the thinking was that although there was too much drink and drunkenness, people felt that outright Prohibition was a step too far.

It might bring other complications like a rise in crime. So Arbroath, like most of Scotland, voted to say "wet" rather than "dry".

November 3 1892

Today's *Arbroath Herald* contains a review of the affairs of the Arbroath Cycling Club.

Cycling is a sport which has become very popular over the past 20 years or so, and the county of Forfarshire enjoys many fine roads on which young men can cycle.

Although bicycles are expensive, they are well worth the money.

The membership of the Cycling Club in 1892 is 53 as against 27 last year, and this reflects the growth of the sport.

For various reasons of seemliness and delicacy, it is not a sport suited for females, but the Arbroath Club has now been in existence for about twelve years and is in a "flourishing condition".

The pneumatic tyre, that great recent invention for cycling generally, has made a great difference to the local club.

The club is proud of the fact that it has, over the past several years, had a member who has been either third or fourth in the County Championships.

This is in spite of the fact that the town of Arbroath lacks any real facilities for training cyclists, and has had to use the beach on occasion.

There have been a few cycling events at Gayfield, but what is really required is a good cinders cycling track in the town.

The Club Champion is G Smith, who gave a good performance in county events, especially when he started from scratch in the 50 miles handicap.

Second in the club performances is W W Craig who won the three mile handicap with a 10 second start.

November 4 1912

The body calling itself the Arbroath Health Congress held its annual convention in the White Hart Hotel.

It was a cheery occasion under the Chairmanship of Dr J D Gilruth with Bailie Smith and James Anderson acting as croupiers.

After a large dinner, various toasts were proposed to the Royal Family, the Armed Forces and the Town and Councillors of Arbroath.

Mr George G Dalgarno, solicitor, said that in the recent election the people of Arbroath had shown that they were very happy with the way that Town affairs were run, and that he could not help feeling that the town was in cheerier spirit than it had been for many years.

The local industries which had been in recession from time to time in the past were now all healthy and full employment was here.

In addition the amount of summer visitors was growing and what seemed to be having a great effect was the new station.

The old station had been gloomy and had scared people off, but "a wave of prosperity had swept the town".

Two depressing notes were struck – one was the state of the harbour which badly needed modernised, and the other was the state of some of the housing in the town.

It was probably no different from other towns, but in this bright new century there was no excuse for it.

The evening ended on an optimistic note with everyone agreeing that in all Scotland, there was no better place to live than Arbroath.

November 5 1960

Guy Fawkes Night!

It was about three and half centuries ago that these chaps tried to blow up the Houses of Parliament, and the event was still celebrated with gusto in Arbroath and everywhere else.

Although it was basically harmless, it did frighten a few animals and people of a nervous disposition.

There were still quite a few men in Arbroath who did not want anything to do with explosions following their experiences in the Second or even the First World Wars.

The fireworks had been on sale since about August and they were appallingly cheap with "one penny bangers" and "two penny bangers" on sale in quite a few shops.

Most people dismissed it as "a penny for a bang". Sometimes the bang did not go off, and it was "a penny for a whiz"!

Incidentally, how could one complain to the shopkeeper if there was no bang? How could you prove it?

There were also rockets. For them, you needed an empty milk bottle or lemonade bottle to stand them in. You lit the paper and the rocket took off and disappeared harmlessly into the air and in Arbroath usually into the sea.

It was all part of childhood. Everyone was warned about the dangers, and accidents did happen but usually of a very minor nature. The real fun was the bonfire in the garden or on the Common, and it was often an opportunity to burn some rubbish.

Tonight the weather was not all that great, but the Fire Brigade were probably quite happy about that!

At Auchmithie, woman leaning against boat, 1881 photograph by James Cox, National Galleries of Scotland

Auchmithie Harbour

On the beach, Auchmithie

November 6 1942

There now seemed little reason to doubt that the British success in North Africa had been a lasting one.

Following the tank battle at the end of October, the infantry were now advancing.

Although one had to be careful about what one read in newspapers which were of course heavily censored, the news seemed to be uniformly good.

The Arbroath Herald even went as far as to sound a note of caution and to make sure that gains were consolidated before further advances were sought.

There was however a distinct lack of detail allowed in letters which reached home from Arbroath soldiers and sailors, and that was ominous.

In the meantime, life continued in Arbroath with several legal cases brought against people for blackout offences, usually brought about by negligence and forgetfulness rather than any deliberate attempt to break the law.

There was a heartening story about "tattie gatherers" from the Mains of Kelly donating £1 15 shillings to Lady Chapel for sending to Prisoners of War from the Arbroath area.

The main local news story was about Chief Constable James MacDonald being sued for the enormous sum of £1500. Burgh Surveyor William Turner alleged he had made false and misleading statements about Turner's involvement in the petrol stored by Arbroath Town Council in the Arrott Street yard.

It was a juicy and interesting case which almost acted as some sort of comic relief for the real horrors of what was going on in the world at the moment.

November 7 1919

The Spanish flu epidemic was still continuing to sweep the country a year after the end of the war.

Tonight in Liverpool, a week after his 53rd birthday, John Edward Doig, commonly known as "Ned" died.

John "Ned" Doig

"Ned" Doig was probably the best goalkeeper that Arbroath have ever had, and one of Sunderland and Scotland's best as well.

Technically he was not an Arbroathian, having been born in Letham near Forfar, but he always considered himself an inhabitant of Arbroath, for whom he played 128 games between 1886 and 1890.

He was good enough to be watched by several English clubs and he turned professional with Blackburn Rovers, then the holders of the FA Cup, in 1890.

But he played one game for them before falling out with them, and being homesick, he returned to Arbroath.

As he had played one game as a professional football player, by an odd legal ruling, he was not allowed to play for Arbroath again.

But he was given another chance in England, this time with Sunderland in what was known as "the team of all the talents" which went on to win the English League in 1892, 1893, 1895 and 1902 (but never the English Cup).

He won four caps for Scotland, including the Ibrox Disaster game of 1902.

When he went on to Liverpool, he won a Second Division medal in 1905.

He remained very fond of Arbroath and was frequently seen here.

He was a small man for a goalkeeper and always, both on the field and off the field, wore a bonnet because he was very aware of his baldness.

November 8 1905

It is not often that the game of billiards holds centre stage in Arbroath, but today and tonight were an exception.

An exhibition match was staged at the White Hart Hotel between Tom Aitken, the Champion of Scotland and J Douglas Johnson, a well-known local player from Perth.

The limited accommodation in the hotel was full of Arbroath people supporting Johnson, but in total admiration of the skill and play of Tom Aitken.

Aitken had been born in Aberdeen but learned his trade in Peterhead, had become Champion of Scotland in 1902 and would remain virtually unchallenged until well after the war.

This afternoon and this evening his skills were much appreciated by the people of Arbroath, and although Johnson was given a handicap of 500 out of 16000, he was no match for Aitken who scored three century breaks and one of 285 which included 47 "nursery cannons".

Johnson did not play at all badly but was defeated by 1800 to 1103. Both men behaved in the manner expected of billiard players and talked cheerfully to the locals after the game.

It was an occasion that would be much remembered in Arbroath and everyone was grateful to Mr Smith of the White Hart Hotel for opening the billiards season in this way.

The game of billiards had grown in the last 50 years, but was not really widely played in Arbroath, being associated in people's minds with gangsters and "ne-er do wells".

It was frequently denounced from Church pulpits for its association with professionalism and betting.

November 9 1954

Shipbuilding has returned to Arbroath!

After an interval of 25 years, the shipyard has been back in action and two keels have been laid.

To say "shipbuilding" is possibly an exaggeration, for the scale is certainly a great deal smaller than what one could see on the Clyde or the Mersey, but nevertheless, there will always be a need for fishing boats and good quality ones at that.

Now two brothers from St Monance in Fife, Alex and Andrew Gerrard, who bought the slipway several years ago and started off with small repairs, have recently moved on to actually building the vessels.

Now there is the constant sound of machinery and the yard bustles with more than 30 workers employed.

The two vessels currently on the slipway at the moment are both Seine-net fishing boats, one of which will ply its trade in the Aberdeen area while the other is likely to be used locally.

They are 50 feet and 53 feet respectively. It is a welcome sight again, but locals have long memories of one previous disaster many years ago when the "Elmgrove" slid gracefully off the stocks into the sea and then promptly capsized in the water.

Fortunately there was no loss of life, but the whole thing was a major embarrassment to the town.

This will not happen, it is fervently hoped, with the Gerrard Brothers, who also have plans for other ventures; they have leased a piece of land which is currently part of the bus station.

November 10 1939

So what was this war all about then?

People were beginning to ask questions about it.

War had been declared, troops had been mobilised, there had been irritating regulations about blackouts and gas masks.

Football had been suspended and then started again. Arbroath are now in the quaintly named Eastern and North-Eastern League.

Schools had been closed but opened again, and everything else was astonishingly normal.

Cinemas were as before, and even local amateur dramatic groups were still functioning.

There had been an absolute wheen of Church concerts.

There were the usual Arbroath things in the newspapers – some poor chap had fallen off a cliff, another had walked into the harbour after having had too much to drink.

Generally speaking, nothing was happening with the Maginot and Siegfried Lines apparently doing a good job in keeping the armies apart.

Poland had been more or less obliterated in the East and divided up between the German and the Russians.

There was talk of Arbroath accepting some refugees, but little was happening in western Europe.

The British Expeditionary Force was in danger of being renamed Back Every Friday, for so many of them had not yet left the British Isles.

There were even quite a few readers' letters in newspapers hinting, ever so gently, that a negotiated peace might not be the worst idea in the world.

The contrast between this "phoney war" and the Great War with its horrendous casualties could not have been more stark.

November 11 1918

Arbroath awoke this morning in confident expectation of the news they had all been awaiting now for several days, particularly since the Kaiser had abdicated on Friday November 8.

The word that everyone wanted to hear was "surrender", but instead the word was a new one called "armistice" namely the cessation of hostilities pending a Peace Agreement.

Shortly after 11.00 am *The Arbroath Herald* put a notice in the window to this effect. A jubilant crowd assembled outside the Town Hall to hear the Provost.

The Burgh flag was run up the flagpole, then the Provost appeared on the balcony to announce the good news of the telegram from the Tay Defences in Dundee to say that an armistice had been signed.

In a very short time flags were hung out of windows and the steeple bells rang merrily for a long time.

It was an unofficial public holiday and dancing took place in the streets to the music of a penny whistle.

Some wounded Tommies who had been living in Seaforth House appeared and those who were able danced with some of the fish girls and the factory girls.

At least six bands appeared by the afternoon –the local Highland Light Infantry, the Boys Brigade, the Burgh Pipe Band, the Burgh Instrumental Band, the Highland Pipe Band and Keith and Blackman's rag time band.

And at night, the street lights went on again!

But there were some who could not be happy.

A grieving widow with two children had to be comforted when she saw the celebrations, and out of respect, the celebrations were paused until she had passed.

Arbroath Instrumental Band in new uniform

November 12 1923

The Palace Cinema (the Pally, as it is known locally) is tonight beginning the showing of a film which should attract local attention and large houses.

It is "The Little Minister" of J M Barrie, the man from nearby Kirriemuir.

"Special and Appropriate Scottish Music will be discoursed (sic) during the showing of this picture".

This means that the piano will play songs like "Loch Lomond" and "Mary, My Scots Bluebell" in the background as the picture progresses, for the films are as yet "all silent".

Now that a radio service has started in Great Britain, it cannot be long before the pictures can become "talkies".

The film is the screen version of a play, and it is supposed to be set in the woods near Kirriemuir.

"The Little Minister" falls in love with Babbie, played by the famous Betty Compson, described as a "gypsy coquette" who makes the Minister forget "every religion except love".

The main film will be shown all week, but there will be a change of supporting programme in midweek including a different "Pathe Gazette" of the news with the obvious intention of encouraging people to come back.

In truth, even in times of financial stringency, the cinema is not expensive at a "siccy" (sixpence) for the cheapest seats, and half price for children.

"The Little Minister" is shown at 7.00 pm, then the supporting programme, then "The Little Minister" again until 10.20 pm and you can watch the "big picture" twice, if you want to.

This is the heyday of the cinema, full of romance, escapism and the chance to forget reality.

November 13 1907

The Women's Suffrage Movement today comes to Arbroath.

The "votes for women" campaign has so far caused little concern in Arbroath, and indeed has been the subject of not a little ridicule locally as well as a few coarse remarks by men.

Today however the National Women's Social and Political Union organised two meetings in Arbroath, the first of them at the YMCA Hall and presided over by Mrs Ouchterlony of the Guynd.

She hoped that any decision that they took should be sent to Mr Morley the present high profile MP of Montrose Burghs.

Miss Dugdale of Aboyne, supported by Miss Lumsden of Glenbogie and Miss Fraser of the Women's Union, spoke eloquently talking about "slavery" and "tyranny" and how outrageous it was that in the strongest country of the world, people were disenfranchised because of their sex.

The second meeting was in the evening at the Good Templar Hall and was clearly aimed more at working class women with references to the need for Factory Inspectors to cut out the "sweated system" and other things.

Both these meetings were well attended, and resolutions were passed. It was probably true to say that the cause of women's voting aroused as yet only mild interest generally.

It was sad that the Liberal Government, which had been in power now for over two years, and which had proved itself so dynamic in other respects of social progress, had as yet shown little interest in the movement.

But times would change.

November 14 1945

"The spotlight is on youth today" said a lady with less than stunning originality at a meeting of the local ladies' guild which worked in favour of the British Sailors' Society.

The war in Europe has now been over for six months, and in the Far East for about three months, and the role of the Royal Navy was a proud one in the defence of the country and the liberation of Europe.

Recently nine young Arbroath lads have been enlisted for the Royal Navy, and it is a great opportunity.

> "Training for life at sea is in itself the very best that any lad could have. Discipline, orderliness and application to work are maintained as in no other apprenticeship. That and the understanding friendship of their instructors and the happy comradeship of their fellow students make for an ideal life for youths at a period when the right direction and environment mean everything".

Not everyone would necessarily agree with the idealistic sentiments expressed by the lady, for there is certainly a downside to living on a ship for any length of time.

There is certainly no doubt that the country will need a Royal Navy for the foreseeable future, and National Service will stay with us for some time.

Meanwhile the trickle back home of soldiers and sailors is continuing with many of the sailors who served on the Arctic convoys, for example, or the battle of the Atlantic, having perhaps a slightly different picture of life in the "senior service".

November 15 1922

It was General Election Day in Arbroath, and indeed in the country.

It was a General Election with a few differences, though.

One was that the sitting candidate for Montrose Burghs, Leng Sturrock was ill and unable to campaign in person with most of the electioneering being done by his brother Percy.

Sturrock was standing as a Coalition Liberal, which was likely to attract the Conservative votes.

His only opponent was John Carnegie, a local man standing for Labour.

It was hard to work this one out because no-one knew the effect that Leng Sturrock's illness would have on things.

Would there be a sympathy vote? Or would the view be taken that there was no point in voting for an invalid?

Carnegie's campaign was vigorous and to the point, as he pointed quite rightly at unemployment, the shocking houses that some people still lived in, and the almost total lack of any medical facilities for anyone other than the rich, problems that Lloyd George's Coalition had failed to tackle.

Polling was steady throughout the day, and a lot brisker in the evening once the factories closed, something that was looked upon as good news for Labour.

Polls closed at 9.00 pm. then the ballot boxes were taken to the police station where they were guarded overnight and then conveyed to Dundee where they would be counted.

Sturrock won, but with a greatly reduced majority of 1,363.

The major talking point was in Dundee itself where the seating Liberal, Winston Churchill, had been defeated by a Prohibitionist!

November 16 1899

Naturally the war in South Africa which has broken out this year is attracting most attention.

At least 39 Arbroath men are known to be already serving in South Africa or currently being trained in England prior to being shipped out. There is naturally concern about the local boys fighting far away.

The Arbroath Farmers Club have been holding their Turnip Competition over the past four days at local farms like Panlathy, Stotfaulds and Downiekin and it finished today at New Downie and Calungie.

It seems to have been a fairly light-hearted few days with a certain amount of "hospitality" distributed at the various places at which they called, but the judges decided that Murroes, Craigie, Panlathy and Stotfaulds were the winners in the various sections of Swedes, Turnips and Yellows.

Turnips or "neeps" as they are locally called, are in plentiful supply this year, which has been a good year for the harvest generally.

The new century is now only weeks away and there is great discussion in the agricultural community about the possibility of motorised "tractors" taking over from horses.

Already several "horseless carriages" have been seen in the environs of Arbroath. Some see them as dangerous contraptions which go too fast, but others see the possibilities.

In the meantime there is also the occasional worry about the health of the old Queen, now past her 80th birthday and apparently getting more and more unsociable and awkward by the day.

November 17 1910

At Forfar Sheriff Court, Sheriff Lee had a curious case to deal with concerning an Arbroath couple.

Mr and Mrs David Ferguson of Waulkmills, Arbroath, appeared on a charge of having undertaken for reward the nursing and maintenance, apart from its parents, of an illegitimate child and failed, within 48 hours of its reception to give notice to the local authority.

This was contrary to the Children Act, whereby they were liable to imprisonment to a term not exceeding six months and to a fine not exceeding £20.

The accused pleaded guilty and claimed that they had omitted to inform the authorities through ignorance of this requirement.

Sheriff Lee wisely accepted their plea and dismissed them, hoping that they would not in future make the same mistake.

What this case was all about is hard to unravel, but it does not seem that there was any dishonesty on the part of Mr and Mrs Ferguson (a childless couple, one assumes) who had effectively agreed to foster an illegitimate child and had come to an agreement for a sum of money with the child's parents.

Illegitimacy was of course a tremendous stigma in 1910 and one assumes that this was a daughter of a middle class or rich family who had fallen from grace, and the family were willing to pay for the child to be looked after.

The fault of the Fergusons seems to have been simply that they forgot to tell the authorities.

November 18 1942

Arbroath wouldn't be Arbroath if there were not some people complaining about something!

The war has taken a turn for the better with news of a great victory in Egypt and continuing good news about the pursuit of the Afrika Korps across the desert.

Such news as has been allowed to filter through tends to indicate that Arbroath men have been heavily involved, and that casualties have been light.

Because of this, churches were allowed to ring their bells last Sunday for the first time for two years. (Previously that would have signified an invasion!)

The Arbroath Churches did so, but apparently they were not co-ordinated and not loud enough! Ah well, "there's aye a something, isn't there?"

Better news comes about a well-known local man, veterinary surgeon Mr A Linton Robertson who has received the Territorial Efficiency Decoration for serving 20 years in the Territorial Army.

Mr Robertson is a veteran of the Great War, having served in France, where he was gassed, with the Glasgow Highlanders (9th Highland Light Infantry) and then served at Salonika, now in his profession as a vet dealing mainly with horses.

After the war he was in Constantinople for a year, but returned to Scotland in 1922 and joined the Territorial Army, and latterly the Home Guard.

He has also helped with the Boy Scouts and been a Past President of the Rotary Club.

November 19 1959

"The times they are a-changin'".

Although it was 1964 before Bob Dylan released the song which provided the catch-phrase of a generation, there is little doubt that the past decade has seen an enormous change in the lifestyle of most Arbroathians.

Prosperity and affluence have arrived to an extent that the older generation would hardly believe possible.

Full employment is now more or less taken for granted, housing has improved, there is a free health service and educational provision is such that University education is now within the grasp of most people.

There are of course undesirable side effects with youth crime now a major factor, or at least highlighted more than before, particularly at dances where "pop" music seems to have such an effect on youngsters.

In Arbroath, The Picture House and The Palace are still going strong with stars like Kim Novak, Bob Hope, Clifton Webb and others making their regular and welcome appearance, but the writing is on the wall now for the cinema.

Adverts are beginning to appear in *The Arbroath Herald* from Reekie-Television encouraging people to buy their television on credit.

Worse still, perhaps is the advert from Grant's which offers the rent of a television set for a £3 deposit and then 10 shillings per week with the guarantee of a new "set" every four years.

This immediately puts TV within the grasp of most working class families, and inevitably with a TV in the house, the weekly (or often more than that) trip to "the pictures" will become less attractive, or necessary.

November 20 1914

Now more than three months into the war, and with winter now upon us, Arbroath remains bullish and upbeat.

The outrageous prophecy of the war being over "before the leaves fall" is clearly wrong and "over by Christmas" is now very unlikely.

Most folk are aware that this will be a long war.

Already there have been significant casualties, and there are clear signs that the rush to enlist of August and September is slowing down, as young men are beginning to entertain serious doubts about the wisdom of it all.

The Arbroath Herald devotes a page and a bit to "Arbroath's Muster Roll" a list of local men who are involved in the war – a clear piece of emotional blackmail to young men who are NOT on the list.

Bob Crumley, captain of Arbroath FC, one of the heroes of Dundee's winning of the Scottish Cup in 1910, and a man who served in the Gordon Highlanders in the Boer War has decided to join the Scottish Horse.

In the meantime, social life in Arbroath continues – Arbroath FC, for example, beat Dundee "A" in a Central League game, and the concert featuring "Scotch Kelly" at the New Palace Theatre was very well attended.

Arbroath being a coastal town, there is a blackout in force and now that the nights are a lot longer, it is having a noticeable effect, although enterprising people have found ways round it.

November 21 1952

Full praise is due to Arbirlot Women's Rural Institute for taking on an ambitious production like "Trial by Jury" by Gilbert and Sullivan and making such a good job of it!

An all-women cast doing this show in a village hall is remarkable.

What was even more remarkable was the audience that they attracted, so large as to be from places other than the small village of Arbirlot. Indeed, a few cars were seen coming from the Dundee direction!

The village hall was filled to capacity and the village had to be scoured to find extra chairs. Even then a few latecomers had to stand at the back.

The story is of a breach of promise case in which a man had broken his promise to marry a lady "doubly criminal to do so, for the bride had bought her trousseau!"

The music like most of Gilbert and Sullivan is very restful and amusing, and the ladies of the WRI did splendidly with lines like

> "since the days of Charles the Second,
> it's been generally reckoned
> a very serious crime,
> to be married to two women at a time",

and full credit has to be given to Mrs Robertson, the wife of the village schoolmaster, for the way in which she directed her group.

The performance of "Trial By Jury" was preceded by a One Act Play called "Mad Hatters in Mayfair" put on by members of the Arbroath Amateur Dramatic Club. That too was a thundering success.

November 22 1896

Today Arbroath was visited by Graham Brown of Lachan and Andrew Wright of Yung K'ang, two Missionaries from the China Inland Mission, who spoke on several occasions on the work of mission in China, a land which was not very familiar to many people in Britain other than as a land of mysticism and exoticism.

Last night the pair addressed a large meeting in the YMCA Hall, Mr Wright being dressed in Chinese costume, something that attracted a great deal of favourable comment.

Today (Sunday) he talked to the fellowship of the YMCA, in the afternoon he occupied the pulpit at Inverbrothock Free Church and in the evening he addressed the Queen Street Church Congregation.

Mr Brown talked to Princes Street United Presbyterian Church, Ladyloan Free Church and the Town Mission Hall.

Between the two of them they reached a large number of Arbroathian people whom they entertained by talking about the traditions of China and the progress being made by the China Inland Mission in converting China to Christianity.

Both speakers made an effort to combine interesting information along with evangelical zeal. Rather to the surprise of many people, they did not ask for a collection.

This, apparently, was part of the traditions of the China Inland Mission that they did not ASK for money, leaving it to the "spontaneous liberality" of the people to support them.

Not everyone agreed with the idea of mission on the grounds that every country should have the right and ability to decide its own religion, but no-one could deny the bravery of the two men.

November 23 1950

Arbroath had a distinguished visitor tonight at the Assembly Hall under the auspices of the Workers Educational Association.

This was the famous Scottish Nationalist and academic Douglas Young. He was a impressive figure of a man, 200 cm (6'7") tall, from Tayport in North Fife, who had spent his early years in India.

He had spent "time" in Saughton Prison during World War II for declining to register as a conscientious objector in "England's war".

On his release he contested a by-election in Kirkcaldy in 1944 and almost won, securing 42% of the vote, and made various unsuccessful attempts to enter Parliament since then.

Tonight, in his deep throaty voice he talked at length about the different attempts by various people throughout history to obtain Scottish Home Rule or independence, not least the good people of Arbroath who signed the Declaration of Independence in 1320.

He then went on to tell them that his earliest known ancestor, a man called John Young, had been an employee of the Abbey at the time, something that raised a few cheers from his audience.

His talk was well received by the WEA, for he admitted that he flirted with socialism from time to time, and that in general terms he was a supporter of the Attlee Government and the social reforms of the last few years.

He was currently lecturer in Latin at Queen's College, Dundee which was then a part of the University of St Andrews, but he would become more famous as a lecturer in Greek in St Andrews itself, a playwright and a poet.

November 24 1920

A rare treat for Arbroath people in these grim post-war days! A group of London artistes appeared at the Webster Memorial Hall.

The artistes were rewarded with a large audience, although the audience was boosted by the fact that at least two of them were well known to Arbroath.

Marcus Thomson and Charles Bruce were already a guarantee of good entertainment. *The Arbroath Guide* is now of the opinion that local people will be grateful to Mr Thomson for introducing a soprano like Dora Labbette and an accompanist of "rare musical insight and sympathy" like Joan Singleton.

Miss Labbette was particularly impressive with "irresistible charm of youth in her appearance" and a "dewy freshness in her clear soprano voice".

She sang three groups of songs and was joined by Marcus Thomson in her duets.

Charles Bruce is a brilliant violinist, playing with "that air of detachment from his surroundings which mark out the true devotee. His tone is pure and resonant and he possesses a highly developed technique".

Joan Singleton was particularly impressive on the piano, and the audience welcomed the opportunity to see such a great artiste in the town, and the feeling was clearly mutual, for Miss Singleton was obviously impressed by her reception as well.

It was clearly a great night of what in the 1920s would become to be known as "high brow" entertainment, but a feature of the audience was that it contained quite a few from all strands of society.

November 25 1938

Sad news was received today of the death of William Cordiner of the Bell Rock Lighthouse.

He had been ill for about a week. Whether or not he would gave survived if he had not been on duty at the lighthouse is a matter of some doubt. He took ill, apparently with appendicitis, a week past Thursday, and his assistants radioed for assistance.

A doctor in Craill was able to telephone emergency instructions to the lighthouse while the emergency ship of the Northern Commissioners relief ship "Pharos" set out from Granton in Edinburgh.

The weather was far from favourable, and a boatswain's chair had to be deployed to transport him to the ship.

Once on the ship, he was conveyed to Arbroath where the Arbroath Lifeboat came out to meet the "Pharos" and he was conveyed to the Arbroath Royal Infirmary.

There he underwent an emergency operation for appendicitis, and for a few days seemed to be well on the way to recovery until last night when he suffered a relapse and died this Friday morning at 11.00.

Mr Cordiner was 58, a native of Peterhead, and had been in the lighthouse service for 34 years, having been appointed to the job at Bell Rock in 1933.

He was survived by his wife and two sons and three daughters who lived in the special quarters kept for lighthouse keepers. It was a salutary reminder of the dangers and difficulties involved in the maintenance and upkeep of lighthouses.

November 26 1931

1931 is the year associated with the Depression.

In theory that should not really affect the fishing industry for there are "plenty of fish in the sea" as Gilbert and Sullivan might have put it.

But of course, fishing is affected, for there is less money around in the economy. The Depression was quite deep.

There had already been in August a change in Government (although not of Prime Minister) in Great Britain, and then a General Election but there had as yet been no improvement.

In various countries in Europe, dangerous demagogues were showing signs of wanting to cash in on the situation.

This week however has seen depression in the Arbroath fishing industry for another reason, namely the inability to get out to sea.

The south easterly gale blowing on Monday prevented anyone going out, a few brave souls ventured out on Tuesday and Wednesday but did not stay for long, and to-day (Thursday) saw the return of quite impossible conditions.

We thus had the spectacle of impoverished and unhappy fishermen brooding about the harbour with even jobs like boat maintenance difficult in these conditions.

Those who did venture out in midweek brought home poor quality fish, but, such is the way of the market, they fetched high prices – a box of selected haddocks, for example was selling at 35 shillings to 42 shillings, and cod were selling for 3/6d to 5 shillings each.

November 27 1893

Photography is an activity which has grown in Arbroath and elsewhere during the 19th century.

Although it is still a very expensive hobby with a camera away out of the financial reach of so many families, nevertheless many people do make an effort to have their weddings photographed, and there are pictures of works outings, football teams etc. and family groups.

There are still those who are frightened of the flashes, and it certainly takes a long time, which makes it difficult for children but there is no doubt that photographs are good to look at.

Tonight in the YMCA Classroom, the Arbroath Amateur Photographic Association held an exhibition of photographs and "lantern slides" shown by a machine called "the magic lantern" and projected onto a white wall by Mr James McLeish.

The pictures were mainly of the local area around Arbroath but there were a few of Forfarshire and Perthshire as well, and all were much admired.

Appreciation was recorded by Chairman, Mr G G Dalgarno, and others of what was a wonderful night reminding people of summer days in the middle of winter.

A competition might have been a good idea, and two other questions were asked about the future of photography.

Might it be possible to have pictures and slides taken some day with all the colours, and not just black and white?

And even more revolutionary, could we even one day have "moving pictures"?

November 28 1925

Arbroath's situation near the coast means that it gets snow less often than inland areas, and the snow tends to turn to rain that bit quicker.

It is therefore very seldom that a freak meteorological set of circumstances means that Arbroath is the only part of the country to get snow.

In addition, Arbroath is often less prepared for wintry conditions than other parts of the world.

This Saturday morning at 7.30 am just as Arbroath FC were boarding their train to go to Glasgow to play Clyde at Shawfield, heavy snow blanketed the area around the station.

Mr McGlashan and his men were very pessimistic about there being any chance of football.

But the further west they travelled the less snow there was, and the game duly went ahead.

But meanwhile back in Arbroath chaos ensued.

The snow fell "in pancakes" according to those who enjoy hyperbole, and by nine o'clock just as business was beginning, the town was at a standstill.

The Cleansing Department were summoned to clear the streets and allow for traffic to move, but the pavements remained treacherous with the unfortunate Andrew Ellis of Rossie Street falling and fracturing his knee cap on the way to his work at Nicol's in Chalmers Street.

The snow cleared quickly, and the footballers came back to find Arbroath free of snow, while they themselves were complaining bitterly about refereeing decisions and other things after their beating from Clyde.

Portrait of Mrs Janet Webster

November 29 1907

Arbroath High School tonight gave an excellent example of how political meetings should be conducted with their own Election meeting which featured all the issues of the day.

This was arranged by the Literary Society of the school and attracted an audience and an electorate of 60.

This being 1907 all the speakers were boys and one assumes that although girls were allowed to attend, they did not get a chance to vote, even though we are told that the "suffragettes were in strong force, but no police assistance was required".

Mr Anderson was the Chairman of the meeting and the Returning Officer.

Speeches were delivered by James Hood (Conservative), ET Vernon (Liberal), GS Robertson (Socialist) James Dick (Labour) and AH Salmond (Nationalist).

This surprises us in some ways for 1907. Two left wing candidates, and a Nationalist (a Scottish Nationalist, one assumes, although there were not many of them around in 1907)!

Was this the way things were going? All the current issues were addressed – women's suffrage, House of Lords, old age pensions, Ireland, trade unions, the right to work, and free trade.

The heckling was much enjoyed by everyone.

It was a model political meeting, and the winner was James Dick who delivered an impassioned speech for Labour and won the poll with 34 votes out of a possible 60.

It was of course an age in which politics were becoming important, because the Liberal Government had now been in power for nearly two years and were beginning to make some necessary changes, not all of them welcome in Arbroath!

November 30 1918

The war has been over for nearly three weeks now, but there is no feeling of triumph in Arbroath.

Still casualties are being reported, often men found dead in the field where they have been lying for months.

Still there are Arbroath women who fear the knock on the door.

The weather is dull and misty with very little sunshine, and there is the all-prevalent flu virus, which can occasionally kill.

On the plus side, there have already been a few happy arrivals at Arbroath Station of the early demobs, and a few not quite so happy arrivals of the wounded, young men who left the town a few years ago in the prime of their youth, but now sadly maimed and damaged.

Today is a Saturday but there is no meaningful football.

The Olympia and the Palace are open and doing business, and now you can walk to the cinema with the help of the gas lights, and can see where you are going! But how sad it is that women clearly outnumber men!

But there is another entertainment tonight, for there will be a General Election on December 14.

Montrose Burghs has two candidates – John Leng Sturrock, a Coalition Liberal candidate who is likely to win and Henry Noel Brailsford for Labour, who is not a local man but talks a lot of sense.

Both men hold meetings tonight, and both have a great deal of "heckling" to contend with.

Reverend D Melville Stewart

December

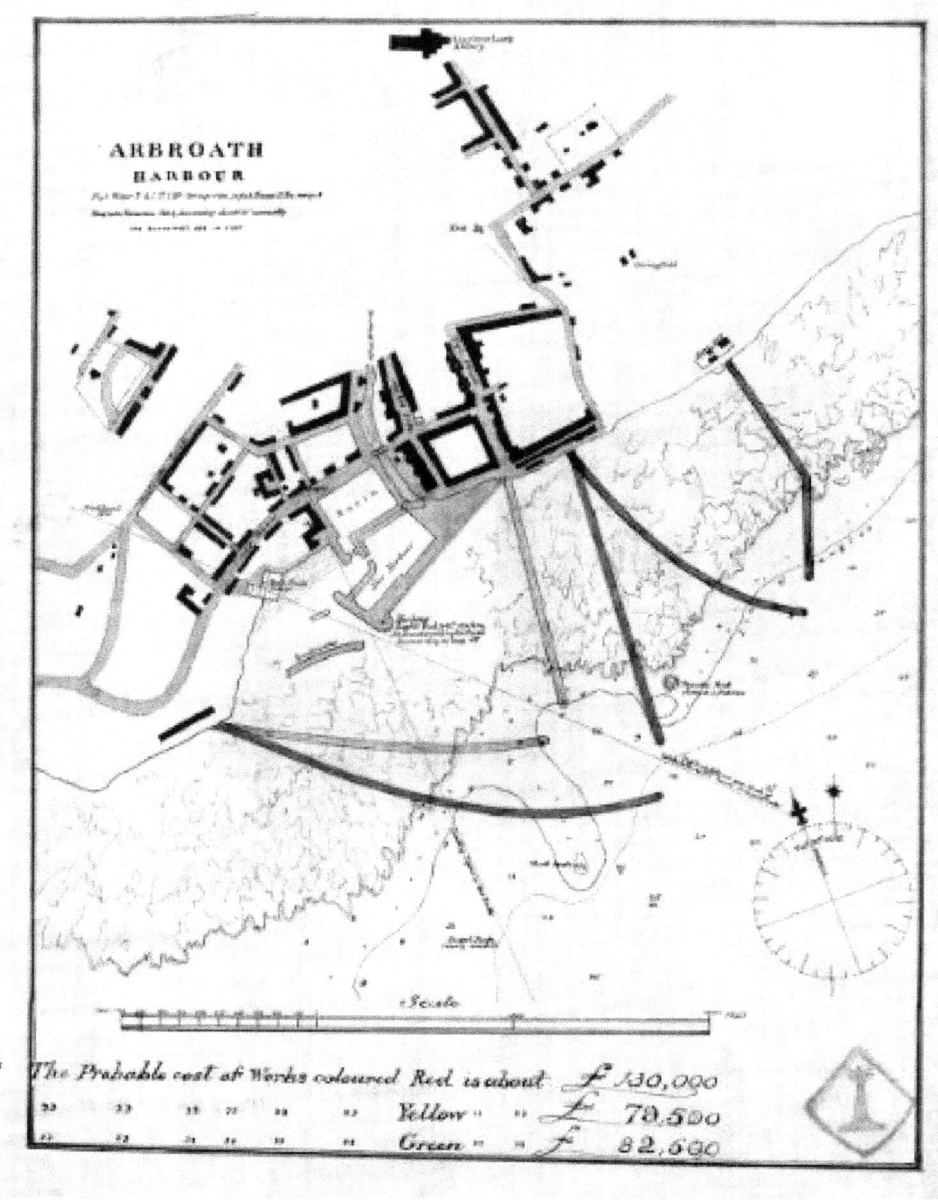

Arbroath Harbour, 1883

December 1 2012

This could have been one of the biggest shocks of Scottish footballing history, but as it was, it was a very creditable result.

Arbroath's part-timers travelled to Celtic Park, where they earned a draw and a money-spinning replay at Gayfield, which would be televised live.

Full credit was due to Paul Sheerin's men, and Chairman John Christison was almost in tears at the end as he was interviewed on BBC.

Arbroath had actually earned a draw against a team which had beaten Barcelona a few weeks previously.

Arbroath were two divisions below Celtic, and the Arbroath fans who travelled were hardly brimming with over-confidence, possibly relishing the chance to visit a big and famous stadium rather than anything else.

Celtic made the mistake of taking the game too easily and fielded men like Miku and Lassad who were a little short of traditional Celtic greats like Billy McNeill, Jimmy McGrory and Danny McGrain.

Celtic scored a bizarre goal when Alex Keddie could not get out of the way of a defensive clearance from Stuart Malcolm and it was 1-0 at half time.

That seemed to be that, one felt, but no!

Arbroath defended pluckily all the second half, and then with three minutes to go, Steven Doris scored from a free kick, also with the aid of a deflection.

The small knot of maroon-clad supporters went mad with delight, as the sparse Celtic crowd turned angry.

But Gayfield it was in 11 days' time, and Arbroath enjoyed a brief moment in the spotlight.

December 2 1929

Motor cars are very definitely in the news these days with much talk in Parliament about speed restrictions and even the idea that before one could get a licence to drive a car, one would have to take a test of competence!

The idea that before one could get a licence to drive a car, the day was approaching that one would have to take a test of competence!

Accidents were simply far too common. But today in Arbroath there was a simpler and yet more basic problem for Bailie David T. Wilson to deal with.

Cars were simply being left unattended in the wrong places and causing obstruction.

Even though there had been several places designated as Car Parks, there were still people like Mr Charnock of Stirling who had left his car in Kirk Square for longer than allowed and was fined 10 shillings.

Mr Mungall of Dunnichen and Mr Garvie of Montrose both claimed that the parking places were not sufficiently well delineated.

This cut no ice with Bailie Wilson, who fined them 10 shillings each, and advised them to "use their eyes" and to use proper Car Parks or simply to park their vehicles in side streets well away from the town centre!

Motor cars were still comparatively rare, but they were no longer the curiosity items that they had been a few years ago.

They were still outrageously expensive, and car owners were usually considered to be rich.

Little sympathy was therefore expressed by the local populace at the fines that Bailie Wilson was imposing.

"It's a' comin aff a broad back" was the general feeling.

December 3 1955

A funeral was held today.

It was the death of the Arbroath to Forfar railway, which had existed since 1839 and had been of great benefit to both towns.

Smokies had been transported to Forfar and jute and linen to Arbroath, Forfar people had enjoyed their day at the seaside thanks to the railway.

Arbroath people had gone to Forfar as a first step to hillwalking in the glens and other things.

And of course, there had always been a heavily packed train on New Year's Day from one town to another, depending on whether the derby was at Gayfield or Station Park.

The reasons for the closure were political and complex, but the bottom line was that there was now not enough traffic, either of passengers or goods, to make it viable.

The nationalisation of the railways in 1948 which might have raised a few hopes that profit was now not so important as people, failed to save the ancient line.

Road was now the main conduit between the two towns.

A train left Arbroath Station at 9.31 pm with a coffin on board and with many mourners including Provost Moir (who had not originally intended to travel) and there were detonator salutes at the various stations en route.

The train reached Forfar Station, was greeted by some Forfar mourners, then returned sadly to Arbroath.

It was the end of an era, and the 116 years had seen many wars, including two major, terrible ones, five monarchs and about 20 Prime Ministers.

December 4 1913

A rather alarming fire was put out today by the prompt action of the Fire Brigade, but there was one tragic consequence.

Shortly before 5 o'clock this afternoon in Lillies Wynd, passers-by were alerted by the barking of a dog in the store of Mr D D Sandeman.

They immediately raised the alarm and someone ran to the grocery stores of Mr Doig who was one of the few in Arbroath who had a telephone.

The Fire Brigade were promptly summoned under the command of Mr Farquhar, the Firemaster.

By the time that they arrived, the fire had taken a hold of the store in the three-storey building, which was contiguous with several others.

Tthe firemen, able to attach two lines of hose to the water main, were able to pump a copious supply of water into the store, thus containing the conflagration to the store itself without damaging the adjacent property.

A great deal of "waste material" was destroyed by fire, smoke and water, but the building itself was not much damaged.

Tragically, there was one fatality. This was the guard dog which had done his job diligently and conscientiously, but had suffocated through the effects of the smoke.

This was a shame, but in addition, do we think that *The Arbroath Herald* may be hinting at something when it says that the material was "all insured"?

The damage was estimated at being between £80 and £100.

December 5 1872

Arbroath today had the opportunity to honour one of its heroes.

Provost James Muir in the Court Room handed over a medal from the Royal Humane Society to 54-year old David Smith, of 9 Old Shore Head.

Apparently a child called George Munro had fallen into the Harbour on September 26 and David Smith had dived in to save him.

Provost James Muir said he was very proud to be the Provost of Arbroath on occasions like this.

Mr Smith had reacted spontaneously without any belief that he was going to be rewarded for his actions, and it was just exactly the way in which he expected people who lived in Arbroath to behave.

Apparently it was not the first time that Smith had been of help in similar circumstances, although nothing like as spectacular as on this occasion and Provost Muir was very happy to be asked to do the needful.

It was in fact the second time this week that something like this had happened, for Councillor Evans had presented a medal to Mr Maxwell for a similar rescue.

David Smith, in reply, said he was honoured to receive this medal but considered that it was only his duty.

The harbour was a very dangerous place for the unwary, but the little boy had recovered and his parents had already expressed their gratitude.

December 6 1923

It was General Election day in Arbroath.

Excitement pervaded the streets of the town with the possibility of Ramsay MacDonald, a boy from the fishing town called Lossiemouth with strong similarities to Arbroath, becoming the first Labour Prime Minister.

This prospect was viewed with either enthusiasm (among the mill workers and the fishermen) or horror (among the middle classes).

For the first time in a long time, we had a very close run thing in the Montrose Burghs constituency with Leng Sturrock, the sitting Liberal, beating John Carnegie, the Labour man, by a majority of 1685.

The election had been called by Prime Minister Baldwin on the issue of Free Trade as against Protection, but as it stood at midnight, there was no clear picture emerging.

The Arbroath Herald is proud of its new "wireless" system which allows it to hear results in England and Scotland more or less as they are declared and to announce them to the crowds waiting outside.

It was after midnight before the result came from Dundee of the Montrose Burghs, and that Leng Sturrock was back at Westminster.

The end result was a hung Parliament with the Conservatives the biggest single party but unable to do a deal with either Labour or the Liberals.

In the end, the Liberals agreed to give some passive support to Labour.

Thus it was that in early 1924 after several weeks of wrangling, the "Lossie loon" J Ramsay MacDonald became Prime Minister.

December 7 1900

The Spink Street Crossing is causing a great deal of concern in the town at the moment.

Normally, there are two possible ways of getting across the railway line – either by the level crossing, when the gates are not shut, or by the tunnel underneath the railway.

The snag is that at the moment because of the recent heavy rains, the tunnel has been flooded and is unusable.

No-one, it seems, either from the Town Council or the railway company is making the slightest attempt to clear the tunnel.

This means that people have to use the level crossing, but the problem seems to be that with all the shunting of engines to and fro, the gates can be closed for up to a quarter of an hour.

A few brave but foolish callants have been known to make a race for it, thus endangering their lives or making themselves liable to a large fine.

Some others have made a long detour of about half an hour.

Most, including some "bare footed urchins", wait in the wet – a piteous spectacle, according to one letter writer of *The Arbroath Herald* – before the "railway man" (who is often subject to some abuse but "Ah'm only daein ma joab") deigns to let people across.

The Arbroath Herald sympathises and says that the whole thing is typical of the cavalier attitude of the railway companies to the people of Arbroath, and continues its campaign for the building of a new station.

December 8 1941

There is, this Monday morning in the streets of Arbroath, a smile on the face and a spring in the step of everyone.

Bizarrely and paradoxically, this has been caused by events on the other side of the world – a brutal and unprovoked attack on innocent people, as they were portrayed in the British press.

This was the Japanese attack on the American base at Pearl Harbour in Hawaii.

It actually happened on Sunday night (British Time) but the first that most Arbroath people heard of it was when they put on their radio this morning or read the morning papers.

It did not take a lot to work out that this meant that the Americans, hitherto reluctant and half-hearted allies of the British, were now in the war, at least against the Japanese.

Hitler, a couple of days later, declared war on them in Europe, so Britain was no longer alone.

And it did mean that now with the Soviet Union and the USA on our side, we were going to win!

It would not happen for a while but *The Arbroath Herald* is correct with its leader which says, simply, One Big War.

The newspaper is also delighted and proud of the £200 that has been raised as part of the town's contribution to Aid To Russia.

1941 has been a very difficult year for Britain and a fair number of Arbroath casualties have been reported in various theatres of war, but at least it is finishing on a positive note.

December 9 1952

These are still the early days of the National Health Service.

It has to be said that there were still a few people who looked upon the new set-up with a degree of scepticism and indeed even suspicion.

In particular, given the almost universal phobia of dentists, the School Dental Service is often looked at askance as if they are "not real dentists", and are only working in schools because they are not able to get a job anywhere else.

Thus tonight when Arbroath District Education Sub Committee were told by Mr J LeBlond, the Secretary, that he had received a complaint that school children were not receiving enough or indeed any local anaesthetic from dentists when their teeth were being extracted, everyone sat up and took notice.

This was apparently because the teeth concerned were what were known as children's "milk teeth" and that so often they fell out anyway (sometimes leading to a visit from the tooth fairy with a penny!) or simply required a sharp tug.

However, some samples of fairly large teeth were produced and Mr LeBlond said "I'm sure you will agree that the extraction of these could be quite painful".

The Sub Committee agreed and decided to send a letter to the medical officer of health to make sure that anaesthetic was administered.

The counter-argument that anaesthetic sometimes causes more problems than the actual extraction was not listened to.

In spite of all this, there was still a substantial number of Arbroath children who grew up with a complex about dentists!

December 10 1936

It would be fair to say that Arbroathians were divided in their opinion today about the mighty events in London.

King Edward VIII had been forced to abdicate because he wanted his mistress Wallis Simpson to become Queen.

If he had been prepared to keep her as his mistress there would have been no problem, but he wanted to make the relationship public, and there were three objections to her – she was American, a commoner and twice divorced.

The choice presented by the Prime Minister and the Archbishop of Canterbury to King Edward was a stark one – either Mrs Simpson or the Throne.

He chose Mrs Simpson.

It had all come about so suddenly, and the issue was much debated. Many people, including *The Arbroath Herald*, and the local Churches felt that "self-abnegation" was a requisite of a King.

Others sympathised with "good old Eddy" whose public and ill-concealed sexual adventures did at least show that the Royal Family had a human, and even likeable, side.

The King had also shown some sympathy with the unemployed, and maybe that was the real problem!

As far as Arbroath was concerned, it now meant that the new Queen was a local one – Elizabeth of Glamis!

She would now have a difficult time helping her shy and stammering husband through the tough times ahead, for the menace of Hitler was a real one.

The Coronation would go ahead as arranged in May 1937 – except with a different King!

December 11 1903

Mary Duff or Early, described as a pedlar of no fixed residence, is becoming a regular at Arbroath Police Court and Bailie William Alexander must be getting used to her.

Yesterday she appeared on a charge of being drunk and incapable in Guthrie Port, claiming that she was on her way to see "Jamie", her husband, who was in the Poorhouse.

She was dismissed by the humane Bailie Alexander, but his patience was put to a more severe test today when she appeared again, this time being found drunk and incapable in the Marketgait.

She pleaded guilty, saying that she had lost her "certificate", by which she means, presumably, her pedlar's licence and she had been "plunging aboot" looking for it.

She then went on to describe herself as a "puir, stupid auld craitur" something which raised a few laughs in the court and even a smile from Bailie Alexander.

This time however, the kind Bailie had to be seen to take some action and he imposed a fine of 10 shillings with an alternative of seven days in prison. There was something rather likeable about this lady, who had no real harm in her, one feels

It is hard to see where she could have managed to get 10 shillings to pay her fine, so the likelihood is that she spent the next few days "inside" which was maybe not the worst place for her, because there was some sort of shelter and food.

December 12 1872

The Arbroath Guide is happy and proud to print a letter from Mr William Briggs of the Chemical and Asphalt Works concerning his recent financial problems.

It says that it is the way that business should be carried on.

Basically about six years ago, Mr Briggs was in serious financial trouble caused by a sudden drop in the market, a succession of fires at his work and the sequestration of assets of a firm that was indebted to him.

As a result of all this, he was obliged to call in his creditors, and it was agreed that he would pay them 10 shillings in the pound of what was owed.

Now things having improved, Mr Briggs felt able to pay the balance making 20 shillings in the pound, and he thanked them all for their patience.

The Arbroath Guide talks about "honourable conduct" and wishes Mr Briggs better luck in the future with his business dealings.

Bankruptcies, sequestrations and liquidations were by no means uncommon in Victorian society, as a perusal of some of Dickens novels would indicate.

There was very little in the way of a safety net for those whose businesses failed with all the humiliation that it would entail.

Here we have an example of creditors accepting what he had to offer and allowing Mr Briggs to continue trading in the hope and expectation of an improvement, and they now had their reward by being paid back in full.

There is clearly a good side to Victorian capitalism as well!

December 13 1954

Two young sailors from HMS Condor made their appearance today before Sheriff Cullen on a charge of theft and reset.

Kenneth Victor James Elford (19) naval airman, was charged with theft of £20 and Charles Murray Geddes (18) ordinary seaman, with reset.

Elford was acting as an escort to an officer who was collecting a large sum of money (for the wages, presumably) from the British Linen Bank at Brothock Bridge.

The officer spoke to a bank official for a while, leaving the money in the charge of Elford. When the officer came back, he noticed that the bag containing the money had been broken into and opened, but he thought no more of it until he returned to base and discovered that the bag was £20 short.

It was later ascertained that Elford had sent money in a registered envelope and had bought some postal orders, and given £5 to Geddes which Geddes had accepted.

Elford's solicitor, Mr Robertson, said that Elford was rather immature, a bit of a misfit in the Services, had failed his exams and was considering another career.

He had sent £8 of the £20 to his parents. He tended to do things on impulse and regret them later.

Geddes was also described as rather immature and had been easily led astray.

Sheriff Cullen was none too impressed by Mr Robertson's gallant attempt, and Elford was sent to prison for 30 days, while Geddes, on the lesser charge, was fined £5.

December 14 1920

The fierce and unpredictable weather of late has led to a few incidents in the harbour area of town.

The Bell Rock lighthouse had been completed in 1811, and the shore station, the Signal Tower, in 1813.

The *Lady Betty Balfour* of Montrose, captained by Mr Chase of Montrose, had been forced to put into Arbroath Harbour a few days ago because of stormy weather.

Today she tried to leave but ran into a bank of sand opposite the Bell Rock Signal Tower and was held fast.

No damage seems to have been done, and it is hoped to re-float her tomorrow morning on high tide.

This followed a slightly more serious and alarming incident when the Pittenweem motor ketch sprang a leak on the port side just beside the Bell Rock.

The ship contained 61 tons of coal, which it was conveying from Leith to Aberdeen, and it had already been forced to put in to harbour at Anstruther.

The two man crew had to take to their small boat to row back into Arbroath having hoisted a blanket which no-one noticed and they then fired flares from their sinking ship which were spotted on the shore.

They were then rescued by William Swankie on his fishing yawl *Catherine* – no easy task in the darkness, but the two men were landed safely ashore none the worse for their adventure which *The Arbroath Herald* describes as "thrilling" – not the word that modern journalists would use!

There is no mention of the cargo of coal which presumably was lost.

December 15 1922

This week Arbroath has been treated to a Feast of Opera, according to *The Arbroath Herald* as the Arbroath Operatic Society have staged an excellent performance of "The Mikado" by Gilbert and Sullivan in the Webster Memorial Hall.

The critic is very enthusiastic about the society and the performance and of course the show itself does lend itself to enthusiastic amateur companies, especially one like this.

There have been very few "stammers or mistakes" even on opening night, and the audience have enjoyed the production, which included a chorus of 40 who sometimes struggled to fit onto the smallish stage.

The Principals included Mr A J B Ramsay as Nanki Poo, Mr Hunter as Pooh Bah and Mr C Y Myles as Pish Tush. Mr E Thomson junior was the Mikado himself. Mr A E Adams however was outstanding as Ko Ko. The Ladies were equally good with The Little Maids from school played by Mrs Kydd, Miss Cowieson and Miss Donaldson, with Miss Evelyn Low singled out for her portrayal of Katisha.

There was even a little "audience participation" as everyone joined in "Tit Willow".

The Musical Director was Mr Robert Scott and he was well served by a competent orchestra.

It was good to see so any people there, some of whom not necessarily fans of Gilbert and Sullivan but who came along to see so many local people in the show who were clearly enjoying entertaining their local townspeople.

It was yet another example of the town now beginning to emerge from the dark days of war and its immediate aftermath.

December 16 1919

Arbroath lovers of Gilbert and Sullivan's "Trial By Jury" would be enthralled to see a real life local drama being played out along the same lines!

Today in the Court of Session, Lord Anderson approved a writ for the trial by jury of an action by Mary Stephen of Montquhir, Carmyllie against widower William Mudie, a blacksmith, of Redford, Carmyllie, for £500 damages because of breach of promise.

Mrs Stephen is 50 years old and since May 1917, Mr Mudie paid her "marked attention" and in August 1917 he asked her to marry him.

From then on he was looked upon as her lover, and in November 1918 he gave her £20 and told her to buy a ring. In June 1919 he gave another £20 to buy clothes.

The wedding was fixed for July 4 1919.

But then a week before the wedding, they both went to Arbroath to buy a wedding ring and she left him to talk to an acquaintance.

Mr Mudie was left alone in the shop and did not hear her calling to him and felt so humiliated by all this, that he called that night to say that the wedding was off.

Mr Mudie, 58 years old and a widower gave a slightly different version of events.

On the day in question, the lady flew into a temper and left him to talk to an acquaintance. He was hurt and annoyed and the wedding was off.

He had offered £100, in addition to writing off the £40.

There is nothing more entertaining that the sight of people old enough to know better making a fool of themselves in public, and Arbroath now waited with baited breath for the trial.

December 17 1946

The war has now been over for eighteen months, but rationing is still very much in force, even though there are a few relaxations in the restrictions.

In practice, in Arbroath there were always more fish for those who had acquired the noble art of keeping their mouths shut.

Nevertheless, the vigorous Labour Government of Clement Attlee is determined to ensure an equitable method of food distribution, and today ex-Bailie John Souttar presided at a meeting of the Arbroath Food Control Committee.

Miss Helen S Pirrie, executive officer, stated that the welfare food scheme continued to play an effective part in the Government's policy.

During the past year there had been distributed 13,953 bottles of orange juice, 1,906 bottles of cod liver oil, 560 packets of "A" and "D" vitamin tablets and 16, 496 tins of national dried milk.

Such was the grim determination at national and local level that the new generation of wartime and post-war babies was to be a healthy one!

The committee also considered and granted four new food retail licences – one for a grocer, two for fish retailers and one for a catering establishment.

It is often suggested that the late 1940s were a time of economic depression and the word "austerity" is frequently used.

Only to a point is this true. Things were a great deal better than in the years after the last war, and in any case, people had become used to food control and rationing, which did at least guarantee that everyone got something!

But more than that, there was hope that things were taking a turn for the better.

December 18 1935

It is clear that some sort of prosperity is in the air, even in the depths of winter.

The bad old days of depression have gone.

There will be an "exhibition bungalow" house on view for everyone in Keptie Road to cater for the new pretensions of those who wish to get away from outside shared toilets, of which there are still rather too many in Arbroath.

And last night the Dean of Guild Court approved a new extension to the premises of Messrs. Carnegie, Soutar & Sons, 118 High Street.

The new extension will involve the demolition of the existing back area and its replacement by a new two storey building with toilets, extra room for diners and eventually a dance area so that weddings can be held there.

The plans were passed unanimously, although Provost William Chapel added that if there was to be a dance area, the stairs would have to be attended to.

The Dean of Guild, Mr Lamb, even congratulated the firm on their initiative "which bespoke their confidence in the future of Arbroath".

There were of course many improvements being made in the town, now that the trade recession was going away.

In particular because things were improving in Glasgow, which was of course the source of Arbroath's holiday "market".

But local industry was picking up too with the jute mills in Arbroath, Dundee and Forfar now working full time.

The wise may have worried that there was a sinister reason for all this, but such concerns were ignored in the current clear and obvious economic improvements.

December 19 1958

This will be the best Christmas ever, it is believed.

There are several reasons for this. In the first place, prosperity is clearly in the air.

In an era of full employment, goods are in plentiful supply and there is more money around to buy them with.

The days of rationing and poverty have clearly gone.

Not only that, but the Government have at last given in to reality and made Christmas Day a public holiday in Scotland.

This is nothing more than a regularisation of the situation because workers were increasingly "voting with their feet" and not coming in on Christmas Day or disappearing at lunch time.

Catching this mood, the Arbroath Amateur Dramatic Club have for the past few years put on a pantomime. This year will be their most lavish ever, for they are putting on Dick Whittington.

It is a very ambitious task for an amateur club, and although it would lack the slickness, professionalism and sophistication that one might get in a professional performance in Dundee for example, this is all made up for by the fact that all the actors are well known local characters, and loads of local children are taking part.

Good audiences are guaranteed when the curtain goes up on December 23 until the show finishes a few days after Christmas.

The show is produced by Gwen Williams and the choreography is done by Elaine Masson. Clearly a great deal of work has been done on the sets and the scenery.

December 20 1884

Glasgow Rangers Football Club have their lovers and detractors in Arbroath, as they do everywhere else, but they were far from popular in town this midwinter day when they came to Gayfield and defeated the home side 8-1.

The result was bad enough, but the conditions were also wintry and it would be claimed in future years that Rangers won only because they had better boots, specially reinforced ones of dubious legality, on them than the local men did.

But the real problem which caused all the "groans, hooting and other marks of disapprobation" as *The Courier* put it were the events of November 15 when Arbroath actually beat them 4-3, but Rangers then protested that the ground was not wide enough (some sources say not long enough) for a Scottish Cup tie.

They claimed to have been "beaten on a back green". Their objections were ultimately sustained and today saw the ordered replay take place.

1884 was far too early for anyone to mutter darkly about freemasons and general jobbery, but it was clear that Rangers had "knocked on a few doors" in Glasgow, and they were not made particularly welcome in town even when walking to and from the railway station.

Even when the Rangers players were finally seated on their train, a "final volley of groans" was given by "a large crowd of home sympathisers".

Fortunately no violence was offered by anyone, not even snowballs, but it was an excellent example of how passions could be roused by this new game of football.

As for the game itself, it was no great contest with Arbroath down 0-3 at half-time and only briefly in with a chance after Crawford pulled a goal back early in the second half.

December 21 1927

Arbroath had seen its fair share of winter weather this December but the snow of the last few days had now turned to rain. The river was threatening to burst its banks.

This did not stop the Women's Guild of the Inverbrothock Parish Church meeting for their Social Evening in the Church Hall under the leadership of the Reverend George Hitchcock.

The main part of the evening's entertainment were three sketches in which members of the Social Circle and the Guild itself took part in what was essentially homespun entertainment.

Two light-hearted sketches were "Robin Tamson's Smiddy" involving Elizabeth Cant, Annie Christison, Lily Petrie, Jean Smyth and John Duncan, "The Coortin' o Leezie McFarlane" with Jean Neilson, Alex Webster and James Cuthill.

The third, more serious, was "Father, Pray With Me Tonight" with Lizzie Anderson, Annie Robbie and Alex Strachan in contrast.

It being close to Christmas, a more seasonal note was struck with the reading by Mrs Alex Hood of a Christmas play, during which carols were sung by the company.

The plays were most efficiently staged under the direction of Mr David Darroch. whose untiring efforts found ample rewards in the success which attended the evening's entertainment.

Much was said about the changing role of women since the Great War with them smoking cigarettes, driving cars and wearing nylons etc. but here there was no shortage of them willing to take part in dramatic performances!

December 22 1916

Conscription has been in force for a year now and there are now very few men of eligible military age in the town.

Only those in charge of a business, or with difficult family circumstances e.g. widowed and left with young children, or in reserved occupations should remain.

There is still scope, according to *The Arbroath Herald* for men to join the Arbroath Volunteer Regiment.

This has 370 men at the moment, mostly those who are too old, too young or too infirm to serve in the Army on a full time basis, e.g. those who have been invalided home with a wound or who have been exposed to gas.

They normally drill on the parts of the beach which have not been sealed off, or in the local parks.

There are actually with them at the moment two young lads who have been discharged from the Black Watch for being too young, having lied about their age and been found out!

One of them actually got as far as France before his age was discovered and he returned with a letter from the Commanding Officer of his Battalion which said that he was a credit to the Battalion, that he would be a good employee back home and that he (the Commanding Officer) would be glad to welcome him back when he was old enough!

In the meantime he did his soldiering with the Arbroath Volunteers!

December 23 1961

Never has the town of Arbroath looked so happy and cheery as it does this Saturday before Christmas.

Trees in almost every window are adorned with electric lights, and the High Street is a kaleidoscope of colours.

The weather is cold but mainly dry, and there is a clear sign of happiness and prosperity in the air.

There has of course been no great tradition of lavish celebration of Christmas in Arbroath – it only became a Public Holiday in 1958, although in practice people had simply taken a day off for years before then – but this year with economic prosperity in the air, things have taken off.

TV ownership is now virtually universal, but the big Christmas presents seem to be Long Playing records for the Record Player or the Gramophone.

Santa Claus has been seen at various local venues, and the Arbroath Dramatic Club have been putting on a brilliant pantomime performance of "Mother Goose" with local people which has gone down very well in the Webster Hall.

Churches are organising Watch Night services, and the pubs and hotels are doing a roaring trade with jokes about "No room at the inn – as usual at Christmas".

1961 has been a good year for the town and 1962 will be even better, one hopes. Only one fly in the ointment however, and that was the football where Arbroath today travelled to Hamilton and went down 0-5.

The Arbroath Herald adds sadly that Arbroath have "fallen away recently", which is a rather kind way of putting it!

December 24 1921

Times remain hard in Arbroath in the immediate aftermath of the Great War.

The influenza outbreak, although definitely on the wane, still retained its baleful grip on the town.

The consequences of the depression this year (including the Coal Strike which affected everything) are still visible in its effect on all industries, even in fishing, simply because there is less money around and therefore fewer people can afford fish!

But at least Christmas this year has given the local economy some sort of a boost.

The Post Office certainly reporting an increase in trade to something like pre-War levels.

Arbroath has also seen an increase in things like Christmas Concerts and visits by carol singers to hospitals with more or less every Church making an attempt to put on festive music.

Christmas Day is not, as yet a public holiday in Scotland, but this year it will not matter because it is a Sunday anyway!

Although Santa Claus is not yet the figure that he will become in later years, he has been seen in a few local venues, sometimes wearing a red cloak, and sometimes a green one.

And of course, Christmas Eve being a Saturday, there is still football. Sadly today the Red Lichties lost to the strong-going Alloa in the Scottish League Second Division at Gayfield.

But for most Arbroathians, Christmas, although it will be celebrated with increasing gusto, is still merely a rehearsal for the New Year next week!

December 25 1914

Well, who would have thought it?

A war that broke out with devastating suddenness in early August in Europe, and now looks like it is going to last for some considerable time, dominates every aspect of Arbroath life.

The optimists said that it "would be over by Christmas".

This is clearly not the case, nor does it seem that the war is going to end any time soon.

Letters to wives and mothers indicate that they are now living in holes in the ground called "trenches" where they can stay indefinitely, it would appear.

The war generally seems to have settled down in Europe after a very busy autumn which saw Belgium fall, but Paris saved.

The initial enthusiasm seems to have passed and it is clear that recruiting is becoming a problem, for *The Arbroath Herald* carries an advertisement asking for employers to put as much pressure as possible on their employees to enlist.

Some soldiers are home on leave, and more are expected to be allowed home for a few days at the New Year. Every effort has been made to make Arbroath as normal as usual – and of course, today is a working day.

The big difference was the shops which of course are not allowed to be lit up because of the black out and the danger of shelling from the sea.

Recently some seaside towns in the north of England had been shelled, something that proved just how barbarous the Huns were.

December 26 1899

"Boxing Day" was a term with which very few people in Scotland in 1899 would have been familiar.

Although there had been a few concessions to yesterday being Christmas Day, today was a normal working day.

Bailie John Duncan was on the bench at Arbroath Police Court dealing with one of his "regulars".

This was the seventh time that John Cavan, a cab driver in the Applegate, had appeared in court.

When sober, apparently a pleasant and sensible man, Cavan was fined £2 with the alternative of one month in prison for a breach of the peace last night (Christmas Night) in Keptie Road and Arbirlot Road, when according to Constable Will and Constable Suttie, he and two others had "conducted themselves in a drunk and disorderly manner" by "cursing, swearing and interfering with passengers".

The three men were then warned by the police, and the other two seem to have "taken a telling" and disappeared, but Cavan continued along Arbirlot Road shouting and swearing until he was arrested at Emislaw.

Even in the cells he "became outrageous" and "it was necessary to take precautions to prevent him doing damage".

Whether this was a tactful way of saying that the police had to use a little "force" or whether it just meant that they removed his boots, we cannot be sure.

It would seem that if this was his seventh appearance, it was taking a long time for the penny to drop with Mr Cavan!

December 27 1944

A great honour was bestowed on Arbroath today with the news that Pilot Officer Norman Garland Sievwright, RAFVR 182 Squadron, had been awarded the Distinguished Flying Cross for gallantry in leading his squadron in an attack on a well fortified German town called Stadtlohn.

In spite of heavy anti-aircraft flak, he had acted with "high qualities of courage and determination".

He was a well-known Arbroath man, aged 23, and the son of Bob Sievwright, the famous cricketer, and he had played cricket himself.

He had joined the RAF in July 1941 and had been adjudged to be good enough to be a pilot. He had been sent to Canada to train, and he had been very much on active service from D Day onwards.

It would be nice to leave the story like that, but a few days later on Hogmanay 1944, Norman was sent on another mission from which he did not return.

Sometime in January 1945, his mother and father received news that he was missing. It was stressed that this did not necessarily mean that he had been killed – he might have been captured and in a POW camp, but the longer that 1945 went on, the more likely it became that he was not coming back.

No trace was ever found, but he was confirmed dead in 1946.

Arbroath has every right to be proud of the Sievwright family for its achievements on the cricket field, but Norman Sievwright provides another reason to be proud.

December 28 1918

Great excitement prevailed all morning outside *The Arbroath Herald* offices at Brothock Bridge as everyone awaited the result of Montrose Burghs constituency in the General Election.

The election had actually been held on December 14 (and it was the first that women had been allowed to vote in) but the counting had been deferred to allow the collation of results from soldiers still in France and elsewhere, and sailors on the high seas.

The result was a foregone conclusion both in Montrose Burghs and nationally, with the Coalition Government of Lloyd George having won the war, now wanting a mandate for the peace.

In Arbroath, although some workers in the fishing industry and in the textile factories showed a slight preference for Labour, most people were happy to continue with the Coalition.

The count was held in Dundee and immediately after the declaration at about 1.40 pm, the result was wired to Arbroath, Montrose and Forfar. A board appeared in *The Herald* window showing

    J Leng Sturrock (Coalition Liberal)   9309
    HN Brailsford (Labour)   2940

Surprisingly, only about 50% of the electorate voted, but the majority was clear.

That afternoon, Leng Sturrock (the grandson of John Leng the proprietor of *The Dundee Advertiser)* came to Arbroath that afternoon to thank those who had supported him, and promised that he would do his best for the town in what looked like difficult times ahead.

December 29 1906

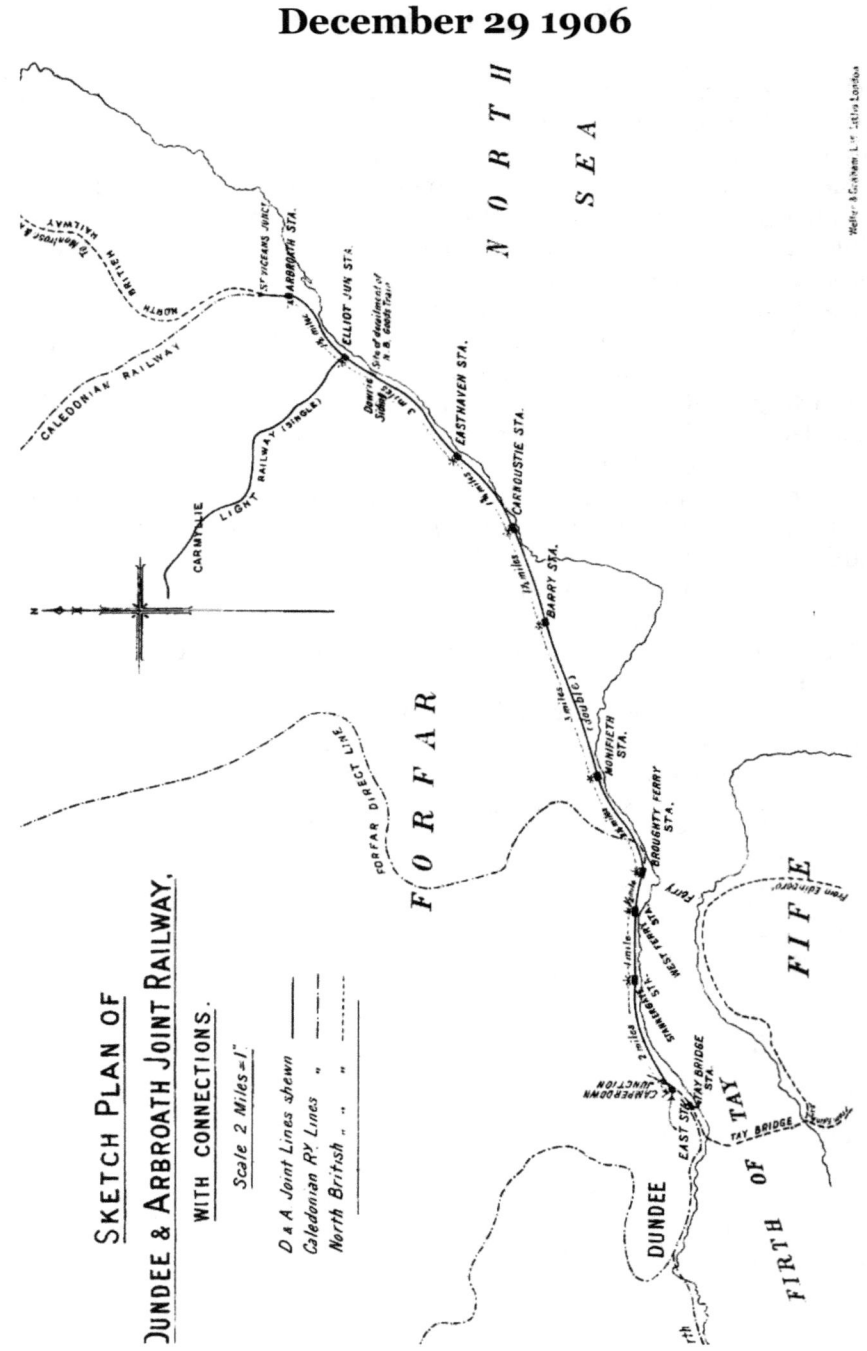

December 29 1906

Today's newspapers carry the full tragic details of yesterday's dreadful railway disaster at Elliot Junction, between Carnoustie and Arbroath.

The total death toll would be 22, including the Liberal Member of Parliament Alexander William Black, who was severely injured in the crash and died shortly thereafter. 24 were injured, eight severely.

It was a consequence of the heavy snow which had fallen on Boxing Day and from which the railway companies had not recovered.

There was a local train to Dundee stationary at Elliot Junction and unable to move any further because of a derailed goods wagon on the line further south.

In the meantime a "fast" train, hauled by North British Railway K Class locomotive 324, had arrived from Edinburgh earlier in the day at Arbroath but couldn't go any further because of snow on the line.

The driver therefore decided to head back south to Dundee with his passengers. He was allowed to go, the operators having apparently forgotten about the stationary train at Elliot and indeed, for that matter, the upturned train further south.

Travelling at about 30 mph, running tender first, with coal heaped high restricting vision, the "fast" train did not see the stationary train.

The Board of Trade Report said "If it is true that [driver George Gourlay] took no more than two half glasses of whisky, whilst waiting at Arbroath, it is evident that this amount of alcohol could not have caused the effects noticed by [porter] David Morrison, [guard] James Briggs and [parcel clerk] Charles Whitton" — to the effect that there was clearly something wrong with Gourlay.

It was still snowing intermittently and also at about 4.00 pm getting quite dark, and he ploughed into the back of the stationary train.

Driver Gourlay, from Edinburgh, survived but Stoker Irvine was less lucky. No passenger on the fast train was badly injured, but those who had been sitting in the back of the slow train suffered terribly, the rescue attempt being hampered by the fact that Elliot Station was comparatively remote and difficult to access by road because of the snow.

It was one of the area's saddest ever days.

Scene of the Elliot Junction railway disaster

December 30 1939

A casual visitor to town would not immediately conclude that there was anything particularly different this year as distinct from last year.

The town was full of soldiers in uniform either home on leave or soldiers from England stationed nearby.

Cinemas are operating as normal, and there is still some football, although the Leagues have been redrawn.

Transport is running as normal with, if anything, the service better and busier than previously.

There has been an absolute rash of weddings, the date determined in many cases by when the groom can get leave.

The social life of Churches is absolutely flourishing with whist drives and talks about food preservation etc. a common phenomenon.

The war has been going for four months now and little worthy of note in the history book has occurred.

It has become known as the phoney war (at least on the Western front where the Maginot line seems to be deterring the Germans) and there is a substantial section of opinion who wonder really what this is all about, and perhaps Herr Hitler is not really as bad as he is painted.

Casualties have been minimal, but the big fear remains of air raids and indeed shelling from the sea.

The big difference is at night when there is a total blackout.

To an extent, Arbroath has got round this problem with a few oil lamps at ground level placed at strategic place in town to indicate junctions.

But the big question is when will there be serious action in Europe?

Or will it all fizzle out in an agreed peace?

December 30 1991

From the Breakwater on Monday 30 December 1991, with a tide so low that some boats were resting on the bottom. The big boat in the centre is Relentless AH136, built at Macduff in 1961. At this time, Relentless had a black hull.

December 31 1959

And so the 1950s were coming to an end!

Generally speaking it had been a good decade with new houses being built and the development of the town into a modern seaside resort.

Everyone was aware that this was an era of prosperity for everyone, but that brought its own challenge to Arbroath.

Glaswegians, for example, were now more and more able to afford to go further afield for their holidays, perhaps even abroad to places like France or Spain, something unheard of a few years ago.

Tonight was an awful night with wind and rain, and although some brave Arbroathians braved the weather in usual gathering places like Kirk Square, more and more decided to watch the new thing that was becoming more and more common every year, namely the television.

And this year, there was an added attraction for the Hogmanay programme was to be hosted by no less a person than Arbroath's very own Andy Stewart.

Andy was no stranger to television of course, but tonight he was the host. How strange it would be to see the boy that so many people remembered from his High School days now hosting a live TV show which would be shown live all over Scotland and England, then would be recorded and sent to Canada, and the USA!

Yes, New Year was changing, but there still remained the traditional bits of it with first footing and the drink that could make you both cheerful and sad, whatever you preferred.

And there would be the football tomorrow – but not Forfar this year for the happy reason that Arbroath were in the First Division.

Mind you, it was a trip to fellow strugglers Stirling Albion!

Cardinal Beaton - Abbot of Arbroath Abbey in 1524, later Archbishop of St Andrews and the last Scottish Cardinal prior to the Reformation.

Index to Traders

Adamson, A.K. clothing	343
Addison, Alex., cycle and motor agent	588
Alexander, J. general linen and woollen draper	82
Alexander, William, licensed grocer	175
Anderson & Hewit, tailors	409, 643
Anderson, C. N., "The Stag,"	591
Anderson, David grocer	101
Anderson, J. R. & Co., joiners	588
Anderson, M., draper	613
Anderson, R. grocer	396
Anderson, R. & Co., fish merchants	646
Anglo-Australian Bank	143
Arbroath and District Economic Building Society	90
Arbroath Burgh School Board	350
Arbroath Burgh School Management Committee	597
Arbroath Coffee House Co	119
Arbroath Electric Light and Power Co.	403, 631
Arbroath French Cleaning and Art Dyeing Works	619
Arbroath Friendly Coal Society	391
Arbroath Gas Corporation	375, 618
Arbroath Herald Limited	112, 134, 140, 163, 177, 407, 415, 420, 626, 649, 651
Arbroath Horsehiring Co., Ltd	401, 636
Arbroath Plate Glass Insurance	393, 620
Astbury, R Wilson, Carnoustie photographer	650
Atkinson, F. H., electrician	578
Balfour, C.L. baker	414
Ballingall, Robert cycle and motor manufacturer	406
Bank Street Hall	173
Barnett, David D. wine and spirit merchant	640
Batchelor, A. & D. tea, wine, and spirit merchants	91
Beatt, Andrew, tobacconist	140
Beattie's Fish Depot	606
Bell Rock Tavern	353, 632
Bennet & Smith (Insurance)	75, 103
Bible and stationery Warehouse	339
Black, George, joiner	637
Black, J. bookseller	593
Boath, Alex, tailor	94
Boath, Mrs, grocer Marketgate	104
Boath, Fred butcher	354
Boath, W. & J. booksellers	80
Booth, Thomas music warehouse	135, 136

Booth, William, tailor	587
Brand, William & Son, slaters	618
Brand, William slater	94, 365
Briggs, William & Sons, Ltd., Asphalte Works	395, 614
Briggs, William, Asphalte Works	84
Britannic Assurance Co	421
British Law Fire Insurance Co.	399, 596
Brown, Mrs J. H., grocer	375, 615
Brown, Robert, grocer	391, 648
Bruce, A., newsagent bookseller	584
Buick, Albert waste and china merchant	369
Buist & Co., linen drapers	639
Burness, J. F. butcher	109
Butchart, R. T., upholsterer	611
Byars, David, milliner	76
Calder Bros., builders	98, 369, 647
Caledonian Insurance Company	410, 625
Campbell, G. A. plasterer	93
Campbell, J. D., electrical engineer	647
Campbell, P. & P. dyers	125
Campbell's Hat and Cap Depot	92
Carnoustie Cooperative Association	167, 424
Carnoustie Equitable Co-operative Society	168
Carse of Gowrie Dairy Company	79
Carver & Symon, architects	108
Central Coffee and Dining Rooms	377, 608
Christie & Anderson, builders	398, 626
Christie, Mrs game dealer	104
Clark, M. M. shoemaker	110
Clark, Thos., cycle agent	410, 591
Commercial Union Assurance Co.	75
Cook, David & Sons, plumbers	86, 400
Cook, James R. plumber	357
Cooper, George, chemist	603
Copland, Charles S. watchmaker	91
Corner Hat and Cap Shop	85
Cowan, D The Ship inn	349
Craig's Glass and China warehouse	74
Craig, William A. cabinet maker	361
Crook & Webster, plumbers	412, 594
Crowe, George hairdresser Commerce St	97
Crowe, Messrs & Co. hairdressers	95
Cruickshank, J.S. ladies' underclothing	379
Cuthbert, James. ironmonger &c	113, 114, 115, 116

Cuthill, George grocer	107
Cuthill, R. A. seeds and plants	95
Cuthill, James, slater	592
D. and A. Preserve Co. Limited	652
Dargie, A. C. house painter	77
Dick, James B., grocer Carnoustie	166
Dodds & Bathie, stock salesmen &c.	154
Doig, James family grocers	126, 127
Donald, Archibald, & Son plasterers	623, 650
Donald, Archibald, sen., plasterer	381
Donald, Archibald C. plasterer	400
Dorward, Geo. grocer	141
Duncan, Howat optician	387, 646
Dundee & Arbroath Confections and Preserve Manufacturing Co.,	72
Dundee & Arbroath Preserve Manufacturing Co.,	373
Dunlop, Mrs, confectioner	633
Duthie George, tailor	111, 383
Dye & Falconer, tailors Carnoustie	166
Dyer Robert, plumber	99
Eddie, J. & R. B , watchmakers	337, 574
Edward & Co., Friockheim	164
Arbroath Equitable Cooperative Society	586
Esplin Geo., fruiterer and gamedealer	109
Ewing, draper	359
Exchange Bar,	363
Fairweather, J. tobacconist	99
Fairweather, Samuel boot and shoe manufacturer	180, 181
Fairweather, S., & Sons, boot mfrs.	653
Farquhar, R. C., joiner funeral undertaker	105
Farquhar, Rowland C. building contractor	426, 572
Farquharson, R. glazier	108
Ferguson, A. draper	389
Ferguson, Mrs, furniture dealer	591
Ferrier, photographer Dundee	142
Ferrier, Wm. tailor Carnoustie	169, 425
Fife, Andrew, builder	174, 367
Finlay, George butcher	87
Finlayson, James grocer	151
Fitzcharles and Co, antique furniture	360
Fletcher, George D., grocer	174, 408
Forbes, Robert, butcher	149
Fox, James licensed grocer	149
Frain, Wm. & Sons glass and china Dundee	121
Fulton, G. hatter	174

Fyfe, Alex, joiner	91
Gall, Mrs D., grocer	395
Geddes, W. H. & Son, photographers	171
General Accident Assurance	355
Gibb, J. P. hairdresser	91
Gilbey, W and A, wine growers	139
Girdwood, Thomas chemist	345
Glass, Robert, butcher	637
Gouck, H. hosier	151
Goulding's Manures	99
Gowans, peter R. stationer	385
Grant & Laing, bakers	379, 609
Grant, Colin boot manufacturer,	73
Grant, Misses J. and C.	389
Grant, T. R., plumber	398, 609
Grant, William L. & Son, painters	402, 604
Gray, Andrew W. Glass merchants	110
Gray, Charles sale and cover maker	385
Greenhill, William, livery stable Carnoustie	165
Greig, J. R. underwear	346
Grewar J. P. & Son cabinetmakers, funeral undertaking	82, 114, 374, 644
Harper, J.W. tea rooms	408
Harris & Kyd, butchers	159
Harris, George, butcher	358, 573
Heggie, Andrew watchmaker	425
Henry's Studio, photographer Carnoustie	165
Herron & Colville, plumbers	411, 624
Herron, Peter, & Sons, blacksmiths	622
High, William, jeweller	348, 589
Hird, Alexander, draper and outfitter	158, 249, 405, 570
Hogg, M. confectioner	402
Hunter, G. R., boot repairer	635
Hutchison, David draper	105, 585
Hutton, George shoemaker	97
Imperial Hotel (Aitken's)	152
Imperial Hotel (S. Banks)	348
Ivanhoe Whisky	85
Jack, James, aerated water manufacturer	370
Jack, James, chemist and aerated water	571
Jamieson & Son, D. plasterers	585
Jenkins A., confectioner	83
Jenkins, A. & M., confectioners	351
Johnston, J. music warehouse	159
Johnston's Emporium	153, 340, 423, 598

Jolly, James photographer	423
Keith, George, sailmaker	592
Kelly, James broker	349
Kerr, David, butcher	96
Kerr, John grocer Carnoustie	167
Kerr, Mrs I, potted meat manufacturer	630
Kerr's potted Meat store	351
Knight, Robert, baker	615
Kyd, David, dealer in antiques	400, 594
Kydd, James, & Sons, joiners	365, 620
Lamb, John, butcher	388, 579
Law, James, & Son, motor engineers	362, 589
Leslie, E.J. solicitor	100
Lesslie, C. H., dentist	352
Lewer, Miss milliner	96
Littlejohn, Mrs, tobacconist	111
Lochland Street Garage	625
Lochlands Bar	583
Lochnagar Bar	411
Low, Alex, watchmaker	175
Low, Charles A. grocer	84
Lyall, W.A. funeral undertaking	383
Lyall, William National Bar	105
McBain, J. M. (Insurance)	163
McBain, Norman (Insurance)	92
McCallum, Colin P. dairy	355
McHardy, W. New Dock Tavern	97
McKay, Andrew fish dealer	85
McLean, Duncan whisky	340
McPherson, W H. dentist	410
McWattie, James. & Sons tobacco manufacturers	147
Macdonald, D. R., hatter	382, 577
Macdonald, James draper	147
MacFarlane, R. A., motor engineer	638
Mackay, David & Co., funeral undertakers	418, 615
Mackay, James D. cabinetmaker	178
Mackenzie, J. R., London Mantle House	376
Mackenzie, John family grocer	158
Mackie, J. Winton, marble cutter Glasgow	156
MacLaren Bros., footwear	613
Maclure, E. & J., dyers	92, 377
Macpherson, Mrs jeweller,	83
Martin, J. B., newsagent	395, 610
Masterton's Paraffin Soap Extract	161

Mathewson, E. W., painter	425
Matthew, Alexander, pipemaker	90
Matthew, M. & Son, clothiers	397, 595
Meekison and Jamieson	353
Meffan, John M., jeweller	359
Melvin & Sons, carriage builders.	155
Middleton & Donald, plasterers	119
Milne, James, photographer	89
Mitchell, Charles P., grocer	633
Mitchell, Charles slater	95
Mitchell, J. & Son, slaters	345, 590
Moffat, Joseph, umbrellamaker	406, 627
Moir, J. K., costumier	602
Moncur, D., & Co. (aerated waters)	335
Moonlight, Charles, tailor	614
Morrison, William, plasterer	626
Muir, Son, & Patton, Thomas, colliery agents	120
Muir, Son, & Patton, Thomas, coal merchants	378, 617
Murdoch, William D. grocer Carnoustie	165
Murray & Co., silk mercers Montrose	98
Myles, C. Y., & Sons, tailors	654
Myles, C. Y., tailor ,	334
Myles, Chas Y., tailor	182, 183
Napier, D. & J. plumbers	102
Napier, John jun. grocer &c.	173
Naysmith, Andrew chemist	106
North British and Mercantile Insurance Company	81, 384
North British Aerated Water Company, Montrose	150
Northern Accident Insurance Co.	157
Northern Assurance Company	372, 607
Norwich Union Fire Insurance Society	390, 616
Ogg, W. S. hairdresser	128
Ogilvie, John bookseller	148
Olympia Picture Theatre	342, 581
Olympia Chocolate Store	605
Palace, The picture house	576
Paterson, Sons & Co. music sellers	184, 593
Paton, T. C., draper	584
Pavilion, Montrose	375
Peddie, W. B., Red Lion Bar	582
Peebles Brothers teamen Dundee	145
People's Friend, The	132
People's Journal, The	132
Pert's, Arbroath furniture	575

Peter, James, tailor	336
Petrie, A. G., blacksmith	398, 614
Petrie, Alex, family grocer	77
Petrie, D, D. Friockheim	164
Pirie, David watchmaker and optician	377, 594
Pladda Iron-Screw steamer	128
Plough and Harrow	346, 589
Popular Stores	343
Porteous, A. W., confectioner	610
Porter, Charles, grocer	585
Prudential Assurance Company	87
Ramsay and Gordon, builders	387
Rayne, John, plumber	418, 638
Reid & Cuthill tailor	638
Reid, Alexander bookseller	168
Reid, Alexander builder	643
Reid, Geo. (Insurance)	144, 356, 371
Reid. Alexander, builder and sculptor	392
Rennie, William grocer	404
Robbie, David grocer &c.	162
Robbie, David cycles and cars	413
Robbie, D. & Co motor engineers	642
Robertson & Son, James joiners	386, 629
Robertson, James grocer Carnoustie	169
Robertson, Misses E. & J. hairdressers	102
Ross, Mrs R.L. wine merchant	408
Ross, William St Thomas Bar	351
Royal Exchange Assurance	347, 641
Royal Hotel, High Street (Calder)	584
Royal Oak Bar	347
Rust, H. L. C., outfitter	599
Ruxton, James, chemist	344, 623
Ruxton, Mrs R. G. tailor and outfitter	88
Salmond, George biscuit manufacturer	117, 118
Salmond, George, baker	363, 635
Salmond, Win. & Co. drapers	160
Savege, T. & Co., painters	635
Savege, T. painter and decorator	170
Scott, Andrew, grocer	131, 416, 628
Scott, David J. glass merchant and glazier	385, 582
Scott, Ernest decorator	104
Scott, Mrs M., confectioner	611
Scottish Boiler Insurance	142
Scottish Union and National Insurance Co.	394, 634

Scottish Widows' Fund (Life Assurance)	123
Seaton, James family grocer	86
Shakespeare bar	587
Shepherd, Robert vintner	160
Shepherd. James, baker	419, 605
Shield, Mill, & Jack, chemists	133, 139
Simpson, James joiner undertaking	368
Singer & Booth, bootmakers	583
Sievwright, J & R W joiners	338
Skea, Charles, salt and whiting merchant	379
Smart, David jeweller	421
Smart, W.B. monumental mason	344
Smith, Alex. The Lorne Bar	99
Smith, James & Son shoemakers	88
Smith, J. P. & Son, tailors	146
Smith, James florist	108
Smith, James rope spinner	90
Smith. Hood & Co., coal merchants	417,601
Smith's Furniture Stores	84
Soutar, Carnegie, baker	416, 624
Soutar, James drapery	380
Souter, James newsagent Carnoustie	166
Station Cycle Works	630
Station Hotel and Bar (James Malcolm)	418
St Ruth's Art studio	348
Steeple Restaurant,	359
Stephen, James horse-hirer	172
Stephen's Fish Mart	630
Stevenson, James grocer	389
Stevenson Bros., dyers, Dundee	78, 404
Stevensons, launderers	612
Stewart, George, butcher	611
Stewart, Miss, fancy draper	603
Strachan & Farquhar, dressmakers	179, 366
Strachan, A. & Son tailors	89
Strachan, George. H. sheriff officer	97
Strachan, R. & Sons tailors	87
Strachan, Wallace, & Whyte	170
Sutherland, Alexander monumental mason	414
Suttie, John blacksmith	171
Swan, James, fish merchant	586
Swirles, A. & Son curriers	172
Sword, James, china merchant	612
Tarbet, Wm. grocer	109

Taylor, David S., photographer	96
Thompson, James R. engraver	381
Thomson, G. Rutherford & Son cabinet makers	137, 138
Thomson, James A., ironmonger	628
Thomson, James, baker, Friockheim	424
Thomson, John, ironmonger	169
Thomson, William, butcher	600
Thornton, David, draper	590
Thornton, D. tailor	393
Thornton, James, joiner	610
Tosh's Stores	102
Tullis, John & Son tanners Glasgow	130
Urquhart, Mrs George grocer	402
Vernon's garden	632
Victoria Cafe	608
Victoria Bar	357
Victoria Cafe, Millgate	352
Victoria Public Buildings Company	93
Walker, D. Y., butcher	367, 593
Wallace, Alex, china merchant	173, 345
Wallace, Alex. S. veterinary surgeon	168
Waterson, George and sons stationers	122
Waverley Temperance Hotel	176, 361, 606
Webster & Littlejohn (Insurance)	150
West Port association	341
Westwater, H. pastry baker	97
White Hart Hiring and Garage Co	364
White Hart Hotel (Ehrlich's)	124
White Hart Hotel (Smith's),	419, 645
White Hart Livery Stables	124
White's Semolina	148, 412
Whitton, Charles P. grocer	603
Whitton, Miss, fancy goods	77
Will, A., Carnoustie stationer	650
Williamson, W. B. baker	604
Willocks, James watchmaker	141
Wiltshire Dairy Stores	422
Winton, James, Arbroath rock	580
Wood, Norah H, dressmaker	592
Yorkshire Insurance	356, 621
Young, D. & Sons, Cartwrights	404, 604

Dickman's Den, from a Raphael Tuck postcard, 1907

Mason's Cove, from a Raphael Tuck postcard, 1904

Index

A

Abbey viii, xiii, 1, 27, 212, 222, 236, 243, 250, 268, 279, 285, 302, 305, 327, 328, 329, 436, 437, 467, 472, 486, 506, 541, 543, 557, 563, 657, 658, 681, 728
Abbey Leather Works 436
Abbey Theatre 43, 44, 45, 196, 197, 200, 201, 222, 557, 558
Aberbrothock 233, 247, 328
Aberdeen Bon Accord 444, 511
Adams, Thomas 564
Adams, A. E. 707
Air Raid Patrols 495
Aird, George 522
Airlie Crescent 546
Airlie, Earl of 323, 447, 562
Albert, Prince Consort 5, 25
Albion Rovers 22, 482
Aldridge, Olive politician 63
Alexander and Sons 29
Alexander, C. cricketer 509
Alexander, William, Bailie, later Provost, 68, 435, 487, 550, 703
Allan Street 306
Alloa 245, 260, 717
Alma Works 287, 551
Almerlecloss 6
Anchorage 517
Anderson, School society chairman 688
Anderson, football player 263
Anderson, G. cricketer 509
Anderson, James 660
Anderson, John 327
Anderson, Lizzie 714
Anderson, Lord, Court of Session 708
Anderson, Professor George 440
Anderson, Provost 303, 433, 454
Angus 13, 15, 20, 27, 31, 32, 42, 47, 49, 69, 193, 198, 216, 238, 252, 301, 309, 316, 323, 447, 466, 467, 491, 503, 513, 535, 536, 537, 542, 562, 564, 567
Angus Agricultural Show 467
Angus County Council 42
Angus Volunteers 513
Angus, A. cricketer 509
Angus, Reverend Henry 551
Annie Smith, boat 518
Antiquary Coach 435
Applegate 719
Arbirlot 216, 223, 238, 485, 486, 491, 566, 679, 719
Arbirlot Women's Rural Institute 679
Arbroath *passim*
_ Abbey Pageant 212, 543
_ Academy 316
_ Amateur Dramatic Club 679, 712, 716
_ Amateur Dramatic Society 10
_ Amateur Operatic Society 26, 34, 55
_ Amateur Photographic Association 685
_ and District Music Festival 70
_ and District Whippet Club 490
_ Artillery 218, 313
_ Artillery Band 218
_ British Legion 486
_ Burgh Instrumental Band 494, 669
_ Burns Club 213
_ Civil Defence 261, 262
_ Co-operative Society 253, 512, 516, 525
_ Common 298, 315
_ Curling Club 190
_ Cycling Club 659
_ District Education Sub Committee 701
_ Epidemic Hospital 293
_ Evening Continuation Classes 205
_ Farmers Club 674

739

_ Football Club - see also Gayfield - 22, 70, 255, 314, 500, 678, 686
_ General Post Office 58
_ Golf Club 474, 523
_ Guide, The xiii, 9, 55, 214, 235, 238, 304, 327, 449, 452, 472, 556, 559, 682, 704
_ Harbour 214, 468, 498, 527, 564, 692, 706
_ Health Congress 660
_ Herald, The xiii, 3, 10, 16, 19, 23, 25, 28, 34, 59, 61, 64, 65, 187, 191, 192, 193, 195, 199, 206, 212, 215, 230, 232, 242, 246, 263, 271, 273, 279, 293, 321, 429, 432, 433, 438, 439, 446, 453, 454, 459, 465, 469, 481, 482, 485, 493, 499, 506, 508, 520, 523, 529, 533, 545, 557, 567, 664, 669, 677, 678, 696, 698, 699, 700, 702, 706, 707, 715, 716, 718, 721
_ High School 13, 22, 46, 50, 64, 205, 209, 222, 305, 316, 331, 332, 429, 440, 446, 499, 510, 515, 533, 543, 549, 688, 727
_ High Street Co-operative Society 525
_ Infirmary 57, 219, 256, 258, 259, 485, 487, 495, 525, 564
_ Instrumental Band 218, 669
_ Ladies Tennis Club 432
_ Mill and Factory Workers' Union 250
_ Museum 9, 55, 281
_ Old Church 291, 323, 564
_ Old Men's Club 551
_ Operatic Society 26, 34, 47, 55, 707
_ Parish Church 442
_ Physical Culture Club 33
_ Police Court 57, 286, 487, 505, 657, 703, 719
_ Presbytery 40, 235, 238
_ Public Baths 187, 248, 504, 514
_ Public Health Hospital 65
_ Public Library 16, 507, 549
_ Railway Station 271, 454
_ Rotary Club 496
_ Royal Infirmary 58, 683
_ Sands 448
_ School Board 13, 68, 533
_ School Management Committee 42, 331
_ Sheriff Court 219, 544
_ smokies 8
_ Station 6, 198, 454, 472, 568, 689, 695
_ Symphony Orchestra 199
_ Tennis Club 190
_ Theatre 500
_ Total Abstinence Society 14
_ Town Council 55, 314, 321, 496, 519, 664
_ Town House 21, 47, 212, 322, 326, 330, 436, 452
_ Town Mission 450
_ Trades Council 204
_ United Cricket Club 23, 30, 324, 438, 441, 442, 446, 458, 460, 465, 478, 488, 492, 509
_ Victoria 22, 517
_ Volunteer Regiment 715
_ Working Men's Club 53
Arbroath–Forfar Railway Company 235
Arbuckle, Sir William 316
Ardenlea 30, 465, 475
Argyll, Dorrie actor 534
Arrott Street 664
Artisan Golf Club 523
Arts League of Service Players 534
Ashdale 22
Asquith 4, 279
Auchmithie 36, 193, 319, 524, 662, 663
Auldbar Road 6
Ayr United 11, 263

B

Bain, Aaron 44
Baird, Robert G 332
Balaclava 32, 235
Balfour, Arthur, Prime Minister 21

Balfour, George 552
Balmashanner Hill 455
Balmossie Bridge 502
Baltic Works 551
Bank Street 63, 250, 282, 306, 549
Bannerman, Campbell, Prime Minister 279
Bannerman, John, Liberal politician 285
Barngreen 483
Barry 313, 491, 503
Battle of Arbroath 27
Baxter, Mary 237
Beaton, Cardinal 1, 728
Becci, Atilio 227, 245
Bell Rock 449, 683, 706
Bell, "Stumpie", teacher 489
Bell, Arbroath Victoria footballer 517
Bell, John, artiste 65
Bell, Reverend W. W. M. 238
Berkshire Aviation Tours Ltd 541
Bertram Mills Circus 315
Bible Training Institute 450
Billiards 188, 290, 666
Black Watch 447, 495, 503, 516, 715
Black, Alexander MP 723
Black, Linda 456
Blair, Andrew 551
Blair, John artiste 65
Blairgowrie 260, 472
blizzard 17, 31, 49
Bo'ness 7, 34
Boath, Miss, young swimmer 514
Bonnington United Presbyterian 561
Bouch, Dr Thomas 48
Bowen, W., shipmaster 17
Bowes-Lyon, Lay Elizabeth 562
Bowes-Lyon, Lieut-Col Hon M 447
Boyes, Charlie 23
Bradshaw's railway timetable 2, 38, 300, 428, 430, 431, 532
Brailsford, Henry Noel, Labour politician 689, 721
Brand, Arbroath FC footballer 245
Brannan, P 207

Breakwater 526, 553, 726
Brechin 18, 22, 23, 31, 32, 33, 49, 58, 64, 194, 204, 233, 249, 260, 273, 296, 301, 474, 478, 486, 502, 508, 540, 548
Bremner, James, publican 203
Brice, Rev Joseph 559
Briggs, James 723
Briggs, William 706
British Linen Bank 705
Brodie, John 191
Brothock, River 247, 269, 275, 286, 439, 473, 519, 705, 721
Broughty Ferry 277, 433, 552
Brown W.O., SSPCA 309
Brown, Alwyn, artiste 534
Brown, Bill, goalkeeper 22
Brown, footballer 263, 535
Brown, Graham, missionary 680
Brown, John, ghillie 291
Brown, Robert artiste 55
Brown, Scott, footballer 194
Bruce-Gardyne, Jock, Tory MP 69, 542
Bruce, Brian actor 557
Bruce, Carol actor 196
Bruce, Charles 682
Bruce, footballer 506
Bruce, swimmer 514
Buchanan, David 332
Buckingham Palace 224, 288
Bummie 455
Burgess, Joseph 279
Burnett, C.G. cricketer 488
Burnett, Darren, bowling green bowler 294
Burnett, F. W. G., cricketer 488
Burnside Works 240, 540
Butchart, W. weight-lifter 33

C

Cadman, billiard player 188
Café Moderne 15
Cairnie Place 282, 312
Cairnie Street 332, 444
Calder, Sergeant 513

Calder's Famous Cinematograph 500
Caledonian Mercury, The 41
Callum, Catherine cook 231
Calungie 674
Cameron Dr 534
Cameron, Joseph 70
Campbell, Dick 11, 194
Campbell, George railway contractor 271
Campbell, Rev 491
Cant, Elizabeth 714
Cargill, Ardenlea FC 475
Cargill, Charles 564
Cargill, David 223, 319, 564
Cargill, Ella 437, 539
Cargill, footballer 28
Cargill, Margaret 228
Cargill, Pieter 196
Carmyllie 19, 566, 708
Carnegie Soutar and Sons 15, 711
Carnegie, Andrew 519, 563
Carnegie, B.A., B.C. and H.G., cricketers 488
Carnegie, James 308
Carnegie, Jessie 237
Carnegie, John politician 673, 698
Carnegie, Lindsay 6, 269, 480, 506
Carnegie, Station Master 521
Carnival 311, 453
Carnoustie 69, 222, 311, 432, 459, 517, 552
Carrie, footballer 28
Carrie, John 522
Carver, footballer 245, 482
Cassidy, Stewart actor 201
Caterthun 32
Cavan, John cab driver 719
Census 210, 221, 223, 228, 229, 231, 234, 237, 306
Chalmers Street 686
Chalmers, cook 287
Chapel, Bailie 475
Chapel, Lady 16, 664
Chapel, Provost Sir William 8, 15, 190, 247, 290, 437, 711

Chaplain, Evelyn 196
Charles, William 237
Chemical and Asphalt Works 704
China Inland Mission 680
Christison, Alan actor 200, 201
Christison, Annie actor 714
Christison, John Chairman Arbroath FC 693
Churchill, Winston 56, 274, 278, 289, 457, 546, 673
Clark, Archibald 57
Clark, dancer 14
Clark, footballer 28
Clark, John (Celtic) 535
Clark, Kelly 460
Clocksbriggs 6
Cobb, James 32
Collace 57
Collie, Arbroath footballer 511
Commerce Street 506, 549
Connon Rev Albert 64
Constable, Briggs politician 279
Convent Churchyard 452
Cordiner, William light-house keeper 683
Corn Exchange 222, 326, 519, 540
Corsar, Charles 231, 555, 561
Corsar, Major, Fire Master 269
Coull, David 290
Coull, Mary 231
Courier, The 439, 455, 713
Covent Garden 19
Cowieson, Miss opera singer 707
Cownie, J cricketer 509
Cowper, Reverend William 540
Craig, Alexander 657
Craig, Mary 502,
Craig, WW cyclist 659
Craigen, James 11
Craigie 674
Crawford, Arbroath footballer 511, 713
Crawford, Earl of 27
Crawford, Headmaster Arbroath Academy 316
Crawford, Mary 237

Crawford, Norman, librarian 496
Crimea 32, 235, 313, 327
Crockatt, Arbroath FC footballer 198
Crombie, Rev David 442
Crowe, William, Inspector of postmen 253
Cruickshank, Andrew 534
Crumley, Bob Arbroath FC captain 678
Culloden Farm 541
Cumbrian, steamer 7
Cumming, Edwin 484
Cumming, footballer 245
Cunninghill Ranges 513
Cuthbert, James 477
Cuthill, James 714
Cuthill, Rev Spence 255

D

Dale School 42, 255, 326
Dalgarno, George G. solicitor 660, 685
Dalgety, Thomas, flaxdresser 487
Dalhousie Estate 491
Dalhousie Place 286
Dalhousie, Earl of 566
Dall, Elizabeth 218
Davidson, William 237
Dancers Bus 29
Danger Point ii, 545
Darroch, David 714
Davidson and Smith, bus firm 29
Davidson, footballer 535
Davidson, soldier 32
Declaration of Arbroath xiii, 69, 212, 236, 243, 486, 681
Delaney, Jimmy, Celtic footballer 227
Dempster of Dunnichen, George 445
Dewar, Arbroath Infirmary 57
Dewar, Dr W.J. 255, 484
Dick, Alasdair 494
Dick, James 688
Dickfield Street 237
Dickson, Lieutenant 313
Dickson, Maurice 438, 458, 465
Dilly, Arbroath FC footballer

Dishland Hill 257, 484
Dishlandtown Street 227
Dobson, David 287
Doig, James grocer 696
Doig, Ned goalkeeper 30, 60, 665
Donald, Miss L.T. 257
Donaldson, Miss, actor 707
Donibristle 193
Doris, Steven footballer 693
Dorward, fire instructor 269
Dorward, footballer 198
Dorward, teacher 14
Downie, J weight-lifter 33
Downiekin 674
Drumkilbo 562
Duff, footballer 245
Duff, James 57
Duff, Mary 703
Duncan, Bailie John 57, 242, 719
Duncan, John artiste 714
Duncan, Sir James MP 20, 316
Duncan, S. cricketer 509
Duncan, Sunday School Superintendent 66
Dundee 18, 22, 30, 33, 42, 48, 49, 52, 63, 65, 193, 195, 211, 214, 231, 244, 246, 261, 264, 267, 271, 283, 284, 286, 288, 289, 291, 297, 304, 313, 315, 318, 322, 327, 330, 444, 454, 457, 469, 472, 474, 475, 482, 492, 495, 501, 502, 511, 520, 521, 530, 536, 539, 540, 541, 543, 549, 552, 555, 560, 566, 568, 669, 673, 678, 679, 681, 698, 711, 712, 721, 723
Dundee and Arbroath Joint Railway Company 211, 722
Dundee and Broughty Ferry Tramways Association 552
Dundee, Perth and London Shipping Company 288
Dunnichen 252, 445, 694

E

Eadie, John 332
Early, Mary Duff or 703

Easson, David footballer 198, 263, 535
East Abbey Street 250, 302
East Craigie 517
East Fife 245, 444
Eastern Cemetery 42, 474, 564
Eaton, Emily 448
eclipse 239
Eddie, rifle club 451
Edinburgh 41, 48, 67, 195, 216, 244, 247, 268, 270, 305, 438, 446, 461, 488, 515, 521, 536, 549, 562, 683, 723
Edward I 243, 445
Edward VII 25, 326
Edward VIII 702
Edward, George PE teacher 474
Edward, Prince Albert Victor Christian 436
Edward, Sergeant 521
Elder, Eleanor 534
Elford, Kenneth Victor James 705
Elliot Junction 211, 434, 521
Elliot Junction Rail Disaster xiii, 722, 723, 724
Elliot Street 242
Elliot, a barque 17
Elliot, Arthur Hingston 286
Ellis, Andrew 686
Emislaw 719
Empire Marketing Board 8
Entwhistle, Miss Jennie 332
Erskine Church 309, 551
Esk, River 519
exhibition bungalow 711

F

Fairport, dredger 270
Fairport, pseudonym 270, 435
Fairweather, cricketer 296
Falconer, James stoker 278
Farmhill 554
Farquhar, Fire master 696
Farquharson, Adam 540
Farquharson, Colin 51
Farquharson, Robert 195
Fauldiehill 485

Fellowes, Horace violinist 199
Ferguson, David 675
Ferguson, footballer 28, 198
Ferrier, cricketer 23, 296
Fettes, Ellen 306
Fettes, John flax dresser 68
Fidelity AH113 217
Fife Herald, The 308
Findlay, Reverend May 56
fish 6, 8, 12, 227, 331, 471, 477, 483, 510, 518, 520, 530, 537, 538, 554, 556, 669, 684, 709, 717
Fisheracre 505
flax 7, 68, 223, 240, 275, 306, 433, 489, 520
Florence, John 332
flu 3, 26, 46, 59, 70, 218, 230, 277, 453, 473, 554, 665, 689, 717
Flucker, footballer 482
Ford, B. N. W. cricketer 488
Ford, J. cricketer 509
Ford, Mary 551
Fordyce, footballer 245
Forfar 3, 6, 15, 18, 22, 29, 31, 33, 42, 62, 64, 69, 194, 195, 198, 222, 231, 233, 235, 243, 247, 249, 260, 267, 271, 279, 281, 291, 293, 295, 312, 317, 324, 327, 434, 446, 449, 454, 455, 460, 466, 472, 491, 506, 511, 513, 519, 520, 530, 540, 541, 549, 552, 563, 566, 567, 658, 665, 675, 695, 711, 721, 727
Forfar Amateur Dramatic Society 222
Forfarshire 30, 198, 249, 433, 517, 552, 556, 659, 685
Forsyth, Bruce 530
Forsyth, Elizabeth 505
Forsyth, Jemima 205
Forsyth, Michael 305
Forth Railway Bridge 434, 454
Fraser, Douglas 287, 493
Fraser, footballer 263, 535
Fraser, Miss suffragist
Friockheim 6, 49, 543, 552
Fussey, Rosemary 201

G

Gable Endies 198
Gallipoli 289
Gallowden Laundry 58
Garden, young swimmer 514
Gardner, David A, Treasurer and Provost 206, 209, 258
Gardner, Isobel 222
Gayfield xii, xiii, 22, 28, 31, 35, 198, 202, 224, 245, 247, 263, 303, 311, 314, 439, 444, 460, 466, 474, 475, 482, 511, 517, 520, 535, 541, 659, 693, 695, 713, 717
Geddes, Charles 705
Geddes, Emma 34
Gedy, John Abbot of Arbroath 328
General Election 21, 34, 62, 69, 207, 295, 457, 547, 563, 673, 684, 689, 698, 721
General Strike 273
George Hotel 242
George Street 57
Gibb, Lance Corporal 289
Gibb, Police Sergeant 317
Gibson, Provost James 452
Gilbert and Sullivan 26, 34, 55, 679, 684, 707, 708
Gilbert, Frank 201
Gilruth, Dr J D 660
Gladstone, William Ewart Prime Minister 21
Glamis Castle 47, 274, 437, 447, 562, 567
Glasgow Celtic 28, 198
Glasgow Fair 450
Gleig, R. cricketer 509
Glencarse 19
Good Templar Hall 192, 525, 671
Goodfellow and Steven's 496
Goodwillie, Councillor 496
Gordon Arabs 298
Gordon Highlanders 56, 678
Gordon, Captain 313
Gordon, footballer 198
Gordon, Michelle 210
Gordon, Miss nurse 57
Gordon, Sheriff 219, 538, 544
Gordon, swimmer 514
Gordon's Mill 489
Gourlay, George locomotive driver 723
Gowanlea Cottages 440
Graham, Billy 264
Graham, Major Howard 302
Grampian Electricity Scheme 552
Grampian TV 530
Grange Cricket Club 283, 488
Grangemouth 7
Grant, Colin Provost 241, 242, 286, 500, 505
Grant, James author 280
Grant, Miss suffragist 330
Grant's, retailer 492, 677
Gravesend 68
Gray, footballer 198
Greasley, Doug cricketer 478
Great War 4, 188, 199, 207, 216, 250, 259, 260, 284, 295, 303, 311, 329, 432, 451, 469, 473, 474, 541, 547, 565, 668, 676, 714, 717
Green Bank House 484
Greig, David 190
Greyhound Racing Track 42
Grimond, Jo Liberal MP 285
Guthrie Port 279, 563, 658, 703
Guthrie, village 6
Guynd 671

H

Hadden, Johnny 455
Hamilton Accies 263, 716
Hamilton, Gavin 314
Hamilton, Ian 268
Hampden 60, 244, 264
Hannah Street 223, 448, 487, 544
Harbour 7, 210, 214, 240, 468, 498, 514, 526, 527, 541, 564, 663, 692, 697, 700, 706
Harcourt, Vernon 279, 550, 563
Hart, T procurator fiscal 219

Hay, footballer 535
Hayes, Maureen 201
Hean, John tanner 215
Hedderwick, Caroline 222
Heinkel 11 5C aircraft 485
Helen Street 242, 290, 310
Henderson, George 237
Henderson, Private 289
High Street vi, 188, 203, 210, 223, 252, 297, 326, 327, 330, 429, 449, 456, 472, 473, 506, 521, 525, 529, 538, 539, 555, 563, 711, 716
Hill of Beath 194
Hill Street 46, 208, 234, 436
Hird, Alexander 252
Hitchcock, Rev George 714
HMS Condor 193, 478, 515, 560, 705
Hobbs, Jack 23, 442
Hogg, A. C. 514
Hogg, Jessie 14
Hogg, Rodney 441
Hogg, slater 220
Holder, Gordon 44
Holyrood Palace 433
Hood, Alex 714
Hood, baker 63
Hood, Emily 429
Hood, James 688
Hood, swimmer 514
Hope Street 657
Hopemount Church 42, 208, 238, 474
Hopkin Gilkes 48
Horner's Wynd 449
Hospitalfield 467
Hotel Seaforth 285, 437
Housing Scheme 453, 565
Howie, farmer 477
Howie, Mrs T. J. 297
Hume Street 232, 439
Hume, farmer 219
Hume, Private 289
Hunter, artiste 707
Hunter, Ian 26
Hunter, musician 65
Hutchison, Dennis 534
Hutchison, Marion 561
Hutchison, Sir Robert 295

I

Imperial Hotel 190, 203, 429
Inchcape 192, 228, 252, 303, 328, 460, 475, 564
Inchcape Lodge Number 619, 192
Independent Labour Party 63
Inverbrothock Free Church 680
Inverbrothock Illustrated 205
Inverbrothock Parish Church 714
Inverbrothock School 255
Inverbrothock Watters Cup 460
Inverkeilor 65, 267, 289, 435
Inverkeilor Players 65
Inverleith Road 42
Inverquharity 27
Irwin, Bailie Tom 295

J

James Street 469, 500
Jamieson Street 32
Jamieson, footballer 245, 482
Jarman's Hotel 455
Jenkins, John Liberal candidate 62
Johnshaven 527
Johnston, Alan 200, 201
Johnston, James and Norman 448
Johnston, Tom MP 244
Johnstone, footballer 198, 482
Joss, theatre director 65
Joyce, A.W. life saving instructor 514
jute 48, 69, 279, 287, 312, 520, 540, 695, 711

K

Kane, David 222
Keddie, Alex 693
Keith and Blackman 493, 669
Keith, George Provost 436
Kemp, Arts patron 16
Kemp, footballer 517
Kennedy, Miss young swimmer 514

Keptie House 429
Keptie Loch 190
Keptie Public School 533
Keptie Road 58, 711, 719
Keptie School 13
Keptie Street 4, 35, 203, 221, 252, 271, 292, 439, 495, 506, 529
Kerr, Margaret 196
Kerr, Matthew farmer 318
Kidd, Ron cricketer 478
Kilpatrick, Douglas teacher 46
Kinblethmont Estate 480
King Edward I 243, 245, 445
King Edward VII 25, 326
King Edward VIII 702
King George V 19, 52, 288, 433, 461, 506, 567
King George VI 47, 274
King of Afghanistan 224
King William IV 308, 322
King, Arthur 205
King, Ellen 437
King's Own Scottish Borderers 46
King's Park 264
Kinnaird, Lord 486
Kirk Square 3, 694, 727
Kirkland, James cattleman 219
Kirriemuir 27, 291, 329, 670
Kydd, Mrs actor 707

L

Ladies Column 61
Ladyloan 475, 487
Ladyloan Free Church 680
Ladyloan United Free Church Mission 66
Lady Betty Balfour, ship 706
Laing, Infirmary doctor 57
Laing, Jack 201
Lakie, Bailie 317
Lamb, Dean of Guild 711
Lamb, Provost John 189, 213, 247, 311
Lamont, W. artist 481
Langlands, Susan and William 237
Lauder, Sir Harry xiii, 230, 245, 462, 489
Law, Christian 237
LeBlond, J. Education committee secretary 701
Leonard Street 286, 490
Letham 60, 252, 269, 316, 566, 665
Leysmill 6, 27
Lifeboat 211, 525, 683
Lillies Wynd 696
Lindsay Street 234
Lindsay-Carnegie 269, 480, 506
Lindsay, Alexander 27
Lindsay, Ian 512
Lindsay, James 19
linseed 468
Littlejohn, David SSPCA 309, 563
Littlejohn, T. cricketer 509
Lloyd George 4, 20, 52, 563, 565, 673, 721
Lochlands xiii, 23, 32, 190, 272, 273, 277, 283, 296, 442, 465, 478, 492, 495, 506, 508, 541, 548, 563
Logan, Rev Angus 564
Lord Burn 237
Lordburn Joinery Works 442
Low, Mary 221
Low Common 450, 465
Low, Evelyn 707
Low, Town House 330
Lowe, footballer 245, 482
Lownie, Miss soloist 14
Lunan Bay 67, 267, 435, 518
Lyall, Edna 280
Lyall, William 52

Mac, Mc

McAllin, Clement 534
MacCormick, John 268
McCurragh, Reverend W 207
MacDonald, Chief Constable 53, 250, 310, 664
MacDonald, Ramsay 295, 507, 549, 698
MacDonald, Town Clerk 563
McElney, Miss matron 256
McEwan, John band founder 218

McFarlane, Helen 258
McFarlane, Leezie 714
McFlannels 62
McGlashan, Bailie Robert 213, 486
McGlashan, Bert footballer and manager 28, 245, 482, 686
MacGregor, Alexina Jessie 330
McInnes, billiards player 188
McLean, Davie 324
McLean, footballer 263
McLean, Lex 470
McLeish, James lantern projectionist 685
McLennan, William flaxdresser 505
McLeod, G.C. cricketer 465
McLeod, hotel keeper 242
McLevy, footballer 263, 535
McMillan, J. cricketer 509
Mackay, Hugh 534
Mackay, James 228
Mackays shipyard 217
Mackie, R. L. Franco-Scottish society 209
MacLennan, Donald chauffeur 544
MacMillan, Harold Prime Minister 20
McNab, Colin footballer 245, 482
McNeil, prosecutor 57
McPhail, Reverend Matthew 238
McPherson, Robert 521
McRae, W weightlifter 33
McVicar, P. cricketer 509

M

Mafeking 286
Mains of Kelly 664
Mann, Fred cricketer 277, 446
Marigold A52 553
Marketgate 223, 447, 495
Marnie, Stewart boat hirer 319
Marshall, footballer 511
Marshall, Henry 28
Marywell 435
Masonic Lodge Panmure (No.299) 551
Masson, Elaine 712

Masson, George 490
Masson, William 314
Mathers, soloist 14
Matheson T 209
Matheson, Frank 544
Mathieson, John dux 205
Matthews, Corporal rifle man 513
Matthewson, Thomas labourer 52
Maule Street 546
Maxwell, life saver 697
Meigle 260, 441
Mellor, footballer 517
Melvin, Bailie Robert 242, 657
Menmuir 32
Merchants' Association 453
Middleton, footballer 28
Middleton, James lorryman 310
Miller, F. cricketer 509
Millgate 52, 506, 563
Millgate Loan 310, 484
Millgate Works 436
Milne, Charles 563
Milne, footballer 511
Milne, Sharon 200, 201
Miniature Railway 318
Miniature Rifle Club 451
Miss Arbroath 456, 504
Mission Hall 24, 66, 524, 680
Moir, Frank 196
Moir, Provost James Kyd 209, 285, 302, 494, 695
Moir, Jean 196
Monifieth 69
Montquhir 708
Montrose 9, 14, 15, 18, 21, 49, 60, 64, 69, 70, 192, 193, 198, 203, 233, 249, 253, 260, 267, 279, 295, 297, 305, 308, 325, 444, 445, 449, 457, 475, 518, 541, 542, 552, 559, 563, 671, 673, 689, 694, 698, 706, 721
Morgan Academy 22
Morley, John MP 21, 279, 671
Morrell, Frank 516
Morris, George 26
Morrison, David porter 723

Mosely, Fred life saver 456
Mowat, I.W. political speaker 20
Mowat, Jimmy goalkeeper 22
Moyston, John dissident employee 314
Muckle Meg (Margaret Swan) 483
Mudie, William blacksmith 708
Muir, Provost James 17, 697
Muir, Reverend James 297
Mungall, car owner, Dunnichen 694
Mungall, Stuart actor 222
Munro, George child 697
Murray, Andy 294
Murray, Helen 522
Murray, Mary 484
Murroes 674
Myles, C. Y. 707
Myles, cricketer 324

N

National Bar 203
National Health Service 50, 457, 494, 701
National Service 503, 516, 568, 672
National Women's Social and Political Union 671
Neave, George missionary 524
Neil, footballer 511
Neilson, Jean actor 714
Netherward 287
New Downie 674
New Palace Theatre 678
New Public Hall 24, 555
Newgate Club 257
Nicoll, Band of Hope 66
Nicoll, Marjory 456
Nolan, cricketer 324
Nolt Loan Road 252
Noran, River 519
Noranside Sanatorium 193
North Grimsby 237
North Inch 30, 503
North Sea xiii, 187, 274, 468, 518, 519, 542, 548
Northern Tool and Gear Company 502
Nourse, Dave cricketer 23

O

Ogilvy Place School 533
Ogilvy, Baron Alexander 27
Ogilvy, Lord 249
Old Shore Head 223, 697
Olympia Cinema 3
Olympia Theatre 255
Onward and Upward 216
Open Air Bathing Pool 437, 504
Ouchterloney 566, 671

P

Palace Cinema 12, 670, 677, 689
Palace Theatre 199, 469, 678
Panlathy 491, 674
Panmure Masonic Hall 565
Panmure Street 30, 218, 290
Park Street Mission 480
Parkhead 465
Parochial Board 304
Parrott, Lady speaker 54
Paterson, footballer 245
Paterson, James Hunter publican 52
Paterson, Moira 200, 201
Paton, Alexander 521
Pennant-Jones, Caroline 196
Pert, Morris pianist 70
Perth 30, 48, 195, 231, 249, 263, 267, 288, 291, 503, 522, 530, 666
Perthshire Courier, The 233, 522
Peter, William 237
Peters, Maureen hotel keeper 203
Petrie M. J. cricketer 488
Petrie, Georgina 231
Petrie, Jimmy 198
Petrie, Jockie xiii, 444, 474, 511
Petrie, Lily 714
Philip Street 220
phthisis 65
Pichon, Ann 534
Picture House 274, 489, 677
Pirrie, Helen s. civil servant 709
planes 67
Playfield Station 6

police 53, 57, 68, 229, 243, 268, 290, 301, 309, 310, 317, 528, 657, 673, 688, 719
Police Court 4, 51, 57, 250, 286, 310, 487, 490, 505, 528, 657, 658, 703, 719
Polish Army 476
Ponderlaw Lane 505
Ponderlaw Street 272
Pont L'Eveque 209
Poor House 321, 326
Port Stanley 17
Post Office 25, 58, 253, 286, 307, 449, 493, 717
potato 331, 452, 477, 548, 550, 556
Premier Troupe of Minstrels 14
Prince Albert Victor Christian Edward 436
Princes Street 448, 680
Princes Street United Presbyterian Church 680
Princess Victoria, ship 35
Proctor, footballer 198
Pryde, Helen W. author 62
Pugh, Dorothy singer 199
Pyper, police inspector 528

Q

Queen Mary 506
Queen Street Congregational Church 56
Queen Victoria 215, 291, 322
Queen's Park 30, 60, 511
Quinn, footballer 263, 535
Quinn, John 540
Quintinshill 289

R

radio 19, 47, 62, 244, 288, 301, 501, 529, 670, 700
Rae, D. cricketer 509
Railton, George Salvationist 272
railway 2, 6, 9, 29, 38, 195, 202, 252, 260, 271, 273, 281, 284, 300, 315, 318, 329, 428, 429, 431, 434, 437, 449, 454, 461, 472, 502, 521, 532, 566, 695, 699, 713, 723, 724
Rait, Lt Walter Garnet 323
Ralley, Robert Parker shopkeeper 539
Ralph The Rover xiii, 247, 328
Ramsay, A. J. B. opera singer 707
Ramsay, C. cricketer 324, 488
Ramsay, John 253
Ramsay, Pat 222
Randall, Derek cricketer 441
Red Lichties 11, 33, 198, 224, 245, 263, 717
Red Triangle Hut 33, 208, 462
Redcastle 435
Redford 708
Reform Act 233, 308, 322
Reid, George school board 13
Relentless AH136 726
Rennie, Arthur 58
Rennie, footballer 511
Rhodes, Wilfred cricketer 23
Riddle sisters, singers 65
Ritchie, F. cricketer 509
Ritchie, Robert 546
Robb, George 57
Robb, Margaret 55
Robbie, Annie 714
Robbie, dancer 14
Robert Street 232
Robertson, Bailie and Provost Alexander McLaren 310, 490 528
Robertson, Elizabeth 237
Robertson, G. S. political speaker 688
Robertson, George 429
Robertson, Helen 522
Robertson, Linton 676
Robertson, Mrs opera director 679
Robertson, Neil 26, 190
Robertson, Solicitor 705
Robertson, Town Treasurer 432
Ross County 194
Ross, Bailie, Mrs J. C. 206
Ross, bar proprietor 528
Ross, Duncan 459
Ross, Horatio 308

Rossie Street 686
Roy, Tommy union official 540
Royal Caledonian Club, The 190
Royal Garrison Artillery 277
rubbish 202, 661
rugby 432, 51
Ruxton, Alexander 221

S

St Andrew's Church 543
St Andrews 1, 305, 332, 440, 446, 486, 681, 728
St John's Methodist Church 272, 440, 554
St Mary Street 237
St Mary's Episcopalian Church 480
St Monance 667
Saint Thamas's market 449, 472
St Thomas Bar 528
St Thomas Lodge 297
St Thomas RC Church 207
St Thomas Swimming Club and Humane Society 448, 514
St Vigean's Church 448
St Vigeans 42, 221, 223, 234, 306
Salmond, A. H. political speaker 688
Salmond, footballer 511
Salmond, George baker 306
Salmond, George cricketer 283
Salmond, J.B. newspaper proprietor 191
Salmond, William 306
Salute The Soldier 189, 311
San Francisco 17
Sandeman, D. D. store owner 696
Sapphire AH79 553
Saucher Farm 57
Savant 465
Sawley, Lex 196
Scott, Alan 490
Scott, David 34
Scott, Rev J Moffat 66
Scott, Robert 707
Scott, the Misses 259
Scott, Thomas 188

Scott, Sir Walter 191, 270, 280, 435
Scott, William 316
Scottish Association of Magical Societies 258
Scottish Coast Mission 524
Scottish Covenant Movement 268
Scottish Modern Arts Association 16
Scottish National Party 285, 542
Scottish Society for the Prevention of Cruelty to Animals 309
Scouts 192, 466, 676
Seaforth 20, 231, 285, 437, 555, 561, 669
Sebastopol 32, 235
Setten, Mrs concert organiser 65
Shalona, fishing vessel 217
Shanks Foundry 493
Shanks, Jane 228
shark 518
sheep stealing 57
Shepherd, George 10, 546
Shepherd, Margaret 223
shipbuilding 667
Shirreffs, footballer 263, 535
Shorehead 306
Sievwright, A. cricketer 509
Sievwright, N. cricketer 509
Sievwright, R.W. xiii, 23, 257, 260, 276, 277, 294, 296, 324, 433, 438, 442, 446, 465, 508, 509, 548, 720
Silver Cloud, fishing boat 527
Simpson, George 521
Simpson, James 237
Simpson, Mrs Wallis 702
Simpson, William, blacksmith 237
Simpson, William, baby 237
Simpson, William, coachman 484
Simpson, Willie 33
Sinclair, footballer 263
Slesser, Malcolm politician 69
Smail, John office manager 286
Small, William Harvey promoter 42
smallpox 254
Smart, footballer 517
Smith, A 435, 666

Smith, Dave 196
Smith G 659
Smith, Alex registrar 538
Smith, Archie 564
Smith, Bailie 660
Smith, Coxswain William 211
Smith, David 697
Smyth, Jean actor 714
snow 17, 18, 28, 31, 39, 49, 686, 714, 723
Society For the Prevention of Destitution 550
Soup Kitchen 9, 287
Soutar, Hugh Hanton, Provost of Montrose 15
Soutar, Pipe Sergeant 325
Soutar, Jeanie 312
South Africa 23, 25, 275, 286, 450, 465, 533, 674
South Angus Liberal Unionist Association 20
South Mains of Ethie 435
Souttar, John 658
Spink Street Crossing 699
Spink, David 317
Spink, Edward 250
Spink, Mary 657
Spink, Miss pianist 14
Sporting Post, The 22
Stanley Street 306
Stark, William 257
Station Hotel 203
Station Park 3, 695
Steel, Nadia Grace actor 44
Stephen, Mary 708
Stewart, Andy xiii, 543, 727
Stewart, Edward 546
Stewart, George 54
Stewart, James 487
Stewart, John
Stewart, Rev Melville 690
Stewart, Scott 11
Stewart, William 287
Stirling 305, 460, 488, 514, 694, 727
Stone of Destiny xiii, 243, 268, 305, 446
Stormont, footballer 511

Stormont, Jim 70
storms 35, 39, 48, 240, 478
Storrier, David footballer 30
Stotfaulds 674
Stott, Irene actor 557
Strachan, Alec 714
Strachan, Mary 34
Strachan, T. W. 20
Strathmore Avenue 456
Strathmore Cricket Club 260
Strathmore Union 260, 324, 441, 442, 478
Strathmore, Earl of 303, 324, 437, 503, 562
Strickland, Sandy 462
Stuart, Conway soloist 218
Sturrock, J Leng M.P. 325, 673, 689, 698, 721
Sutherland, Mary convict 522
Suttie, Constable 719
Swan, Anne 280
Swan, Margaret 483
Swankie, Harry 564
Swankie, Margaret 10
Swankie, William 706
Swimming Baths 519

T

table tennis 459
Tackett, footballer 511
Tasker, Hilary 44
tattie gatherers 537, 664
Tay Railway Bridge 48
Taylor, Ann 505
Taylor, Elizabeth 220
Telstar AH63 526
Tennis 190, 432, 455
Territorial Army 313, 461, 503, 676
The Antiquary 191, 270, 435
The Blossom, pleasure boat 319
The Grange, Edinburgh 283
The Robert Lindsay, lifeboat 564
Thomson, jnr E. opera singer 707
Thomson, John 242
Thomson, Marcus 682

Thomson, Provost Rutherford 248, 320, 325
Thornley, Mary actor 534
Thornton, F. W. A. pageant commentator 486
Tomlinson, Albert engineer 502
Townhead Road 278, 516
Tracey, Inspector of lifeboats 211
tuberculosis 30, 65, 252, 256
Turnbull, Helen actor 10
Turner, William burgh surveyor 664
Turnip Competition 674
Tuttie's Neuk Hall 551
Tweedie, Rev J. A. 289, 429

U

unemployment 233, 274, 287, 302, 331, 447, 458, 547, 550, 673
Union Street East 223, 483
United Free Church 66, 297, 429, 491
Urquhart, footballer 245

V

vaccination 254, 538
Vannet, Joe cricketer 478, 517
Vernon, E. T. political speaker 688
Vernon, Rev Edward 216
Victoria Hall 14, 500
Victoria Park 527
Victoria Park Church 64
Victoria, locomotive 5, 6

W

Waddington, Thomas 528
Walker, Miss musician 199
Walker, referee 198
Wallace Street 502
war xiv, 3, 4, 12, 16, 25, 35, 41, 46, 50, 52, 55, 56, 59, 189, 193, 204, 210, 227, 230, 235, 245, 248, 253, 256, 259, 261, 263, 273, 274, 275, 278, 284, 288, 289, 292, 295, 301, 309, 311, 315, 320, 325, 329, 331, 432, 445, 447, 453, 455, 457, 458, 461, 465, 468, 471, 473, 476, 485, 493, 494, 501, 512, 513, 516, 517, 529, 533, 536, 546, 547, 548, 554, 560, 658, 665, 666, 668, 672, 674, 676, 678, 681, 682, 689, 700, 707, 709, 718, 721, 725
War Savings 189
Ward Dykes 269
Watt, Alexander fish merchant 538
Waulkmills 675
Webb, Clifton 677
Webb, Sidney 550
Webster Memorial Hall 10, 26, 54, 55, 62, 70, 218, 258, 259, 268, 285, 295, 332, 470, 476, 494, 534, 536, 682, 707, 716
Webster, Alex 714
Webster, Alfred 282
Webster, Francis and Sons (Alma Works) 551
Webster, Mrs Janet 687
Webster, Provost John F 47, 202
Welcome Home Fund 261, 476
Welsh, Andrew SNP MP 542
West Common 57
West Grimsby 487
West Links Park 318
West Port 253, 487, 506, 539
West Port Co-operative Association 253
White Hart Hotel 435, 561, 660, 666
White Hart Stable 269
White Heather Club 543
White, J. picnic supervisor 480
White, P. weight lifter 33
White, Peggy 470
Whitson, Don radio engineer 512
Whitton, Charles 723
Whitton, William 658
Whyte, A. band conductor 494
Will, Addison opera producer 26
Will, Constable 719
Williams, Bert 494
Williams, cricketer 508
Williams, Gwen 712
Williamson, footballer 263, 535

Wilson, Bailie David 4, 51, 250, 259, 282, 325, 565, 694
Wilson, Councillor 545
Wilson, D.D. headmaster 209, 332
Wilson, Harold Prime minister 542
Wilson, Lieutenant rifle marksman 513
Windmill Hotel 258
Wiseman, Reverend D.C. 208
Workers Educational Association 253, 681
Wright, Andrew 680
Wright, footballer 535
Wright, Wilbur and Orville 541
Wynds 450

Y

YMCA 54, 188, 208, 474, 486, 555, 671, 680, 685
Young People's Day 554
Young, Douglas politician and poet 681
Young, footballer 263, 535
Young, Gas Manager 314
Young, George 491
Young, Mary S 479
Young, Miss picnic supervisor 480
Young, Sydney 534
Yule, Dr 219

Years

1320 236, 247, 486, 681
1396 328
1445 27
1746 249
1772 272
1789 41, 233, 445
1816 270
1817 41
1832 233, 308, 464
1839 5, 6, 29, 191, 221, 281, 434, 541, 656, 695
1841 210, 306, 522
1842 2
1844 9, 449
1846 300, 452, 556
1850 304
1851 221, 237, 306
1855 327
1856 235
1857 281
1861 221, 228, 237, 306, 332
1870 214, 221, 489
1871 48, 228, 306
1872 48, 66, 697, 704
1880s 18
1881 231, 306, 662
1882 240, 272, 474, 489
1883 228, 267, 692
1884 491, 713
1885 xiii, 191, 444, 475, 511
1886 190, 665
1887 60, 191
1889 291, 298, 321, 454, 455, 520, 540
1890 71, 187, 434, 484, 665
1891 234, 252, 280, 306, 555
1892 40, 446, 467, 659, 665
1893 218, 287, 313, 436, 505, 665, 685
1894 24
1896 14, 17, 21, 479, 480, 566, 680
1897 17, 195, 215
1898 63, 472
1899 30, 68, 674, 719
1900 30, 211, 221, 242, 275, 286, 323, 561, 699
1901 25, 30, 191, 223, 269, 312, 474, 500, 551, 657
1902 28, 30, 198, 326, 487, 549, 665, 666
1903 30, 55, 61, 253, 523, 533, 541, 703
1904 7, 21, 241, 293, 491
1905 57, 442, 524, 665, 666
1906 34, 38, 198, 256, 435, 499, 722, 723
1907 23, 205, 221, 252, 491, 513, 671, 688
1908 66, 253, 254, 279
1909 448, 477, 528, 541
1910 30, 221, 271, 550, 563, 675, 678
1911 221, 228, 229, 271, 519
1912 xiii, 23, 32, 221, 246, 253, 438, 521, 539, 545, 660

1913 13, 67, 330, 440, 538, 696
1914 3, 13, 17, 55, 216, 227, 310, 320, 429, 461, 465, 468, 481, 493, 501, 538, 549, 678, 718
1915 248, 289, 320, 333, 451
1916 248, 253, 320, 439, 715
1917 4, 248, 273, 320, 458, 506, 708
1918 12, 46, 52, 207, 261, 320, 495, 554, 669, 689, 708, 721
1919 3, 46, 59, 207, 230, 253, 277, 325, 451, 453, 474, 665, 708
1920 191, 259, 296, 331, 433, 447, 473, 514, 538, 565, 658, 682, 706
1921 188, 204, 239, 273, 284, 481, 506, 544, 717
1922 18, 51, 54, 192, 228, 295, 303, 455, 525, 673, 676, 707
1923 19, 219, 244, 250, 288, 295, 318, 670, 698
1924 199, 288, 295, 432, 507, 698
1925 58, 232, 329, 569, 686
1926 250, 273, 483, 490
1927 244, 253, 314, 541, 552, 714
1928 224, 260, 319, 474, 475, 547
1929 55, 250, 260, 295, 297, 446, 469, 694
1930 39, 438, 451, 466, 567
1930s 15, 65, 213, 256, 309, 470, 559
1931 208, 256, 282, 539, 547, 684
1932 8, 53, 65, 227, 228, 444, 489, 508, 509
1933 53, 55, 190, 220, 543, 683
1934 53, 324, 437, 534, 559
1935 245, 309, 318, 324, 469, 474, 482, 711
1936 33, 47, 190, 297, 450, 512, 702
1937 vi, 15, 26, 216, 279, 470, 518, 702
1938 255, 290, 529, 683
1939 227, 245, 262, 263, 274, 278, 301, 442, 459, 495, 501, 512, 546, 668, 725
1940 208, 278, 440, 485, 548
1941 210, 700, 720
1942 56, 227, 471, 664, 676
1943 485, 517
1944 189, 307, 311, 681, 720
1945 16, 227, 261, 274, 457, 471, 476, 672, 720
1946 42, 217, 227, 247, 263, 709, 720
1947 64, 193, 315, 442, 443, 486, 536
1948 257, 494, 502, 695
1949 213, 527
1950 62, 243, 253, 515, 516, 543, 562, 681
1950s xii, 50, 62, 270, 318, 512, 543, 562, 727
1951 202, 206, 243, 268, 428, 431, 512, 516
1952 47, 512, 679, 701
1953 35, 55, 194, 209, 218, 238, 302, 512, 516, 564
1954 305, 317, 512, 667, 705
1955 10, 29, 264, 446, 695
1956 70, 212, 492, 568
1957 22, 285, 446, 504, 562
1958 49, 258, 440, 712, 716
1959 263, 535, 677, 727
1960 20, 478, 492, 661
1961 50, 212, 317, 332, 462, 496, 512, 530, 551, 716, 726
1962 203, 206, 212, 316, 456, 503, 526, 560, 716
1963 537
1964 222, 677
1967 292, 535
1974 69, 542
1976 294, 305
1978 31
1984 557, 558
1990 69, 217
1995 283, 305
1997 196, 197, 305
1998 441
1999 283, 294
2001 200, 201, 460, 510
2009 460
2012 693
2013 43, 44, 45, 460
2015 194, 488
2016 194
2022 11, 210

www.ingramcontent.com/pod-product-compliance
Lightning Source LLC
Chambersburg PA
CBHW051551230426
43668CB00013B/1810